The Philosophical Foundations of the Late Schelling

New Perspectives in Ontology
Series Editors: Peter Gratton, Southeastern Louisiana University, and
Sean J. McGrath, Memorial University of Newfoundland, Canada

Publishes the best new work on the question of being and the history of metaphysics

After the linguistic and structuralist turn of the twentieth century, a renaissance
in metaphysics and ontology is occurring. Following in the wake of speculative
realism and new materialism, this series aims to build on this renewed interest in
perennial metaphysical questions, while opening up avenues of investigation long
assumed to be closed. Working within the Continental tradition without being
confined by it, the books in this series will move beyond the linguistic turn and
rethink the oldest questions in a contemporary context. They will challenge old
prejudices while drawing upon the speculative turn in post-Heideggerian ontology,
the philosophy of nature and the philosophy of religion.

Editorial Advisory Board

Books available

The Political Theology of Schelling, Saitya Brata Das
Continental Realism and its Discontents, edited by Marie-Eve Morin
The Contingency of Necessity: Reason and God as Matters of Fact, Tyler Tritten
The Problem of Nature in Hegel's Final System, Wes Furlotte
Schelling's Naturalism: Motion, Space and the Volition of Thought, Ben Woodard
Thinking Nature: An Essay in Negative Ecology, Sean J. McGrath
Heidegger's Ontology of Events, James Bahoh
The Political Theology of Kierkegaard, Saitya Brata Das
The Schelling–Eschenmayer Controversy, 1801: Nature and Identity, Benjamin Berger
    and Daniel Whistler
Hölderlin's Philosophy of Nature, edited by Rochelle Tobias
Affect and Attention After Deleuze and Whitehead: Ecological Attunement,
    Russell J. Duvernoy
The Philosophical Foundations of the Late Schelling: The Turn to the Positive,
    Sean J. McGrath
Schelling's Ontology of Powers, Charlotte Alderwick

Books forthcoming

Collected Essays in Speculative Philosophy, by James Bradley and edited by
Sean J. McGrath

www.edinburghuniversitypress.com/series/epnpio

The Philosophical Foundations of the Late Schelling

The Turn to the Positive

SEAN J. McGRATH

EDINBURGH
University Press

Edinburgh University Press is one of the leading university presses in the UK. We publish academic books and journals in our selected subject areas across the humanities and social sciences, combining cutting-edge scholarship with high editorial and production values to produce academic works of lasting importance. For more information visit our website: edinburghuniversitypress.com

Edinburgh University Press Ltd
The Tun – Holyrood Road, 12(2f) Jackson's Entry, Edinburgh EH8 8PJ

First published in hardback by Edinburgh University Press 2021

Typeset in 11/13 Adobe Garamond by
IDSUK (DataConnection) Ltd

A CIP record for this book is available from the British Library

ISBN 978 1 4744 1034 2 (hardback)
ISBN 978 1 3995 1119 3 (paperback)
ISBN 978 1 4744 1035 9 (webready PDF)
ISBN 978 1 4744 1036 6 (epub)

Contents

Preface

Upon completing my 2012 book, *The Dark Ground of Spirit: Schelling and the Unconscious*, I decided I had to write a book on the late Schelling's philosophy of religion. The goal was to demonstrate the contemporary political-theological relevance of the late Schelling's Philosophy of Mythology and Revelation, in particular its relevance for the post-secular debate. I realised some time into the project that I could not say much about Schelling's approach to secularism without first explaining his heterodox theories of the Trinity and Incarnation. Schelling's notion of the three ages of the Church, for example, would appear arbitrary without explaining how this theory is a consequence of his revisionary readings of the central Christian dogmas of the Trinity and Incarnation. The three ages of the Church are three ages of the Trinity, and in each age one of the three members of the Trinity is actualised as a divine person through the mediation of human history. Secularism, properly understood as the advent of what Schelling calls 'philosophical religion', is nothing short of the culmination of the full personalisation of the third person of the Trinity, anticipated (in Schelling's reading of him) by Paul in 1 Cor. 15:28.

In the course of digging deeper into the reasons for Schelling's renovations of sacred tradition, new surprises awaited me; for example, my discovery, somewhat late into the work, of the sociopolitical relevance of Schelling's idiosyncratic interpretation of the hypostatic union of the divine and the human in Christ defined at Chalcedon in 451. The human is never more free, never more autonomous, then when it has been singularly identified with the divine in the person of Christ. As Marcel Gauchet put it, without any apparent dependence on Schelling's Philosophy of Revelation, but interpreting the same paradoxical, ancient formula of *fully human, fully divine* which inspired Schelling to draw similar conclusions a century and half before him, the incarnation *autonomises* the human. Secular modernity is a consequence of Christendom, not a negation of it.[1] The freedom of the Son to obey the Father grounds our redemption, as the freedom of the Father grounds creation. The freedom of the Spirit frees humanity to decide (or not) to participate in the divine production of perfect community. This notion of free obedience is the fundamental presupposition of Schelling's prophecy of a coming philosophical religion, which he argued, to no one it seemed (the initial curious crowds at Berlin had long since left), will bring the history of religion to its end. Free obedience is central to understanding Schelling's significance for the post-secularism debate. Only a free reception of revelation will be fully adequate to the Christ event, Schelling argues, and a free reception is one that need not occur, and only occurs, if it does occur, as a rational, volitional decision of one who is free to believe or not to believe.

The primacy of freedom, for both God and creation, is not an entirely original thesis of Schelling's. It is a retrieval of a Hebraic position that in its extreme form was declared heretical at the Council of Nicaea in 325, when the Church defined the orthodox doctrine of the Trinity. The pre-Nicene Greek theologians who asserted a Hebraic sense of the freedom of the divine to enter into relation, or not, in opposition to certain neo-Platonic, logical conceptions of the co-eternity of the three persons, included both Origen and the much-maligned Arius. The late Schelling fearlessly rehabilitates these controversial theological figures in a bid to rethink the meaning of Christianity for today. This discovery not only helps us understand much in Schelling which might otherwise appear arbitrary; it also renders the late Schelling's Philosophy of Mythology and Revelation of great interest to historians of theology, particularly a new generation of scholars reviving interest in the Greek Church Fathers.

All of this entailed a much more expanded work than the one I conceived of in 2012, a work which divides clearly into two books: a first book, *The Turn to the Positive*, which deals with the logical and ontological issues related to the distinction between negative and positive philosophy, especially the decisional grounding of the latter (the late Schelling's existentialist turn, which begins with the 1809 Freedom Essay), and a second book, which I will publish with any luck within a year of this one, under the title *The Speculative Theology of the Late Schelling*. The first book is primarily concerned with Schelling's triadic logic, ontology and anthropology. The second book will more explicitly treat Schelling's heterodox theory of Trinitarian relations (with his Christology as the centrepiece), and offer an interpretation of his concept of philosophical religion read not, as it sometimes is, as the victory of philosophy over revelation, and the emancipation of humanity from historical Christianity, but, quite the contrary, as a Trinitarian eschatology.

Together these two books will constitute one of the few elaborated, theological interpretations of Schelling's late philosophy of religion to have appeared in English (given the paucity of work on the late Schelling in English, no great achievement), and the only interpretation to put Schelling into discussion with post-secularism.

I expect that with the translations of the major pieces of the positive philosophy appearing now or scheduled to appear in the next few years,[2] these two books will soon be accompanied by many others, no doubt more learned than mine. The theological interpretation of the late Schelling is a work that calls for scholars of Patristic theology, for specialists in Greek Christianity, Kabbalah and Ancient Hebrew. I am none of these.

The other thing that only came to light when things were quite far along might be my most important finding in the past eight years. Schelling's critique of Hegel, like his subordinationist theory of the Trinity, I have discovered, is not primarily a critique of Hegel's logic (a repeated misreading in the literature, which Schelling encouraged in those oblique passages in which he writes explicitly on Hegel); Schelling's critique is primarily directed at Hegel's account of human psychology. Schelling's often fantastic, speculative theogony, which begins as a Boehmian-inspired narrative of the birth of God from the unground, and ends with a complete overhaul of the central doctrines of the Christian Churches, is based on Schelling's alternative to Hegel's dialectic of recognition, an alternative which I call 'non-dialectical personalism'. For Schelling, a person is not one who stands logically in need of recognition by another, but one who is internally self-mediated and hence logically and morally free in their relations to the other. Only free persons are capable of producing love, which is Schelling's final answer to the question that tormented him for most of his life: Why is there something rather than nothing? There *is* 'something', or rather many things, which combine, struggle and conflict with one another, so that among them personal beings can evolve, beings who are free from each other and thus capable of freely uniting with one another, that is, beings capable of love.[3]

In this book, I offer Schelling's reasons for his defence of what could only be called a theory of individuation in an age that has become increasingly obsessed with the social and collective constitution of persons. In the second book, I will trace Schelling's non-dialectical personalism back to his retrieval of the ostensibly heretical notion of the primacy of divine freedom found in some of the Greek Fathers, notably Origen and Arius. The dispute between Hegel and Schelling on the freedom of the person is a revival of the dispute between Athanasius and the subordinationists (Origenans and Arians) at Nicaea, Hegel adopting the Athanasian line and insisting on necessary, that is, logical relations among the persons of the

Trinity, and Schelling backing the anathematised alternative of the primacy of the Father and the freedom, that is, the non-necessity, of the Trinitarian relations. Through Schelling, the concept of free self-mediation constitutes a minor canon, alongside the more mainstream uptake of Hegelian recognition (Buber, Husserl, Gadamer). Schelling's notion of free self-mediation as presupposition of personal relations is passed on to Kierkegaard, the Russians, Soloviev, Dostoevsky and Berdyaev, and finds echoes in the twentieth century in surprising places, in Jung, in Heidegger and in Levinas. A person for Schelling is not one who always already stands in dialectical relation to another but one who has overcome an internal necessity (or in other language, appropriated a dark ground, mastered an internal chaos, and achieved a functional relation with the unconscious). This insight put the new work on Schelling into a closer relation than anticipated to *The Dark Ground of Spirit*. It also proves the original point of the project even more emphatically than I first dreamed it could be proven: secular, philosophical psychology, political theory, even economic theory, unconsciously depend upon forgotten theological controversies.

14 December 2020
Feast of St John of the Cross
Holyrood, Newfoundland

Notes

1. Gauchet (1985).
2. See Klaus Ottmann's translation of the *Paulus Nachschrift* (Schelling 2020). As this book goes to press, I am aware of a translation of the *Urfassung* (1831) being prepared for SUNY Press.
3. See Schelling's definition of love from the Freedom Essay (1809: 409/70). A first formulation of this notion of love appears in, of all places, the 1806 *Aphorisms on the Introduction to Nature-Philosophy* (SW 7: 174, n. 163): 'This is the mystery of eternal love, that that which would like to be absolute for itself is rather only in and with other things. Nevertheless, it regards this as no theft of its being for itself. If each were not a whole but rather only a part of a whole, then love would not be: but this is love, where each is a whole, and yet is not and cannot be without the other.' See also the 1811 draft of *The Ages of the World* (in Lawrence's translation) (Schelling 1811: 64/124): 'It is only in this way [through the personalisation of the three potencies], moreover, that the highest essence of love reveals itself. It is nothing to marvel at when principles coexist peacefully because they are compelled to do so by a binding force that pulls them together. Love comes into play, however, only if, where existential independence prevails, free beings are freely drawn to one another.'

Acknowledgements

Too many people have contributed to the production of this book for me to be able to thank them all by name. Among my colleagues, Andrzej Wiercinski at the University of Warsaw, Markus Enders at the University of Freiburg and Jason Wirth at the University of Seattle were each seminal interlocutors at key points in the project. My graduate students at Memorial University heard much of this material, rough and ready as it were, in seminars over the years. Memorial University PhD candidates Kyla Bruff and Alisan Genc in particular helped me refine my arguments. At McGill University, where I finished this book during a pleasant year as visiting professor at the School of Religious Studies, I profited from vigorously debating Schelling and related matters with Garth Green and George di Giovanni, and with graduate students Jason Blakeburn, Daniel Heide and Hadi Fakhoury.

I would also like to acknowledge all that I have received from my scholarly collaboration with the members of the North American Schelling Society. NASS was founded by myself and Jason Wirth in 2012 to redress the isolation of the Schelling scholar and the marginalisation of Schelling's work. The society has grown exponentially since then. The original meeting was comprised of a dozen senior scholars who had written important works on Schelling but who had never met each other; the upcoming NASS meeting, planned for Toronto, will have more than sixty presenters, the majority of whom are graduate students or new scholars. While academic philosophical work is the product of countless solitary hours, philosophy still remains as communal an enterprise as it was in Socrates' day. Many of the pieces that make up this book were presented at meetings of NASS and I have learned from too many of my fellow NASS members to be able to name each of them here. Let me at least say thank you to Iain Hamilton

Grant (the last, true *Naturphilosoph*), Tyler Tritten, Daniel Whistler, Joseph Lawrence, Bruce Matthews, Tilottama Rajan, Joan Stegerwald, Lore Hühn and Marcela Garcia, and offer my apologies to the many others whom I cannot name here for lack of space.

Some of the material published here appeared earlier in a different form, notably in the following articles: 'German Idealism', in *The Meillassoux Dictionary*, ed. Paul Ennis and Peter Gratton (Edinburgh: Edinburgh University Press, 2014), pp. 80–2; 'On the Difference Between Schelling and Hegel', in *Rethinking German Idealism*, ed. Joseph Carew and Sean McGrath (New York: Palgrave Macmillan, 2016), pp. 247–70; 'Is the Late Schelling Still Doing Nature-Philosophy?', *Angelaki*, 21:4 (2016): 121–41; 'The Ecstatic Realism of the Late Schelling', in *Continental Realism and its Discontents*, ed. Marie Eve Morin (Edinburgh: Edinburgh University Press, 2017), pp. 38–58.

I dedicate this book to my deceased friend and former colleague, the one who most encouraged my research on Schelling, and who taught me pretty much everything I know concerning the logic of the Trinity, Professor James Bradley (1947–2012).

Note on Sources

All translations from the later Schelling are my own unless otherwise noted. SW refers to Schelling's *Sämtliche Werke*, the 1856–61 fourteen-volume edition of Schelling's collected works, edited by K. F. A Schelling. In addition to this edition, which is still the standard (until the *Historisch-Kritische Ausgabe* is complete), I refer frequently to the 1831 *Urfassung der Philosophie der Offenbarung* and the 1841 *Philosophie der Offenbarung* (the *Paulus Nachschrift*). Where a published English translation of a cited text of Schelling is used, I give the English pagination after the German. I have preferred the King James Bible for most English biblical passages because it is what best corresponds to the Luther Bible, which Schelling used, but on occasion I have used the New International Version. I have kept theological capitalisations to a minimum. Exceptions are 'the Word' and 'the *Logos*' when it refers to the second person of the Trinity; 'Father', 'Son' and 'Spirit', in a Trinitarian context; 'Church', when it refers to the collective body of all Christian denominations; and 'State' when it refers to the formal idea of administrative governance.

I have moved freely between the various published editions of the different parts of the seven-book positive philosophy. The earliest written form of Schelling's Philosophy of Revelation is the 1831 *Urfassung*, which is based on a transcript of lectures that Schelling gave in Munich that year. The text was prepared for the crown prince of Bavaria, Maximilian II, whom Schelling was tutoring at the time. Maximilian could not attend the lectures and asked that the transcript be prepared for him to study. The manuscript was discovered misfiled at the University of Eichstätt and edited and published by Walter Ehrhardt in 1992. Ehrhardt argues that while the text was transcribed by an auditor of the lectures, it was corrected by Schelling himself (Schelling 1831: 731). This would seem to position the *Urfassung* as the definitive version of the Philosophy of Revelation inasmuch as it is the only written version we possess which we know that Schelling approved. It cannot stand as that, however, for crucial additions were made in the following two decades, including the clarification of the movement from negative to positive philosophy and the critique of Hegel. Moreover, the *Urfassung* is not the most historically influential version, since it was never published in Schelling's lifetime. The 1841 version, the *Paulus Nachschrift*, is an unauthorised transcript of the lectures which Schelling first gave in Berlin in the winter semester of 1841/42 (and repeated, with variations, every year until he stopped lecturing in 1846). It was published by a fierce critic of Schelling, the rationalist H. E. G. Paulus (a theological revisionist who denied revelation as a possibility altogether) in 1843, without Schelling's permission. Paulus intended to humiliate Schelling by exposing the folly of Schelling's last system to the world – he thought it enough to simply publish Schelling's words verbatim without comment and let the old man hang himself with his outrageous claims. Schelling sued Paulus for publishing his work prematurely and against his wishes, but to no avail: the book went to press and was widely read. Schelling's polemic with Hegel is explicit in the *Paulus Nachschrift*, where it is only indirect in the *Urfassung*, and this critique could be the most influential part of Schelling's late philosophy, for it inspired a generation of post-idealist philosophers in Germany, including Kierkegaard and Marx. As I finished this book, a translation of the *Paulus* was published by Klaus Ottmann (Spring Publications, 2020). I have also made use of Schelling's Munich lecture of 1833, *On the History of Modern Philosophy* (Schelling 1833).

The official version of the Philosophy of Revelation is that edited by Schelling's son, K. F. A Schelling, and published as the last two volumes (13 and 14) of Schelling's *Sämtliche Werke* between 1856 and 1858. It is preceded by two volumes on the Philosophy of Mythology (volumes 11 and 12). This version is heavily edited and constructed from a multiplicity of sources, the deciphering of which ought to keep the Schelling Kommission der Bayerischen Akademie der Wissenschaften busy for the better part of this century. It has the advantage of completeness, and includes Schelling's revised philosophical introduction to the Philosophy of Mythology, the crucial *Darstellung der reinrationalen Philosophie*, which according to Schelling's last wish, was to replace *The Grounding of the Positive Philosophy*.[1] Here, in Schelling's final work (he was working on these notes, which he never lectured on publicly, until his death), he turns back to negative philosophy to revise the doctrine of potencies and the theory of natural history in the light of the Philosophy of Revelation. This text contains some of Schelling's most fertile thoughts on the political, and demonstrates, if demonstration is still needed, that while nature-philosophy is not abandoned at the end, it is significantly revised, and rendered propaedeutic to a history of spirit and a positive philosophy of God.

The table below outlines the seven books of Schelling's Philosophy of Mythology and Revelation as arranged and edited by K. F. A. Schelling in the fourteen-volume *Sämtliche Werke* (SW; I. Abteilung: 10 Bde [= I–X]; 2. Abteilung: 4 Bde [= XI–XIV]) and in the Schröter edition, the twelve-volume *Originalausgabe* (OA, six main volumes or *Hauptbande* [1–6], plus six supplementary volumes or *Ergänzungsbande* [1e–6e]). I have also indicated where these lectures and texts originated.

Book	SW/OA	Original title	Numbered lectures and date	English translation	Reference used[2]
I	SW 11: 1–252 OA 6: 1–254	*Historish-kritische Einleitung in die Philosophie der Mythologie*	Lectures 1–10 First given in Berlin 1842	*Historical-Critical Introduction to the Philosophy of Mythology,* trans. Richey and Zisselsberger (2007)	1842a
II	SW 11: 253–572 OA 5: 431–574	*Philosophische Einleitung in die Philosophie der Mythologie oder Darstellung der reinrationalen Philosophie*	Lectures 11–24 Never given as such	Paraphrased and partly translated by Hayes (1995: 131–99)	1854a
III	SW 12: 1–132 OA 6: 255–387	*Philosophie der Mythologie. Erstes Buch. Der Monotheismus*	Lectures 1–6 First given in Berlin 1842	Not translated	1842b
IV	SW 12: 133–674 OA 5e	*Philosophie der Mythologie. Zweites Buch. Die Mythologie*	Lectures 7–29 First given in Berlin 1842	Not translated	1842c
V	SW 13: 1–174 OA 6e: 1–174	*Einleitung in die Philosophie der Offenbarung oder Begründung der positive Philosophie*	Lectures 1–8 Given in Berlin 1842	*The Grounding of the Positive Philosophy: The Berlin Lectures,* trans. B. Matthews (2007)	1842d
VI	SW 13: 175–530 OA 6e: 175–530	*Philosophie der Offenbarung erster Theil [Kurze Darstellung der Philosophie der Mythologie]*	Lectures 9–23 Never given as such	Not translated	1854b
VII	SW 14: 1–334 OA 6: 389–726	*Philosophie der Offenbarung zweiter Theil*	Lectures 24–37 Never given as such	Paraphrased and partly translated by Hayes (1995: 201–334)	1854c

Notes

1. Horst Fuhrmans published Schelling's Literary Testament dated from 1853 in *Kant-Studien* 51 (1959/60), 14–26. The document corresponds with Schelling's dictation of the five parts of his positive philosophy and their order to his son Paul in 1852, which K. F. A. Schelling, who was responsible for the edition of the complete works, communicated in a letter to Waitz on 12 January 1855. On the basis of these texts Thomas Buchheim concludes that according to Schelling's final statements on the matter, the positive philosophy is composed of five parts, none of which includes *The Grounding*. The parts are 1) the Historical Critical Introduction to the Philosophy of Mythology (Schelling 1842a; SW 11: 1–252); 2) the Philosophical Introduction to the Philosophy of Mythology (Schelling 1854a; SW 11: 253–572); 3) the monotheism treatise (Schelling 1842b; SW 12: 1–132); 4) the Philosophy of Mythology proper (Schelling 1842c; SW 12: 133–674); 5) the Philosophy of Revelation (in two parts: Schelling 1854b; SW 13: 175–530; Schelling 1854c; SW 14: 1–334). See Buchheim (2020).
2. These references are based on the date of the original lectures. In the cases where the material has been compiled posthumously from various sources by K. F. A. Schelling, I have given the date 1854, the year of Schelling's death, and the last point at which he could have worked on it.

Freedom is the highest for us and for God.

Schelling, *Urfassung der Philosophie der Offenbarung*

Chapter 1

Introduction

After his death in 1831, Hegel's chair in Berlin was deliberately left open by the Prussian regime. The conservative crown prince of Prussia, Friedrich Wilhelm IV, aiming to stem the tide of Hegelianism sweeping across Germany and to preserve something of the old Christian culture, refused to appoint any of Hegel's many eligible disciples to the post (Frank 1977: 10–14). The left Hegelians were clamouring for a revolution that would dismantle the class system by once and for all disentangling politics from religion. The right Hegelians were calling for the opposite: the realisation of a bourgeois egalitarian state in Prussia such as had already been achieved in France, with maximal political freedom and religious tolerance. In the face of what for him were equally undesirable alternatives, Friedrich Wilhelm IV left Hegel's chair vacant for a decade. Negotiations began with Bavaria to bring Schelling, at the time a senior bureaucrat in the Bavarian administration, to Berlin. Who better to cleanse German philosophy of Hegelianism than the man who had invented German idealism? Schelling after all had given Hegel his start in philosophy, and had since, according to reports out of Munich, become aware of the limitations of idealism and the enduring value of Christian culture and tradition. The elder statesman of German romanticism was offered the highest salary of any German professor in the history of modern Germany up to that time to purge Prussia of the 'dragonseed of Hegelian pantheism'.[1]

On the opening day, the Berlin lecture hall was filled to capacity with everyone who was anyone in German intellectual life. Venerable scholars such as Jakob Burckhardt stood alongside young revolutionaries such as Friedrich Engels and Mikhail Bakunin, and a new generation of still unknown thinkers, among them Søren Kierkegaard. Everyone, friends and enemies of Hegelianism alike, wanted to know what the old man was going to say. After several decades of overblown idealism, Schelling proclaimed the advent of a new realism in philosophy and culture. The announcement was met with enthusiasm from the younger generation. Kierkegaard gushed into his diary that 'the child of thought leapt for joy within me as in Elizabeth, when he [Schelling] mentioned the word "actuality"' (cited in Kosch 2006: 105). Schelling quickly disappointed most, including Kierkegaard, as he used the Berlin chair to expound his final system, the outlines of which had already been worked out years before, as a reading of the 1831 *Urfassung* makes clear. Not only was Schelling offering yet another speculative philosophy of history; he was, like Hegel, privileging Christianity as both the end of the ancient world and the beginning of the modern. Also like Hegel, Schelling was arguing that modern secular culture was not the demise of Christianity, but its fruition: Schelling's late philosophy, like Hegel's earliest work in the philosophy of religion, culminates in a theological affirmation of the legitimacy of European secularism and a secular affirmation of the truth of modernity's theological origins. Philosophy in the late Schelling, as in Hegel, offers a speculative repetition of Christian theology as the definitive form of thinking. What was new about this?

We know from his correspondence at the time that Schelling was full of trepidation about the Berlin lectures, having worked himself into a paroxysm of insecurity about how the Hegelians would receive him. He was pleasantly surprised at the respect and genuine interest shown to him, at least at first, by everyone, including the Hegelians (Kasper 1965: 35–8). It was the end of a period, the closing of an age of speculative philosophy second to none, perhaps even more dramatic in outcome than the golden age of Athenian philosophy. What did they all expect from Schelling? What were they crowding into the room for? It was the same room in which Hegel had lectured for years and in which he had, week after week, progressively unfurled the most comprehensive system of philosophy ever constructed. What more was there to say? That Schelling's Berlin audience were for the most part disappointed at what they heard, and that within five years the attendance at his lectures would plummet so precipitously that Schelling was forced to retire (Boenke 1995: 69) – none of this changes the fact that on that November day they were all there, jostling for a spot in the room, leaning forward in expectation, straining to hear what the old hero of German philosophy had still to say.

I think that what is most impressive about this story, the reason it is told over and over again in the history books, is that it is such an open display of philosophical hope in an era of great transformation. They were there, not only to hear Schelling trounce his old nemesis Hegel (some of them looked forward to that perhaps), but because they still, after Kant's three critiques, after Fichte's *Wissenschaftslehre*, after Hegel's *Encyclopedia of the Philosophical*

Sciences, longed for, and therefore believed in, the possibility of true *knowledge*. German idealism is rightly taken to task for substituting the presumption of the possession of knowledge for the more modest Greek 'love of wisdom'. Socrates says he knows only one thing, that he knows nothing; Hegel, in sharp contrast, systematises all human knowledge into an absolute system and proclaims the end of philosophy as love of wisdom, that is, the end of philosophy as the longing and search for knowledge. One can well imagine the cynicism of this generation worn out by the system builders and speculative architects of the absolute.

And yet the lover of wisdom who does not genuinely believe in its possibility, the possibility of knowledge and an end to the quest, is a fake. He or she is just someone making a living off the most human of human needs, not by satisfying it, but by exacerbating it. The German idealists claimed to have reached the goal, to have found the Holy Grail, and they were no doubt mistaken; but we, late modern cynics, we should be cautious that our objection to them does not become one of legislating disbelief, turning Socrates' quest into the presumptive, un-Socratic claim not just that we have found no one who is wise, but that no one is or could be wise, because there is no wisdom to be found. When Schelling stepped up to the podium in Berlin, he was riding on a wave of collective and almost childlike hope that perhaps he, the one who had inaugurated the whole German idealist enterprise, and had outlasted those who had eclipsed him in output and reputation – perhaps *he* had found it. Perhaps he knew something. They came to Berlin hoping for wisdom, not only critique; and not mere scientific knowledge, but ultimate wisdom, guidance and intimations of what is finally and definitively true about human existence.

Schelling's famous failure in Berlin – let us think about it in the context of the extraordinary expectations laid upon him. Let us think about his Berlin lectures not only, or even primarily, as a failure, but as in some way, inadequate to be sure, but nevertheless in *some way*, rising to the occasion. For what Schelling offered the Berlin audience was nothing less than what he regarded as wisdom. Certainty about ultimate things was not possible, Schelling said in so many words, at least not in the current age of the world, and perhaps never in the way that the audience longed for it. Genuine wisdom could only be eschatological, not just a *docta ignorantia*, but, under an old symbol for a placeholder for a knowledge still to come, a promissory note, an IOU from the absolute, a divine *revelation*. Schelling offered his Berlin audience revelation; not a new revelation, but the old revelation, the revelation that in his view had set Greek, Roman and European civilisation in motion and directed it towards modernity. You want absolute knowledge from me, he said, and I cannot give it to you. I can only give you what Paul called 'the wisdom of God' which is 'folly' to humankind (1 Cor. 3:18–20).

But perhaps, he said, we can together prepare philosophy for a new reception of this now well-known revelation, a reception no longer constricted by creed and cult, no longer proclaimed by an authority and received in that alienated form, but a revelation which, by means of its own inscrutable power to widen the human heart to the compass of divine love, may one day become knowledge. They did not want to hear this. Most left the room shaking their heads or ridiculing the incorrigible idealism of the father of the failed movement.

Perhaps it is time, now, in our anatheistic age, after the death of the death of God, on the cusp of technological and ecological transformations of our civilisation that have no precedent prior to the birth of agriculture, perhaps it is time to hear Schelling again. What is left of the Judaeo-Christian revelation? What more has it to offer us? There is no denying that the late Schelling traverses terrain that had already been explored and mapped by Hegel, particularly the relation of Western philosophy to Christian theology, and the question concerning the theological origins of modernity. He does so deliberately. Hegel's mistake, in Schelling's view, was not that he attempted to unite the worlds of philosophy and theology; it was that he did it badly, at the expense of both. Schelling's career ends where Hegel's began: in a philosophical interpretation of the New Testament, albeit one entirely at odds with Hegel's. Only in his old age did Schelling come to see what Hegel grasped at the start of his career, that the political and spiritual history of the West, and the destiny of the world, is incomprehensible without an appreciation of the radically new era that begins for humanity with the failed Jewish messiah and the community who proclaimed his death and resurrection to the Roman Empire. Hegel's early works (his so-called *theologische Jugendschriften*) are about little else.[2] In essays such as 'The Positivity of the Christian Religion' (1795–96), 'The Spirit of Christianity' (1798–99) and *Faith and Knowledge* (1802), Hegel pursued the line which he was to fully develop in the *Encyclopedia of the Philosophical Sciences* and the *Lectures on the Philosophy of Religion*, namely, the thesis that the first form of the absolute system is found in the earliest preaching of the Church. No matter that it is for modern philosophy to finally free the truth of Christianity from its sensuous and pictorial form; the truth of philosophy is also the truth of Christianity as Hegel understands it: that God overcomes the alienation between Godself and God's creation by dying on the cross. The transcendent becomes immanent in the Christ event and reveals the dialectical, reciprocal dependency of the infinite on the finite.

For Hegel, the history of the world is the history of God recognising Godself in God's other, the dialectic of recognition described in a few famous pages of *The Phenomenology of Spirit*, recast as a theogony and history of being. As in the interpersonal struggle, recognition involves a negation of the negation, an abolition of the difference between the two (alternatively self and other or God and humankind), which cancels the immediate, negative appearance of otherness and preserves it as the mediator of sameness. As early as his 1802 *Faith and Knowledge*, Hegel sees the dialectic of recognition as the spiritual truth of the New Testament. Christ's death on the cross is the death of God Godself, who in dying is identified with God's other: not only the creature Jesus, but the sin and Godforsakenness of creation itself. This identification is simultaneously the qualification of transcendence (the negation of the one-sided Jewish notion of the infinite as the wholly other, as well as of the equally abstract neo-Platonic notion of the One, the Good beyond being) and the immanentisation of divinity. In this identification, all that was previously regarded as above and beyond is hereafter recognised as here below – or not at all. The Father dies on the cross along with the Son, and the human is deprived of the transcendent; but this moment of absolute Godforsakenness is to be affirmed as the full maturation of the human, who now realises or sets about realising within the human community all that was previously projected on to heaven. The climax of this redemption is not the resurrection – which is for Hegel a purely mythic expression of the truth coming to birth in the New Testament – but the ascension, when Jesus finally leaves the disciples so that the Spirit which unites him to his Father can now be distributed among them, rendering them Church, the visible and material presence of the divine on earth. The history of the Church culminates, then, in the birth of the modern world, wherein Western culture is finally emancipated from the religion of its infancy and realises in a secular key all that was once deferred to the afterlife: freedom, justice and communion with one another.[3]

What does Schelling offer to compete with Hegel's magnificent speculative reconstruction of Christianity? What more could there be to say?

Schelling's Philosophy of Revelation articulates the politico-philosophical core of the New Testament, that which makes Christianity hermeneutically volatile and perennially subversive. And it does so by interpreting the Christ event in terms of a non-dialectical theory of personhood, which Schelling first unveiled in his masterpiece, the 1809 Freedom Essay. A person, Schelling argued in 1809, is not one who stands in a logically reciprocal relation to another, but one who has overcome internal necessity, internal otherness, and so achieved freedom.[4] Only on the basis of this mastery of necessity is a person capable of relatedness, just as God must first overcome the blind act of being which precedes God before God can create a world. Personal relations are radically contingent according to Schelling, that is, they are, without exception, whether divine relations or human relations, whether relations of love or hate, good or evil, always irreducible expressions of freedom. Applied to the Trinity, this means that God need not beget a Son, the

Son need not obey the Father (as both Origen and Arius claimed, against the tradition which won the day at the Council of Nicaea in 325); the begetting of the Son and his *kenosis* of divinity before the Father are contingent, free and unprethinkable historical events, which literally change everything. On the basis of this counter-Hegelian theory of the Trinity, Schelling constructs an alternative account of how Christianity produces modernity and how the secular legitimately succeeds the sacred. What is ultimately at stake in the Schelling–Hegel dispute, then – and this is still not sufficiently recognised by the new generation of scholars of German idealism – is the philosophical interpretation of Christianity, or as I will put it in this work, the interpretation of the end of Christianity. What is the meaning of its central symbol of redemption through the death of God? What is Christianity's future, and how is the future of Christianity bound up with the destiny of all humanity?

I believe that Schelling's dispute with Hegel on the meaning of Christianity is not only an underexplored chapter of the history of modern philosophy (although it is surely that). Schelling has something important to say to the philosophy of religion now – precisely now – at this moment of the apparent unravelling of the theological narrative that once united the Western world. Both Hegel and Schelling insist that modern secularism is not a contradiction of Christianity but its fulfilment: what began on the hill of skulls outside the walls of Jerusalem will end in a world that needs neither creed nor cult. Hegel argues that this fully realised human community is already here, now, among us; it is nothing other than the modern, liberal, democratic state. And with this extraordinary endorsement of the status quo, Hegel discloses the resignation if not the cynicism that underwrites his philosophy: we are to stop longing for a better world, for this is as good as it gets. While Hegel's language sometimes appears to suggest otherwise, the note of cynicism at the heart of Hegelianism is made explicit by Hegel's Lacanian interpreter, Žižek. Philosophy realises the truth of religion, the truth that religion in itself has no truth. There is no God; there is only us and what we do.

> Finite (determinate, positive, substantial) reality is in itself void, inconsistent, self-sublating. From this it does not follow that this reality is just a shadow, a secondary reflection, etc., of some higher reality: there is nothing *but this* reality . . . The starting point, immediate reality, deploys its nothingness, it cancels itself, negates itself, but there is nothing beyond it. (Žižek and Milbank 2009: 107, n. 134)

Schelling's answer to Hegel's apotheosis of the status quo is to censure the present, not by denying the possibility of justice, but by deferring its actuality and proclaiming, with Paul (whom he follows at almost every juncture of the Philosophy of Revelation), the still-outstanding *eschaton*, the advent of the end of history. In short, in place of Hegelian resignation, Schelling gives us reason to hope that the future, the absolute future, might be wholly different from the past.

The Schellingian deferral of the advent of justice should be distinguished from the messianism-lite popular in poststructural or 'continental' political philosophy. The end is not infinitely deferred, and thereby rendered innocuous (a regulative ideal for the stabilisation of liberal democracy). Justice is not a figure of speech. The Church of St John, Schelling's metaphor for the final age of history, which will fulfil Paul's prophecy of the definitive victory of Christ over an unbelieving world (1 Cor. 15:28), is not a regulative ideal, nor is it merely a point on the horizon which gives us an orientation but at which we never arrive. Schelling in effect proclaims absolute justice to be real and active if not yet fully actual: it is the promise which has from the beginning motivated and inspired Christendom. And if it has fallen into forgetfulness in the nineteenth century, it is anything but finished with us. To the degree that we acknowledge the claim of the promise on our conscience and commit ourselves to the advent of justice, we cannot be indifferent to the injustices of the present. Far from confirming our present state of existence as insurmountable and 'good enough', genuine political eschatology mobilises us to do something about the dire political, social and ecological state of the present.[5] Without hope there is no will to change the present, and without the transcendent there is no hope.[6]

In this way, Schelling brings back the radicality and political potency of early Christian eschatology. The first Christians did not need temple and priest to mediate a relation to the holy; they were redeemed by the crucified and risen Christ. They did not see the cross, as Hegel did, as the end of the road, as the abolition of transcendence. On the contrary, the cross *relocated* transcendence – from the above to the future and in such a way as to illuminate *this* present world more directly by its light. Transcendence was relocated from the spatial beyond of the Greek mystery religions and Platonic philosophy to the temporal beyond of Judaism. The primitive Christian transcendent is not a place, but a time: it is the future of the earth. It is this understanding of transcendence that Schelling reactualises for our era. According to Schelling, we live at the end of the second age of revelation, the end of institutional Christianity, and at the threshold of philosophical religion or what I will call religious secularism. To anticipate the third and final age of revelation is, in a way, to stand in solidarity with atheism – for we no longer project the destiny of the earth on to heaven. In another way, it is to refuse the closure of the question of meaning, which is the atheists' recurrent error. Atheism typically claims to know more about our situation than is given to us to know. It may be that justice is not above us in heaven, but neither is it within us, among us now or already actual in the community. Justice, according to Schelling, is ahead of us, calling to us, challenging us to rise to the occasion of its advent. I believe that this thought, which is at the very heart of Schelling's Philosophy of Revelation, remains as relevant today as it was in the first half of the nineteenth century, or in the first century of the Common Era.

When Schelling unfurled his Philosophy of Revelation in Berlin, Hegel's system was the dominant philosophical paradigm. The centrality of Christianity to Hegel's thought – in which it was placed at the pinnacle of history as 'the consummate religion' and the most adequate representation of speculative truth (if, for all that, still only a representation) – was not controversial, for Kant, Fichte, F. Schlegel and their many followers had done the same, namely, interpreted history as progress towards the pinnacle it reached in European Christendom. Those who heard him in Berlin in 1841 could be excused for thinking that there was nothing very new in the old Schelling after all. They were mistaken. Nevertheless, Schelling's Philosophy of Revelation was soon forgotten, along with the other great systems of the nineteenth century. God was declared definitively dead (and not merely speculatively transformed into philosophy). The twentieth century dawned as an era in which philosophy's most essential questions capitulated to science, and philosophers were compelled to make their home in what Weber famously described as a disenchanted world.[7] Theologians went into a defensive posture in a battle they were destined to lose. Theology was no longer a speculative partner to philosophy; rather, it was deployed to consolidate an identity for embattled churches in a culturally indifferent or even hostile environment. Few early twentieth-century theologians directly engaged the question of the objective truth of revelation: objectivity had been given over to science, which treated things and their properties, not God and his attributes. The question of the objective truth of revelation, which was the foremost topic of nineteenth-century theology, was no longer of interest. Neo-Thomism, Protestant liberalism and neo-orthodoxy did not put the objective truth of revelation into question (which is not necessarily to doubt it), but assumed it as a manifesto, a constitution around which to organise micro-societies.

Since the mid-twentieth century, when Catholic religious orders were bursting at the seams with young men and women seeking refuge from modernity, theology has declined considerably. The defensive theologies of the religious orders have disappeared with the churches they defended, and we are left with this question: What *was* the revelation? What truth was there in it? No one acquainted with intellectual history can easily deny that revelation functioned as a presupposition of Western society (and to a lesser extent, of Middle Eastern societies), and perhaps made possible our greatest achievements (the declaration of human rights)[8] as well as our greatest follies (capitalism), but a pressing question remains: Can it continue to do so? Or, more to the point, now that 'Western' has become a meaningless distinction (for what is it distinguished *from*? 'Eastern'? 'Southern'? 'Northern'?), now that the global village predicted by McLuhan has been achieved in a way he never expected – as a single, world market with endless flows of communication and exchange and little communion (Deleuze's 'integrated world capitalism') – can the revelation possibly still mean anything? In our post-Christendom context, Schelling's Philosophy of Revelation assumes a relevance it has never previously had. The question is not only, What truth *was* in the revelation? It is also, What is still true about it?

For Schelling, working out his Philosophy of Revelation in the 1830s, as romanticism, grown old, entered a conservative and more contemplative phase, the question of the scientific, historical and philosophical truth of revelation could no longer be ignored. Among many others of his generation, for example Hölderlin, F. Schlegel and Hegel, Schelling believed that the advent of the end of Christianity was upon Europe in the middle of the nineteenth century. The end was not Christianity's dissolution as an antiquated and irrelevant religion of the past, but its consummation in a global religious secularism that would bring about world peace. The end of Christianity could only be the end of the Church as we have known it, and the overcoming of the State (which the early Romantics had already anticipated). For Schelling, the State would cease to exist when it was no longer necessary, that is, when the freedom of individuals, which it grounds, would be synchronised through a transformed moral and spiritual life which would bring about the achievement of perfect community on earth. Striking an uncommon eschatological note in an era of increasing cynicism, Schelling proclaimed that now was the time for the revelation to shake free of 'the old, narrow, stunted, puny Christianity of the prevailing dogmatic schools', to emancipate its truth from 'a Christianity thinly confined to miserable formulae which shun the light' – but not so as to be privatised or 'whittled down to an exclusively personal kind of Christianity'; rather, the time was ripe for the revelation to found 'a truly public religion', 'the religion of all mankind in which mankind will, at the same time, find the supreme knowledge' (Schelling 1854c: 328).

Can anyone still believe this? Perhaps not many. Nevertheless, it is my claim that Schelling's vision of 'philosophical religion' enucleated and thematised the conceptual core of the Gospel. His challenge to a world already weary of philosophical systems was to present revelation as a real-world philosophical and political option, not just for Europe and its colonies but for all people on an interconnected globe.

Theologians, especially Barthians, might be tempted to categorise Schelling's Philosophy of Revelation as an apologetic version of fundamental theology, perhaps even a correlationist theology that tests the revelation against universal criteria drawn from the secular sciences, and so submits revelation to the tribunal of general (fallen) human reason. This judgement would be wrong. To read Schelling as a modern apologist is to miss the radicality of his innovation and to confuse his 'naturalism' with 'natural theology'. In his 1812 answer to Jacobi, the *Denkmal*, which I analyse in detail below, Schelling defends a religious naturalism against Jacobi's 'non-philosophy', a naturalism which thinks nature *in* God, and thinks God as the God *of* nature (in both subjective and objective senses of the genitive: nature's God, and the God who is Lord of nature).[9] Schelling's late approach to both nature and God, which begins in earnest in 1809, but only finds its footing in 1812, is not by means of deductions or *a priori* rational certainties. The questions demand a new method, which Schelling will spend the rest of his career perfecting. His approach is neither foundationalist nor correlationist. Foundationalism begins with secure premises and deduces certain conclusions. Schelling does not begin with premises, but with facts – that there is something rather than nothing, that human beings are capable of good and evil, that God has revealed Godself in creation – and speculatively endeavours to think the premises that could explain such facts. Who is God such that nature exists? Who are we such that good and evil exist? What is history such that God could be claimed to have revealed Godself in it? The answers to these questions will not be facts, nor will they be certainties: they will be speculative explanations, which invite falsification.

Correlationist theology (I have in mind Tillich and his followers) presupposes an inside/outside dichotomy dividing theology: *inside* the community of belief, theology proceeds on the sure foundations of faith; *outside*, in the public sphere, theology cannot presume faith but must justify its existence in other, purely philosophical or historical-critical terms. Correlationism mediates between Church and world, providing public justification for the very existence of theology in categories that the non-Christian and the unbeliever can in principle accept. The basic concepts of Schelling's Philosophy of Revelation – the knowledge of God's existence, the historicity of revelation, the relation of revelation to knowledge of nature – no doubt fall within the purview of 'fundamental' or 'apologetic' theology as it has been traditionally conceived. Nevertheless, it would be an egregious error to read Schelling's Philosophy of Revelation as a philosophical prolegomenon to theology proper, as a species of apologetics or correlationism, for this would be to separate in Schelling fundamental questions (that is, philosophical questions) from dogmatic questions. Schelling is no longer working with the inside/outside dichotomy that the discipline of fundamental theology presupposes. The point of the Philosophy of Revelation is to think from out of *the future* of Christianity and provide the outlines of a theology that is thoroughly public, for in the end, as Paul says (in one of the late Schelling's favourite texts), Christianity will belong to all people, for all people will belong to Christ (1 Cor. 15:28).[10] The Philosophy of Revelation does not divide the human community into two camps – believers and unbelievers, Church and world – and therefore Schelling does not divide theology into fundamental and dogmatic theology. Correlationism is not on the agenda for him, for he intends to transcend the distinction between the Church and the world, the sacred and the secular sciences (which would only need to be correlated insofar as they were opposed).

Most problematically, Schelling rejects the traditional argument, still widely endorsed in systematic theology, that the redemption and its conceptual presuppositions, Trinity and Christology, presuppose the faith of the Church and cannot be understood without it. While Schelling recognises that revelation has been mediated historically through the Church, and has been conceptually developed in the light of faith, he claims that it is not the destiny of revelation to remain an intra-ecclesial or faith-dependent dogma. The redemption is a reasonable and rationally defensible (if not apodictically demonstrable) interpretation of certain historical events, and therefore it can and ought to be expounded without presupposing faith. If the extraordinary events which the redemption purports to explain lack apodictic foundations, so too do all historical events. As a theological *explanans* of the events, moreover, the redemption has a coherence and explanatory power which extends beyond the historical *explanandum*. The doctrine of the redemption, Schelling claims, not only addresses the most profound longing of the human heart, for *personal* salvation, it also satisfies the deepest demand of reason, for a self-explanatory ground of being.

Schelling has little sensitivity for a theology of revelation. This, I will argue, is one of the weaknesses in his late thinking. By a theology of revelation I mean a theology which assumes, not blind fidelity to authoritatively pronounced propositions, but an ordinary intellect 'illumined' by faith. Theology in this more traditional register proceeds scientifically, that is, self-critically and in methodically moderated dialogue with others, but because of this presupposition of faith, it does not expect universal agreement, and is not disappointed when it finds itself contradicted at every turn by unbelief. Not all are so illuminated, for whatever reason. The theology of revelation is no less rational for this presupposition, nor is it unspeculative and rigid. On the contrary, closely aligned with the presupposition of intellectual illumination is the assumption that grace founds communities of believers, the Church itself, within which the theological enterprise of understanding what has been revealed, and continually revising that understanding in the light of new questions, new problems and new historical contexts, proceeds not only scientifically, but as the highest form of science, as what Thomas Aquinas calls *sacra doctrina*.

Schelling's work is a philosophy of revelation, as distinct from a theology of revelation, and it neither presumes faith nor does it shrink back from the scientific ideal of at least aiming at universal human agreement. To the neo-Orthodox theologian who would charge Schelling with judging the things of God by means of fallen human reason, Schelling would reply: reason may be fallen, but it was never *merely* human. The objectivity of reason was the early Schelling's innovation over Fichte and the Kantian tradition. Reason is not 'in us', merely human, subjective, and so on; it is 'out there', that is, it is nature, the eternal order, which thinks itself through me even as it gives rise to all natural forms.

In Schelling's defence against the theological objections to him, is it not central to Chalcedonian Christianity to recognise humanity as de facto redeemed and divinised? Schelling dares to think from out of the future of Christianity. To think out of the future of Christianity is to think from out of a fulfilled New Testament, which means to believe the promise. In that fulfilment, in that *eschaton* (the end of Christianity), reason can no longer behave as though revelation were alien to it, as if transcendence meant that God is not also immanent in nature and human culture. Everything hinges on the temporal qualifier of this claim: Schelling does not assume that we have reached the standpoint of the absolute, and so his Philosophy of Revelation remains fallibilist (Schelling more or less invents the fallibilist logic that will be taken up by the American pragmatists). Schelling's fallibilism does not so much place God's word under censure as confess, with Paul and the tradition, that the end has not yet come, and that we still see the things of God as in a glass darkly (1 Cor. 13:12).

It is important to note that Schelling does not deny the need for an inside/outside distinction at certain periods in the history of theology, including even the present age. He is not denying that revelation develops in the incubator of the faith community, as a gift of grace that in decisive ways interrupts philosophy and science and contradicts the judgements of historical reason on several points, and that it could only so develop insofar as it protected the revelation from the unbelief that surrounded it. He is, however, denying that revelation can *remain* the special knowledge of a particular historical community without betraying its very essence. Schelling is daring to think revelation as the common intellectual and moral inheritance of humankind. We are not yet there – Schelling is clear on this point. 'We must not misjudge our time' (Schelling 1815a: 206/xl). Philosophical religion, which will succeed historical Christianity, does not yet exist; the Philosophy of Revelation is not philosophical religion. It is not the fulfilled form of divinised reason and the final universalisation of the Gospel. The

Philosophy of Revelation is to philosophical religion as John the Baptist was to the Christ, the herald but not the one, a voice crying in the wilderness, preparing the way for the philosophy to come, the coming of which will render it redundant.[11] In Schelling's view, Hegel mistook the present age for the age to come and prematurely endeavoured to transform Christian dogma into general principles of knowledge, with the end result of distorting both theology and philosophy. Schelling's Philosophy of Revelation, as distinct from Hegel's philosophy of religion, is anticipatory and therefore provisional, to be succeeded by the philosophical religion of the future. Schelling is audacious, but his audacity consists neither in a rationalisation of dogma nor a theologisation of philosophy (and he has been accused of both), but in his daring to think Christianity in view of its end, even if that end has not yet occurred.

Neither this book nor its sequel attempts to summarise the labyrinthine narrative of Schelling's Philosophy of Revelation, which could not be recounted without a survey of its equally massive prolegomenon, the Philosophy of Mythology. The whole story takes up seven books and 2,100 pages of Schelling's collected works, and this is not including the preliminary sketches, the Erlangen Lectures (1820–27) or the Munich Lectures (1827–40). The task has not yet been done, in English at any rate, and I do not attempt it here. I wish to make a more modest contribution to the growing literature on Schelling in English, and present, in a general way but with careful attention to principles, the structure of Schelling's Philosophy of Revelation, and offer hermeneutical readings of several of its essential claims.

A word on the title of the present book is perhaps apposite here. By addressing 'the philosophical foundations of the late Schelling' I do not wish to create the impression that Schelling has philosophical foundations to offer theology or intends to revive natural theology in any way. There is no logical connection between the negative and the positive philosophy; that means that no certain foundations secure the turn to the positive, no deductions or demonstrations mitigate the risk involved. Nevertheless, Schelling offers philosophical reasons for his non-foundationalist philosophy of religion (alongside non-philosophical or historical-critical reasons). Schelling refuses a deductive turn but offers philosophical reasons for this refusal, reasons that have repercussions for other areas of philosophy as well. The foundations of the positive philosophy are not to be found in nature-philosophy or in identity-philosophy, both of which Schelling associates with negative philosophy. The foundations are not even to be found in the revised negative philosophy that Schelling called *die reinrationalen Philosophie* (Schelling 1854a), because the foundations are, and must be, positive, not negative. One cannot begin positive philosophy in the negative;

what begins in the negative remains in the negative. The entry point to the positive is always *the philosopher*, the one who decides to think his or her existence, and to exist in his or her thinking. The freedom of this beginning, the personal quality of it, means that everyone will have to do it for themselves, and there will be as many ways to begin as there are philosophers. The striking disclaimer that Schelling offered in 1842 in Berlin should be kept in mind at every stage of the following work: 'The positive philosophy is the truly free philosophy; whoever does not want it should just as well leave it alone. I propose it to everyone freely. I only maintain that if one wants the actual chain of events, if he wants a freely created world, and so on, he can have all of this only via the path of such a philosophy' (Schelling 1842d: 132/182).

That Schelling's Philosophy of Revelation is non-foundationalist does not mean that he has no arguments to make for the turn to the positive. It is with these arguments that I am concerned in the present book: I mean to outline, elaborate and evaluate the logical, moral and existential arguments Schelling offers us for assuming revelation as an explanation for nature, the human situation and history. At least insofar as the English literature is concerned, this has not yet been done. Not that it required any great inventive skill to do it. It required only patient reading of the late Schelling without ideological editing. 'Whoever seeks to listen to me', Schelling said in Berlin in 1841, 'listens to the end' (SW 13: 143). Aside from a school of first-generation disciples so small they scarcely show up in the records, no one did.[12] Not only did the Berlin lecture hall, which was filled to capacity on the opening day of Schelling's much-anticipated 1841 lectures, empty out within a space of weeks; even sympathetic auditors, such as Kierkegaard, who stayed on halfway into the winter semester, had no patience for what Schelling was doing. Most of them left, often with some purloined Schellingian concept gleaned from the narrative, which they would put to use in their own philosophies, usually without acknowledgement.[13]

We would be mistaken if we assumed from the lack of uptake that Schelling's last work was one of pure philosophical-theological speculation, with few real-world consequences. On the contrary, this is Schelling at his most political.[14] Employed by two kings to quell the revolutionary fires breaking out all over Europe and threatening to engulf Germany – principally, to stem the tide of republicanism – Schelling took his job seriously. Like most of the great thinkers of Christianity (Augustine, Aquinas, Luther), it was impossible for Schelling to speak of the religious without also speaking of the political, or to speak of the political without also speaking of religion. It is noteworthy that in correspondence at the time of the turn in his thinking, Schelling speaks of religion as primarily a sociopolitical affair. Because Schelling is repeatedly misunderstood as a mystic, his reasons for reconsidering religion in 1806 are worth citing here. 'In my solitude in Jena, I became more preoccupied with nature and less with life . . . Since then I have come to learn that religion and public faith are the pivot point of life in the State around which everything revolves, the point at which the lever must be applied which could jolt the moribund masses.'[15] This passage makes it explicit that Schelling's turn to religion in the years 1804–9 was not a turn inwards, not a turn to mysticism and contemplative life after his years as a busy and public academic, but quite the opposite: it was a turn outwards, towards sociopolitical problems which he believed could only be solved through religion.

As a political-theological thinker, Schelling writes in the tradition of Joachim of Fiore: he is prophetic, and deeply, if carefully, critical of modernity, looking towards nothing less than the fulfilment of Christianity (that is, of human history) in the fusion of the Church with the world and the full appropriation of revelation by secular reason, that is, the sacralisation of the secular and the secularising of the sacred. In terms of the contemporary political spectrum, which divides political possibilities between the left, which defends a maximal notion of the interventionist State, and the right, which defends the economic individual (i.e., the market) against the State, Schelling is neither left nor right, neither liberal nor conservative. With the left, he believes that it is only in society that the person is truly free, and therefore that the State should make possible and protect society (Schelling 1854a: 436). With the right, he believes that society exists *for* the individual, not the other way around (Schelling 1854a: 551, 554). Against the left, Schelling believes in neither original goodness nor the predominance of rationality in the individual, and denies the contractarianism which presumes both. He argues, against classical liberals, that freedom is the product of social relations and cannot, therefore, precede them. We cannot freely enter into contractual relations with others in the mythic constitution of the State, for we are only free through our State-protected relations with others. The lowest level of governance is to be preferred: given the degraded situation of the human being, who cannot be trusted to will the good on his or her own, the State is necessary, a punishment for sin (Schelling 1854a: 547), but it should be kept as small as possible, render itself invisible and function as the hidden and enabling ground of society (Schelling 1854a: 551). Against the right, Schelling believes that the State is a historical manifestation of the eternal law. Schelling is with the left in anticipating a definitive emancipation of human beings from all forms of bondage, but he is with the right in denying that we possess the political means to bring this about. With the left, he believes that moral life is only possible in society; with the right, he denies that the purpose of the State is to produce such moral living. He advocates reform, not revolution, and believes that we should be cautious when deciding which institutions should or should not be preserved and protected from the vicissitudes of change. He believes, with the right, that social inequalities are natural, but he does not therefore follow some rightists in arguing that they are therefore just. Against the conservatives, who have too quickly concluded that we have already done the best we can do, Schelling preaches the Gospel of eschatological emancipation from inequalities and the punitive State needed to mitigate it – a Gospel he takes up from the letters of Paul and the Gospel of John. If Schelling is neither left nor right in the simplistic terms of contemporary politics, neither was early Christianity left or right: it neither rushed headlong into social and political revolution, nor did it retreat from the political into mysticism or fetishise the status quo. Early Christians resisted injustice while still awaiting, 'with eager expectation', the unveiling of 'the sons and daughters of God' (Rom. 8:19).

All of these positions converge on Schelling's political eschatology: Schelling looks towards the culmination of human history in the coming of the perfect community. This future is the end of Christianity (in the sense of its *terminus ad quem* or goal), the 'third age of revelation', 'the Church of St John', the advent of philosophical religion, to succeed the first or Petrine age (Catholicism) and the second or Pauline age (Protestantism). The third age will see both the demise of the State as well as the end of the Church, in both senses of the term 'end', that is, both its closure (*eschaton*) and fulfilment (*telos*). It will bring to an end the need for the Church as the spiritual authority on earth, compensating for the State's external and legal authority and holding in check the State's totalitarian tendencies. It will free us from the political as well, for it will fulfil the deepest desires of the human heart, for perfect community or, more prosaically, for the unity of equality and liberty. This democracy to come (we can with some justice borrow Derrida's phrase here [Derrida 2005: 78]) is what Christianity was always intended to be. The third age is not yet the end of history. It is preparatory for the promised *eschaton*, the moment in time foretold by Paul, when time itself will come to an end and the Son will deliver the world back to the Father. 'When everything is subject to Christ, then the Son Himself will also be subject to the One who subjected everything to Him, so that God may be all in all' (1 Cor. 15:28). Schelling is not usually a practitioner of indirection and is rarely ironic. He is not flirting with a religious tradition in which he does not believe, nor is he playing with biblical metaphors as stand-ins for other concepts. The *eschaton* is not a regulative ideal, as it is in Derridean discourse, a fantasy on the horizon of the political, unattainable ('impossible') but necessary for a functioning democracy. The third age is for Schelling the true meaning of the Gospel and a real-world political possibility, one that at the end of his life he earnestly believed we ought to *actively* anticipate, that is, work towards.

With a few exceptions, the Schelling renaissance in English remains silent on Schelling's unmistakable theological commitments.[16] In some highly visible cases, the new Schellingians are even openly hostile to Schelling's theology, endeavouring to extract a kernel of logic from the late Schelling, or a kernel of ontology, or politics, or psychology, cleansed of its indigestible Christian husk.[17] These authors regard Schelling's theology as an accident, an excess, perhaps the occasion for the development of something interesting for logic, ontology, politics or psychology, but not essential to these contributions. If the late Schelling has anything to say to contemporary thought, they assume, it is not concerning Christology, Trinitarian theology or eschatology. On these points, Schelling is embarrassingly out of step with our post-Christian times. For Schelling insists, in no uncertain terms, that Christianity is the true religion, the culmination of human religious history; that the essence of Christianity consists in the succession of theism by Trinitarianism; that the history of the Trinity is narrated, not deduced (even if anticipation of the logical structure of the Trinity is native to reason); that the narration is based on certain historical facts (the events recounted in the New Testament), which can be reasonably defended in a fully secular context; that the Trinity is the proper explication of the Christ event; and finally, and most importantly, that Christianity is not yet finished. As the future religion *par excellence*, Christianity will only be complete when the world becomes Church.

At issue in the late Schelling, then, is the question of the degree to which modern philosophy can even *recognise* the intelligibility of Christianity, what we might loosely call the sense of Christianity, without either reducing it to something already known, something which is true *a priori* and merely dressed up in historical terms (Schelling's reading of Hegel's position), or formalising it to the point where the New Testament is deprived of any substantive content (the early Heidegger's approach).[18] To sum up Schelling's argument as succinctly as possible, reason's assent to the irreducible truth of the Christian revelation is no leap of faith but the discursive culmination of a sober and fearless assessment of logic, metaphysics and history. In this assent, which is not logically compelled but willed by the philosopher who refuses to remain content with the phantoms of idealism, with modernity's disavowals, or with the quiet despair of contemporary politics, reason must first negate itself and renounce an interior, virtual infinite in favour of the real infinite, only so that it can then receive itself back transformed. This is what Schelling calls 'the ecstasy of reason', that rational act whereby reason steps outside of itself, recognises its negativity, and opens itself to the reception of knowledge that it did not produce nor could produce for itself.[19]

Anyone writing about Schelling today must first dispel the prejudice that has haunted this figure through most of the twentieth century, the assumption that Schelling is merely a transitional figure, and that his later lectures peter out into obscurantism and mysticism. The research of a new generation of Schellingians has gone some distance towards putting this presupposition to rest.[20] With regard to Schelling's later work, there is still much interpretation to be done. It has become fashionable in new Schelling research to argue against the periodisation of Schelling typical of mid-twentieth-century scholarship. There is only one Schelling, we are told, and the appearance of distinct periods, internal diversity or apparent contradiction, which in another age earned Schelling some less than flattering designators ('the Proteus of philosophy' and so on), is a sign of the commentator failing to grasp the essential unity of Schelling's thought. What many of these protests in favour of Schelling's continuity have in common is a tendency, more or less expressed, to downplay the significance of the biblical revelation for Schelling's late work. If Schelling's late turn to Christianity is mentioned by certain defenders of his continuity, it is usually regarded as an inessential swerve of the older Schelling, a forgivable idiosyncrasy, and nothing that threatens or qualifies the pantheistic earlier work. It strikes me that such a sidelining of the Philosophy of Revelation in the interest of emphasising the continuity of Schelling's work produces the very opposite of what is intended; it in fact amounts to a denial of continuity. To deny the relevance of the religious content of Schelling's Philosophy of Revelation is to deny the continuity of Schelling's work as such. The Philosophy of Revelation, insofar as it defended 1) the existence of the creator God and 2) the truth of the basic claims of orthodox Christianity – incarnation, redemption and Trinity – is, in the view of some high-profile scholars, a non-essential eccentricity of the ageing philosopher, who probably should be forgiven his pious recidivism. Schelling is thus not, on this view, entirely continuous, for at the end he appends to his philosophy something discontinuous with the central thrust of his thought, namely Christianity. Since this pious appendix is neither intrinsically connected to his philosophy nor particularly interesting in itself, it does not disturb the continuity of all that precedes it in any important way, and occasionally allows Schelling to supplement his earlier work with interesting new concepts. We forgive the old man for lapsing into the religion of his upbringing at the end of his life.

To read the Philosophy of Revelation as the essential completion of Schelling's path, by contrast, as I do in this book, is to *defend* Schelling's continuity, the continuity of his purpose, sustained over seven decades, to think the problems of philosophy as comprehensively as his times and abilities would allow. Schelling never abandons a principle once discovered and demonstrated, for example, the principle of polarity or the law of the ground, which is not to say that he never thinks beyond it. Would it not be strange otherwise? What is reasonable about an a man in his sixties thinking the same way he did as a teenager? In the nature-philosophy/identity-philosophy of his early works, Schelling produced his basic ontology, what he later called 'rational philosophy' (which is no less true for being negative, that is, *a priori*). This ontology is not altered by the Philosophy of Revelation, for what is revealed in Christianity, according to Schelling, is not a new philosophy that contradicts the rational philosophy. What is revealed is the *unprethinkable* existence of the creator God – unprethinkable because it is the being of a personalising divinity, one who can only be known, like any person, to the degree that they reveal themselves. Schelling's God is not an onto-theological first principle, dragged in at the last minute to shore up a shaky metaphysics. Schelling's speculative path, from his early transcendental idealism, through his identity philosophy, to the experimental theosophical metaphysics of the Freedom Essay, to the final cycle of lectures on mythology and revelation, is a journey towards the genuinely divine God, the God of history. The evidence for this personalising divinity is the whole of natural and human history. What makes the Philosophy of Revelation a *philosophy* (and not a theology) is Schelling's application of the concepts of his basic *naturphilosophische* ontology to the interpretation of revelation, an application that does not change the ontology even if it changes everything else Schelling might have previously thought about God, history and human destiny. To conclude these qualifications, let us be clear: Schelling is no Tertullian, divorcing reason from revelation, nor is he Wittgenstein, producing two antithetical philosophies. The thinker whom Schelling most resembles in his approach to revelation is Thomas Aquinas, who famously wrote *gratia supponit naturam* ('Grace does not destroy nature but perfects it' [*Summa Theologica*, 1a, q. 8, ad 2]). Or in Schelling's own words, 'Revelation must contain something transcending reason, yet something that one cannot have without reason' (Schelling 1841: 97). Revelation is not a deduction or intuition of reason, even if the only means we have to think it is rational. To hold that reason is suitable to the thinking of revelation is not to reduce revelation to nature-philosophy or to any other philosophy, but rather to recognise that the unprethinkable source of the one is also the unprethinkable source of the other.

Schelling's career spanned six decades of productive work as a writer, university lecturer and public speaker, opening and closing the era of German idealism, a field which has resurged into popularity of late alongside its ally, romanticism. He inaugurated the movement with his speculative amplifications of late Kant and early Fichte into a style of metaphysics that was foreign to both of them, and brought it to a close with his late turn to what I call 'ecstatic theological realism'. No one can any longer deny that

Schelling is literally the first and last word in German idealism. And yet the English philosophers who wrote the first histories of post-Kantian philosophy in Germany (British idealists and their followers) were content to leave Schelling as a transitional figure between Fichte and Hegel. They expended some energy on understanding Schelling's *Naturphilosophie*, for Hegel had always praised it, and followed him up until the 1800 *System of Transcendental Idealism*. They ignored Schelling's crucial middle and later works, in which the first major critique of Hegelian idealism is unfurled and the death knell of German idealism is sounded from the very academic lectern occupied by Hegel up until his death in 1831. For a representative example of this kind of selective historical memory – and a statement of prejudice that still dominates mainstream philosophical interpretations of Schelling – let us look briefly at John Watson's widely read early study, *Schelling's Transcendental Idealism: A Critical Exposition* (1882).

Watson was a well-known historian of philosophy educated in England by British idealists, and a founding member of one of the first departments of philosophy in Canada, at Queen's University in Kingston. His study of Schelling contains a detailed and mostly reliable summary of Schelling's *System of Transcendental Idealism*. Most interesting for our purposes, however, are the concluding eighteen pages of Watson's book, which deal with Schelling's later philosophy. From the opening of the book, we are in no doubt about Watson's assessment. He damns Schelling's work as a whole with faint praise. 'His [Schelling's] philosophy is in large measure a failure; but then it is one of those failures that are more significant than the petty successes of others' (Watson 1882: 3).[21] If Schelling's early philosophy is of interest to Watson because it contributes to 'the transition from Kant to Hegel through Fichte' (Watson 1882: 3), Schelling's later philosophy is bluntly dismissed as 'mystical' (Watson 1882: 218). Even more revealing of his Hegelian prejudices, Watson writes:

> That he [Schelling] can give no other than a mystical solution [to the relation of God to the world] results partly from the limitations of his philosophical genius, and partly from the false course on which he embarked when he coordinated nature and spirit instead of subordinating the one to the other. (Watson 1882: 220)

Leaving aside for the moment the questionable use of the term 'mysticism' here,[22] Watson sums up in a word the deliberate misreading by which several generations of English historians of philosophy justified their neglect of the late Schelling. It is mere 'mysticism', that is, without rational justification. 'The conception of God, as by his very nature compelled to reveal himself in the world, undoubtedly contains a truth of pre-eminent importance; but it is not arrived at by any rational and well-ordered method, but is simply accepted on the guarantee of a flash of poetic insight' (Watson 1882: 232).

There are two points worth making about this passage, which is so typi-cal of its time. First, Watson betrays his careless reading of the Philosophy of Revelation, which had been published for over twenty-five years in Germany when he wrote this book (it is not even clear that Watson had read it at all, although he feels justified in passing judgement upon it). Watson conflates the middle Schelling of the Freedom Essay, who writes a theogony of the creator God, with the late Schelling who expressly rejects this earlier abrogation of God's freedom and transcendence.[23] In the Freedom Essay, Schelling becomes a Boehmian, and describes a natural process by which God becomes conscious of himself by creating the world, more or less defin-ing for his generation the position made popular by Hegel, what I have elsewhere called historical immanentism.[24] Twenty-two years later, when the 710-page manuscript of the Philosophy of Revelation (the *Urfassung* of 1831) was complete – a text Schelling would use in his lectures with little deviation for the next twenty-two years – God is defined as the necessary being who in fact exists, and who is complete in Godself. While the creator God *decides* to become vulnerable to the world (as a lover chooses to become vulnerable – to need – the beloved), God does not need to create in order to become conscious or free.[25]

> The perfect spirit, insofar as he is he who will be who he is, he who is not bound to himself but can go out of himself, he who is the living spirit, can alone be called God strictly speaking. Not a lifeless substance that is merely capable of logical rela-tions, even less a substance which is mobile but which moves only out of blind necessity, which through successive negation of every determinate being presents itself at last as the nothing, could be God; only that bears the name God which says: I will be what what I will be; that is, what I chose to be. There is nothing prede-termining my being. No one can predetermine what I will be – it depends entirely upon my will. (Schelling 1831: 89)

This passage leaves little doubt that by the 'substance which is mobile but which moves only out of blind necessity, which through successive negation of every determinate being presents itself at last as the nothing', Schelling has Hegel's self-mediating absolute in mind. Nor can we doubt that by the God who 'is he who will be', Schelling is referring to the God revealed to Moses, the one who names himself *ehyeh aser ehyeh*, commonly translated 'I am that I am' (Exod. 3:14). Schelling anticipates the Hebrew scholarship of the twentieth century which sees in the divine name the future tense of the Hebrew verb 'to be', indicating that Yahweh refuses to be confined by any-thing that would limit God's possibilities, that Yahweh is a God of possibil-ity, a God who stands open to the future.[26] Hence, those interpreters are to some degree correct in seeing in the late Schelling a return to an orthodox Jewish-Christian notion of God and a rejection of the idealist pantheist God whose being is bound up with the dialectic of infinity and finitude.

However, before we jump to any conclusions regarding the late Schelling's 'conservativism', or celebrate the triumph of 'Christian metaphysics' over 'German idealism' (Laughland 2007), it is worth pointing out the heterodoxy of Schelling's late position on the relationship of the Christian Trinity to the world. Schelling's highest principle, his basic presupposition, is divine freedom. A God who *needs* the world in order to be divine is not free. Hegel's God needs to create the world in order to be God, Hegel's God needs to mediate divinity by means of creation, negate infinity by means of the finite, in order to realise Godself as spirit. A process that can only subsist by means of negation is no God, Schelling writes.[27] To be sure, in creating the world, God sets a divine process in motion which begins in the negative and ends in a recapitulated and higher unity, but God does so out of no inner need, Schelling insists. God is free not to do so and would remain entirely Godself had God never created anything at all. 'Monotheism is only compatible with a system of free creation' (Schelling 1831: 125).

Schelling's late notion of God is the archetype for his non-dialectical personalism, one of the three pillars of Schelling's late philosophy. A person for Schelling is not, *pace* Hegel and the tradition of dialogical personalism which he inaugurated, one who needs to be recognised by another in order to be a person, but one who has overcome necessity and otherness within his or herself and so is free to enter into relations with others. God does not create the world in order to have another who can recognise God; God, having personalised Godself by overcoming the blind act of being which is God's origin, creates the world out of love, out of the pure desire to communicate God's being. That said, Schelling breaks with the Augustinian and Thomist tradition, which maintains that the Trinity subsists in perfect indifference to creation, receives nothing from it, and is unaffected by it.[28] The perfection of the Augustinian-Thomist Trinity, which enjoys full actuality and personal communion among the three fully actual, divine persons independent of its relation to creation, raises the question, Why does such a God create the world at all? One might question further, with Moltmann, and ask, Can a God who is invulnerable to creation legitimately be described as loving? What kind of lover remains invulnerable to his beloved? Schelling's late position on the Trinity is subtle and carefully developed over the course of the Philosophy of Revelation. A detailed discussion of it will occupy the second part of this two-book project. Suffice it to say here that God is not 'compelled to reveal Godself in the world'; God *decides* to be so revealed. In that revelation, the triune God steps out of eternity, where God is real but not actual, into time; that is, the persons of the Trinity become actual, fully differentiated personalities in the creation and redemption of the world. This means that, for Schelling, the economic Trinity adds something to the immanent

Trinity: actuality in time. The Father actualises his Fatherhood in creation, the Son actualises his Sonship in redemption, and the Spirit actualises itself as Spirit in becoming actual in the human community. Prior to these events, these Trinitarian relations are only potentially personal relations, for the condition of their actualisation is their freedom from one another, a freedom that they only truly achieve in the creation, redemption and sanctification of the world. Each of the persons must in turn overcome an internal necessity specific to each and so achieve a free relation to each of the others. So God is not *compelled* to reveal Godself in the creation of the world; but were the world not created, God's three personalities would remain unrevealed even to Godself.

Watson declares that Schelling's late philosophy is not the product of a 'rational and well-ordered method, but is simply accepted on the guarantee of a flash of poetic insight'. The aim of this book is to demonstrate how deeply wrong Watson is. Neither Schelling's philosophy of freedom nor his Philosophy of Revelation has much to do with mysticism (by whatever definition), and if Schelling's speculation occasionally takes poetic flight, it is not properly characterised as poetry. Even if method is never permitted to supplant content in Schelling's late philosophy (a deliberate and rationally defensible move), and even if Schelling remained throughout his career sensitive to the insights that exceed the grasp of discursive philosophy, a consciousness of method – the need for it and the danger it poses to thinking – pervades the whole work. No doubt the Freedom Essay is a literary and religious masterpiece, and is often cited for its poetic power. One could call it 'mere poetry' only by ignoring or misunderstanding the steely rigour of the logic elaborated in the first pages and operative at every conceptual turn of the succeeding narrative. The late Schelling rarely waxes poetic about the history of religion, is highly critical of theosophy, and is deeply hesitant about mysticism (Schelling 1842d: 119/173).[29] Rather than translating mysticism into metaphysics, he applies certain well-tested principles (the same logic worked out in the Freedom Essay two decades earlier) to the reading of history in such a way as to enact the very pattern of scientific thinking (what Peirce, a much more careful reader of Schelling than Watson, will call 'abductive logic').[30] Schelling not only rejects any philosophy that would presume to justify itself on the basis of intuition or 'poetic insight' (in *The Grounding of the Positive Philosophy*, this illegitimate move is elaborated as the central error of theosophy);[31] at no point in the seven-book narrative that constitutes the cycle of lectures of the Philosophy of Mythology and Revelation does Schelling resolve a conceptual issue through recourse to poetry or intuition.

On close inspection, Schelling's arguments are shown to be underwritten by a rigorous adherence to an admittedly idiosyncratic but brilliant reading of informal logic; in many ways, the narrative of the personalisation of God through the creation, the fall, and the redemption of the world is an elaboration of these principles (which is not to say, *pace* Hogrebe and Gabriel, that Schelling's ontology is reducible to this logic).[32] If we were to compare Schelling and Hegel on the question of following a rational and well-ordered method, it is not at all clear who would emerge as the more rigorous thinker. Certainly, no one can miss the method that Hegel brings to everything he does: on every page of the *Encyclopedia*, one can watch Hegel hammering reality into the mould of his dialectical logic. Schelling, by contrast, is deeply sensitive to the gap that forever divides thought and being – a gap that was misunderstood by Kant as one constituted by the structure of knowledge rather than the structure of being – and so never demands that reality fit into a schema pre-established by reason. Schelling's method is neither inductive nor deductive; rather, it proceeds in such a way as to invite a rewriting of the rational assumptions that he brings to the study of the real. Watson drew the false conclusion that because Schelling's Philosophy of Revelation remains open-ended – for it is the narration of a history that is not yet finished rather than a deduction of the forms of history – Schelling has no method.

Methodological rigour and certainty are not the same thing.[33] The insistence on closure is not in itself reasonable; in the context of the philosophy of history it is in fact dogmatic. In the work of the natural sciences, closure is methodologically precluded. If Popper is followed, to be scientific is to be open to falsification by facts (Popper 1963). In this regard, Schelling is the most scientific of all the German idealists. Kant, Fichte and Hegel, each in their own way, were beguiled by the craving for closure so typical of modernity and preferred a deductive method, even if such deductions, as in Kant's case, left philosophy in a merely phenomenal order with unclear relations to the real. Reason – Fichte, Kant and, in another way, Hegel insist – must be deductive, advancing to necessary conclusions and producing closure. It is precisely this Spinozistic assumption of his generation that the late Schelling challenges as the most unreasonable of all. We are never more reasonable than when we abjure the false certainty of the ideal for a genuine knowledge of the real. What Watson missed entirely is that the ecstasy of reason in the late Schelling is not a mystical rapture or a poetic flight but a rational act, the most reasonable thing reason can do. Science does it on a mundane level all the time: it is the creative leap that so often follows the scientist's wrestling with a recalcitrant, inexplicable fact, and precedes scientific breakthroughs. *Systematic thinking* and *system building* do not necessarily coincide. All system building is systematic but not all systematic thinking is system building. Where Hegel is the builder of *a* system, *the* system, Schelling builds and apparently destroys multiple systems throughout his career. As is often pointed out, this is because Schelling does not believe that the construction of a single system adequate to reality is humanly possible. Every human system is partial and to that degree inadequate to the whole. Yet Schelling is always systematic in what he does; there is no abjuring of reason in his refusal of a closed system.

One who refuses system might disavow the principle of sufficient reason, as in contemporary forms of obscurantism and cynicism. Schelling never does. He is neither obscurantist nor cynical in his refusal of a closed system. The obscurantist declares that life is too infinitely mysterious for rational philosophy; only the poets and the mystics can do it justice. The cynic finds nothing mysterious about life, but with the same premature certainty as the obscurantist, rejects the principle of reason, declaring that all thought, language and action, co-opted as they are by constitutive ideology, inevitably shipwreck in parallaxes.[34] The obscurantist and the cynic are in one sense opposed: for the obscurantist, life is too richly meaningful for philosophy to be anything other than an idle exercise of ignorant rationalists; for the cynic, consciousness is too constitutively self-deceiving for philosophy to be anything other than self-reflective critique, and one that can never stop because consciousness will always incline towards the safety and stability of a new ideology. The one finds life too meaningful for philosophy, the other, too meaningless. Obscurantism and cynicism share a position that sets them both against the primordially scientific attitude that I hold to be Schelling's. Both obscurantism and cynicism foreclose the range of questioning. Both presume to definitively know something about the fit (or lack thereof) of truth and thought. The obscurantist says, definitively and without qualification (as though speaking out of some privileged, non-rational gnosis): philosophical thought is always distortive of the real because it simply cannot handle it. The cynic says, just as definitively and without qualification, and with just as much presumption of secret access to the truth, precisely the same thing. Where the obscurantist finds something to affirm in this – the excessively meaningful nature of reality – the cynic finds something to smugly mock – the comic ineptitude of false consciousness. It might seem surprising to line up New Age gurus next to professional critics of culture (Eckhart Tolle alongside Slavoj Žižek), but from a Schellingian perspective they have much in common. Both renege on the principle of reason; both presume to know something that Schelling would never claim to know; both are manifestly lacking in the philosophical humility that refuses system for the same reason it refuses closure: because it refuses, in the light of historical being, any *a priori* limitation on the range of questioning.

The refusal of system could, on the other hand, be motivated by genuine philosophical humility: fidelity to both the imperatives of reason (coherence *and* adequacy) and the strangeness of things. On this view, no system of thought is possible because truth is not identical to intelligibility. That thought cannot complete its task of giving an account of the real does not necessarily render it futile. It is in the interest of an open exploration of systematicity that Schelling at every stage of his career rejected any rendering of the truth as a secure possession of conceptual thinking. Peirce admired this element of restless experimentation and self-critique in Schelling.[35] Because of the irreducible exteriority of the divine to thinking, philosophy in Schelling never assumes primacy over other forms of discourse, as it does in Hegel. Insofar as reason cannot explain its own existence, philosophy never achieves closure. In the late Schelling, this leitmotif of the poverty of reason generates a new figure for systematicity without system. Reason is most rational when it empties itself, renounces its *a priori* concept of being as sufficient to the real (however necessary it remains to thinking), and stands ecstatically oriented to that which is beyond reason.

No one who knows Schelling's late work endorses the standard history of philosophy account of him as a mere 'transitional' figure. First of all, it is unfaithful to Schelling's output. Schelling was still a young man when he published the *System of Transcendental Idealism*, with five decades of philosophical activity ahead of him. It is true that Schelling's major publications came to a halt with the 1809 Freedom Essay (Schelling's pivotal answer to Hegel's *Phenomenology of Spirit*); nevertheless, Schelling's lectures on nature, art, logic, mythology and revelation cover thousands of pages of densely argued speculative philosophy. Most of this literature was available by the time Schelling's son published the fourteen-volume edition of his *Sämtliche Werke* between the year 1856 and 1861. And while that edition has been understandably criticised by Schelling scholars, no one can say that we did not know what the late Schelling was up to. One must ask, why the long neglect in English of a figure that no German scholar ever regarded as marginal? If Schelling is such a big deal, why did mainstream philosophy never recognise him?

No doubt the influence of Hegel on British idealism played a role. Watson is an example of two generations of English-speaking historians of philosophy who accepted the damning verdict of most of the (Hegelian) British idealists: the early Schelling made some important contributions, but the late Schelling lost the plot. However, I believe that something more is at stake in the forgetting of Schelling in English than the hegemony of Hegel, something that concerns not so much the influence of British Hegelians as it does the demolition of British idealism by analytical philosophy.[36] The significance of this event is generally underestimated: the analytical revolution, spearheaded by Russell's critique of the speculative philosophy of F. H. Bradley, bifurcated philosophy in the English-speaking world into two incommensurate, mutually excommunicating fragments, 'analytical' and 'continental'.[37] My contention is that there is something about Schelling – as distinct, for example, from Hegel – that leaves him homeless in the twentieth century. Hegel was never forgotten by continental philosophy and has, via the Pittsburgh school of Brandom and Macdowell, secured a position in analytical philosophy (Rockmore 2012). Apart from scattered if influential studies (Heidegger 1936; Habermas 1954; Jaspers 1955), Schelling was not received by continental philosophy until Andrew Bowie's 1993 study. The split between analytical and continental philosophy divides Schelling himself right down the middle.[38]

Philosophy in English changed radically in the early part of the twentieth century. The extensive reception of German idealism by English speculative philosophy came to a halt with the Fregeian-Russellian reduction of being to instantiation. At a single stroke, speculative philosophy (German, British and American) – which was united in regarding the question of being as fundamental for philosophy and saw the answer to the question as inevitably interrogating theology – came to an end, was made literally impossible: for existence was no longer to be thought of as an activity which might have a variety of modes, but as a quantifier.[39] To say that something exists is simply to posit some bearer of predicates or to introduce in front of the predicate F the existential quantifier $\exists$, substituting for the predicative judgement, $\exists x F x$, which means, for the predicate F, there exists something, x, which answers to it. While illusory subjects such as 'the present King of France' are thereby rendered the chimera of a false description before a sentence about them can get off the ground, the move comes at great expense to ontology, and makes assumptions which can no longer be interrogated. The question of the meaning of being is elided by this notation, for the answer is assumed: to exist is to instantiate predicates. The question of the *manner* of existence, the modes of being, and above all, the question concerning the distinction between the being of a subject and the being of a predicate – questions which inescapably lead into the history of speculative philosophy (for concepts of an infinite mode of existence, a necessary existence, and a pure act of being arise along this line of inquiry) – is rendered impossible, literally unrepresentable by this logic.

While continental philosophy followed an opposite path and, in the wake of Heidegger, made the question of the meaning of being basic to philosophy again, it did so by refusing so-called 'onto-theology' at the outset, which meant that infinite ontologies were no longer permissible. The early Heidegger's phenomenological ontology is deliberately constructed in such a way as to surgically remove the idea of God – Aristotle's *actus purus*, Anselm's *quo maius nihil cogitari potest*, Aquinas's *ipsum esse subsistens*, Scotus's *ens necessarium*, Descartes' *idea substantiae infinitae*, Kant's *Ideal der reinen Vernunft* – from the discourse of philosophy. Heidegger redefines the terms of inquiry so as to make the question of the being of infinity incoherent. That this was primarily a move in logic is generally missed by most Heideggerians. *Being and Time* began as a critique of Aristotle's ten categories – a project that had occupied Heidegger since his *Habilitationsschrift* on Duns Scotus – and ended in an atheist existential philosophy of time, which owes a great deal to Schelling.[40] Shortly after its publication in 1927, Heidegger argued that the whole business of category deduction was a dead end. Phenomenology, for Heidegger, is hermeneutical and ontological, rather than epistemological or logical.[41] Nevertheless, the basic logical move of *Being and Time* remained in place, even for the later Heidegger, and has determined the course of continental philosophy ever since: the categories of philosophy are inextricably finite, anchored in human experience, and can only refer beyond themselves at the expense of coherence.

It is worth noting that Husserl's phenomenology on its own terms harbours other, less restrictive possibilities for the philosophy of religion.[42] It is not recognised widely enough that the early Heidegger did two things to Husserl's phenomenology that transformed it beyond recognition: he not only foregrounded phenomenology, which in the early Husserl is preoccupied with epistemology, in ontology; he also sidelined Husserl's overarching logical concerns. Husserl was deeply interested in questions concerning logical sense, validity and verification. So too was the young Heidegger.[43] Heidegger has perhaps less to answer for in this regard than his countless followers. When Heidegger wrote in 1929 that 'the idea of "logic" itself disintegrates in the turbulence of a more original questioning' (Heidegger 1929: 105), he did not mean that henceforth we could ignore our logical presuppositions, and philosophise in ignorance of the rules governing the formation of our concepts. Heidegger himself certainly knew what he was doing, but it is not clear that the industry of continental philosophy, which grants doctorates to students who demonstrate that they can fluently speak and write using the rhetoric of their favourite European author, knows what it is doing. Heideggerianism, if not Heidegger himself, is guilty of the forgetting of logic in the twentieth century – and where logic is forgotten, Schelling will be misread. The twentieth-century analysts, who took logic seriously, however, had little or no interest in speculative metaphysics or speculative theology. The reduction of the copula in judgement to a conjunctive that becomes inessential when being is expressed as $\exists(x)$ renders metaphysics in the grand sense moot. If to be means to be a bearer of predicates, then ideas, principles, divinities, the infinite are all chimeras produced by grammar. And wherever the question concerning the being of ideas, principles, divinities and the infinite cannot be asked, Schelling will not be read.

What followed the reduction of being to instantiation was a century of philosophers who either relied exclusively on a reduced logic, posing and answering clear and usually trivial questions framed in such a way that the question of the meaning of being could not be asked, or who pursued ontology with little regard for logic. Schelling simply could not fit into this century. Too logical for continentalists, he was too speculative for analysts. Things have changed, and many are promoting the withering away of the continental/analytical distinction, which largely survives these days only as a matter of departmental politics in North American universities. With speculative realism and object oriented ontology, logic and infinity are once again on the agenda, and in a non-reduced modality. The work of high-profile writers such as Slavoj Žižek, Iain Hamilton Grant and Markus Gabriel has reminded us that not only is Schelling a great speculative philosopher, he is also a great logician, one whose apparently meandering paths of thought are underwritten by a thinking of the problems of logic which anticipates much of what has lately come into vogue. English scholarship is finally realising something that has been well known in German scholarship, at least since the great studies of the late Schelling appeared in the mid-twentieth century, namely that just as German idealism is inconceivable without Schelling, so too is Schelling much more than a Romantic. Many of the most pressing topics in philosophy today, such as the relation of language to logic, the contingency of existence, the irreducibility of mind and the being of infinity, are anticipated if not well worked through by the German idealists. Schelling launches German idealism with his *Naturphilosophie*, which is far more ambitiously speculative than Fichte's efforts to systematise Kant (typically read as the inception of German idealism). Schelling deepens the post-Kantian reinvention of metaphysics with his philosophy of art and its allied system, the philosophy of identity. And he brings German idealism to an end, to the point where it can go no further because it has begun to unravel its own foundations, in the Freedom Essay, the *Ages of the World* drafts and, above all, in his lectures on the Philosophy of Mythology and Revelation.

The task at hand in the present work relies upon the excellent revisionary readings of Schelling done by Žižek, Grant and Gabriel, and yet turns a new page. For in all of the fuss around the late Schelling, a glaring omission stands out like the proverbial elephant in the room: no one has much to say about Schelling's philosophy of religion, and more specifically his philosophy of Christianity. No one seems to want to touch it. The new Schellingians avoid it as though it were marginal to the late Schelling's work. Theologians avoid it because it seems to be either incoherent, or worse, pantheistic, or worst of all, gnostic. The Philosophy of Revelation is a speculative reconstruction of the New Testament, especially the epistles of Paul and the Gospel of John, on the assumption that these texts offer us an historically reliable clue to the riddle of existence. In this specific sense, Schelling is returning us to the third-century Alexandrian idea of Christian *gnosis*. Schelling is proposing that the New Testament should be taken as offering us knowledge of ultimate things, knowledge that can and should be appropriated by philosophy in a post-Kantian register. As a work of speculative biblical interpretation, Schelling's Philosophy of Revelation belongs alongside the theologies of the later Schleiermacher and the mature Tillich. To be clear, Schelling's Philosophy of Revelation is not a finished project and cannot substitute for a complete systematic theology, such as both Schleiermacher and Tillich produced. It is full of theological insight and daring reconstructions. But it is also full of holes and puzzles, and the reader must compensate for these with interpolations and biblical interpretations of his or her own. This is perhaps true of all of Schelling's works, but especially so of the Philosophy of Revelation. Avid readers of Schelling will know that this fragmentary style is one of the sources of the fecundity of Schelling's thought. Schelling does not create disciples, but followers who think like he does, even if they are driven by their times, their questions and their own insights to think thoughts that the master himself never thought. The tragedy of Schelling's career consists in this, not that he could not produce a system (this was literally child's play for him, something that preoccupied him in his juvenilia), but that what he painstakingly constructed over the course of the last four decades of his life, his final and definitive philosophical position, stands largely unread today.

There are also contingent reasons for this neglect. The reading of the late Schelling today is hampered by the theological ignorance that reigns in contemporary academia. Few philosophers working in English-speaking universities in the twenty-first century have a generous enough knowledge of the history of Christianity to be able to fully grasp the theological and sociopolitical significance of Schelling's Philosophy of Revelation. This partially explains why Schelling's late philosophy, which has been on the shelves of major libraries for 150 years, has had so little impact on the philosophy of religion.[44] It also partially explains the cherry-picking which prevails among the many academic philosophers now working on Schelling in the English-speaking world – including their tendency to read the Philosophy of Mythology as Schelling's last word, and not, as it was designed, as the prolegomena to the Philosophy of Revelation. *If* the Philosophy of Revelation is read at all, it is not usually read with the knowledge of the New Testament and the early Church requisite for appreciating Schelling's subtle argumentation. Schelling was a master of Greek, Latin and Hebrew, and possessed an encyclopaedic knowledge of the scriptures and Church history which few philosophers working today can parallel. He is not generally read as the eschatological thinker he undoubtedly was because the distinction between eschatology and utopianism is no longer widely understood. His later turn towards the person is not appreciated, because the intrinsic relation between eschatological thinking – particularly the concept of eventful time which prevails in eschatological literature – and the ethics of the person is not appreciated. And Schelling's late political thought is misunderstood as reactionary, the conservatism typical of an ageing Romantic, because the history of political theology in general is not well-enough known.

But the real reason for the neglect of Schelling's Philosophy of Revelation has, I fear, more ideological causes than the decline of theological education in our secular age. When Schelling begins to interpret the scriptures, to unfold the Gospels as the meaning of history, we simply do not want to listen to him any more. We make the mistake of assuming, as did the auditors in the Berlin lecture hall in 1841, that we have heard all of that before. Nothing could be further from the truth. It is, then, to a generous hearing of the old master, and to the renewal of the Christian philosophy of religion, that I dedicate the following pages.

On the heated question concerning Schelling's continuity, let me be clear on my position: there are two Schellings. Schelling I is a philosopher of nature; Schelling II is a philosopher of revelation. Schelling's *Erzeugungsdialektik* means that Schelling II can still be a philosopher of nature even if Schelling I was not yet a philosopher of revelation.[45] Schelling I begins with the 1793 Timaeus Essay. Schelling II begins with the 1809 Freedom Essay. While the two Schellings are primarily distinguished in terms of subject matter, there are also crucially important methodological distinctions between them. But there is no contradiction between them. Schelling is like Heidegger, on a path that leads him to a place he could not have anticipated when setting out, a path leading to what is a substantially different philosophical position than the one with which he began. That this thought is anathema to so many who study Schelling today has many causes, some of which are not philosophical. The trend today is to assert, against earlier, largely Hegelian readings of Schelling as 'the Proteus of German philosophy', the continuity thesis.

I agree with the continuity thesis insofar as it asserts that the later Schelling is continuous with the early Schelling. The one who heads south on a meandering path through the forest does not change his mind when he continues as the path leads north. Schelling is a deeply consistent thinker, and if his consistency was missed by former generations of readers, it is because it is not on the surface but in the depths of his thinking. Insofar as advocates of the continuity thesis are arguing that there is no substantial difference between the later and the early Schelling, that the positive philosophy is *naturphilosophie* throughout, or that the Philosophy of Revelation concerns matters that were already discussed in the early works, then

I must disagree. And before I say why, consider first of all how strange it is to assume that a philosopher such as Schelling, who was nothing if not original, possessing a mind made restless by its native fertility, would not have adjusted his position over the course of six decades of productive work – that the old man would have the same convictions and philosophical interests as the young man. One could make the point in yet a more Schellingian way. If there is continuity between the early and the late Schelling, if the two are to be identified such that the later Schelling is still, at least in part, the early Schelling, then they must first be disjoined, like the subject and the predicate in any judgement. Or in yet another Schellingian figure, if the late Schelling had not dissociated from his past, then he would have never emerged from it, and had no past.

Let me briefly situate my position on Schelling's continuity in the history of this debate from Horst Furhmans to Iain Hamilton Grant. Furhmans offered the strongest argument for discontinuity, and provoked Schulz's counter-thesis, the strongest argument in favour of continuity. In Furhmans's view, Schelling breaks with idealism, not only Hegel's but also his own, when he recognises the incompatibility of all forms of idealism with revealed Christianity in his first Munich period (1806–20). The themes that preoccupy Schelling's writings and lecturing during this time – historicity, the freedom and personality of God, the moral accountability of the human person before God – are incompatible, according to Fuhrmans, with the objective idealism of his early period, the subjective idealism of Fichte and the absolute idealism of Hegel. Idealism for Furhmans equals determinism. Christianity, which presumes the freedom of God in creation and the freedom of humankind under God, breaks with all forms of idealism/determinism. The fragmentary and searching works of Schelling's middle period (the Freedom Essay, the drafts of *The Ages of the World*, the Stuttgart Seminars) do not so much resolve the tension between idealism and Christianity as exacerbate it, and become in their very failure the catalyst for the late Romantic recovery of Christianity in German thought. By the time of the positive philosophy, Schelling has lost the insight, according to Furhmans, and settled back into a more familiar idealist mode, and become again a system builder. Furhmans is thus the strongest voice for discontinuity in Schelling's work, not only the discontinuity between the middle period and the early works on nature-philosophy and identity-philosophy, but also the discontinuity between what he regards as the retro-idealism of the Philosophy of Mythology and Revelation and the more powerful insights barely systematised in Schelling's middle period.[46]

Schulz took exception to Furhmans's strong discontinuity thesis and argued precisely the opposite.[47] Schelling's late work is continuous with the middle and the early works: it is the fulfilment of what was begun earlier, a fulfilment (*Vollendung*) of idealism as such. With Schelling's positive philosophy idealism reaches its end and is over, for it can go no further. Idealism sought from the beginning to demonstrate the identity of thought and being, to recover reality in reflection, and only because it aimed at this could it discover in the end that reason cannot think existence. Hence Schelling's late philosophy, which does not so much fail to reconcile thought and existence as demonstrate the impossibility of such a reconciliation, inaugurates post-idealism and the philosophy of existence (Marx, Schopenhauer, Nietzsche, Kierkegaard). It should be noted that Schulz finds this continuity in Schelling by downplaying the theme of revelation in the positive philosophy. Schelling's theological turn is of little importance to the larger teleology of idealism working its way through him, according to Schulz.

Walter Kasper's major work on Schelling belongs to this German *disputatio*, for he ventures an early reconciliation of Furhmans and Schulz.[48] According to Kasper, Schelling was on the path to the positive from the beginning. Idealism in Schelling's early thought was already a philosophy of freedom, the product of a deed, and at least potentially a philosophy of Christianity. Schelling's earliest insight was that the absolute could not be known through anything other than the absolute: it could not be deduced or epistemically secured in any way. There was no way for the Cartesian subject to know the absolute, any more than there was a path from Scholastic syllogisms to the absolute. Knowing the absolute was the same as presupposing the absolute. With Schelling's positing of the absolute as non-object and the decisional beginning of philosophy, his path to thinking the historicity of the human being, which is fulfilled by the theological turn of the positive philosophy, begins. In Kasper's view, these three assumptions, 1) the decisional beginning of idealism (the absolute as starting point, as presupposition), 2) freedom as the essence of the human being and the *sine qua non* of philosophy, and 3) history as the manifestation of freedom, as the arena of freedom, as the play of the infinite in the finite, remain Schelling's foundation until the end. Kasper is thus a strong advocate of continuity, and a follower of Schulz, but the continuity is now found along the lines of the positive philosophy, not, as in Schulz, the negative philosophy. Schelling was ostensibly a positive philosopher from the start. Kasper sees Schelling's dialectic of negative and positive philosophy as both a recognition of the dialectic of law and Gospel in Luther and an improvement on Scholastic externalist interpretations of the relationship of nature to the supernatural. The supernatural presupposes the natural and fulfils it, but the relation between the two is one of freedom, not necessity. The notion of a natural presupposition of revelation is Catholic, the notion of the freedom of the fulfilment is Protestant.

Kasper's Schulzian reading of the late Schelling as an idealist grounds his critique of the late Schelling as committing the idealist fallacy of domesticating the transcendent.

> He [Schelling] knew that it was not possible to deduce what is from God as intellectually necessary, but he nevertheless thought that it was possible *a posteriori* with the Absolute. Thus he believed that it was possible, at least in a later phase, to understand God's path. The fact is thereby left aside that God is always the greater precisely in that God cannot be known. Schelling forgot that precisely the path of the negation of the negation must, in the knowledge of God, be an indication of the fact that every human thinking is and remains finite thinking, and that it therefore cannot adequately follow infinite thought. (Kasper 1965: 168)

This is, in my view, too strong a critique, if nevertheless one that is to some degree justified by Schelling's alignment with thinkers of *univocatio enits*, from Scotus to Descartes. Kasper identifies philosophical knowledge of the absolute with revelation. Positive philosophy aims at the latter, and hopes, with all the saints, for the former at the end of time, when we shall see God face to face (1 Cor. 13:12). Even the knowledge of God which is promised us will fall short of idealist self-transparency, according to the late Schelling. Kasper underplays the role of the indivisible remainder, which remains the insuperable condition of the human knowledge of God, even at the end of history. Reason will never gain the upper hand on the absolute, in Schelling's view, and will always remain finite in relation to God, because of the abyssal freedom out of which divinity and all things have emerged.

In his bid to align Schelling's absolute with Catholic theology, Kasper seems to have missed the radicality of Schelling's notion of ground. If God contains something in him which is not Godself, an origin of God, which God can never antecede, then transcendence is absolute. Put another way, if God remains a mystery even to God, how then can human beings hope to achieve an adequate knowledge of the divine? To do so, to demand such idealist certainty and self-transparent understanding of the being of God, is to reject the God who *is* in favour of a God more suited to the categories of reason. This is not only an error that Schelling does not commit, it is one that he expressly forbids, and constructs his last philosophy to avoid.

With Furhmans I argue for a turn that requires us to clearly distinguish (but not separate) the early and the later Schelling. Against Furhmans, I argue that the turn renders the middle and the late Schelling to some degree continuous, as it also renders the early Schelling and the middle Schelling to some degree continuous, in the same way that a hinge is continuous with both the door and the door frame which it connects. With Schulz I argue that idealism reaches its end in Schelling and discovers that it cannot be a philosophy of existence. Against Schulz (and Kasper, who follows Schulz in this regard) I argue that this is a breakthrough of Schelling's late period, not something that was always there from the beginning. There are harbingers of the breakthrough in the early philosophy, but the full actualisation of this thought of the difference between thinking and being depends upon Schelling's late turn to Christian revelation.

In more recent literature, Iain Hamilton Grant has revived the continuity thesis, but with a different emphasis than Schulz. What is continuous in Schelling is not, *pace* Schulz, the idealist goal of self-reflection, but the original Schellingian emphasis on nature as absolute. 'Schellingianism is naturephilosophy throughout' (Grant 2006: 5). In *The Dark Ground of Spirit* I wrote that Grant is correct (McGrath 2012: 141). Nature-philosophy plays a role in all of Schelling's works, early, middle and late, because a thoroughgoing theory of nature is also a theory of reason. The principle of the objective existence of reason remains fundamental for Schelling from the beginning to the end of his career. Nevertheless, the Philosophy of Revelation is not merely nature-philosophy, any more than the philosophy of freedom of 1809 is merely nature-philosophy. My point, as I have argued in print (McGrath 2016a), is that *naturphilosophische* principles remain binding on the Philosophy of Revelation, because they are not merely principles of nature, they are principles of reason. *Naturphilosophie* plays a role in all of Schelling's works, including Schelling II, because a thoroughgoing theory of nature is also a theory of reason (the principle of the objective existence of reason remains fundamental for Schelling from the beginning to the end of his career).

We cannot deflate Schelling by means of a monolithic substantialisation of his *naturphilosophische* approach to questions concerning spirit, ethics and religion, as though he is on board with a speculative realist denial of the human difference, or a contemporary flattening of the hierarchy of nature, or as though his philosophy of religion is mere window dressing for continued reflections on immanentism. Schelling's philosophy remains grounded in nature-philosophy throughout both of the main phases of his career; but in the first phase, the ethical and religious questions that preoccupy him from 1809 onwards, and that require that he look beyond nature for answers, are deferred (they are there implicitly, but rarely directly engaged). And in the second phase, when biblical revelation becomes the object of inquiry, the principles of nature/reason remain the means of the investigation; for Schelling, unlike, for example, a theologian of revelation such as Barth, does not see revelation as fundamentally altering reason so much as giving it something new, a knowledge that is essentially above nature (*übernaturlich*, as Schelling describes revelation in the *Darstellung* [Schelling 1854a: 82–3]). In the *Denkmal*, Schelling spoke of a naturalism that is contained by an expanded sense of theism, as nature is contained by God (Schelling 1812: 68–9). Philosophical monotheism will not, then, contradict nature-philosophy, but will nevertheless go beyond it.

The whole question of the role of nature-philosophy in the late Schelling should be reframed. What is at issue is not nature as such, the sensible/intelligible order (as good a definition of nature as I can think of); it is nature as absolute that is the problem, unconditioned nature (Schelling 1799a: 13/77), 'nature as infinite productivity (*natura naturans*)' or 'nature as subject' (1799b: 284/202). In short, it is the Spinozistic identification of nature and God, *Deus sive natura*, and Schelling's early appropriation of the idea in his works between the years 1797 and 1806, that is at issue. The question should be reframed in the terms in which the later Schelling poses it repeatedly, namely as the question concerning pantheism. From 1809 to the end, the question for Schelling is not whether or not nature remains normative for philosophy – for it must always remain so. The question is whether God has been properly conceived as substance, as the unconditioned, or in the early Schelling's terms, as the absolute.

But the matter quickly becomes more complicated. Given that pantheism at least does not commit the theist's error of constructing a philosophy or theology of God without offering an explanation of nature,[49] and given that the actual infinite is that which has no outside, pantheism must be, on some abstract level, true: God *is* in some sense everything. Analytically, it is true that God = being.[50] Kant brings this whole line of inquiry to a head by arguing that God *means* reality; God is the totality of all predicates (Kant 1787: A 560/B 608). But granted the truth of the claim, is it true to say that being = nature? The answer must be no. We cannot substitute the term 'nature' for 'being', any more than we can substitute 'reason', or as Gabriel would have it, 'fields of sense' (Gabriel 2015). Nature, reason, fields of sense – all figures for the same triune logical structure – are included in being, to be sure, but being is more than nature. The analytic statement, God = being, belongs to negative philosophy, and is without relation to the 'actual chain of events' (Schelling 1842d: 132/182). The matter must be rethought in the light of the positive. The whole of the positive philosophy can be summed up in a single thesis: pantheism is not true . . . yet (Schelling 1809: 404/66; 1810a: 484/243; 1854c: 66). God *will be* 'all in all' (*panta en passin*; 1 Cor. 15:28; Eph. 1:23), but only after passing through a historical process of triune personalisation, which encompasses all of geological and human history.

I argue for two main phases of Schelling's thought, which are genetically connected to one another but irreducible to each other. The principle that differentiates the two is the hypothesis of history as the theatre of the revelation of the personal and triune God of the New Testament.[51] This is the thought that does not enter into the orbit of the early Schelling's central concerns; and it is the thought without which nothing of the later Schelling can be properly understood. It divides the two phases of Schelling's career, just as it divides contemporary Schelling scholars. Schelling I is concerned with spirit as nature, that is, spirit that is *necessarily* self-productive. Schelling II is concerned with spirit as personality, that is, spirit that is *freely* self-productive. Spirit that is necessarily self-productive is nature. Spirit that is freely self-productive is divine by origin (the creator) and human by participation. The hinge of Schelling I and II is the Freedom Essay. Here Schelling takes up the themes that will concern him for the rest of his long career; problems in religion, ethics and politics, above all the problem of personality – topics about which he had very little to say prior to the essay. In the preface to the book in which he published the Freedom Essay, Schelling claims to have said nothing about such matters hitherto (Schelling 1809: 333–4/4). This is surely an exaggeration, meant to refute those who assumed, either critically or supportively, that Schelling's nature-philosophy was at least implicitly a theory of divinity, an ethics and a politics. Schelling did write on these matters before 1809, but tangentially, and often in a way that seemed somewhat conventional and that stands in undeniable tension with what he had to say about them later on.[52]

The Freedom Essay outlines, programmatically and tersely, all of the major moves of the Philosophy of Revelation: the primordial nature of freedom, the contraction of the infinite in creation, the thesis of non-dialectical personalism, the theorem of absolute transcendence, the personalisation of God in history (or rather, history as the personalisation of God), the fall of creation (the real distinction between good and evil and the historical actuality of the latter), the end of the age of mythology, the Trinitarian redemption, the coming sanctification of the world, when God shall be all in all and pantheism will have become true. But here's the catch: a hinge moves both forwards and backwards. The Freedom Essay is to some degree a continuation of nature-philosophy by other means. Schelling is as concerned with naturalising freedom and personality (non-reductively, to be sure) as he is with opening up a new theme in his work (namely the religious or revealed). So wherein precisely lies the distinction between Schelling I and Schelling II? It lies not only in a change of topic, but also in a subtle but decisive change in method. *Naturphilosophische* principles remain in play throughout the later work. They are nothing less than the principles of reason itself, and Schelling does not reinvent reason in the end, nor does revelation essentially alter it (even if it gives reason something new to think). Nature-philosophy is no longer deployed to the same ends, because Schelling's position is different. He has a higher standpoint, as he himself said.[53] And since nothing is ever 'cancelled' in Schelling, the lower standpoint, the *naturphilosophische* standpoint, is still operative, but as the ground, not as the essence or being of the new philosophy.

One can put the change in method in the following way. The 'of' in the philosophy of nature is not only an objective genitive; it is also a subjective genitive, and herein lies the radicality of the early Schelling's approach. To do nature-philosophy is no longer simply to observe and describe what is; to do nature-philosophy is, as Schelling says cryptically, to create nature (Schelling 1799a: 67/5). The nature-philosopher has a mantic vocation, to speak not only *of* nature but to speak *out of* nature, to assume the subjectivity of nature on the presupposition that the human is nature become conscious of itself (Schelling 1799a: 78/14). The human difference is in no way underplayed by Schelling's naturalism; on the contrary, nature's infinite drive to reveal itself is only fulfilled in the human being to whom it could be revealed. The whole point of rendering teleology constitutive, rather than, as in Kant, regulative, was to argue that the faculty of judgement, which appears in the human being alone, is a part of the natural process: the organism needs us to put it all together conceptually, to recognise it, as it were (Schelling 1797b). The nature-philosopher is called by nature itself to raise nature to the conceptual by thinking it through as a systematic whole.[54]

By contrast, the 'of' in the Philosophy of Revelation is never a subjective genitive. Revelation is here object, not subject. Revelation is *revelation* because the one who thinks it, the one to whom it has been revealed, never gets behind it. The *a priori* of revelation is hidden in the mind of the revealer. Where Schelling I could speak from *out of* nature, could write *as* nature, Schelling II never presumes to speak from *out of* revelation, never assumes the voice of the revealer, nor presumes to produce revelation in his philosophy. To do philosophy of revelation in the subjective genitive sense would be to create philosophical religion, and this, Schelling says, does not yet and cannot yet exist (Schelling 1842a; 1842b). In the end, we shall possess the mind of God, as does the Christ, and we shall possess it *through* the Christ. But the end is not yet here. The still mostly unknown God, the creator, redeemer and sanctifier of the world, remains the lord of revelation. To claim to speak for God would be worse than sheer presumption; it would be a denial of the revealedness of revelation as such. That said, the revealed is not simply to be left as bare statement, symbol or story, repeated and believed on authority. It is to be understood, and if it were not to some degree understandable by human beings, it would not be a revelation. It is not merely fact without explanation that is revealed; it is explanatory fact. The revelation lights up the world and makes things that were previously incomprehensible to some degree explicable. We to whom the revealer reveals the revelation have a duty to understand it and to strain our minds to think it, which will mean widening our categories to be capable of receiving it.

My interpretation of the late Schelling is based on the assumption that the fundamental principles governing his turn to the positive remain more or less the same, from 1809 onwards, even if many of the details change. The principles are three, and I enumerate them here as a heuristic aid for the readings that follow. I call them the three pillars of the philosophy of the late Schelling. Each is more or less in place in 1809, and on no one of them does Schelling's view substantially change. On the contrary, in each instance it could easily be shown that Schelling's commitment to these three principles only deepens over the years. They may appear arbitrary as presented here. It is my hope that the internal coherence of the three pillars, and their close relation to the doctrine of potencies, as well as to Schelling's reading of the Patristic theological tradition, will become evident by the end of this study.

1. *The theorem of absolute transcendence*: A complete system of being is not possible inasmuch as being itself is transcended by its own origin. Even God is horizoned by that which exceeds God. Philosophy is therefore an infinite task.
2. *Non-dialectical personalism*: *Pace* Hegel, a person is not one who stands in a necessary relation to another person, but one who has overcome an internal necessity. Such freedom is the condition of the possibility of love, as it is of good and evil. The history of the world is nothing less than the history of the personalising of the divine: God's overcoming necessity, the blind act of being, upon which God, like all things, depends.
3. *Trinitarian eschatology*: The world is factically fallen and in process of being redeemed by a God who is not only one, but three. The three divine potencies become fully persons in history, a history in which they are free of one another, and free for each other. Their finding one another and becoming unified with one other in the end (the *eschaton*), 'one in being' (*homoousion*) out of love, not necessity, constitutes the three ages of the Church.

The first two principles will preoccupy us in this book, which treats of the path from negative to positive philosophy, and the structure and conditions of the initial decision that is the transition between the two. The third principle is the subject of the second book, which will explain Schelling's theory of the Trinity and situate it, and his related Christology, in the history of Trinitarian theology, and show how both are essential to Schelling's late theory of the State, the Church and the philosophical religion that will render the essential distinction between State and Church obsolete. Insofar as these three principles are the support structure of everything Schelling has to say about positive philosophy, some remarks on the Trinity are needed in the first part as well. I am asking a lot of my readers, as Schelling asked a lot of his auditors in 1841, for what follows is not a selective reading such as is more common today, but a commentary on the interdependent logic, ontology, ethics, politics and theology of the late Schelling. I am convinced that one cannot treat any of these in separation from the other. Nevertheless, there are readers who will be drawn to one part over the other. This first book, *The Turn to the Positive*, will be of most interest to those with a concern for Schelling's logic and ontology. The second book, *The Speculative Theology of the Late Schelling*, will be of interest to theologically inclined readers, as it directly treats Schelling's contributions to Trinitarian theology, to Christology and to ecclesiology. If both these books serve to raise anew the religious questions that were of utmost concern to the late Schelling – questions that many today have decided to ignore, but that have for whatever reason always preoccupied me – I will have succeeded.

Notes

1. Friedrich Wilhelm IV's ambassador to Munich, C. J. Bunsen, in his 1841 letter inviting Schelling to Berlin, cited in Matthews (2007: 6).
2. See Hegel (1948). Saitya Das has recently proven that political-theological motifs can be traced all the way back to Schelling's early works as well, admittedly when the latter are read through the lens of the Philosophy of Revelation. See Das (2016). If we follow Das (and we should), the late Schelling's apparently abrupt turn to political theology may be thought of as akin to Radiohead's turn to ambient electronics in *Kid A*: on hearing the album, so strange in tone that the band is scarcely recognisable as the grunge guitar heroes of the 1990s, fans suddenly realised that the blips and beeps and electronic voices that foreground *Kid A* are in fact the background of the guitar rock of *The Bends* and *OK Computer*. Similarly, political theological tropes are scatted throughout Schelling's nature-philosophy and identity-philosophy, but they are easily overlooked, for the main theme of Schelling's early work was, as he put it later, negative philosophy, not positive philosophy – and while the political can and must be discussed in negative philosophy, it raises questions that can only be answered by positive philosophy, specifically by revealed religion.
3. While the full story is only recounted in Hegel's 1827 *Lectures on the Philosophy of Religion* (Hegel 1827: 389–489), the philosophical interpretation of the speculative and historical significance of the death of Christ is one of Hegel's earliest thoughts: the 'speculative Good Friday' of *Faith and Knowledge*. See Hegel (1802: 190–1). H. S. Harris suggests that Schelling influenced Hegel on this point. See Harris (1989). Schelling offered a speculative interpretation of the Christian Trinity in 1802/3 at the time that he was editing the *Philosophisches Journal* with Hegel, a theory of God's *kenosis* in creation and the cross which is in rough outline the same as Hegel's 1927 interpretation. See Schelling (1803: 286–95). As we shall see in the second book, Schelling's late

Trinitarianism differs significantly from his 1803 sketch and from Hegel's theory. The late Schelling, I will argue, is not a death-of-God theologian at all. On Hegel's notion of the death of God, see Altizer (1997) and Žižek and Milbank (2009).

4. 'Only in personality is there life, and all personality rests on a dark ground' (Schelling 1809: 413/75); 'Only the human being who has the strength to rise above himself is capable of creating a true past for himself' (*Weltalter*, SW 8: 259); 'That there is something in God that is merely power and force [*bloß Kraft und Stärke*] should not come as a surprise if one does not hold that God is only that and nothing else. It is rather the contrary that should come as a surprise. For how can we fear God if in him there is no force and how can he himself, with all his wisdom and goodness, subsist [*bestehen*] without force, since force is exactly what subsists while all that subsists is a force? Where there is no force, there is no character either, no individuality, no real personality, but rather a vain dispersion [*eitel Diffluenz*], as one can verify everyday in men without character. And the old saying is just as good, if not better, when inverted: without force, not even supreme goodness would have attained its majesty' (Schelling 1812: 65, translation Hadi Fakhouri). What is named variously in these passages from Schelling's middle period as 'the dark ground', 'the past', as 'power and force', can more technically be named 'necessity' or in the most formal sense of the term 'nature'. The overcoming of nature in this precise sense, and not in a gnostic sense, as sensuality or finitude, nature as destiny, as what you have been given to be, is what Schelling means by personality.

5. Among recent commentators on Schelling, Jason Wirth has gone furthest in showing the ecological significance of Schelling. See Wirth (2015).

6. This point was made trenchantly by Ernst Bloch (whom Habermas called 'a Marxist Schelling') in his three-volume work *The Principle of Hope* (Bloch 1959), and applied theologically by Jürgen Moltmann (Moltmann 1967).

7. See, for example, Sellars's seminal piece, 'Philosophy and the Scientific Image of Man' (Sellars 1963), in which the 'manifest image' of the world (which is human-centred) is distinguished from the 'scientific image' of the world (which is objective), in effect decommissioning all forms of philosophical ontology. The classic statement of the triumph of science over religion and mythology is still Weber (2002).

8. In addition to Gauchet on the Christian roots of liberalism (Gauchet 1985), see Berman (2008), who proves through careful historical analysis that our modern political ideal of 'equality' and universal 'freedom' has no analogue in any ancient culture other than the Hebraic.

9. See Schelling (1812).

10. See Schelling (1854c: 61–6).

11. See Schelling (1854a: 255): 'The philosophy of religion, which we call for, *does not exist* . . . [it is] to be reached in the course of a great and lengthy development.'

12. On the reception of the late Schelling in the nineteenth century, mostly, as it turns out, by Roman Catholic theologians, see Kasper (1965: 7–9, 30–8) and O'Meara (1982).

13. There are some notable exceptions to the general lack of influence of Schelling's Philosophy of Revelation: Franz Rosenzweig's *Star of Redemption*, Paul Tillich's *Systematic Theology*, Russian Sophiology (Vladimir Soloviev, Sergei Bulgakov), and last but not least Nicolai Berdyaev's Christian existentialism.

14. The late Schelling's political philosophy, already sketched out in the 1810 Stuttgart Seminars (Schelling 1810: 458–65), is the theme of the final three lectures of the *Darstellung der reinrationalen Philosophie* (Schelling 1854a: 516–90). These have recently been translated by Kyla Bruff. See Bruff (2020).

15. Schelling to Windischmann, 16 January 1806, in Fuhrmans (1975: vol. 3, 294).

16. See especially the works of Tyler Tritten, an author who is not only unafraid of Schelling's theological commitments, but also capable of understanding them (2012a; 2014; 2017). Tritten's careful studies are replete with extremely precise exegeses from which I have benefited greatly. I have also made use of Paul Tillich's more or less forgotten doctoral thesis, *Die religionsgeschichtliche Konstruktion in Schellings positive Philosophie* (Tillich 1910). Even at the inception of his brilliant career, Tillich had a sense for what is theologically significant in Schelling, and manages to fill the sparse 120 pages of his dissertation with penetrating observations accompanied by a judicious selection of citations from primary texts. Laughland's slim and somewhat one-sided book (Laughland 2007) has its problems (among them, the author's insistence on scholasticising Schelling), but at least he does not fall prey to the contemporary tendency to unify Schelling's work at the expense of the coherence of the Philosophy of Revelation. Laughland sees the turn from the early to the late Schelling, as do I, in the Freedom Essay, particularly in the breakthrough to a real distinction between good and evil (which is notably lacking in the identity-philosophy), and the retrieval of a robust (and Lutheran) doctrine of the fall. None of these points were missed by the twentieth-century German and French commentators, who were less allergic to Christianity than are the new Schellingians. See Fuhrmans (1940), Kasper (1965), Hemmerle (1968), Tilliette (1970), Marquet (1973) and Courtine (1990).

17. See Rush (2014: 232) for a representatively biased dismissal: 'What is the path forward for philosophy, according to Schelling, after the pretensions of negative philosophy have been reined in? This is where positive philosophy, Schelling's most arcane invention, comes in. It seems to me that the Berlin audience took fair measure of what Schelling had on offer, at least in the form he offered it. Still, one might hesitate to dismiss positive philosophy quite so out of hand, if one could reconstruct its impetus and structure in such a way that it did not depend quite as much as it seems on revamped Christian theology.' Markus Gabriel goes to some pains to dismiss Schelling's theology, even while endorsing its logic. See Gabriel (2015: 82): 'For Schelling, it is crucial to note that "God" refers to nothing more or less than the incessant and polymorphous becoming of intelligibility. God is sense, the almost trivial fact that the ways we access the world (our sense-making practices, which generate fields of sense) belong to the world itself.'

18. I analysed Heidegger's formalising of Christian themes in detail in my first book (McGrath 2006a).

19. The ecstasy of reason first makes its appearance in Schelling's 1821 Erlangen lecture (SW 9: 230). It is the basic methodological move of the positive philosophy and is elaborated in some detail in *The Grounding of the Positive Philosophy* (1842d: 147–74/193–212).

20. From a large and growing literature, see Bowie (1993), Beach (1994), Snow (1996), Žižek (1996), Grant (2006) and Wirth (2003; 2015).

21. The trope of the failure of Schelling's late philosophy is widespread in the histories of German idealism and partly accounts for its neglect. See, for example, Harris (1989: 62): 'I am so convinced that Schelling's late philosophy is based on a mistake that I have never bothered to read it.'

22. Clearly Watson does not mean by mysticism a doctrine of the union of the human spirit with the divine godhead, but what we today would call 'obscurantism'. For the proper understanding of the term, see Enders (1993: 17–21).

23. See Durner (1979: 226): 'The demand to take "the absolute freedom of God in the creation" (XIII, 310; see also X, 281) as the point of departure of philosophical

reflection, is first sufficiently realised with the new methodical approach in the actual *late philosophy*, according to which the inversion of the immanent determinations of Spirit to transitive potencies no longer takes place "naturally" . . . First in this conception is God truly free not only to posit the world – as this deed of activation of a possibility does not change His own selfhood – but also just as free not to posit the world, since He does not need the world in order to be Himself.' See also Kasper, who makes the freedom of God from creation the decisive point of difference between the early and the late Schelling (Kasper 1965: 223–327).

24. By the term 'historical immanentism' I mean the meta-narrative, common to many idealists, Romantics and followers of Jung, that describes the history of being as a dialectical process through which God achieves consciousness of Godself. Its roots lie in theosophy and the until recently widely neglected tradition of Western esotericism. See McGrath (2012: 6–11).

25. On this distinction between a God who needs the world to complete Godself and a God who needs the world because God has made Godself vulnerable to it, see Moltmann (1993: 45): 'If he [God] longs for his other, it is not out of *deficiency* of being; it is rather out of the superabundance of his creative fullness. If we talk about this divine longing, then we do not mean any "imperfection of the Absolute" when we transfer the principle of historical movement in this way. On the contrary, *the lack of any creative movement would mean an imperfection in the Absolute.*' On this point, Moltmann cites Berdyaev, another profoundly Schellingian thinker: 'For creative movement, indeed . . . is a characteristic of the perfection of being' (Berdyaev 1939: 51).

26. See Von Rad (1962: 180) and Kearney (2001). For an argument distinguishing Schelling's understanding of the possible God from Kearney's, see Tritten (2017: 7–10). I discuss Schelling's interpretation of the tetragrammaton in more detail below at pp. 218ff.

27. It seems that current Hegel scholarship, which is for the most part deflationary, agrees. The Hegelian absolute is a mere metaphor for the conditions of intelligibility. See the work of Robert Brandom, Wilfred Sellars and John McDowell, or 'the Pittsburgh School'. For a summary of the school, see Rockmore (2012). Markus Gabriel is trying to do the same with Schelling: offering a deflationary reading, palatable to contemporary atheism, that flattens Schelling's late ontology into conditions of meaning or 'fields of sense'. See Gabriel (2015). Schelling proves to be less susceptible to such a deflation. Who knows, perhaps Hegel really was an atheist in the end. Schelling certainly was not.

28. See Augustine, *De civitate dei*, Book XI, ch. 21; Aquinas, *Summa theologiae*, 1a. q. 3.

29. The late Schelling regards the doctrine of *unio mystica* as an expression of the existing person, which does not, however, break through to the really existing God. See Schelling (1854a: vorlesung 24). On the one hand, Schelling has the highest praise for genuine mysticism or contemplative life (the same thing, in his view), which rises above the abstractions of the moral law and seeks a personal relation to the absolute; on the other hand, he regards mysticism as subordinate to the positive philosophy, whose highest expressions are ethico-political, not mystical and quietistic.

30. See Peirce (1901; 1908).

31. See Schelling (1842d: 119–26/173–8).

32. Cf. Hogrebe (1989).

33. Some of what follows was published previously in McGrath (2017a).

34. I have Slavoj Žižek in mind. See, for instance, Žižek (2006). But cynicism is so widespread among philosophers and theorists today that it might be described as the

reigning ideology of the educated class. The essential difference between ancient and modern cynicism is that the modern cynic, unlike the ancient cynic, sees no possibility for truthful speaking or virtuous action. Hence modern cynicism is self-referential and endlessly, unproductively critical. Ancient cynicism is a moral theory; modern cynicism is a surrender to the absurd. On the difference between ancient and modern cynicism, see Sloterdijk (1988).

35. In a letter to William James of 28 January 1894, Peirce confesses the depth of the influence of Schelling on his work: 'I consider Schelling as enormous, and one thing I admire about him is his freedom from the trammels of system, and his holding himself uncommitted to any previous utterance. In that, he is like a scientific man.' Quoted in Esposito (1977: 203).

36. British idealism is not synonymous with Hegelianism any more than it is restricted to philosophy written in Britain. In some respects, 'British idealism' is a misnomer, since the school should arguably include American speculative philosophy, which was in both style and substance related to British speculative philosophy. The term would then cover not only T. H. Green, F. H. Bradley, Bernard Bosanquet and J. M. E. McTaggart but also the American transcendentalists Emerson and Thoreau as well as the so-called pragmatists, Royce, James, Dewey and Peirce. Both American and British philosophy in the latter half of the nineteenth century developed under the influence of a generous reception of German idealism. It was not just Hegel that the Victorians read; the early Schelling was made popular in England through Coleridge's 1817 *Biographia Literaria*, which includes an extensive paraphrase of the *System of Transcendental Idealism*. Less well known is the fact that the first of Schelling's Berlin lectures was translated into English in an American transcendentalist journal while Schelling was still giving them (see Schelling 1843). The translation amounts to less than ten pages, but that it was translated at all indicates interest and reception in America in the mid-nineteenth century. While the scholarly reconstruction has not yet been done, I consider it highly unlikely that Peirce did not read the late Schelling, which he easily could have, since Schelling's *Sämtliche Werke* would have been available to him through Harvard Library. In short, British idealism is not just British, and is much more pluralistic than the characterisation 'neo-Hegelian' would indicate. Even the more Hegelian of the British idealists, such as Bosanquet, leavened Hegel with British empiricism in such a way as to produce a hybrid philosophy that has much in common with Schelling. See Bradley (1979a and b). On the reception of Schelling in England in the nineteenth century, see Whiteley (2018). On Coleridge and Schelling, see Hedley (2000). On British idealism in general, see Mander (2011) and Grant and Dunham (2010).

37. See Candlish (2007) and Bradley (2012).

38. We have seen both in recent years: the Hogrebe–Gabriel reading of the late Schelling as a mytho-poeticising of the logic of the predicate (Hogrebe 1989; Gabriel 2013), and the Heideggerian reading, of which Krell is representative (2005), which finds in Schelling questions that only find 'answers' in the encrypted aphorisms of the late Heidegger.

39. See Carnap (1932). It is worth noting that the same reduction of existence to quantifiable instantiation has demolished speculative philosophy in Germany as well. With the exception of Freiburg, Heidelberg and a few other universities, German departments of philosophy have become centres for the study of Anglo-American analytic philosophy.

40. On Schelling and Heidegger, see Schwab (2013).

41. I reconstructed this history in my first book, *The Early Heidegger and Medieval Philosophy* (McGrath 2006a).

42. Husserl himself was undecided on the issue of the infinite. The 'French turn in phenomenology' (Levinas, Marion, Henry), which anchors itself in Husserl rather than Heidegger and revitalised theology at the turn of the twenty-first century, demonstrates the point.

43. Heidegger's 1913 dissertation was on logic, and his 1915 *Habilitationsschrift* on Scotus is predominantly concerned with logic. See McGrath (2006a: 88–119).

44. I speak here only of philosophy and theology in the English-speaking academy (which includes most of what goes under the rubric of 'continental philosophy'). We may, of course, explain the situation by referring to the paucity of English translations of the later Schelling. But the general decline in theological research and education in North America cannot be discounted. The situation in Germany and France is quite different. The late Schelling's influence on philosophy and theology in Germany and France has been considerable. The degree to which major German and French thinkers, for example Von Balthasar, Pannenberg, Moltmann, Marion and Levinas, are indebted to Schelling is in need of study. Certainly the work of German and French scholars such as Fuhrmans (1940; 1954), Hemmerle (1968), Kasper (1965), Jankélévich (1933), Marquet (1973) and Tilliette (1970; 1987) did not go unread. In Italy, the influence of Schelling passed through Pareyson (1975), among whose students are counted Vattimo and Eco.

45. On the crucial distinction between Hegel's dialectic of sublation (*Aufhebungsdialektik*) and Schelling's dialectic of production (*Erzeugungsdialektik*), see Beach (1994: 84–91; 1990).

46. See Furhmans (1940; 1954).

47. See Schulz (1955).

48. See Kasper (1965).

49. See Schelling (1812: 68): 'A theistic system that excludes the explanation of nature does not at all deserve its name, for without a determined concept of God's connection to nature the very concept of God remains uncertain' (trans. Hadi Fakhoury).

50. In the *Darstellung*, Schelling singles out Malebranche for explicitly identifying God with being (Schelling 1854a: 272). But one also finds the claim in various forms of expression throughout the Middle Ages, in Eckhart for example. *Darum ist Gott ledig aller Dinge – und [eben] darum ist er alle Dinge* (Eckhart 1963: Predigt 32, p. 306). God is 'pure naked existence' (*Commentary on Exodus*, in Eckhart 1986: 45, n. 14). The identification of God with being is a leitmotif of Christian neo-Platonism and is even made, with qualification, by Aquinas. God is subsistent being itself (*ipsum esse subsistens*) (*Summa Theologica*, 1a, q. 4, a. 2). Malebranche's advantage, according to Schelling, is that he does not mean God is being in a general sense, the universal being which is the empty category of thought (*ens omnimodo indeterminatum*); God, for Malebrache, is being in a concrete sense; God is *das Seyende*, not merely *das Sein* (Schelling 1854a: 272). It is not clear that this is any different from Aquinas's identification of God with *esse* rather than *essentia*.

51. In *The System of Transcendental Idealism* (1800: 570–606), Schelling considers history as the revelation of the absolute, a thesis to which he returns in *On University Studies* (Schelling 1803: 286–95) and *Philosophy and Religion* (Schelling 1804); but a close reading of these texts shows the difference between these early conceptions of history as emanations of divinity and the much more theologically nuanced notion of historical revelation in the later work. For Schelling I, history is a spontaneous showing of divinity, much as nature is a showing of divinity for neo-Platonism, a necessary emanation of multiplicity from the absolute. It is not strictly a self-revelation of God because God

is not here conceived as a person who might or might nor reveal themselves, but rather, along pantheistic lines, as an impersonal absolute.

52. It would be romantic to see a conversion subsequent to the death of his beloved Caroline Schlegel on 7 September 1809, only the Christian themes were already explicit in the Freedom Essay, which was completed at the beginning of that year (Tilliette 1999: 168). Certainly, in later years Schelling openly identified with Christianity, which he did not as a young philosopher. In the 1827 Munich lecture, *System der Weltalter*, Schelling declared, 'I have derived my comfort [*Beruhigung*] from the texts of the New Testament, and hope that others will too. The truly decisive name of my philosophy is Christian philosophy, and I assume this decision seriously' (Schelling 1827: 9). Thanks to Hadi Fakhoury for pointing this out and for translating the passage.

53. Schelling said as much to the journalist Nicolas Melgunoff in a conversation in Augsburg in 1836, when asked about the relation of the Philosophy of Revelation to his *Naturphilosophie*. 'The foundations that support me are the same, but I stand higher.' Schelling cited in Tilliette (1999: 290).

54. 'The spirit of nature is only apparently opposed to the soul; in itself it is the medium of its revelation: it sets things in opposition to one another, but only so that one being can emerge as the highest benignity and reconciliation of all forces. All other creatures are merely driven by the spirt of nature, and assert through it their individuality; in man alone the soul arises as the centerpoint, without which the world would be like nature without the sun' (Schelling 1807: 311).

Chapter 2

The Ideal

Thus far from man and his endeavours making the world comprehensible, it is man himself that is the most incomprehensible and who inexorably drives me to the belief in the wretchedness of all being, a belief that makes itself known in so many bitter pronouncements from both ancient and recent times. It is precisely man that drives me to the final desperate question: Why is there anything at all? Why is there not nothing?

Schelling, *The Grounding of the Positive Philosophy*

The turn to the positive only occurs when the philosopher decides that the above question can no longer be ignored. The turn is a decision, not the conclusion of a rational process. In it, the philosopher confronts what existentialists will later call 'the feeling of absurdity' (Camus 1955: 9–11). The philosopher can 'turn' to the positive philosophy because he or she is already in the positive. The philosopher exists, and thinks from out of that unprethinkable fact, which at first astonishes (*ertsaunt*) philosophy and renders it silent (Schelling 1841: 157/119; 1821: 229–30). The difference between Schelling and the existentialists is that where the latter regard the absurdity of existence as a gloomy conclusion of the search for meaning, Schelling regards it as a premise. Eternal existence, unprethinkable existence, the sheer thatness of the world (*das reine Daß*), silences reason, but awakens the philosopher into a new line of questioning (Schelling 1841: 157/119). Every explanation offered by rational philosophy leaves out the heart of the matter, the fact of the givenness of things. The task is not to give up philosophising in the face of the inexplicably real; the task is to philosophise in a new way, to enter into philosophy with one's actual existence hanging in the balance. It is on these grounds, and only on these grounds, that the New Testament appears to philosophy as revelatory, as an unveiling of the secret hidden in God and revealed to children (Matt. 11:25; Col. 1:26).

The decision always has a context, and these contexts are as varied as are philosophers themselves: any situation is an opportunity for remembering the riddle of existence. For Schelling, the context is idealism in Germany, which he helped construct. Schelling assumes the voice of his age and offers an entry point into the positive after Kant, Fichte and identity-philosophy, in a new critique of reason. This time, however, the critique will not silence metaphysics and religion but give it a voice.

Identity-philosophy, which is the fruition of various sketches of nature-philosophy, nature-philosophy brought as far as it can go, is a system of *the rational*, not a system of *the real*. It deals with essence, not existence. It knows possibilities, and suspends knowledge of historical actualities. Insofar as identity-philosophy aimed to be an absolute system, one that left nothing out, the late Schelling regards it as a failure. But insofar as it never presumed to include the historical within it – in its Würzburg form it even denied the reality of history (Schelling 1804a) – it was, and is, superior to Hegel's confusion of reason and history, negative and positive. We might want to absolve some version of nature-philosophy of the limitations of identity-philosophy, but on what grounds would we do so? What is the difference between the two such that we could defend nature-philosophy from the later critique levelled against any negative philosophy that overlooks its own negativity (Schelling 1841: 121–39)? The identity-philosophy that knows its negativity is the fullest expression of freedom, 'a poem composed by reason itself'.[1] In its explicit acknowledgement of its self-referentiality identity-philosophy is higher than any metaphysics prior to it. It did not begin in truth but aimed at it. That it failed to achieve historical being in no way diminishes its rationality, or the validity of its achievement. By taking truth to be an end rather than a presupposition, something outstanding for it, something to be sought, identity-philosophy proved itself to be that much closer to actuality than any philosophy before it.

In the light of the 1809 distinction between nature and God, the absolute of identity-philosophy is unveiled as the innate idea of the unconditioned, reason's own inalienable content, 'the figure and form of reason itself' (Kasper 1965: 142). This idea, the late Schelling writes, Kant was right to regard as a merely regulative ideal (Schelling 1842d: 45/120–1). The idea could be described as *unconditioned nature*, or *absolute identity*, or *the system of reason*, or all three. The inescapability of the thought, the way all paths of thinking lead to it (for it is the idea which alone makes thought possible), leaves open the question: Does being in fact hold sway as God? Nature certainly exists, but it need not exist, and its contingency thus raises the question: Is it created or an accident? With this question, which is not a logical but an existential and ethical conclusion, the philosopher awakens to the real. The awakening is not an experience of God, but a realisation of God's absence.

The limits of nature-philosophy

We might be inclined to locate the turn in Schelling's thought to a changed attitude to religion, as though he rediscovered Christianity sometime between 1806 and 1809, after losing it in his early adulthood – and we would not be entirely wrong.[2] However, neither would we be entirely right. The turn to the positive also pivots on Schelling's rethinking of reason and its relation to reality. In fact, it remains richly undecidable what came first, the renewed sense of the reality of Christianity, or the new sense of the transcendence of the real. At the centre of the ontology of Schelling II is an argument for the finitude of nature that is hard to square with the famous works of his youth, and with it, an emphasis on the limits of nature-philosophy. He had argued before, it is true, that nature-philosophy was not the whole of philosophy and should be complemented by transcendental philosophy (Schelling 1800: 340–3/6–7). The opposition between these two (nature-philosophy and transcendental philosophy) was a different kind of thing than the opposition between negative and positive philosophy. What bounded nature-philosophy in 1797 was the necessity of a parallel account that takes as its point of departure transcendental subjectivity, reflectively available to itself, and irreducible to the material conditions of its existence, but mirroring in all essentials the results of nature-philosophy. In the late work the outside is demarcated by that which entirely eludes nature-philosophy, and indeed, thought itself.

Few commentators seem to notice this dramatic change in Schelling's conception of nature. Félix Duque is an exception. In a 2007 article entitled 'Nature–in God, or the Problems of a Dash: Schelling's *Freiheitsschrift*', Duque writes:

> The irreducibility of Nature can help to explain what is perhaps the most spectacular turn of Schelling's *Denkweg*. In 1806 the *Nature-philosophy* is erected explicitly as the essence of Philosophy *tout court*, and this precisely because God (the Truth) must be put to the test in Nature and as such a Nature (Being). In the late *Philosophy of Mythology*, on the contrary, Nature remains degraded to a mere moment – always past, always at the bottom – of the Coming of God into History. Or, more precisely: Nature is the revolted and always unsettling basis not only of this Sacred History, but above all of its Mythological *Pre-History*. Nature is the lowest bottom of God, much more sinister that that which the Fathers of the Church denominated *ta batheia tou Patros* – one could say, *The Abyss of the Father*. What has happened? (Duque 2007: 65)

For Schelling I, nature = reason = the absolute. Subjectivity is a trick of the light, the 'disease' of 'reflection', which creates the appearance of separation where there is unity, and of duality where there is identity (Schelling 1797a: 2/169). By refusing to foreground ontology in epistemology, nature-philosophy breaks free of reflection and allows 'nature' or 'the infinite knowledge which God has of himself', that is, 'reason', to speak through us (Schelling 1806: 47). For Schelling II, nature is the ground of God, less than absolute, the antecedent of fully actual, that is, personalised spirit. Reason, which might still be regarded as equal to nature, is no longer equal to God. Human subjectivity participates in nature/reason but is less than both reason and God. A subordinationism has undoubtedly occurred where before there was identity: nature/reason transcends humanity and God transcends nature/reason. Reason has now been finitised in the human being, and Kant rehabilitated to a certain degree. Human reason, subjectivity, is reconceived, to be sure in a post-transcendental fashion, as an unsurpassable limit to thought; on the one hand, rendering us *subjects of* ideology (mythology), on the other, making us possible receivers of revelation, that is, recipients of an act of knowledge originating outside of reason and nature. The central shift is summed up, as Duque points out in the passage cited above, in the distinction between nature and God, which Schelling introduces in the 1809 Freedom Essay. I have called this text, Schelling's masterpiece, the *hinge* of Schelling's career. A hinge does not break; it joins two things that might be otherwise separated. The Freedom Essay is thus the mediator between the early Schelling and the late Schelling, between nature-philosophy and the Philosophy of Revelation (Schelling 1841: 97–8). The much-disputed unity of Schelling's work as a whole depends upon a proper understanding of its argument.

The earlier nature-philosophy posited an 'unconditioned nature' as the origin and ground of visible nature, a blind striving of the unconscious infinite for consciousness, manifestation or appearance, a striving which, because it cannot reach its goal, endlessly produces finite beings, only to sacrifice each and every one of them to the non-manifest, the universal or ideal. And then, without warning, in 1809 nature is downgraded, as Duque puts it, defined in the Freedom Essay as 'ground', not even being but a principle of being, that which does not fully exist but longs to, and makes possible existence, understanding and love. Where nature-philosophy suggests an identity between nature and divinity (conceived pantheistically and impersonally), a suggestion that comes full term in identity-philosophy, which more or less deifies reason, the Freedom Essay clearly and irreversibly differentiates nature from God. And yet Schelling himself insists on the continuity of the early and later phases of his career. Nature-philosophy, he says, never presumed adequacy; and the positive philosophy leaves room for 'a purely rational philosophy', which would be the complement, if not the presupposition of the Philosophy of Revelation (Schelling 1841: 111–21). Negative philosophy is the native possession of reason, culminating in the deduction of the triune schema of potencies which articulates the very structure of nature and reason; positive philosophy is the *experience* of the eventfulness of history, the disclosure, which can only be empirical, of *meaningful* history. History can only be meaningful as a whole; thus no historical event is meaningful in isolation but only as revelatory of a system of meaning, a system, however, that can neither be deduced nor intuited (for then it would not be historical), but only revealed. The three potencies are not refuted or expanded by positive philosophy but are revealed to be, at least with respect to history, empty forms in need of content, which they receive through revelation.

While the method of nature-philosophy was plainly *a priori*, it is not entirely clear that nature-philosophy was *merely* negative. In his 1841 retrospective on negative philosophy, Schelling says that nature-philosophy was impelled by a genuine search for the real. 'After Kant, the Germans held onto metaphysics, but interwoven with experience: *this is nature-philosophy* ... Nature-philosophy was the child of that new spirit that longed for the real' (Schelling 1841: 128). The Kantian turn in Germany had inspired an intense interest in the empirical, but not, as in other parts of Europe, at the expense of metaphysics. Metaphysics was to be *applied* in such a way as not only to explain the empirical but also to stand to be corrected by it. But nature-philosophy is not therefore a positive philosophy, for the nature with which it deals is an *ideal* not an *existing* nature, of the order of essence, not existence.

> Nature-philosophy isn't concerned with deducing real plants; each real, existent plant is something here and now. But just as in the archetypal world, everything ought to be contained *genikos*, or according to kind, so pure science contains only species and genera. It has *all sensible things* only *as capable of being outside thought*, not as [existing] being [*seiende*]. Even this last, it has only as that which is absolutely incapable of being drawn from thinking. And in this way, as never transcending thinking, this science is *thoroughly immanent, never transcendent*, so purely *a priori* that it would be true even if nothing existed, the way geometry would be true even if nothing like a triangle existed. (Schelling 1841: 118)

In this passage, Schelling draws nature-philosophy so close to identity-philosophy as to render the two indiscernible. What, if any, is the difference between the two? Apriorism determines the method and content of both *The First Outline of a System of the Philosophy of Nature* (Schelling 1799a) – a high point in the early nature-philosophy – and the Würzburg system (Schelling 1804a), which is arguably the definitive statement of identity-philosophy. Different but complementary aims motivate Schelling's early nature-philosophy and the final form of nature-philosophy, the 1804 system of identity. The theme of the 1799 *First Outline* is the deduction of the basic powers structuring matter; it is an effort to organise and so explain, *a priori*, the findings of the new natural sciences, especially magnetism, chemistry and physics, by rendering them indicative of the system of nature as such. The theme of the 1804 Würzburg system is unity and multiplicity, and the grounding of the apparent difference between sub-jectivity and objectivity – and all apparent differences among things – in absolute identity. The mature identity-philosophy is a purely speculative effort to give an account of the universe in such as a way as to maintain the primal identity of reason and nature. The *First Outline* endeavours to explain the experienced world; the Würzburg system analyses certain logical difficulties associated with the concepts of knowledge, identity and multiplicity. One can discern a 'longing' for the real in the *First Out-line*, whereas the Würzburg system, with its austere formal refutations of time and multiplicity, could easily (if inaccurately) be described as a flight from the empirically real into the transcendentally ideal. Reading the early Schelling through Peirce, who might well be thought of as having perfected the method of nature-philosophy, one might see in nature-philosophy the seeds of a properly experimental focus; it is some kind of empiricism, which if not exactly free of 'the nets of the understanding' (Schelling 1833: 143–4/147), *abductively* invites falsification by the recalcitrant datum.[3] It is a challenge to see any empiricism at all in the Würzburg system.[4] The upshot of identity-philosophy is the denial of the discursive and finite real-ity of the empirical world itself.[5]

In spite of these ambiguities, the concept of revelation in the Berlin lec-tures makes it clear that there is no more possibility within nature-philosophy for a philosophy of revelation than there is in identity-philosophy, if only for one reason: a transcendent act of knowledge which is wholly the product of a free cause (revelation) can neither be deduced nor intuited. Revelation is 'unprethinkable' (*unvordenkliche*); it is knowledge to which we have no *a pri-ori* access. And while the positive philosophy is more than the Philosophy of Revelation, it presupposes revelation, which it can only access *a posteriori*, or more precisely, *per posterius*, that is, through history. One might object that nature-philosophy too deals with positive being – the material singularity of existing individuals. But it deals with these only insofar as their essences are available *a priori*, as secure intuitions of reason. The being analysed by nature-philosophy is not unprethinkable being (*unvordenkliches Sein*); on the contrary, it is eminently pre-thinkable. Nature-philosophy deals with the empirical in terms of genera, species and the universal laws governing their relations, that is, with concepts of the empirical, not the contingent singularities that appear in time and the irregularities associated with them. Similarly, negative philosophy possesses a genuine, *a priori*, idea of God – the *ens necessarium*. The intellectual intuition of this, the highest of concepts, is the culmination of negative philosophy. But the *personal* existence of God, what we might call the divine *character*, is only revealed in history through God's free acts, and so entirely exceeds any native category of reason, just as it is beyond any experience of nature. We jump the gun if we take Schelling's meaning here to be the demotion of nature-philosophy and its subordination to theology. With this move (the dissociation of nature as ground from God), the Freedom Essay puts nature-philosophy on solidly empirical terrain for the first time, for it sets it free from theology. Now, with the distinction between nature and God established as the lower to the higher, nature can be known genuinely scientifically, that is, independently and in the absence of an adequate knowledge of God, which clearly we do not yet possess. To understand what nature truly is, we will need to know who the God of nature is, but this God will not contradict what we know about nature. Our concept of God should make sense of what we know scientifically about nature.

Even in its longing for the real, nature-philosophy still did not know exactly what it was looking for. It wanted a really existing God, but it did not know that. It did not know what, or more exactly *who*, a really existing God could be. Only a revelation which comes to meet the natural longing for God from outside could answer this question. If we wanted to use Aristotelian-Scholastic language, we could call nature-philosophy's longing for the real a passive potency for revelation.[6] Nature is not outside God, for nothing is outside God, but God is outside or, better, beyond nature, as the whole is greater than the part. To deploy Franz von Baader's image for the relation of I-hood or the principle of individuality to a creature's life, which Schelling himself uses to illustrate the relation of ground to existence (Schelling 1809: 367/35), nature is the centre of a circle, the periphery of which is the really existing God. The being of God transcends the being of nature just as existence transcends ground: something more is manifest in God, something that cannot be reduced to nature, just as existence cannot be reduced to its ground.

The difference between ground and existence (introduced already in 1801)[7] first becomes a real, qualitative difference between nature and God in 1809. God's free decision to create, that is, to allow something to be which is genuinely other than God, is only possible because it is rooted in that which God is not (the ground). The difference, which is founded upon the distinction between 'being in so far as it exists' and 'being in so far as it is merely the ground of existence', renders genuine knowledge of God unprethinkable, that is, only possible through God's free revelation. The ground of God or nature is opposed by the existing God as antecedent is opposed to consequent, as part to whole, as subject to predicate, potency to act. If the condition of the possibility of opposition is a hidden mediator, an X that is indifferent to the opposition but prevails in the being of both sides of the opposites, what *is* this 'same thing' which is the essence both of nature and God? It is, Schelling says in 1809, the unground, which can undergird ground and existence, nature and God, because it is not opposed to either but is 'indifferent' to both (Schelling 1809: 406/68).

The first thing to notice is that while the language of indifference is reminiscent of the absolute of identity-philosophy, important changes have occurred in Schelling's thought on the matter. Both identity-philosophy and positive philosophy undergird oppositional relations by a principle of indifference, but the former does so on a plane of immanence (to borrow a phrase from Deleuze), while the latter introduces hierarchical relations. The formula for the triadic structure of identity-philosophy is:

$$\frac{\text{Subjectivity} \neq \text{Objectivity}}{\text{Absolute Indifference}}$$

In the Freedom Essay, the formula is:

$$\frac{\text{Nature} \neq \text{God}}{\text{Unground}}$$

While structurally the models are the same and the relations among the terms more or less isomorphic, content-wise the models are quite different. First, there is no hierarchical relation between subjectivity and objectivity in identity-philosophy (they are mirror images of each other), whereas God is higher than nature in positive philosophy in two senses: as ground, nature is subordinate to God; as creation, nature is a product of God and hence subordinate to God. Second, the early distinction between subjectivity and objectivity is merely apparent, obtaining on a phenomenal plane, and grounded in deep identity (absolute indifference); the difference between nature and God articulated in 1809 is *real*, even if it is grounded in inscrutable indifference (the unground). Third, identity-philosophy culminates in an intellectual intuition which posits a rational if pre-conscious grasp of the deep identity undergirding the difference between subjectivity and objectivity; positive philosophy, which begins with this 1809 distinction between nature and God, culminates in a revelation, that is, an *a posteriori* disclosure of that which could not otherwise be known.

In the *Dark Ground of Spirit* I referred to Schelling's 'neo-Platonic logic' (McGrath 2012: 23–6), and perhaps caused an unnecessary amount of confusion by not fully explaining myself. If Schelling is a neo-Platonist, he has, as Tritten argues, turned neo-Platonism upside down: matter is still the lowest order of being, but for Schelling it is prior to mind, not, as for Plotinus, the last emanation of it.[8] In 2012 I meant by 'neo-Platonism' not any particular doctrine of *henosis*, and certainly not the Plotinian denigration of matter which Augustine transmits to Christianity. What I assumed (and still do) as essential to neo-Platonism is what I call in this book 'the theorem of absolute transcendence'. It can be defined as follows. The intelligibility of any structure depends upon relations that ultimately cannot be justified in terms of that structure. On the basis of this well-known logical puzzle, one path leads to nominalism, the positing of an accidental or merely conventional correspondence between thought and reality, and the other leads to Platonism, the assumption of an original, if now distorted, identity of thought and reality.[9] For the Platonist, relations are indexical of a transcendent ground of intelligibility. That I understand to be the essentially neo-Platonic claim which is common to all neo-Platonic thinkers, pagan, Jewish, Christian or Muslim.

The simplest way into this neo-Platonic logic is through the problem of the one and the many. Many things are said to be of the same kind by virtue of a common nature or essence, in which each participates and with which none can be identical. Imagine that the universe consisted of only two things; drawing on Dr Seuss, we can call them thing 1 and thing 2. The two things are different from one another, and therefore countable. They are the primordial opposites: the one is what it is only by virtue of not being the other. And yet they belong together in a rudimentary collection, the first and most basic class of things. That the two can be counted means 1) that they are opposites (we prescind from the later distinction between contraries and contradictories) and 2) that they are of the same kind, since there is only one 'kind' at this point. The two are both things, and the two exclude one another according to the principle of non-contradiction: when and where one is, the other is not. Now what is this 'thingness' by virtue of which thing 1 and thing 2 can be opposed, counted and regarded as members of the same class? It is manifestly not a third thing but a relation between the two things that allows us to group the two together. This relation (which is a third element in the basic ontology we are building) needs to be both identical in each and different in both. It needs to ground the two in something common, serve as the principle of intelligibility of the two, and transcend the two, because it must also possess different qualities from the two. Where thing 1 and thing 2 are determinate, occupying space and time, thingness must be free enough of determinations to be able to be identified with opposing determinations. Where thing 1 and thing 2 can be counted together, thingness cannot be counted among them. From the perspective of thing 1 and thing 2, that is, according to the terms in which thing 1 and thing 2 exist, the third element, thingness, does not exist. And yet it must *be* in some sense if thing 1 and thing 2 both are and are of the same kind.

The point of this thought experiment is this: in any judgement of identification or attribution, a relation is assumed but not defined, required but never present as one of the relata. Nominalists part company with Platonists on this point by declaring that grouping things together is just a convention of speech made possible by abstracting from the reality of the basic and inexplicable differences between things. Relations for the nominalist ('universals') are all external, that is, unreal and merely assigned to things for the sake of speaking about them. To continue down this line is to fall into Wittgensteinian silence, to be rendered incapable of speaking truthfully about anything that really matters to human beings. One gives up philosophy altogether for more sensible pursuits, as Wittgenstein did, when upon finishing the *Tractatus* with the elliptical, 'Whereof one cannot speak, thereof one must be silent' (Wittgenstein 1922: prop. 7), he fled Cambridge to become a gardener. Or one finds oneself squirming uncomfortably on Lacan's couch, endlessly engaging a symbolic order that has no intelligible relation to the real but upon which one depends for one's sanity. Down the other path we meet all of the followers of Plato who said in many different ways that relations are real and must be internal to the things related.

Plato discusses certain paradoxes associated with this logic of internal relations in *The Parmenides* (130e–131e). Having heard the theory of forms from Socrates, Parmenides asks him the following, apparently devastating question. Granted forms are what makes different things similar, and granted that similar things participate in the same form, does each thing possess the whole of the form or only part of it? If each possesses the whole of the form, then the form is rendered non-identical with itself. But if each thing only possesses a part of the form, then no thing can be identified with the form. The form would be separate from itself by being wholly immanent in things that are separate from each other (*Parmenides* 131a-b). Socrates, as is typical, answers with analogies that to some degree clarify matters but also produce further confusion. One and the same daylight can be in many places he says, as one and the same sail of a ship can cover many sailors; so too can one and the same form be in many participants. Parmenides counters that this would mean that the second of the two options outlined above is true. As no place receives all the daylight, and no sailor is covered by the whole sail but only by a part of it, so too is only one part of the form possessed by the participant. But if that is the case, then the form is not one in many but many in many, and its function of unifying a multiplicity is lost. Either the participated (the form) is wholly immanent in the participating (the things), in which case the participated is divided against itself, or the participated transcends the participating, in which case the participated is wholly different from the participating. Socrates has no answer.

Proclus tackled the puzzle in his *Elements of Theology* and staked out a solution which Schelling more or less repeats in the Freedom Essay (among other places).[10] All relations of participation lead inexorably, 'by upward tension', to the absolutely transcendent, the 'unparticipated' (*amethekton*), beyond the opposition of the participated (*metechomenon*) and the participating (*metechon*).[11] The unparticipated must have 'a place of honour', it can never become a property of the participating particulars, for then it would be divided and 'the particulars would no longer participate the same principle' (Proclus 1992: prop. 23, pp. 27–9). In short, a transcendent fourth that is not a term in the triad of two identified things and the relation between them is essential to the ontology of participation (*methexis*). Thing 1 and thing 2 can both be things because their relation is grounded in a fourth that is neither a thing nor a relation.

Let the following stand for any judgement, A = B. Let us note that there are three signified elements to the judgement, two terms, A and B, and the equals sign which stands for their relation to one another. The question is, how does the relation relate the two together? The Proclean-Schellingian answer is that there must be a fourth element, which is unsignified in the judgement, because it is wholly other than A and B, and is not reducible to the relation between them. The fourth makes the relation between the two possible by not participating in the relating. Every judgement of identity or attribution is on the surface a triad (A = B), but in the depths, a tetrad, pointing towards some unknown and unknowable ground of determination; let's call it X (Schelling 1809: 340–2/12–13). To say A is B is to say some X is in one way A and in another way B but in itself is neither A nor B, yielding the Schellingian formula for absolute transcendence:

$$\frac{A = B}{X}$$

In Proclus's terms, A and B are the participating, = is the participated, and X is the unparticipated. That which allows us to relate two particulars to one another is neither one of the particulars nor is it opposed to the particulars. This Proclean logic recurs in various neo-Platonic thinkers through the ages. It is found in figures as varied as Origen (the freedom of the Father), Eckhart (the Godhead beyond the Trinity), Cusa (the *oppositio oppositorum*), Richard Hooker (the unparticipated divine law), and Boehme and Schelling (the unground). In the Freedom Essay the move from the triad of the judgement to the hidden fourth occurs through the ungrounding of the nature/God relation. If God and nature are to be related to one another there must be a fourth transcendent element which is neither God nor nature. The fourth is indicated by the relation, but it must be more than the relation. The unground is the unparticipated in Proclus's language, the absolutely transcendent. The unground does not appear, is not 'intellectually intuited', and can only be understood partially and indirectly.

What more is there to be said of it, according to Schelling in 1809? The unground is free, preceded by nothing, compelled by nothing and limited by nothing. The clue to the freedom of this oldest of all origins, Schelling argues, is the fact that only comes from 'the ideal part' of philosophy: nature not only produces products which endlessly and necessarily strive to make the absolute concrete (an impossible task, the failure of which is productive of the universe of things); it also gives rise to an order of being in an important way opposite to this, beings who are free to will the good, or not, and so concretise or obstruct the absolute. This is the domain of freedom, and its first citizen is God himself.[12] God divides from nature, contracts himself, and masters the necessity that grounds God's being, so that God's essence might be revealed in beings who are free as God is free. The God of nature, Schelling argues at length in the Freedom Essay, is personal, a self-revealer. God can only be such because God is *not* nature. The ungrounding of the nature/God relation allows Schelling both to naturalise freedom, explaining how something like freedom is possible within a dynamic account of nature, and to transcendentalise nature, explaining how nature is productive of both necessary and free beings. Nature is productive of necessary beings, beings which act in accordance with the necessity of their respective natures, and free beings, who *will* the universal *deliberately*, and who therefore can just as deliberately refuse it. The order of freedom stands opposed to the order of necessity, but no longer in the old terms which had spirit on one side and mechanism on the other. Spirit inhabits both sides of the binary: on the one side is the dynamic and endlessly becoming order of *necessary* self-production, and on the other side, the order of freedom. Beneath necessary nature and free nature lies the unparticipated and transcendent origin of both, the unground. The X that is in one respect bound is in another respect free, in one respect objectified, in another respect morally free. These two, necessary natural production and free natural production, can be one at root by virtue of their sharing a common ungrounding in that which is not nature at all.

The somewhat sudden appearance of the personal God in 1809 spells an end to Schelling's Spinozistic phase and the beginning of his Christian philosophy, the turn that distinguishes – without separation – Schelling I from Schelling II. The challenge in connecting the late Schelling to the early Schelling generally is that where the late Schelling is clear that God is eternally self-conscious and personal, and freely creates nature, the early Schelling thematises nature in the absence of a notion of a divine creator of nature. The Freedom Essay introduces the notion of a divine creator, but problematically, as one who is not conscious and free eternally but only comes to be so through creation. These three positions on the relation of nature to God – respectively Spinozistic pantheism, historical immanentism and Trinitarian monotheism – cannot be entirely reconciled. I can only conclude that Schelling's views on God developed dramatically between 1799 and 1827, and that these conflicting models are traces of that transformation. That said, the late Schelling never repudiated nature-philosophy and even returns to take another stab at it in his last work, *Darstellung der reinrationalen Philosophie* (Schelling 1854a). The late Schelling sees in nature-philosophy, if not a positive philosophy, at least a movement towards the positive.

The difficulty is that in its final form (post-1799), Schelling's nature-philosophy evolved into identity-philosophy, and an identity-philosophy which, the late Schelling himself admits, never explicitly acknowledged its own negativity. As identity-philosophy, nature-philosophy becomes a thoroughgoing monism that identifies the universe, reason and the absolute. The dualistic appearance of a material universe over and against a mental world is resolved in the positing of an indifference of both objectivity and subjectivity in the absolute. The two orders of appearances (subjectivity and objectivity) seem to be different but are not: the difference between them is merely quantitative. A preponderance of objectivity renders the appearance objective; a preponderance of subjectivity renders the appearance subjective. Objectivity is mind in a different form, subjectivity is matter in a different form: everywhere and in everything one undivided reality prevails. The intellectual intuition that grasps this identity is no longer one's own: it becomes the absolute's own contemplation of itself, and in this absolute knowledge all individuality ceases to be real.[13] We could not be further from the non-dialectical personalism of the Freedom Essay, with its affirmation of the reality of difference, of individual freedom and autonomous existence, and its elevation of personality above being.

In any case, the point of the turn to religion in the Freedom Essay is not to naturalise God, to absorb religion into nature-philosophy – quite the opposite. The point is to free the really existing God from nature, and in that act, to free nature from God so that it could be something for itself. God personalises by productively dissociating from nature, just as a person individuates by productively dissociating from his or her past. The free God is free to reveal Godself, or not, and in this free self-revelation leaves us equally free to affirm God, or not. This is the sense of the claim that the genuine and life-giving opposition of modern philosophy is not nature/spirit but necessity/freedom (Schelling 1809: 333/4). The natural necessity overcome in the productive dissociation of the personalising God is still to be conceived dynamically; it is not dead mechanism, but (unconscious) spirit made visible (Schelling 1797b: 73/202). Nature demoted to ground has not ceased to be the activity of self-manifestation, the unconscious subject (slumbering spirit) which exteriorises itself endlessly through the production of natural beings. The explication of freedom as the spontaneity of personality is new for Schelling in 1809, as he himself admits.

> Since the author has confined himself wholly to investigations in the philosophy of nature [note the implicit identification of nature-philosophy and identity-philosophy] after the first general presentation of his system (in the *Journal for Speculative Physics* [i.e., the Würzburg system]), the continuation of which was unfortunately interrupted by external circumstances, and after the beginning made in the work, Philosophy and Religion – which, admittedly, remained unclear due to faulty presentation – the current treatise is the first in which the author puts forth his concept of the ideal part of philosophy with complete determinateness. Hence, if that first presentation [nature-philosophy including identity-philosophy] should possess any importance, he must first place alongside it this treatise, which, according to the nature of its topic, must already contain deeper disclosures about the entire system than all more partial presentations . . . Up to now the author had nowhere expressed himself regarding the main points that come to be spoken of in this treatise, the freedom of the will, good and evil, personality, and so on (excepting the one work, *Philosophy and Religion*). (Schelling 1809: 333–4/4)

The significance of this autobiographical prefatory note to the Freedom Essay is routinely overlooked. In three sentences, Schelling 1) identifies nature-philosophy with identity-philosophy; 2) denies the adequacy of the nature-philosophy/identity-philosophy system (for it could not account for freedom, morality and personality); and 3) asserts the complementarity of his later philosophy with his early philosophy. It might be argued that Schelling is hardly a trustworthy interpreter of himself, sensitive as he was to the repeated charge of inconsistency. Nevertheless, the point is hard to deny that something begins in the Freedom Essay which is absent in nature-philosophy, and which culminates in positive philosophy, namely a philosophy of freedom, a theory of personality and the hypothesis of a freely existing, personal God (as distinct from an impersonal absolute), that is, a God who could reveal Godself.

The transcendentally free, self-revealing personality (human or divine) is *not* properly described as a natural product; as personal, he or she is one who has overcome necessity, one who has taken up his or her own natural history, the ground of the self which the self could not have laid for itself, and by mastering it, rendered it the ground of a free and spontaneous self-authoring. It is not nature-philosophy but transcendental philosophy or 'idealism' which we have to thank 'for the first complete concept of formal freedom' (Schelling 1809: 351/21).[14] Freedom is not the absence of necessity; to be free is to have overcome or appropriated necessity, or, in another idiom, to have rendered the unconscious the ground of consciousness.[15] The opposites in question in the Freedom Essay, then, are nature, properly conceived *dynamically*, not mechanistically, as auto-production, and freedom transcendentally conceived as moral, that is, free, self-production, the archetype of which is the personal God. Schelling argues that we must allow each of these opposites the fullness of their reality, even exacerbate the contradiction between them, if we are not to lose the true insights of nature-philosophy, on the one hand, or transcendental philosophy, on the other. For nature-philosophy has still not made an advance on transcendental philosophy in the conceiving of freedom. This is no regression to traditional theism. The freely existing God does not have nature outside of God, for 'nothing is prior to, or outside of, God' (Schelling 1809: 358/27). Nature is the inner condition or ground of God's freedom; it is that knot of necessity without which God could not personalise.

As is well known, Schelling turned to religion before he rediscovered Boehme, Christian theosophy and mystical theology in 1809.[16] Religion becomes a predominant theme for Schelling in the transitional years of 1804–6, when having completed the Würzburg system, he attempts to integrate nature-philosophy with the neo-Platonic monism of identity-philosophy.[17] The 1804 *Philosophy and Religion* argues that history is only possible if we posit a break with the absolute, a cleft in being or a 'fall' or 'break' from identity (Schelling 1804b: 41/29). This fall, we are told, is the proper theme of religion. But in 1804 we are still far from a religion of revelation. In the 1806 *Aphorisms*, the true *Naturphilosoph* is held to be also a philosopher of religion, for he or she follows the self-revealing infinite into the unfathomable depths of its dark productivity. To be religious here is to be a genuine scientist, refusing to reduce nature to things but genuflecting before it as before the divine mystery. 'The religion of the philosophers has the colour of nature. It is the might of the one who descends with bold courage into the depths of nature' (Schelling 1806: n. 22). One might say that nature-philosophy was always on the verge of the religious, for in its refusal of the epistemological split that would have the subject building an access to the real via propositions of varying self-evidence and certainty, it identified, at least implicitly (by leaving indiscernible), objective reason with the divine. And yet, in the *Aphorisms*, the premature absolutism of nature-philosophy is made explicit. No more than we are permitted to reduce nature to natural things are we allowed to reduce reason to a human capacity. When we reason we awaken to our true position vis-à-vis the infinite: thought moves in an intelligible sphere whose centre is everywhere and whose circumference is nowhere: 'Reason is not a capacity, not a tool, and does not allow itself to be used. In general there is no reason which we have, but only a reason which has us' (Schelling 1806: n. 46). Reason is participation in divinity. 'Even reason is not an affirmation of the One which would be external to the One itself. Rather it is a knowledge of God which is itself in God. If there is nothing outside God, then the knowledge of God is only the infinite knowledge which God has of himself in eternal self–affirmation' (Schelling 1806: n. 47). Even more directly, 'Reason does not have the idea of God but rather is this idea and nothing else' (Schelling 1806: n. 48). To reason is to participate in the One's non-dual knowing of itself (if such an intelligibility without intellection can be still called a knowing). To know this is always already given to reason: it is not a discursive conclusion but an intellectual intuition, which is nothing other than reason's immediate presence to itself. Just as the *Naturphilosoph* can reason confident that his or her expressions are just as much products of *natura naturans* as the things which he or she endeavours to comprehend, so too can the *Identitätsphilosoph* intuit the oneness of all things with perfect confidence that this unity includes his or her grasp of it. In the terms of positive philosophy, this is nothing more than negative philosophy: a philosophy which reproduces reason's inalienable content as a system of (ideal) reality.

Schelling's early identification of nature/reason with the absolute without remainder (i.e., the differences between them being merely quantitative) rendered a philosophy of revelation redundant, for nothing could be revealed that was not deducible or intuitable by reason. Only where nature and God are *really* different are both idealism and its nemesis, Spinozistic immanence, overcome, and only where immanence is overcome can philosophy recognise a free act of knowledge outside of consciousness. A purely immanentist philosophy can no more recognise revelation than it can the freedom of human persons. If the positive philosophy is to exist, a reception of revelation must occur, and this can only occur on the supposition of God's freedom. Not only are human beings free of God (as evidenced in actual evil) but God is free of creation. God is free of nature; therefore God can love it. 'God himself is linked to nature through voluntary love. He does not need it, and yet he does not want to be without it' (Schelling 1810a: 453/221). The precarious relation of freedom, which on the one hand, makes love possible, and on the other, evil, goes both ways: 'Nature, too, is drawn to God by love' (Schelling 1810a: 453/221). God depends on nature (God's ground) to be God; nature depends on God to exist at all. In its crown, as the human being, nature can freely love God, as God in Christ freely loves the world, or it can reject God, crucify Christ, and hate the world – herein lies the whole plot of the Philosophy of Revelation.

This is not to say that positive philosophy employs a different kind of reason than nature-philosophy, as though in thinking the revelation, reason is essentially altered, purified and elevated, such that philosophising without the revelation inevitably substitutes falsehoods for truth.[18] Schelling's late notion of philosophical religion is meant to correct precisely this excessively pessimistic account of reason, attributable to Luther. Positive philosophy does not rest on faith, but on reason, and the reason which it employs is not other than the reason whose full operation is first manifest in nature-philosophy. Hence we see so many of the themes that are first worked out in nature-philosophy return in the positive philosophy, for example the law of the ground,[19] the ground/being distinction, the transitive nature of the copula, even the doctrine of the potencies itself – all have their root in the early nature-philosophy. The way positive philosophy thinks about revelation, the tools it has as its disposal, the concepts and principles by which it thinks the revelation, all of this is firmly in place in nature-philosophy, for they are the principles of reason itself. And yet positive philosophy thinks differently than nature-philosophy about almost everything, about the relation of God to the world, about the limits of reason, about the finitude of nature, because it has something fundamentally new to think.

Religious naturalism

Schelling's 1812 *Denkmal der Schrift von den göttlichen Dingen, etc. des Herrn Friederich Heinrich Jacobi* is among the most important texts of his middle period for understanding the complex relationship of *Naturphilosophie* to his late philosophy of religion.[20] Not only is this seldom studied work crucial for interpreting the wildly ambiguous Freedom Essay, it also contains clues for understanding the continuity of the early and the later Schelling. What is most striking about the *Denkmal* is Schelling's struggle to break through to a *religious naturalism*, a theory of nature that is not only *compatible* with monotheism, but is systematically and essentially related to a conception of a free and personal divine creator. Also notable in the treatise is Schelling's express aim, which began in the Freedom Essay but would only be fully achieved twenty years later in his Philosophy of Revelation, to construct a philosophical-theological alternative to traditional, foundationalist, natural theology, a philosophical theology which is open to revelation, and at once avoids onto-theology, fideism and rationalism.

The first point of contention between Schelling and Jacobi in the 1811–12 controversy concerns Jacobi's simple formula: rationalism = pantheism = fatalism.[21] Already in the opening pages of the Freedom Essay, Schelling had rejected this claim on logical grounds (Schelling 1809: 338–56/11–26). Pantheism can be fatalistic, as it is in Spinoza, but it need not be. There is no necessary contradiction between the claim that God is everything, and the claim that the human is free. Absolute causality in one being and total dependence of all things on God does not entail that no being except God is free. The solution to the pantheist-fatalist problem lies in a proper understanding of the copula. *God is everything* does not necessarily mean that *everything is God*; it means that God is the deepest origin of everything, the antecedent of everything, but the things God causes can be really different from him such that there is no contradiction in attributing freedom from God to some of God's creatures. The 'is' in statements of attribution and identity does not indicate sameness; on the contrary the 'is' distinguishes two for the sake of identifying them.

One sees from this argument that everything hinges on the conception of what God causes; the fatalism issue cannot be decided formally, but only on the basis of the content of what is being thought. For the sake of argument then, Schelling begins the Freedom Essay by defending pantheism and, by playing devil's advocate, endeavours to show that Jacobi is wrong, that there is no essential necessitarianism in pantheism. Since pantheism, he agrees with Jacobi, is at a certain stage of investigation an inevitable conclusion of rationalism, there is no essential necessitarianism in purely rational philosophy. One can rationally elaborate a non-reductive pantheism, a non-eliminative pantheism, a pantheism that does not confine itself to the thought of nature as mechanism, nor deny the human difference, and so does not collapse creatures into the creator, by paying more careful attention to issues in logic. The two following propositions can be rendered consistent with one another: 'God is everything' and 'the human being is free', provided we know what we are saying. The consequent is always other than the antecedent, even in a statement of identity. Thus human freedom can in principle be the consequent of God's power without for that reason being any less free. Jacobi's critique misses its mark, even if the motivation is well placed, to defend freedom and personality against rationalist fatalism. The point here is not that Schelling wishes to defend or advance a Spinozistic or rational pantheist position in 1809 – he does not. It is that he wishes to locate the flaw in Spinoza elsewhere than in Spinoza's notion of the dependence of everything on *Deus sive natura*.

Spinoza's mistake is that he has a lifeless understanding of God as the infinite substance of which everything is mere attribute or mode, and related to this, he has no appreciation for the difference between subjectivity and substance. Spinoza has failed to think God as absolute subject who stands in a living relation to all that God causes, who is therefore an agent of history in both sense of the genitive, and consequently he has failed to think human freedom beyond the dead end of the concept of *liberum arbitrium* of late Scholasticism (Schelling 1809: 350/20). God is the chief agent of history and inhabits it as the medium of self-revelation. Human freedom, the capacity for good and evil, is our means of participation in divine history, and in the end is not properly explained as a power for arbitrary choice. Freedom is not the absence of determination but the presence of self-determination. Pantheism is not a problem, so long at is properly conceptualised. In his later monotheism treatise, Schelling argues that pantheism is the impulse needed to correct the static, ahistorical transcendence of theism (Schelling 1841: 190–1).

To the end of his career, Schelling would defend the logic of pantheism. In 1 Cor. 15:28, Schelling sees a figuration of eschatological, 'Pauline pantheism'. At the end of history, Paul writes, all things shall freely be made subject to Christ, who will in turn freely subject himself (and everything under him) to the Father, and God will be 'all in all' (*panta en passin*).[22] Then, Schelling adds, pantheism will have become true (Schelling 1854c: 66). An absolute future when pantheism will be real, when God will actually *be everything*, without any diminishment of the reality of individual things, the eventfulness of time or the freedom of the human being – this is the master-thought of the late Schelling, the keystone holding together the sprawling seven books of the Philosophy of Mythology and Revelation and related writings, and the nascent idea struggling to emerge from the Freedom Essay, the *Denkmal* and the *Weltalter* drafts. I call it the theory of deferred pantheism. It is crucial to understanding the relationship beween Schelling I and II and lies at the core of Schelling's reading of the New Testament. Pantheism without loss of love and personal relations, the late Schelling argues, is nothing less than the goal of history, the *telos* of the Trinitarian theogony.

> We see the consummation of the Trinity in three persons who are independent from each other. At first there is *hen kai pan* [the one and all]; at the end there is, inversely, *pan kai hen* [the all and one]. Each [divine person] is one, is God; each potency exists as a self-standing personality of its own. God is then all in all . . . This Christian pantheism is in point of fact the most consummated monotheism. (Schelling 1841: 266)

Back to 1809. That Schelling begins the Freedom Essay with the logic of pantheism does not mean that he intends to defend an ahistorical pantheistic model of the divine–nature relation. Even if he had not yet broken through to the theory of deferred pantheism, Schelling is clear enough in 1809 that pantheism, at least in the ahistorical terms in which he had developed the concept in the identity-philosophy, is not adequate to certain facts of historical experience. Above all, it could not explain the fact of moral evil. The pantheism defence in the Freedom Essay is really nothing more than a prolegomena to Schelling's main argument, which is, I think, decisive for his moving beyond Spinozism without, with Jacobi, abandoning speculative reason. The main argument is not about rehabilitating Spinoza at all, or revamping *Naturphilosophie*. It centres, rather, on Schelling's Boehme-inspired reconceptualisation of nature as *less* than absolute but *of* the divine, a point that he reiterates even more emphatically in the *Denkmal* (Schelling 1812: 71).

Nature is not the totality of things, but the ground of being, the *ground*, not being as such. Nature as ground renders possible the historical unfolding of divine life, the ongoing revelation in time of personality, the personality of God and human personality, that is, free, self-reflective and individuated beings. The positing of nature in God as God's ground strikes Jacobi as even more misguided than Spinozism.[23] But it is, in any case, not Spinozism. In Schelling's pointed critique of him in the *Denkmal*, Jacobi is alleged to have solved nothing by leaving the question concerning nature unasked, and instead woodenly defending personalist theism, as though a concept of God as personal absolves us from asking the question, Why would a divine person create a non-personal order of material being? Jacobi commits the fallacy of dualism, which consists not in seeing the inevitability of two opposed positions, but in deciding for one to the exclusion of the other. '*Everything* exclusive, even if it reveals the better side, is bad in philosophy. Jacobi excluded nature from his philosophical reflection from the very beginning' (Schelling 1833: 176/173). The decision to suspend the question of nature leaves philosophy with bad science and empty theology.[24] The problem of explaining what and why creation is cannot simply be waved away with the theological sleight of hand, 'Nature exists because God wills it so.'

The question, why is there something and not rather nothing, draws Schelling into the most intractable questions of theodicy. 'God' cannot be the answer to the question, for it is precisely our static concept of God as pure act that is at issue. Granted an all-perfect and timeless divinity, why is there the non-divine? The question amounts to asking, why would the perfect create imperfection? Or in more traditional terms, whence evil? What is God such that nature, with its irregularities, innocent and malevolent, should also be? Conventional theism has always exonerated God, the *actus purus*, of any involvement in evil. As Leibniz put it, God does not so much create evil, something that ought not to be, as create something other than himself, which can only be other insofar as it is less than perfect, and this imperfect being is the source of all evil (Leibniz 1710). Such an answer, according to Schelling, leaves nature, the originally imperfect, still unexplained. Nature either vanishes by virtue of its ontological dependence on God, as in some emanationist, neo-Platonic models, or nature becomes something mutely alien to God, standing over and against God as a thing that should not be, but is, and which exists independently of God's will – the gnostic alternative. Schelling is struggling to give an account of God *and* nature in his middle works, a non-dualist account that would avoid both these impasses. If nature is to be something for itself, then an explanatory account of how the imperfect arises from the perfect, how the finite emerges from the infinite, nature from the divine, must be ventured.

Schelling's gamble in 1809 is to answer this question by reversing the Aristotelian-Scholastic assumption: what is first is not pure act, the perfect, but the imperfect, or more accurately, possibility and the perfect arises out of the imperfect.[25] Thus God needs to be explained as much as nature does, and since we begin with what we know better, nature, the explanation must not annul what we do know. God does not create evil, nor does God arise from it; but imperfect matter and evil (which are not the same thing, but which 'subsist' on the same ground) originate in something *in* God that is not God, a power (or 'potency') which God has let loose so that something other than God might exist. Jacobi, or indeed orthodox Catholicism and Protestantism, could never be happy with such a solution, for it appears to draw Christianity dangerously close to pantheism (again), implicating the divine in natural processes of becoming, however eternally achieved or prior to creation. Schelling, however, sees no other way to solve the problem, and even in his final Philosophy of Revelation of 1841–54, he insists that cosmogony, if it is to be intelligible, must be preceded by theogony.[26] Spinozistic pantheism is no help here, for it is too mechanical an account. What is needed is a doctrine of divine becoming, or better, divine personalisation, which could then serve as the archetype of natural becoming: cosmogony, the emergence of things out of nothing, the dynamic of nature naturing, which is the theme of Schelling's early works, must be shown to repeat theogony, the emergence of God from that which is not originally God. An imperfect nature can arise from a perfect divine being only because the perfect divine being itself emerges from what could be called the imperfect, but not in the sense of that which is malformed, flawed or morally perverse, not the absolutely un-divine, but rather the *implicitly* divine. The imperfection at the origin of divinity is not external to the divine but internal to it.[27]

Naturalism must support theism, Schelling argues, not by producing deductive arguments that can found a belief in God, but rather, from within religious philosophy, by expanding our understanding of who God is. This is a direct answer to Jacobi's charge that only two paths are left open after Kant: one, taken by Fichte, developing a moral philosophy without nature, the other taken by the early Schelling, advancing a natural philosophy without morality. Moral philosophy might be able to say something about personality and freedom, Jacobi argues, and this no doubt has some relevance for religion, but religion and *Naturphilosophie* are strictly speaking separate discourses: the rules of the one do not apply to the other, and what is presupposed in the one is unknowable by the other. *Naturphilosophie*, according to Jacobi, must remain silent on religious matters. 'It must never desire to speak of God and divine things, of freedom, or moral good and evil, of true ethics', writes Jacobi, 'for according to its innermost convictions these things for it do not exist, and whatever it says about them could not be truthfully intended. Whoever should do so would be lying' (Jacobi 1811: 154, cited in Ford 1965: 82).

What is at stake on this point, from Schelling's perspective, is Jacobi's misreading of nature-philosophy as a monism. Here, as throughout his career, we see Schelling defend non-dualism, as distinct from monism, in a fashion reminiscent of the best Zen masters. Monism denies duality; non-dualism presupposes it, and says only that reality is *not two* (which is different from saying, with the monist, that reality is one). That is, non-dualism does not deny duality as such; it only denies that the one and the other exclude each other, and are incompatible with one another, and compel the thinker to choose one over the other. A genuine non-dualism is not a one without another. To exclude the other would be dualistic, to one-sidedly take a stand in favour of one of the two at issue. *Naturphilosophie* is not exclusive; it lets its other be, even recognises its relative necessity, or at least the claim to legitimacy of that which it does not include. In 1800 the other of *Naturphilosophie* is cast by Schelling as transcendental philosophy. In 1809 Schelling refines this position: the other in question is the creator God of monotheism and the moral order which God makes possible. That said, Schelling in effect agrees with Jacobi that Spinoza's pantheistic formula, *Deus sive natura*, leaves philosophy with no resources to conceptualise God's personality. The God of whom Schelling speaks in 1809 is not *the same as* everything (the 'is' in the sentence 'God is everything' does not indicate sameness). God is not simply identical with nature. If God is personal and free, God is manifestly not nature. It is perhaps because in his 1811 polemic Jacobi misses this new turn in Schelling's thinking that Schelling is so indignant in his 1812 reply. In 1809 Schelling shares Jacobi's a commitment to divine personalism. But where Jacobi remains content to assert that God's personality is immediately known and must serve as an inexplicable presupposition to any thinking that is to avoid the rationalist/fatalist trap, Schelling in the Freedom Essay goes to some trouble to demonstrate the coherence, the explicability, partial and open-ended, of divine freedom and personality.

If nature is not God, but grounds God and is contained by God, what more precisely is it? Here Schelling keys into his Platonic meontology, which dates back to the *Timaeus* commentary, which he wrote when he was 19.[28] The question cannot be answered so long as we fail to distinguish two senses of nothing, the *ouk on*, of pure nothingness, and the *me on*, non-being, or the absence of determination. If the ground is nothing in the first sense, then history, time and finite beings are illusory, and the debate is moot. Nothing founds nothing, as the ancients insist (*ex nihilo nihil fit*). If, on the other extreme, nature is being in the sense of substance, and by virtue of its contingency, difference and unfinishedness, outside of God, then God would be limited by it. As a blemish on perfect being, a surd, something which ought not to be but is, we would ultimately need, with the gnostics, to account for the existence of nature by tracing it to something other than God. In short, if nature were outside of God, God would not be God. Nature must be in God in some sense, as everything must be in God – and most Christian thinkers would not disagree. But where for traditional Christian neo-Platonism, nature is in God, first as idea in the divine mind, and then as being which is created by God and subsists according to God's gracious and ongoing act of preserving power, for Schelling, the matter is thought in the direction of both a more robust notion of nature's independence and a more personal notion of God's involvement with it. Nature, according to Schelling, is *in God as differentiated from God*, as the meontic origin of God Godself, and if it were not, God would not be capable of producing beings which are free of God. The law of the ground applies here as well, as it applies to everything, for it is the principle of order, as such, the essential truth of the principle of reason. The ground must not be confused with that which it grounds, for if it is, everything becomes groundless, orderless and meaningless.

This is Boehme's central idea, although he was lacking the training in metaphysics to draw the distinction between *ouk on* and *me on*.[29] Nature, if it is a real, dynamic power of producing beings such as ourselves, must be more than merely natural. It must be archaic spirit, a primordial power that lies at the basis of God's personality, or better, God's personalities (since there are three), as desire and drive lies at the basis of every human personality. And while this greatly complicates our conception of God, it also helps us understand two phenomena that go completely unexplained in more traditional conceptions of God as pure act that excludes potency: it helps us to understand why and how evil comes to be, and what divine personality is such that it can produce good or evil. In defence of his 1809 retrieval of Boehmian theogony, Schelling argues that a perfect, eternal God who has not overcome necessity or passed through a process of 'birth' from darkness could have no essential relation to the nature God ostensibly created. For this reason, possibility in some new sense of the term (distinct from Aristotelian potency) must precede all acts and their correlative potencies. God's actual perfection is consequent, not antecedent; God, too, depends upon an origin in which God Godself was not yet God.

That this raises serious problems for understanding the infinity and perfection of God, Schelling recognises. He spends the rest of his long career trying to square the primacy of possibility with the perfection, sovereignty and transcendence of God. Nevertheless, a static and eternally actualised divinity, such as Jacobi defends, creates worse problems. Through-out the monotheistic tradition, theology has been unable to explain why God would create anything at all, and thus 'nature' has not existed for it.[30] Schelling protests that the idea of a God who contains possibility within Godself has biblical as well as metaphysical warrant. A God who does not possess a dark ground a pure, pre-conscious power and strength which God has eternally mastered, is without character, without individuality and life-less. The Old Testament itself recognises the wrath of God as the root of the properly theological fear of God in the believer.[31]

It is important to note that Schelling refines his view quite dra-matically on this point in later years. In 1809–15 he defends what Ford has called 'explicative theism' and what I have called 'historical immanentism'.[32]

> God is seen in terms of a temporal process with two extremes, an absolute begin-ning in *Deus implicitus*, in whom all perfections exist potentially, but none actually, and an ultimate culmination in *Deus explicitus*, a final synthesis containing all the divine perfections as actualised together with conserved values of the creative order. The created world is involved in this process, not as its vehicle to be sure, but as its principal product. (Ford 1965: 86)

It was a standard idea in Scholastic theology that everything in the world is a repetition and finite differentiation of an idea in the mind of God. What Schelling does with divine exemplarism is insist on including not only the perfections of things in the divine being, as, for example, Aquinas does,[33] but also their imperfections. Those aspects of creation which are most material, the dynamism of its actualisation, the growth and decay of things, the diversity of beings which is attributable not to their posses-sion of diverse species but to their failure to perfectly embody the species, the desire and conflictual forces which push nature into constant move-ment and evolution – Schelling includes all of this materiality as well in the divine economy. Rather than regarding becoming as the mere appearance of being, as the play of nothingness on faculties that are too dim to discern the absolute, Schelling sees becoming itself as an ectype, the archetype for which must be located in God. If God has not in some sense become, passed through a process of growth, and negotiated the countervailing forces of contraction and expansion, which *Naturphilosophie* has identified as the essential ingredient of all natural becoming, then nothing else could become anything. Schelling will later come to see that his historical imma-nentist account of divine exemplarism indeed falls prey to what Jacobi most suspects of it; it renders God a creature among creatures, and he will draw in particular on the doctrine of the Trinity to explain how God undergoes a divine process in a first act of creation, which is then finitised and repeated in all natural process, in a second act of creation. Theogony precedes cosmogony, and is therefore to be distinguished from it.

A crucial take-away point from the *Denkmal* is that not all naturalist approaches to divinity are foundationalist or onto-theological. The difference can be seen in Schelling's very precise definition of the kind of naturalism that he is interested in defending, a naturalism that assumes that if there is a divine being, it is not simply other than nature; it is not simply the transcendent, the wholly other, the strange and inscrutable First Cause. If there is a God, God transcends nature by containing it within Godself. God is above nature, more than nature, to be sure, as the whole is above and more than the part, but God is not unnatural. This is enough to prove that Schelling's naturalist approach to the absolute, which he followed in all of his early works to their ultimate logical end, the identity-philosophy, was never entirely abandoned. What changed in 1809 was his youthful presumption that such a *naturphilosophische* path towards the genuinely divine could remain with the terms of the impersonal, pantheistic absolutism of Spinoza. It was not enough to recognise, as Schelling did in his early works, that the human being is the consciousness that nature needs in order to be complete, for consciousness of nature is not necessarily personality. In the pivotal years of 1804–9, Schelling came to see that an impersonal 'divine' substance was not only *not* the highest, it was not God at all. The middle works are precisely an effort to forge a path from nature to God, and if they ultimately fail in execution, the goal is never dropped. It remains Schelling's project until the end, to avoid the impasse of a philosophy of nature without God, or a theology of God without nature, 'an unnatural God and a Godless nature' (Schelling 1812: 70). Beyond the Jacobian impasse of either naturalism or theism, the late Schelling constructs a speculative monotheism, which recapitulates the central moves in the historical formulation of the Christian doctrines of the Trinity and incarnation, but in a fundamentally original way. God is all, and all will be in God – at the end of time. The true concept of God, which Schelling comes to see is revealed to us (not deduced or divined), is not the work of reflection. God reveals Godself. God gives us something to think. That which is to be thought is not only the true concept of religion, it is also the true concept of nature.[34]

The final doctrine of the potencies

This first thing to note in venturing an interpretation of Schelling's late doctrine of the potencies is that an important change occurs between the 1809–15 schema of ground/existence/personality, and the 1831 sequence of determinability (*das sein Könnende*)/determination (*das sein Müssende*)/self-determination (*das sein Sollende*). No doubt the two models are logically related: ground is determinability, the potency for determination, which must exclude all actual determination if it is to serve as ground. Existence is determination. The essence of personality is self-determination. But where in 1809 the three potencies emerge spontaneously from the unground and in that emergence give birth to God, in 1831 the potencies are dependent on God's decision to be God. This is the very axis of the turn from the middle Schelling's theosophical concept of God to his later, properly theological notion. The confusion of the biblical, self-revealing God with a natural process is the principal error of theosophy according to the late Schelling (Schelling 1842d: 121/175). Schelling names Jakob Boehme in this regard, the figure who was so decisive for him in 1809. He probably also had the Speculative Pietism of Friedrich Christoph Oetinger in mind, that vital post-Reformation tradition which blended a romanticised Christianity with esoteric mysticism (Kabbalah) and the philosophy of nature (alchemy) in order to combat the Enlightenment, and which had decisively inspired his younger self, as well as his childhood friends, Hegel and Hölderlin.[35]

By the time he gets to Berlin, Schelling wishes to be done with the Boehmian/Speculative Pietist theogony of the free and self-conscious God who 'gives birth to himself'. Theosophy had certain advantages over orthodoxy, Schelling admits. Most notably, where the traditional theology of creation left the world as only accidentally related to its divine cause, theosophy offered an explanatory account of materiality. The potencies which constitute God are externalised by God in creation as the forces of nature (expansion/contraction, attraction/repulsion, and so on), and the doctrine of *creatio ex nihilo* is rendered consistent with the Kabbalistic *creatio ex Deo*. Boehme defended the theogony of the birth of God from the unground on the basis of mystical intuition, but this need not mislead us. In his assimilation of late medieval and Renaissance neo-Platonism, his deconstruction of modern science and his internalisation of the Luther Bible, Boehme was hardly irrational or unspeculative, and certainly did not derive his theories from private revelations. The motive of Boehme's theosophy was twofold: 1) to give an account of evil that neither explains it away (as does the *privatio boni* tradition), nor allows its existence to compromise the goodness and sovereignty of God; and 2) to explain the relationship of God to creation in such a way as to show that material nature is neither evil nor accidental; theosophically conceived, nature is a self-manifestation of the divine nature. Without the model of Boehme's theosophy, Schelling could not have written the Freedom Essay, which is in many ways an effort to provide metaphysical arguments for theosophical claims.[36] What is crucial for our purposes is to note *why* the late Schelling becomes so critical of theosophy. He praises the depths of Boehme's insight and concurs with Hegel on his place in the history of German thought (Schelling 1842d: 119–26/173–8; Hegel 1896b: 188). But unlike Hegel, he now disapproves of Boehme's notion of God. Boehme wants a free creation but ends up with a God who is 'the immediate substance of the world' (Schelling 1854b: 125), thus a God from whom the world emerges with necessity, as the mediator of God to Godself. The later Schelling's God is always already realised in Godself and creates in perfect freedom. Creation adds nothing to God, but is a pure joy, a theophany, which God undertakes out of the excess of God's perfection (Tritten 2017: 145). 'The God of a truly historical and positive philosophy does not move himself; he acts' (Schelling 1854b: 125).[37]

In a sentence, this passage sums up the ambiguous relationship of the late Schelling's philosophy of God to the Freedom Essay and related writings of the middle period. In 1809 Schelling holds that primal matter, the ground, produces God spontaneously but not deliberately. In the positive philosophy God is self-produced: God's act of existing is deliberate and free, the axial decision whereby God wills to be the creator, and in that act wills that there be something rather than nothing, order rather than disorder, love, with all of its presuppositions (duality, struggle, precarity and the possibility of evil) rather than a silent and undifferentiated infinity of existence. The language of birthing, even the concept of the unground (which does not appear as such in the Philosophy of Revelation), is accordingly dropped and replaced by the language of decision, deed and that which is decided, the fate of eternal, unprethinkable existence (the non-potency, A^0). The God of the Freedom Essay *moves* (and so is moved, albeit by Godself) and produces God's own consciousness, freedom and capacity to love; the God of the Philosophy of Revelation is always already free: God *acts* and produces divinity, and subsequently, out of no need or compulsion, a world other than God.

Since order – tenuous, contingent and precarious – rules over disorder in the universe as it in fact exists, and since order is neither necessary nor eternal, something must have occurred which had as its consequence the *existence* of the potencies which constitute any and all order whatsoever. This event could not be a passage from potency to act; it could only be a passage from act to potency, since potency as such (essence/intelligible being/the conceptualisable) is the product of the event. An event that is not preceded by potency cannot be comprehended *a priori*: the event of being is unprethinkable, as Schelling says. The event itself has no essence which predetermines it, it only has an essence *post factum*. Since the event is the production of reason itself it would be strange to call it irrational. Better to call it the non-rational, unprethinkable event which has as its end the rational, the ordered and the freely willed.

'Something' is determined by the event; 'something' precedes the event which is not strictly speaking a thing at all, but which is essentialised and determined *as* something in the event. The event of grounding is preceded by eternal, unprethinkable existence (*ewige . . . unvordenkliche Sein*), as the cardinal number 1 is preceded by 0 (Schelling 1831: 32–8; Schelling 1841: 162–5/127–30; Schelling 1842d: 156/199, 174/212; Schelling 1854b: 268–9). Without question, this is the late Schelling's most theologically problematic and most fertile concept. Eternal existence is pre-divine, pre-personal and pre-predicative. It is impossible to directly think but impossible *not* to think, because it is co-thought with anything categorically thought. It is impossible to define because it is essence-less. It is impossible to directly experience, but is co-experienced in everything we experience. It is that which exists *as* God, but is not itself God. As the ground of God, it is contingent on God's decision to be God, but in itself contingent on nothing. It is non-modally or existentially necessary, which is the same as saying it is non-modally or radically contingent (groundless). Schelling calls it 'holy, that is, supernatural and inscrutable *Ananke*' (Schelling 1854b: 268), after the Greek goddess, who has no parents but is self-produced. Being without a reason, eternal existence is 'the primordial contingency itself' (*der Urzufall selbst*), 'the contingency which is through itself, which has no cause outside of itself and from which all other contingencies are derived' (Schelling 1854a: 464). It is to be distinguished from the *essential* necessity of the divine nature, which is, in relation to it, a 'contingent necessity' (Schelling 1841: 166–7/132). Eternal, unprethinkable existence is the source of the strength and character of God, 'the sheer power and force' (*bloß Kraft und Stärke*) of the divine (Schelling 1812: 65). On a psychological level, it is the inextricably unconscious, that ground of the soul which gives the personality character, but which can never be made conscious. It is the knot of necessity which, overcome (but not sublated), serves as the ground of the individuated person.[38]

By rendering God's necessity contingent, Schelling threatens the Nicene approach to the Trinity; indeed, he seems to have undermined the infinity of God. 'The act of having existence (*der Akt des Existirens*) is not foreseen and willed by God' (Schelling 1841: 166–7/132).[39] Here is Schelling at his most heterodox. We shall have to examine this problem carefully. For the moment, let this be said. Eternal existence is, for Schelling, not a limitation on the power of God, but the presupposition of God's freedom and sovereignty, since without it there would be nothing over which God was eternally 'lord'.

While semantically A^0 puts eternal existence into sequence with the potencies, A^1, A^2, A^3, it is important not be misled by this symbol into thinking of existence as a potency. A^0 is not a potency; it is the absence of potency, the absolutely first, the *prius*, the act which produces potencies. Schelling sees this as the speculative truth of Aristotle's axiom that potency is originally determined by act, and the universal depends for its being on the individual (Schelling SW 14: 337; 1850: 588). The zero in A^0 means that in eternal, unprethinkable existence there is no A, not even as a potency. A^0 is the absence of potency, but in a different sense than A^2: for the second potency excludes potency and is therefore preceded by it, where A^0 is not preceded by potency but succeeded by it. Negative philosophy arrives at the concept of A^0 or the non-concept of A^0 'only through exclusion, thus negatively' (Schelling 1854a: 562), by moving deductively from potency to non-potency. In the transition to positive philosophy a reverse move must occur, from A^0, where nothing is decided, to A^1 / A^2 / A^3 as principles of actually existing being. A^0, which is excluded from negative philosophy, is the presupposition or the 'absolute *prius*' of positive philosophy. The positing of A^0 is not an act of faith, but an act of the will of one who demands an explanatory account of really existing being (the positive), and in this demand, recognises the surd of existence as such. Positive philosophy ventures the hypothesis that A^0 is not meaningless, not an accident that evacuates all events of ultimate meaning, but the act whereby God eternally wills to be God.

Where Hegel makes the contingent necessary, Schelling absolutises contingency – herein lies his radicality – extending it even to the being of God. A^0 is the primordial freedom that in the Freedom Essay was identified with original being (*Ursein ist Wollen* [Schelling 1809: 350/21; 1831: 40]). It is the unprethinkable ground that becomes the act by which God decides eternally to be a God of reason and love, and in so deciding, eternally wills reason over non-reason, order over nothingness. The point bears repeating, for here the way swings off from Spinoza, Leibniz, Hegel and all necessitarian doctrines of God, as it does from Aristotelian-Scholastic foundationalism, and returns to the metaphysical voluntarism at the origins of the Jewish, Muslim and Christian traditions. Here the way swings back to the pre-Nicene voluntarists, to Origen and Arius. Because A^0 is not subsumable into the potencies, because it is the presupposition of the potencies, God is absolutely free. God is not answerable to anything for God's being: there is no divine nature preceding God's existence that necessitates that God be as God. And there is no necessity that from God order, reason, nature or even the *Logos* should emerge from the night of God's infinite actuality. What A^0 (un)grounds is order as such, the order of nature, and its intelligible structure, formally expressed as the order of the three potencies: A^1 or determinability (or $-A$), A^2 ($+A$), determination, and A^3 ($\pm A$), self-determination.

When trying to understand the late Schelling's doctrine of potencies it is vitally important to keep two things in mind: first, these three formal ontological structures should not appear to us as novel but familiar. We have met them before, in Plato, in Aristotle, in informal logic, and their explication should succeed in demonstrating their obviousness. Schelling's late doctrine of potencies is anything but esoteric. It is Schelling's take on a theme that is as old as philosophy itself: the theme of the triadic structure of being. We should think of the Pythagorean *monas*, *duas* and *trias*. We should remember what Aristotle described as the indeterminate dyad of Plato, the dialectic of 'the limited' (*to peras*) and 'the unlimited' (*apeiron*), which gives rise to the third, 'something mixed' (*hen ti symmisgomenon*), the thing that becomes what it is in time (*Metaphysics*, Book 1, 987b). We should see the subject/object/copula structure of informal logic. We should recognise in the three potencies a speculative expression of the logical laws of identity, non-contradiction and excluded middle. Finally, we should always remember that however logically necessary the potencies are in relation to one another (A^1 cannot be conceived without A^2), as a triadic whole the potencies are contingent upon A^0.

Like the ground of the Freedom Essay, the first potency, A^1 (or $-A$), the formal essence of determinability as such, which can be denied of nothing that in fact exists, does not exist but is directed towards existence, which it is impotent to reach. As the possibility of being or the desire to exist, A^1 is non-being, not nothingness but the *me on* of Parmenides, the *apeiron* of Anaxagoras and Plato (*Philebus* 23c). The second potency, A^2 (+A), is being in the sense of existence rather than essence, but now qualified as preceded by potency; it is the potency-dependent *actus purus*, the Platonic principle of form (*to peras*), which cannot exist without A^1 (its presupposition). First potency is the subject prior to any predicate, the undetermined subject, 'pure ability to be without any being' (*reines Können ohne alles Seyn*). Second potency is the object without its subject, pure determinacy without any mobility, 'pure being without any ability to be' (*reines Seyn ohne alle Können*) (Schelling 1854a: 292).[40] The third potency, A^3 (±A), as in the 1809 triad, is the unity of the first two, the potency that can pass over into actuality without entirely losing itself in the act, because it holds itself in potency for future acts. Only in the third do we have freedom, spirit and the potency of personal existence, that is, personality. Much of this terrain was mapped and explored by Schelling between 1809 and 1815. What is new in the Philosophy of Revelation is the qualification of the three potencies as *negative*, a basic grid of *a priori* concepts, the triadic principles of reason, which stand to be supplemented by an unprethinkable revelation of God's free acts in time.

Since primal being is will, the three potencies are also three modes of willing, and it is as modes of willing that they are most easily understood. First, there is that mode of willing which *can* be (−A, *das sein Könnende*), that which could will anything but in fact wills nothing, or that which holds itself back and does not go out of itself; second, there is that which *must* be (+A, *das sein Müssende*), that which actually wills something and therefore cannot will nothing, or that which holds nothing back and goes out of itself into what it wills; and third, there is that which *shall* be (±A, *das sein Sollende*), that which in willing something does not lose its capacity to will otherwise, or that which in going out of itself still remains with itself. Using other language, Schelling describes the three potencies as that which is in-itself (*das in-sich-Sein*), that which is out-of-itself (*das ausser-sich-Sein*), and that which stays with-itself (*das bei-sich-Sein*) (Schelling 1854a: 290). The first potency is the *subject* of willing, the second is the *object* of willing and the third is the subject-object that together comprise the whole triadic act of willing anything whatsoever. In any act of will, say the willing of this book to come into existence, we can distinguish the one who wills from the act of willing itself. The one who wills is the subject, the 'I' in the sentence 'I will write this book.' The object of the will is the willing to write the book or the predicate of the sentence. We could thus rephrase the above more accurately as 'I *will* to *be* the one who *wills* to write this book', and thus underscore the distinction of the subject of willing, the 'I' (first potency), from the object of willing, the willing to write the book (second potency). The complete act of will, the willing agent in conjunction with the object of its willing, is not just two added together, but a whole, a third, which is irreducible to its component parts. The provisionality and contingency of the whole is crucial here. While the 'I' is actualised in the will to write the book, it is not exhausted in it. I might will other things besides (presumably I remain more than just the author of this book).

This, then, is the psychological insight at the heart of Schelling's late doctrine of the potencies: 'the subject is in itself a void that must be first filled by the predicate' (Schelling 1842d: 77/142). 'Subject' here is equally the logical subject and the psychological subject. One can see what caught the attention of Žižek. Is this not the Lacanian subject, the psychological subject of desire, the cleft in being, the one who only exists insofar as he or she desires being, determinacy, and so who can never fully be?[41] The resonance with Heidegger is also clear: Dasein *is not*, that is, it is never categorically determinable as thus and so; Dasein is always only its possibilities, it is its 'to be'. The fundamental existential is 'existence' of the 'to be' (*zu sein*) of Dasein.[42] Both these interpretations of Schelling, the Lacanian and the Heideggerian, which are fundamentally connected,[43] need to be qualified by Schelling's positive assessment of the meontic essence of the psychological subject. Only because the psychological subject is essentially indeterminable is it also free for novelty, relation and ongoing self-determination. A person is never exhausted or fully determined by his or her relations. The one who wills to be a certain way or enters into a relation with another does not entirely empty his or herself into that way of being; something retreats into inaccessibility; an 'indivisible remainder' (*der nie aufgehende Rest* [Schelling 1809: 359/29]) retreats behind every act of willing, a one who in fact has not appeared and cannot appear, insofar as he or she has conceded actuality to the one who does appear. One thinks of Sartre's analysis of bad faith illustrated in his unforgettable example of the waiter (Sartre 1943: 101–2). We watch the waiter bustle to and fro in the Paris café; we see his impeccable uniform, identical to the uniform of every other Paris waiter: white shirt, black tie, black trousers, white apron. We notice his absolute dedication to the needs of his customers; the man appears to be entirely invested in his role, perfectly identified with his predicates. And yet we know that it is only a role, that he is only pretending to be entirely invested in serving diners, and that behind this façade someone hides and perhaps suffers our objectification or smirks at us, one who is not at all a waiter, who understands himself in terms of a whole range of other possibilities, and who perhaps could not care less whether we enjoy our dinner or not.

That said, Schelling's doctrine of potencies, especially in its later articulation, is also a logical theory of predication, as Wolfram Hogrebe famously pointed out (Hogrebe 1989). It can be a theory of predication as well as a psychology because for Schelling, the principles of logic and the principles of psychology are principles of being. It is not because there is thinking that there is being, but because there is being that there is thinking (Schelling 1842d: 161, n. 1/203, n. xx). In any judgement, then, we can distinguish three elements: the grammatical subject, the grammatical object and the verb. –A is the grammatical subject, +A is the grammatical object, and ±A is the union of the two. The subject is exteriorised and concretised, rendered actual in one respect and potential in another, by the object. The object is not reducible to the subject but neither is it separable from it. The subject (the *hypokeimonon*) *bears* the object, renders it actual, by slipping underneath it and being in turn reduced by it back to potency.

> Once again, the being [*Seyende*] we seek is immediately and in the first thought the potency of being [*Seyn*]. It is subject, but subject that immediately contains within itself its fulfillment (the subject is in itself a void that must be first filled by the predicate) . . . And since in the subject – or potency – being [*Seyn*] is immediately also an *object*, a complete concept of being [*Seyende*] must also incorporate this (the third element), which is a subject and object thought as one inseparable subject-object, so that this must still be distinguished as a third determination. (Schelling 1842d: 143/77, translation slightly altered)

Take, for example, the judgement by which I assert knowledge of a physical object, say an apple. I assert what I know of it in the proposition, 'This is an apple.' Insofar as it is a 'this', a sheer and ineffable singularity, an existing being occupying a specific space and time, the thing is not an apple at all, for in its singularity it is distinct from whatever classes of things it might otherwise belong to. It is not with the class of things called 'apples', or the class of things called 'physical', or the class of things called 'fruits' that we immediately have to do, or even with a particular apple in this respect, but with a *this*, a predicateless *it*. Considered as a singular being without predicates, it could be anything at all. It could be a stone, a memory, a mathematical formula, a tree, the Queen of England, since all these are in one respect ineffable singularities. But nothing can exist without existing in such and such a way: the singular is always a particular, an instance of a class. The thing we are discussing belongs to the class of things called 'apples' (among other classes) and in that sense it cannot be anything other than *an apple*. The subject–predicate structure of every proposition (e.g., '*this* is an apple') is composed of these two potencies, a subject which is exteriorised, concretised and defined by its predicates, without, however, becoming identical with them. The difference between a subject and its predicates is not a difference between two things; it is a difference between two equiprimordial senses of being: being means, first of all, that which can be thus and so, that is, the subject of predication (*das sein Könnende*, what Peirce calls 'firstness', the capacity for determination), and secondly, being means object, the various predicative determinations of a subject, which Schelling describes, confusingly, as necessary being (*das sein Müssende*).[44] The being of the subject and the being of the object are two equiprimordial senses of being, neither of which can be reduced to the other. Determination, actualisation in this or that way, is the opposite of determinability or the capacity for actualisation. And thirdly, being means the union of the first two senses of being, the union of a subject with its predicates, or the grammatical subject with its object. This third sense of being is equally irreducible to the first two and is represented by the copula in any predicate sentence. The 'is' joins the subject with its predicates but is not for that reason nothing.

Schelling can make these distinctions – distinctions which were certainly understood, albeit in a different way, by ancient and medieval philosophers – because he is a proponent of being as an activity rather than mere instantiation.[45] He would, therefore, stringently object to those schools of analytical philosophy which dispense with the concept of being by making the copula irrelevant through the substitution of the existential quantifier, $\exists$, for the verb 'to be'. For Schelling, such a symbolisation, while it might simplify logic, conceals the whole phenomenon of existence. The 'is' in the sentence 'A is B' is not merely a conjunction, nor are we simply positing B in existence: the 'is' should be understood transitively: 'A actualises as B', or 'A exteriorises and manifests as B'. The verbal sense of being, which we might try to capture by rearticulating the subject–predicate structure as 'A being B', is the third potency, that which shall be (*das sein Sollende*). In Schelling's informal logic, the copula is always transitive, even in identity statements, always taking an accusative object, and never merely conjunctive. This means, according to Schelling, that neither the subject nor the object precedes the act of predication but both come into being as subject and object in the judgement, which first disjoins them so as to be able to identify them. The assumption that the subject precedes predication and subsists independently of it may be characterised as the chief error of nominalism; the assumption that the object precedes predication and subsists independently would be the two-world Platonic realism that Schelling opposed as early as 1794. Schelling's view avoids the reductionism of the former and the many pitfalls of the latter by making the copula the transitive ground of both. Schelling's theory of the transitive copula is clearly related to Hegel's speculative proposition, but the difference between the two theories is as important as their similarities. Where, for Hegel, the predicate is the truth of the subject, the truth that the subject in itself has no truth, for Schelling the subject is never exhausted in the predicate, and a duality of subject and predicate, antecedent and consequent, remains the condition of the possibility of real existence. Hence the copula in a Schellingian act of predication is always refractory, for the subject is an excess of possible determination for which no predicate is adequate. An indivisible remainder is always left out in any act of predication.[46]

I have described the three potencies as, respectively, constitutive parts of the personality, as forms of will, and as parts of the judgement. What unites these figures and makes them repetitions of one triune structure are the three potencies as principles of being. Being is triadic, as Plato and Aristotle were the first to point out: it contains a principle of determinability, a principle of determination, and a principle that can mix the two; the unlimited, the limited and the mixed; matter (*hyle*), form (*morphe*) and substance (*ousia*). While Schelling follows Plato rather than Aristotle in holding the first potency or matter to be a dynamic principle and not merely the passive receiver of form, the triadic structure is common to both. It is as principles of being that the potencies are defined in the Philosophy of Revelation. Let us sum up, then, with a purely ontological exposition of the potencies, such as Schelling repeats in various places (Schelling 1831: 32–62; 1841: 100–7).

The first potency (–A), we have said, is *determinability* – not nothingness, the *absence* of all determination, but non-being, the possibility of all determination. –A is prior to actual being, as are all of the potencies, but in a specific sense: it is that which could be but is not (*das sein Könnende*), that which could be anything because it is not yet something (hence the negative sign before the content, A). It neither is nor is not, and it is therefore free in a negative sense, to be or not to be. But this freedom to be or not to be is purely virtual, for –A cannot *actually* be without losing its freedom not to be. –A is potency without actuality. It includes everything except actuality. It is in one sense infinite, but in another sense, limited. –A is the potential infinite, not the actual infinite; it is not that which has nothing outside of it, but that which never comes to an end because it lacks actuality. It includes *essentially* everything but exists as nothing: it refuses to discriminate and commit to any one determination over another.

The inclusion of everything in –A is only possible by virtue of its exclusion of actuality. The first potency is like the adolescent who stands immobilised before the future. He or she thinks they can do anything whatsoever with their life precisely because they have actually not yet done anything. –A posits the actual outside itself, as a second potency (+A) which opposes it. This exteriority of actuality to the first potency shows that –A is not *immediately* related to being, nor can it be conceived apart from its opposite. If –A were the absolute, then it would *be* immediately, that is, it would pass directly into actuality. 'If that which will be is merely that which can immediately be, then we would only encounter blind being in reality' (Schelling 1831: 32). All systems that deny the contingency of being identify –A with absolute being, without distinction, as does Spinoza with his notion of substance. The move is typical of negative philosophy and as such is also found in Schelling's early identity-philosophy, for which history and multiplicity are ultimately illusions. If something is *to be* in a contingent and historical sense, or if something is to be *finite*, then a determination and a mediation must come into play. The constitutive conditionality of being renders all being, even the being of reason, the laws of thought and the being of God, contingent.

Lacking all actuality, –A is impotent to carry itself into being or to actualise any one of its possibilities. Schelling describes –A as 'the unlimited potency for being', or the *ens omnimode determinatum* of Scholasticism (Schelling 1841: 100). We can call it substance or essence. It is that which could be brought to pass over into being, but cannot actually do so itself, for if it were to do so, it would cease to be what it is, pure possibility. We can associate –A, then, with the first law of thought, the principle of identity, but prior to any principle of differentiation and therefore prior to the principle of non-contradiction (which is of course an abstraction, but the distinction of the potencies is only possible in abstraction). –A is bare identity without differentiation (A = A), the simple positing of the possibility of being something, but prior to the differentiation from other things requisite to actually be *something*. The primary quality of the first potency is its inclusiveness: as bare identity, it excludes nothing possible. This would appear to make it actually unlimited, for if it includes all possibilities, nothing is outside of it. However, the very principle of inclusion is paradoxically a principle of exclusion. If −A includes all possibilities, then it must exclude actuality, for actuality is a principle of difference and exclusion. Schelling hereby touches on the same paradox that besets the liberal notion of tolerance. The liberal can tolerate everything but intolerance and hence cannot tolerate everything.

> The *primordial potency* (the unlimited potency to be) excludes nothing and *allows for two contradictory opposites.* That which is the potency for transcendence [*das Übergehenkönnende*] is immediate potency, the absolutely self-same and identical. The ability to be [*das sein Könnende*], the primal potency, refuses to take on any decisive character; according to its nature it can be equally that which transcends itself, or that which stays with itself. (Schelling 1841: 102)

The contradiction consists in the following logical conundrum. Among the possibilities included in −A is the possibility *not* to be, a possibility that would be foreclosed by an immediate, inevitable or logical passage into being. The first potency is open to all possibilities. But to include everything is to exclude one thing, the possibility of annulling possibility in actuality. Hence the first potency presupposes the second potency, which it posits insofar as it excludes it from itself.

> The immediate ability-to-be [*das unmittelbar Seinkönnende*] is the most fortuitous, and therefore appears as the most ungrounded, for the ground of its being is not found in that which precedes it, but in that which follows it, in relation to which it is mere subject [*hypokemenon*], relative non-being. However, it finds thereby its grounding. For itself it has lost it. Insofar as it is subordinated to that which is higher, it can become again its own master [*suae potestatis*]. What it serves as support, of it one can say: it is something, but not a being [*Seiendes*]. The first [potency] is the prime matter of all being, but only becomes determinate when it offers itself as support for a higher ability-to-be. (Schelling 1841: 104)

The second potency (+A) is posited after the first potency. It is the precise opposite of non-being: it is pure act without potency, or the *actus purus*, being itself. It has no potency because it is entirely given over to the determination that it is. Where −A holds back from determination, +A is entirely fastened to being. The second potency is the principle of form, the *to peras* of Plato, the principle of limit or difference, which stands opposed to the *apeiron*, or the unlimited. As form, it contains nothing but the determination that it itself is. It has no possibility to be anything other than what it is, for it reserves no part of its being, and holds nothing of itself back, which is the same as saying it has no self. If −A is the principle of identity, +A is the principle of difference, expressed in the law of non-contradiction (A ≠ not A). We get a glimpse here of why Schelling will associate the second potency with the second person of the Trinity. The second potency is the kenotic potency, the one that has no self or subjecthood which could be thus or so, but which reflects the first potency back to itself, like the mirror of wisdom in Proverbs 8, or pours itself out entirely into its other, like the Christ in Philippians 2. Where the first potency affirms only itself and therefore affirms nothing whatsoever (for it itself is no particular thing and is associated with no particular predicate), the second potency negates itself and affirms only its other. +A is A become entirely predicate or object.

The two potencies exclude one another as No excludes Yes, potency excludes act, and, as mutually excluding, they both posit each other and depend on one another. +A is excluded from –A inasmuch as –A 'wills to occupy all space itself' (Schelling 1841: 104). Echoing the Boehmian conception of potencies of 1809, –A is the self-oriented potency, the principle of ipseity (which is not yet egoism, but could become egoism if actualised), or the potency that by refusing to will anything other than itself in effect wills only itself, and so negates its other (+A or actuality), which means it expels its other outside itself (McGrath 2012: 55). As expelled, the second potency is posited in being in its own right, and in that positing rendered active or 'torn out of its serenity [*Gelassenheit*]' (Schelling 1841: 104). The second potency does not pass from the potency of willing to actual willing, it is posited as always already actual, which means it does not have the freedom to be active or not be active; rather it *must* be active. It is the being that must be (*das sein Müssende*) and, as such, lacks potency, to be or not to be, and stands as the modal opposite of the first potency (–A, the ability to be – *das Sein Könnennende*). Second potency's activity consists primarily in its counteracting the 'selfishness' of first potency, 'negating the first, through which it was itself negated' (Schelling 1841: 104). It subsists in an act of de-substantialising itself and reversing the act by which it itself was posited.

If the first potency is the principle of ipseity, the second potency is the principle of alterity: it is 'brought back from act to potency' in that it renounces its own actuality. The two potencies mirror each other in that what the first possesses as potency but does not actualise, the second de-actualises. The first has a self which it holds back from actuality; the second has a self which it renounces. Second potency is pure will and cannot hold itself back – it does not pass from not-willing to willing, but is always willing, but what it wills is not itself but the other. 'The pure desire [*das rein Wollende*] is nothing other than that which absolutely does not will itself but wills another. The pure desiring will is an absolutely selfless [*unselbstisches*] will. Its will is directed to another' (Schelling 1831: 40). Between these two forms of will (both of which will nothing, but in different ways) lies a crucial moral distinction between one who wants nothing, and so does not risk oneself or exit from one's own will, and one who empties oneself, gives oneself away, who is in some sense nothing but desire, passion and will, but precisely because the object of this desire is not oneself but another, is selfless. Do we not see here a basic distinction between two models of holiness, one Stoic, the other Christian? The Stoic saint wants nothing, is moved by nothing, has transcended desire and suffering, and is at peace; the Christian saint, by contrast (think of Francis of Assisi, or Teresa of Avila) is all motion and activity, tormented by desire, the desire for justice, and tirelessly sacrifices himself or herself in pursuit of it. The Stoic saint possesses a peace that seems to elude the Christian, but never reaches the love that is the essence of the latter: because they never risk themselves, never give themselves away, and renounce all desire (even the desire for justice), the Stoic saint remains imprisoned in potency. The Christian saint who is so driven by love that he or she never bothers to consider their own needs reaches a degree of selflessness that shows Stoicism to be a form of pure egoism. These moral and spiritual implications of the opposition between first and second potency will become clearer when we pass into the positive philosophy, and discover that the two potencies are logical schemata for two divine personalities, the Father, who is invisible, and, as a Christian Kabbalist might put it, is in himself pure wrath, and the Son, who makes the Father visible, but in the form of his opposite, as mercy.

The first potency is a form of will that actually wants nothing because in it the potency for wanting something or not wanting something remains unactualised. Schelling says of it that it has nothing before it that it could will. In not wanting anything it remains in itself and so never passes from not willing into actual willing. To actually will something one must *want* something that is other than oneself (even if what one wills, as in evil, is one's self to the exclusion of others). This actual willing is only achieved by the third potency, which both wills and wants. The second potency has something other than itself which it can will, for it is preceded by the first potency, but because it renounces itself as will, it in effect wills nothing. The first potency wills *nothing*, has nothing beside itself which it could will; the second potency *wills* nothing, that is, has no self-will.

Where the first potency is pure power, it is entirely ineffectual for it cannot emerge into act. Second potency is curiously more real and at the same time less powerful than first potency. First potency is the most precarious and groundless form of being, since its ground is not found prior to it but in what follows it, in second potency (Schelling 1841: 104). Schelling hereby decouples act from power: the Scholastic notion of *actu purus*, which in the Middle Ages rendered God the highest of all beings by denying potency of divinity, is now identified with powerlessness.[47] Second potency has no agenda of its own. Its lack of potency is to be understood not as the fullness of being but on the contrary, as absolute poverty. It reaches out with empty hands towards the first potency. And yet, in its negation of the negation by which it is posited, the second potency is purely positive: it is determinate being, by contrast to the pure and undetermined being of the first potency. But its actuality is not to be confused with real existence – we are still speaking of a potency for actuality, not the actuality of actuality. We remain in the foregoing discussion entirely within the conceptual, or the negative, the domain of essence, even in the second potency, when the essence of existence itself is at issue.

The third potency, ±A, is in one respect potency and in another respect actuality: it is a potency that can pass into actuality without ceasing to be in potency. This is not 'the unity of opposites', or any spurious suspension of the principle of non-contradiction, quite the contrary. ±A is the potency that is expressed logically in the principle of the excluded middle. A and not-A (potency and act) cannot be both affirmed of the same thing in the same respect. ±A can be both potency and act because it is not identical to either of them, but is in one respect in potency, in another respect in act. It includes both determinability and determination within itself, but as neither cancelled nor coincident. To the degree that it is determined, it is not undetermined, and to the degree that it is undetermined, it is not determined. The middle is excluded because ±A actually *is* in one way or another. It is A that is in one respect B, but in another respect free not to be B, free to be C, D, E, and so on. ±A is therefore self-determination or freedom. In being B it does not lose its power to be other than B. Only with ±A is being that can stand on its own, being which could actually exist (*das Bleibende*), achieved (although still only as a potency, not as actuality). The third potency is logically implied by the exclusions necessary in –A and +A. –A excludes (posits outside itself) actuality; +A excludes an actuality that is grounded in potency, or ±A. ±A excludes one-sided possibility or exclusionary potency (–A), and one-sided actuality or exclusionary actuality (+A), which means it negates the negative in each of these preceding potencies and so excludes nothing positive. ±A is therefore freedom in a positive sense, and spirit (*Geist*) in the precise sense of that which can determine itself:

> That which is potency in being and never ceases to be potency, and vice versa, that which is potency which can pass over into being without losing its power (over being), that which can be being and non-being, this is the perfectly free, that which can do what it wills with its ability, because it never ceases to be in potency, and in order to be this, never ceases to be active. It is spirit, that does not endanger itself in being, and also without effort, never ceases to be in potency. (Schelling 1841: 106)

As for Plato, where 'the mixed' is clearly the higher and only genuinely plausible being, even if 'the unlimited' and 'the limited' are its presuppositions (and component parts), so too is ±A the only real candidate for being in any concrete sense. But the third potency has no more immediate a relation to actual existence than the first or the second. It is still only a possibility of being, and if it is to pass from possibility into existence, it needs to be mediated by an act of existence.

Each of the potencies stands for a law of thought: the law of identity (−A), the law of non-contradiction (+A) and the law of the excluded middle (±A). The first potency says 'being is', but does not specify what being is, or differentiate being from nothingness; the second potency says 'non-being is not', but does not relate this difference between being and non-being to what preceded it. The third potency says 'being and nothing are not the same'. The laws of thought are necessary according to essence but contingent according to existence, which means they are laws of being. *If* something is, then it must be self-identical (−A), it must be differentiated from other beings (+A), and it cannot be and not be in the same respect and at the same time (±A), which means, in any proposition concerning it, either that proposition is true or its negation is true. But if nothing is, these laws do not hold. The laws of thought structure nature itself − expressed in terms of potency, they are the architectonic of the intelligible as such (nothing can be intelligible in any other way than this). But thought is contingent upon existence (it is not because there is thought that there is being, but the reverse). Hence we cannot simply and without qualification call the laws of thought *necessary*.[48] They are necessary according to essence and contingent according to existence. The contingency of their existence is demonstrated in the reasonableness of the question, Why is there reason and not rather un-reason? The doctrine of the potencies can be elaborated purely negatively as a self-consistent system of reason, and the result is idealism, or negative philosophy. There is nothing in the doctrine of the three potencies itself which compels the existential question, why? However, the doctrine can also be elaborated questioningly, in an existential vein, as the inexplicable fact of order that places the questioner in question. The doctrine of the potencies might then give rise to the theological question: Is order itself an accident? Or is it somehow and by someone willed to be? The transition from the one register to the other hinges on the will of the thinker who adverts to the astonishing fact of there being anything whatsoever. If negative philosophy can avoid the *question* of the existence of God (by assuming God's necessity according to the formula above, nature = reason = God), positive philosophy begins with it.

The critique of Hegel

After close to two centuries of scholarship, the relationship of Schelling to Hegel remains obscure. There are too many versions of Hegel and too many versions of Schelling to compare. The Hegel who proclaims the implacable march of reason and the total intelligibility of the world (the 'panlogicist' Hegel) is not the Hegel who inscribes negativity, desire and contradiction at the centre of every rational process. The Hegel who proclaims the end of history, its culmination in his *Encyclopedia of the Philosophical Sciences*, is other than the Hegel who modestly lays out the conditions for the possibility of intelligible discourse. The Hegel who achieves absolute knowledge by demonstrating that the divine is immanent in every act of becoming is different from the Hegel who merely elaborates how reason pragmatically adjusts itself to changing historical circumstances and endlessly varying positive data. Just so, the Schelling whose work represents the completion of the German idealist project of a total recapitulation of being in rational reflection is other than the Schelling who discovers, mid-career, that revelation always exceeds reflection, as personality is always opaque to us (even to itself) until it is self-revealed in deeds. The Schelling whose life project is to think the relation of the infinite to the finite is not the Schelling who aims only to show the necessary limits of every discourse. I will offer my own take on the relationship of the late Schelling to Hegel here, one that admittedly requires a commitment to a certain reading of Hegel, which is not the only one, and may not even be the right one. But it was Schelling's reading of Hegel.[49] One no more challenges the originality of the late Schelling's thought by dismissing his critique of Hegel as missing the mark than one challenges the originality of Aristotle's thought by dismissing his critique of Plato.

Schelling's first explicit and extended critique of Hegel appears in his 1833 Munich course, *On the History of Modern Philosophy* (Schelling 1833: 126–64/134–63). The critique focuses on certain issues in Hegel's logic. This has led to some misunderstandings in the literature, as though Schelling's objection to Hegel was primarily a logical objection. In fact, the late Schelling's own approach to logic, the negative philosophy of potencies, bears more than a passing resemblance to Hegel's. In later versions of his critique, for example in the 1841 Berlin lectures, Schelling is more ambiguous about the validity of Hegel's logic. He affirms it as the highest expression of the negative philosophy (Schelling 1841: 358–97). Hegel, we are told in 1841, 'brought about the conclusion of the system with the greatest energy'. He 'alone has saved the basic thought of my [Schelling's] philosophy for a later time' (Schelling 1841: 121–2). Even more unequivocally, Schelling declares, 'I agree completely with the Hegelian definition of philosophy: it is the science of reason insofar as it becomes conscious that it is all Being' (Schelling 1841: 122/71). Hegel 'has expressed accurately the essence of rational philosophy' (Schelling 1841: 129/78). 'Lest anyone believes that the work itself is to be condemned and the merit of the author denied, it might now be desirable to go to the core of Hegel's logic to emphasise the methodological arguments and the acumen manifested in its particulars' (Schelling 1841: 129/79). From such remarks, it is plain that the important differences between the late Schelling and Hegel are not reducible to disagreements about logic.[50] It is the relationship of logic to the world that is at issue between them. Hegel totalises logic in a way that Schelling believes is fundamentally confused. Had Hegel better understood the limits of reason, the power of his logic would have cleared the way to the positive philosophy.[51] Schelling's critique of Hegel's logic draws the attention of Schelling scholars away from other equally central issues of dispute between then, for example concerning matters in philosophical anthropology and the philosophy of religion. Let us deal with each of these in turn.

Concerning logic (on transcendence)

Edward Beach has precisely summarised Schelling's crique of Hegel's logic in a set of 25 theses. Of crucial importance are the following:

> Hegel erred in supposing that logic in principle can include everything. (X: 126; B: 134) . . .
>
> Hegel failed to see that negative philosophy can only treat the possible *qua* possible, not the actual as such. (X: 127; B: 135) . . .
>
> Only a method that places nature and natural consciousness *before* logical concepts can successfully develop a genuinely *a priori* progression of categories. For *a priori* concepts necessarily originate as abstractions derived from nature and from natural consciousness. (X: 140–1; B: 145) . . .
>
> Logic may well be a *necessary condition* for all that exists, but Hegel is wrong in supposing that it is also a *sufficient condition*. There is obviously something other and something more than mere reason in the world – something that goes beyond all rational limits. (X: 143–4; B: 147) . . . (Beach 2020)

Each of these statements centres on the same problem: Hegel's blurring of the distinction between the possible and the actual. It has been noted before that Schelling's alternative to Hegel's logic is based on the retrieval of a medieval distinction between essence (*essentia*) and existence (*existentia*).[52] Hegel is an essentialist, in Schelling's critique of him, and like all essentialists he conceives the relation between the essence of a thing and its existence to be a logical relation.[53]

The relationship of the late Schelling to medieval philosophy is even less clear than his relation to Hegel, and has received little or no attention in recent research. The numerous references to the Scholastics and the frequent repetition of Latin tags in Schelling's late philosophy, which are conspicuously absent in his earlier works, suggest that a careful reading of medieval philosophy occurred sometime during Schelling's first Munich period (1806–20), a time, it should be added, when Schelling was in constant contact with Catholic intellectuals. It also appears reasonable to assume that this move towards medieval realism was key to Schelling's qualification of his earlier idealism as negative philosophy and his critique of Hegel. The Thomist school, reacting to Scotus's *univocatio entis*, insisted on a real distinction between *essentia* (*quidditas*) and the act of existence or *esse* (which came to be known in the Thomist tradition as *existentia*).[54] *Essentia* is the 'what' of a thing, the quiddity or concrete intelligibility which is abstractly known in a concept, rendered universal and applicable to a multiplicity of individuals; but the 'that' of the thing, or the singular reality of the thing, is, for the Thomist, of a different order: it is not another 'what' or a second thing (this was a misreading of Aquinas attributable to Giles of Rome), but an act, the divine act by which the *what* of a thing, which in itself is a mere conceptual possibility, an *ens in anima*, is made real. By calling the existence of the thing 'the act of being' (the *actus essendi*), Thomas introduces another level of potency/act distinction, not explicit in Aristotle: where the form or essence of the thing actualises its matter, which is its potency, the existence of the thing actualises its form. Thus the Aristotelian form/matter distinction requires recourse to a higher sense of act. Form itself is in one respect, act, and in another respect, potency. Form is act insofar as it actualises the matter of a thing, while it is potency insofar as it is actualised by the existence of the thing. If form is as dependent on a different kind of act as matter is dependent on form, a new distinction is required, which is more fundamental than form/matter, a distinction between essence and existence.[55]

The distinction is crucial to the history of objections to the ontological argument from Aquinas to Kant, and Schelling's critique of the argument is clearly situated in this line (Schelling 1842d: 157ff./200ff.). Most importantly, however, Schelling's argument that the idea of God tells us nothing concerning God's existence is just as plainly directed at Hegel as it is at Anselm, Descartes and Leibniz. Just as the whole of Hegel's system can be interpreted as an elaborate form of the ontological argument for the existence of God, so can Schelling's negative philosophy be considered a refutation of it.[56] In Lecture Ten of *The Grounding of the Positive Philosophy*, Schelling concedes to the proponents of the ontological argument that reason possesses an innate idea of God, the idea of *ens necessarium*, but agrees with Kant, and to a certain extent Aquinas, that existence is not a predicate, and that there can therefore be no logical transition from thought to being (Schelling 1842d: 157/200).[57] In the course of formulating this critique, Schelling draws a distinction between essence and existence that is even more radical than Aquinas's *distinctio realis* between *essentia* and *esse*, for it runs all the way down and applies, *mutatis mutandis*, to God. God exists contingently not necessarily, even if God's essence is to exist necessarily. This paradoxical statement is not a contradiction in terms, because essence and existence are radically distinct and irreducible to each other, even in the case of the infinite being. The claim is easily misinterpreted as the ascription of limitation to God. Its meaning is quite the opposite. The concept of a necessity in the divine which has been overcome secures the freedom of God, and thus allows us to recognise the genuine sovereignty and omnipotence of the divinity. God is God because God is free to be and not to be; God is lord of being (SW 10: 260–1). A being which is bound to exist because it is its essence to be is not properly called lord of being, and therefore is not God at all. In God's freedom from being, which means God's freedom from self, God is the archetypal person. God's freedom from being, God's overcoming of the necessity of existence, renders God free for others.[58]

Aquinas never went that far. For Aquinas, God is subsistent being itself, *ipsum esse subsistens*. The Thomist *distinctio realis* between essence and existence applies to all created beings and renders them contingent upon the will of the creator, who wills or does not will them to be; it does not apply to God, the purely subsistent being, the infinite being, which admits no distinction, which is absolutely simple, the one being in which essence *is* existence. Here is the point of Schelling's radical divergence from Aquinas and the root of their different critiques of the ontological argument. Where Aquinas agrees in principle that the concept of God ought to be enough to know the existence of God, Schelling disagrees and in effect argues that even God's existence is not necessary and cannot be known *a priori*. Aquinas does not deny the assumption of the ontological argument, that God's essence is to exist; he denies that we can know this essence *a priori*. Schelling agrees with the proponents of the ontological argument that reason possesses an adequate *a priori* idea of God, but denies that it – or any idea – is sufficient to prove the existence of anything, with the exception, perhaps, of the existence of reason itself, an existence that shows itself in the fact of there being any ideas and mind to think them whatsoever. But even in reason's recognition of its own being, its own having somehow or other come to be, its own being posited, there is no logical move from the idea to the fact: it is not any particular content of reason which indicates reason's existence but the fact that there are contents in the first place.[59]

It might be argued that Schelling's insistence on reason's *a priori* structure and the applicability of the ontological difference between essence and existence to all modes of being, finite and infinite, amounts to a tacit assumption of a univocal notion of being and a concession to Duns Scotus. Scotus characterised being as a univocal *a priori* concept, possessing a single sense which can be modally qualified as infinite or finite, but which is in itself indifferent to both. Here the way swings off from Aquinas, who argues that the ontological argument is wrong because its presupposition, reason's *a priori* possession of an adequate and univocal notion of being, is false.

In any case, Schelling believes that the problem with the ontological argument lies elsewhere than where Aquinas locates it, in the incapacity of reason to conceive the divine essence; for reason, according to Schelling, indeed possesses an *a priori* idea of being.[60] The great transformation effected by Kant's critical philosophy, the analytic of the *a priori*, cannot be reversed. Kant's master move is the exposure of the metaphysical notion of God, the *ens necessarium*, as a confusion of 'the ideal of reason', the conceptually necessary sum of all predicates or the unconditioned, with the God of the Bible. Onto-theology, which Kant first names, is thus boiled down to its essence by Kant, so that it can then become the keystone for an entirely different philosophical project, the Kantian system of reason. Kant shows how, first of all, reason is led inevitably to the notion of the unconditioned, and secondly, that such a notion cannot count as knowledge since it lacks a corresponding intuition, thus failing the minimum condition for the possibility of knowledge. Without subscribing to what he regards as Kant's confused limit of knowledge to sensibly filled-out concepts, Schelling believes Kant is exactly right on one point: reason is led inevitably to the *ens necessarium*, the idea of the infinite potency (which is the whole of the three potencies as a complete and, therefore, unconditioned system), and it therefore cannot avoid the idea of God – Schelling would say reason must posit God – but it oversteps its limits when it assumes that the certainty and transparency with which it grasps the *essence* of infinity can be used as a bridge to demonstrate the *existence* of the infinite being. In the idea of infinity, reason knows nothing more nor less than itself, and in abstraction from its own existence. Reason only understands the conditioned insofar as it measures it against the unconditioned, which is its innermost content or ideal. But this unconditioned is not the really existing God; it is only the *idea* of God. Of it we can and must ask: Does anything exist that could be denominated by this idea? Given that the idea of the 'infinite potency' is the lynchpin of the system of potencies, the architectonic of reason as such, and therefore the keystone of the ideal system of nature, Schelling asks a more basic question: Is there an outside to reason? The idea of God is nothing less (and nothing more) than the highest achievement of thought. But after the negative philosophy has culminated in this thought, Schelling asks, does a being exist whose essence is thought in this idea? It is one thing to say that God's *essence* is to exist necessarily (not contingently); it is something else to say that God's *existence* is necessary. No existence is necessary for Schelling. If God exists, then God exists as the being that must be, as the (only) necessary being, for that is the very idea of God, as negative philosophy shows. But it remains possible that God in fact does not exist.

We must be careful not to misunderstand Schelling's point, perhaps his most radical thought, that God – if God exists – exists contingently.[61] A contingently existing God is not a God who becomes God in time or who might someday cease to be. Schelling's God is 'a being' that is what it is eternally (for to be God means to be the *ens necessarium*), but the existence of which is no less contingent on something other than itself. In the case of God, that which is other than God and conditions God's existence is not outside God but is rather in God, not as essence, but as primal act of being (in 1809, the ungrounded ground, in 1841, eternal existence or A^0). God wills to exist as the one who exists necessarily. It is evident that while the late Schelling abandons theogony, he still maintains the claim of the Freedom Essay that the ground of God is in God but not identical to God, that is, that there is distinction in God, something in the divine, which the divine depends upon for being, which is not God. God is only God insofar as God has mastered the blind act of being which precedes God.[62]

Schelling's argument that, *pace* Aquinas, we *do* possess an adequate idea of God is a signature modern move, placing him squarely in the lineage of Descartes, Spinoza and Leibniz, for they all said as much. But where each of these others failed to distinguish essence from existence, they fell prey to the fallacy named by Kant, of assuming that existence is a predicate. Schelling's innovation consists in arguing, against Aquinas, that we do have an idea of God, and with Descartes, that the idea is inseparable from our reason, and yet also against Kant, that existence cannot be reduced to position in space and time. Schelling, like Aquinas, is an advocate of what James Bradley calls 'existence as an activity' (Bradley 2021): actuality is neither predicate nor position, but the primal activity of being in its verbal and accusative sense. Thus Schelling and Aquinas are agreed that knowledge of *what* and knowledge of *that* are two distinct operations of the intellect. But for Schelling, the difference runs through all of being, even the being of God.

At stake in the critique of the ontological argument is not only the *a priori* proof for the existence of God but the legitimacy of any idealist transition from logic to history, both natural and cultural history. Hegel blurs the distinction between the possible and the actual (essence and existence), according to Schelling, and this is his fundamental error. While he is drawn to the positive, and endeavours in his own way to overcome the negative, Hegel, in Scholastic terms, lacks the real distinction and consequently essentialises existence. While Hegel believes that the ontological argument is formally valid, he regards it as abstract and dualistic, assuming a distinction between thought and being which it then attempts to bridge. 'Thought, the Notion of necessity implies that the Notion does not remain subjective; this subjective is on the contrary abrogated and reveals itself as objective' (Hegel 1996: 605). Insofar as, according to Hegel, it is reason itself that draws the distinction between essence and existence, between the merely conceptual and the actual, existence and actuality are not outside reason but determinations which depend on reason. The rational flow of 'the notion' is to pass necessarily from essence to existence, and this passage does not bring thought outside of reason, for there is no outside to reason. Properly understood, reason is not a subjective faculty but spirit and reality itself. 'What is rational is real; and what is real is rational' (Hegel 1896a: xxvii). Herein lies the crux of the matter for Schelling: Hegel, with all other proponents of the ontological argument, is like Narcissus, bewitched by his own reflection: reason gazes at itself and takes what it sees to be the whole of the real. It can only be so bewitched because it has something of its own: it contains an *a priori* concept that is nothing less than an anticipation of the really existing God.

We have seen how the logical relations among the potencies are a progressive intensification of the *a priori* notion of being, a progression which is wholly immanent to reason, or transcendental, in Kant's sense of the term. Hegel takes the 'movement' of the three potencies to be something more than what it is, something more than a potentisation or intensification of a concept merely immanent to reason, and thus *mistakes* the transition of −A to +A to ±A, which is no doubt *conceptually* a transition from infinite possibility to infinite actuality, as a movement from essence to existence, a self-actualisation of the notion. The logical transition from essence to existence is the movement in Hegel from logic to the philosophy of nature, a movement that occurs both conceptually and existentially at once.[63]

> Thus arose those wrongful and improper expressions of a *self-movement* of the idea, words through which the idea was personified and ascribed an existence that it did not and could not have ... Yet precisely this advance from relative nonbeing to being, to that which according to its nature or *concept* is being, was viewed as a successive realization of the concept of being, as the successive self-actualization of the idea. This advance, however, was in fact merely a successive elevation or intensification of the concept, which in its highest potency remained just a concept, without there ever being provided a transition to *real* being [*wirklichen Daseyn*], to existence. (Schelling 1842d: 73/139)

+A is pure act in its exclusion of potency; it cannot be thought of as in any respect non-actual. The second potency is pure being, but this is still only the *idea* of determinacy, it is not existence. A movement in thought, Schelling argues, signifies nothing in reality:

> In this [essence] nothing else occurs save thinking; it is not a real process that develops here, but a logical one; the being into which potency passes over is a being that itself belongs to the concept and, thus, is only a being in the concept, not outside it.

The transition is *simpliciter*, a becoming other: in the place of the pure potency, which as such is nonbeing, there appears a being. The determination 'a being' is itself here a mere *quidditative*, not a *quodditative* (Scholastic expressions, but expedient designations). I am here only concerned with the *quid*, not with the *quod*. A being or something is just as good a concept as *being* or potency is a concept. A being [*ein Seyendes*] is no longer being [*das Seyendes*] – it is something other than this, but only *essentially*, that is, according to its concept, but not *actu*, something different. The plant is not being, but is rather already a being. But it is a being even if it never really existed. It is, therefore, only a logical world in which we move in a science of reason. (Schelling 1842d: 65–6/134)

The failure to heed the distinction between essence and existence, concept and its existential non-conceptual conditions, is, according to Schelling, the logical misstep behind Hegel's inclusion of the positive within the negative, which so confuses history and reason as to domesticate the positivity of the former and occult the negativity of the latter. Schelling is upfront that his early philosophy is for the most part negative philosophy and therefore proceeds in abstraction from existence (Schelling 1841: 111–21). Schelling never presumed that identity-philosophy was exhaustive of the real, even if he failed to explicitly acknowledge the positive. Hegel went much further and explicitly claimed to have included history and particularity in the purely rational philosophy (Schelling 1842d: 149/86–7). This is related to Hegel's other basic error, his failure to acknowledge how nature interrupts logic (Schelling 1842d: 150/88). Schelling's *Naturphilosophie* no doubt presumes an objectivity to reason: the intelligibility of things is not internal to reason, but gives the lie to the modern dichotomy between matter and mind. Nature-philosophy remains a philosophy of *nature*, not a complete and final account of spirit. Mind is here manifest as nature itself and rendered thinkable as such. Visible nature, rooted as it is in *natura naturans*, the unconditioned, which is never manifest and always producing the new, could never be reduced to logic or concept; hence the *Naturphilosoph* could never agree with Hegel's neo-Fichtian claim that the mind is the truth of nature, the truth that nature has no truth in itself.[64] Insofar as nature-philosophy never took itself to be the whole of the truth, never assumed existential adequacy, it never succumbed to the Hegelian temptation to logicise or essentialise the positive.

Negative philosophy is anything but arbitrary, and so there is an undeniable truth to the Hegelian system. In it, reason follows its own immanent logic, but for all that remains no less inured to the real. Only the fearless advance of metaphysical questioning, the refusal to silence the question, Why is there something rather than nothing? Why is there reason and logic in the first place? – only this can open reason to the outside upon which it depends. The late Schelling rejects Hegel's pretension that philosophy could be an absolute discourse (sublated science, sublated religion), along with his own youthful effort at the same, in favour of a realist philosophy of transcendence. Idealism consists in reason's *a priori* dialogue with its own innate concepts – without any living connection to the real or the existent. Schelling does not deny that reason *appears* to 'sublate' nature, and that concepts seem to penetrate beings to their intelligible core. But what is reason itself? Whence intelligibility as such? The question is at least intelligible, for philosophy cannot coherently deny the existence of reason. And so we come to Schelling's now famous statement, his critique of Hegel and absolute idealism *in nuce*:

> Everything can be in the logical idea without anything being *explained* thereby, as, for example, everything in the sensuous world is grasped in number and measure, which does not thereby mean that geometry or arithmetic explain the sensuous world. The whole world lies, so to speak, in the nets of the understanding or of reason, but the question is *how* exactly it got into those nets, since there is obviously something other and something *more* than mere reason in the world, indeed there is something which strives beyond those barriers. (Schelling 1833: 143–4/147)

Notice that Schelling's argument with Hegel is not a denial of the rationality of the real; Schelling agrees with Hegel on this point. What is missing in Hegel is the shattering question, which destabilises the rationality of the real with the possibility that it need not have been, the question, Why is the real rational? Why is it ordered, and not rather disordered? Insofar as reason cannot explain the existence of order as such, it cannot claim the completeness which it presupposes. Totalising positions, such as Hegel's, are philosophies of *essence*, and their outside is forever demarcated as *existence*. The latter cannot be deduced, transcendentally or dialectically: it can only be known *per posteriorus*, that is, *through* experience, more precisely through an existential act of self-problematisation, which disrupts the ideal, the dream of reason, and awakens the existing subject by refusing to allow it to continue to suppress the inexplicability of individual existence.[65] Because of the surd of existence a philosophically adequate discourse can never presume absoluteness; it must always stand open to a *revelation* of the transcendent, whether this be the transcendence of existing being to thought, the transcendence of the divinity to reason, or the more quotidian but equally mysterious transcendence of the reality of personality to consciousness.

Concerning personality (on non-dialectical relations)

Schelling objected to Hegel's dialectic of recognition as early as the 1809 Freedom Essay (although Hegel is not mentioned by name) – long before he asserted his version of the medieval doctrine of the distinction between essence and existence or constructed an alternative philosophy of the

Trinity. Hegel renders interpersonal relations necessary to individuation, and hence, according to Schelling, abrogates the unassailable freedom of the individual. Evil becomes necessary, as does love, which means evil is no longer evil and love is no longer love.[66] As shall become clear in the second book, Schelling's and Hegel's contesting theories of the person are rooted in alternative accounts of the Trinity and can be traced back to third-century debates between subordinationist Trinitarians and Athanasius.

For the moment it is enough to note that Schelling's theorem of absolute transcendence is the presupposition and condition for his non-dialectical personalism. In love, the beloved still eludes and transcends the lover, and it is precisely because of this transcendence that love as such is possible. In clear opposition to Hegel's dialectic of recognition of 1807, Schelling developed in 1809 a non-dialectical theory of human relations. A person for Schelling is not one who stands in a necessary relation to another person, as in Hegel, but one who has overcome an impersonal and internal necessity. Personal relations are free relations or else they are not personal. A person is one who is free to enter into relation with another, who is free for reciprocity, who is free to love, or not. The person is no less a person when he or she refuses relations. The devil, if he existed, would still be a person, even if he subsisted as nothing other than the spaceless, timeless point of one who denies all otherness. God is still personal before the *Logos* exists as another in whose eyes God can recognise Godself. With Schelling's notion of personhood as the overcoming of necessity, the relations between human beings, between human beings and God, and between God and creation, or, as we shall see, between the divine Father and the Son, become in each case free relations, that is, they are each of them contingent on the good will of the persons involved. In short, none of these relations upon which the order of things, the good itself, depends, need be. That they *are* to some degree is the facticity of creation, the *positum* that Schelling takes as starting point for positive philosophy.

In the master–slave dialectic, Hegel describes the struggle of self-consciousness striving to rise above externality, materiality and objectivity, in order to achieve being-for-itself or spirit (Hegel 1807: 111–19). In short, he describes exactly the struggle of freedom with necessity, and the process whereby the latter is overcome or, in his language, sublated by the former. And yet this achievement of freedom over necessity is impossible by the individual alone, for it requires a dialectical encounter with another self. The other with which spirit deals is and must be a second self, for spirit, like everything else, must be mediated; only in this instance, the mediation is a self-mediation. Spirit mediates itself to itself. Concretely this occurs in the I–Thou relationship. In recognising the other as a subject like myself (thus with his or her own dignity and freedom), I establish the conditions requisite for my own recognition, for now I can see myself reflected back to me in the subjectivity of the other. I call the other Thou and so receive myself back as an I in that very act. The master–slave dialectic recounts the impossibility of ultimately resisting this level of reciprocity. The master would deny the slave his or her subjectivity and treat the other like an object, but in doing so he denies himself his own subjectivity. For none can exist in isolation: the master as much as the slave needs another in order to mirror the self back to itself. As is well known, in Hegel's account the slave is higher than the master, for the slave recognises the subjectivity of the master and so finds a mirror for subjectivity in the master, in spite of the cruelty of the other. The struggle between the two can only be resolved when slavery gives way to reciprocity. Only when the master frees the slave, lets the slave be the subject that he or she is, a being who exists for themselves, only when the master says 'Thou' to the other who confronts him with a claim to dignity and freedom equal to the master's own, only then will the master achieve his own self-recognition.

The dialectic of recognition is a microcosm of the dialectic of creation in Hegel's philosophy of religion: God creates the world, loves it, sets it free to fall and redeems it because God needs it in order to become self-conscious and free (Hegel 1827: 432–69). It is like the older sibling who bullies the younger one, strikes him in the sandpit, only so that she can then console him when he bursts into tears. Hegelian reciprocity is finding in the other something one needs in order to be oneself. Love, like every movement in the Hegelian universe, is a necessary movement. I am driven to the other by a *need* for recognition: self-love is the motive of my recognition of the other. Recognition describes not only the interpersonal relation but above all the absolute's relation to itself, an absolute which does not exist outside of the system of negations by which it comes into existence. The Hegelian absolute is nothing other than self-mediation in a positive sense, or spirit recognising itself in its other.

> Only this self-restoring sameness [*sich wiederherstellende Gleichheit*] or the reflection in the being-other in itself – not an original unity as such or an immediate unity as such – is the true . . . The true is the whole. But the whole is only the essence which completes itself by its development. One can say of the Absolute that it is essentially a result, that it is only at the end what it is in truth. (Hegel 1807: 10, 11; para. 18 and 20)

We could not be further from the Freedom Essay, in which Schelling argues exactly the opposite, that love is not necessary, it is not driven by need but is the product of a decision of one who is already free. The self does not need to be mediated by the other in order to be itself: the self has an immediate if unconscious relation to itself. Self-consciousness is not reflexive. Not everything can be mediated: in all acts of mediation an indivisible remainder remains that precedes and always escapes the circle of reflection (Schelling 1809: 359/29). On the level of the self, the indivisible remainder is freedom itself: at some level, the self must be free to enter into relations with others or not. To argue that the self is always a mediated self is to argue that it only first knows itself in recognising itself in its other. Every intersubjective relation would then be like looking in a mirror: I see in the other myself for the first time. Such recognition would not be possible, Schelling essentially argues, unless there was an original relation of the self to itself. The self that had no relation to itself prior to the I–Thou relation would not be able to *recognise* itself in the other.[67] Love is only possible, Schelling argues against Hegel, where there is difference, unlikeness and opposition. Love does not unite two that are the same and that mirror each other and belong together by nature; love unites two that are other to one another, opposed to each other, and could will to be separate, but do not. The contingency of the unity achieved in love is essential to it. Where necessity prevails, as in Hegel's dialectic of recognition, love is not possible.

From this perspective, Schelling's decisive move against Hegel is already made in 1809. The point of the Freedom Essay, as elaborated above, is to productively dissociate God from nature, to qualify the pantheism which Jacobi is right to see as a perennial form of rationalism. Why is this productive dissociation so significant for Schelling's late philosophy? The answer to this question requires that we read Schelling to the end, to the final lectures of the positive philosophy. God dissociates from nature so that a community of persons might exist. God is personal before God creates, but God is not yet a trinity of actual persons, and this God can only be through creation. Notice: a person is not one who is untouched by necessity, as in a certain reading of Kant's ethics; a person is one who stands confronted by necessity, and yet does not succumb to it. The necessity which God overcomes in willing to be God before the creation of the world is within God. It is 'the ground of God', that in God which is not God, which even resists God in a certain way, in the same way that the foundation of a building resists the weight of its walls, or the way gravity resists the flight of the eagle. This necessity is the very strength of God.[68] *Contra* the dialogical personalism which begins in Hegel's dialectic, and which has its roots in the Nicene doctrine of the Trinity, it is not relations which personalise the individual for Schelling; it is the freedom to enter into relation which personalises. Freedom does not exist without necessity, but freedom and necessity are not opposed to each other like the ideal and the real in identity-philosophy; they are not merely quantitatively distinct, the appearance of otherness, the same thing in a different form. They are opposed to one another like two opposed forces in physics, or better, like the light fire and the dark fire in the Boehmian theogony, or like mercy and wrath in the Kabbalah. A person does not 'strike a balance' in the opposition, equalising the tension between them; a person orders the two so that necessity is mastered in a certain way – not abolished but subordinated, so that necessity can serve as a ground for freedom. Necessity is wrestled into submission by a person, and at the same time maintained, even revered as the condition without which the person could not be. Such self-mastery should be sharply distinguished from repression.[69] Moreover, the tension between freedom and necessity, or to speak in another register, consciousness and unconsciousness, always remains, and at any moment the precariously won freedom of the individual can be toppled by a necessity which has broken out of its subordinate position, for necessity longs to abolish its master, to render it like unto itself, not free but bound.

No necessity binds the I to the Thou. The dialectic of recognition in Hegel, which determines most subsequent thinking about personhood from Feuerbach to Buber and from Husserl to Gadamer – all thinkers of the indissoluble, necessary relation of the I to the Thou, the necessary 'pairing' of ego to alter ego as Husserl put it (Husserl 1931: para. 51)[70] – evokes a minor canon which begins with Schelling, a tradition with nowhere near the influence, but which quietly persists nonetheless, in Kierkegaard ('The self is a relation which relates itself to its own self' [Kierkegaard 1848: 13]), in Heidegger (Dasein individuates by taking over the ground of itself, which it did not lay for itself and which it can never gain power over [Heidegger 1927a: ¶ 58), in Levinas (the relations of the psychism to the other are non-reciprocal [Levinas 1961: section II, A]) or even in Jung ('Only the man who can consciously assent to the power of the inner voice becomes a personality; but if he succumbs to it he will be swept away by the blind flux of psychic events and destroyed' [Jung 1934: para. 308]).[71] This minor canon has been misinterpreted as individualist, as ignorant of the social nature of the person, even as fascist. Read back to its roots in Schelling, it appears differently. The self relates itself to its own self, Dasein self-authenticates by taken over its ground, the psyche individuates, not for the sake of asserting itself over and against the other, but for the sake of entering into genuinely personal relations with the other. The I that needs a Thou to be an I, by contrast, is always vulnerable to the critique that its relations to the other are instrumental relations: I love you because I need you, I cannot be myself without you. How is such love not narcissism? The person in Schelling can instrumentalise its relations to the other, for evil is one of its primordial possibilities, but it can also free the other, which is to say, it can relate to the other in love.

The disturbing moral consequence of Schelling's non-dialectical personalism is this: the person who instrumentalises the other is no less a person for that. We prefer to think of evil human beings, Hitler, Stalin, Eichmann, and so on, as subhuman monsters, or in the latter case, a pre-moral idiot. The thought consoles us by underscoring our difference from them. Far more disturbing is the possibility that evil people are actualising a potency in themselves which also exists in us, and indeed, are doing something distressingly human. Evil is the reduction of all relations to instrumental relations: the evil person recognises no one but themselves, inflates the self into the God without another, but is still personal in that inflation. The instrumentalisation of the personal extends even to the self itself: evil instrumentalises itself, but it remains in its own hand in that self-violation. Here is the most disturbing feature of evil in Schelling's account of it. Evil is personal: it is not mechanical, it is never just the compelled action of one who has failed to personalise. It would be somehow easier to tolerate if if it were. We prefer our psychopaths to be victims of circumstance, like Joaquin Phoenix's Joker, failed by the social system and spurned by everyone. Phoenix's Joker is pushed into violence by the system; he is manifestly not a free agent. Is it not the unrepentant spontaneity, the hint of the self-authorship of the disfiguration that makes Heath Ledger's Joker truly terrifying, where Phoenix's Joker is sad and to be pitied? 'Do you know how I got these scars?', Ledger's Joker asks, and although we never get an answer, it is easier for us to think that they are traces of abuse, the scars of the trauma that is the root cause of the Joker's pathology. Christopher Nolan masterfully leaves the matter undecided, and we must also consider the far more disturbing possibility that the Joker has disfigured himself, that he is as free in his psychopathology as we are in our normalcy. Evil for Schelling is always personal, and this is why it is so violent. The worst Nazi guard is the one who could have treated the inmate otherwise, the one who knows what he is doing. The worst abusive parent is the one who recognises the vulnerability of the child, who has the capacity for love and violates it. Evil, as Schelling says in 1809, is due to what is most perfect in us (Schelling 1809: 396/36).[72]

Schelling's point concerning the freedom of personal relations is hardly news. It can be gleaned from pop psychology which distinguishes 'co-dependency' from 'genuine love'. The one who stays with the other because he needs him or her to be complete is not the genuine lover. The co-dependent wife stays with the abusive husband not out of love but because she has become one who needs the abuse of the other to confirm her own sense of self. If I need my friends to bolster my ego, or to divert me from the burden of my solitude, I do not genuinely love them. Hence the psychotherapeutic cliché: true love does not love because it needs but needs because it loves. The truth in this overused phrase is that love is free or it is not. Or in Schelling's superb statement:

> For love is neither in indifference nor where opposites are linked which require link-
> age for [their] Being, but rather (to repeat a phrase which has already been said) this
> is the secret of love, that it links such things of which each could exist for itself, yet
> does not and cannot exist without the other. (Schelling 1809: 70/500)

Crucial to note in this oft-cited passage is the essential temporality of love:
the two that are linked *could* have existed for themselves and apart from
each other – but this possibility is past and irrecoverable, for the decision
for love has opened up a new situation, one in which the two are now
linked in such a way that they can no longer exist apart from one another.
Love entails no loss of freedom, for the link that unites the lovers is constituted and maintained by freedom. In just this way, the being of God is
now indissolubly linked with the world. God loves the world and, as in
all genuine love, has freely willed to be the one who is now and forever
vulnerable to it.

This lyrical passage should not mislead us: Schelling's poetic expressions
are underwritten by a strict logic, summed up in the following two phrases:
'For every essence can only reveal itself in its opposite, love only in hate,
unity in conflict. Were there no severing of principles, unity could not
prove its omnipotence; were there no discord, love could not become real'
(Schelling 1809: 373/41).[73] Evil is the refusal of the unity essential to love,
a perverted dualism that sows discord in place of love. Because it refuses the
unity of the interpersonal, it wills the nothingness prior to being, that is,
prior to the production of duality. Evil wills the nothingness that precedes
creation, but in an untimely fashion: it wills that nothing should be *after*
something has been. It is the refusal of the will of love which is the ultimate
reason why God creates being in the first place. If it cannot have nothingness, it would have difference without order, separate beings without the
possibility of being at one with one another; in short, it wills chaos. It is
clear, then, that the possibility of love is also the possibility of evil, for both
are consequent upon an original eruption of difference in being. Only a
universe that runs the risk of evil can also produce love.[74]

Concerning religion (on Trinitarian eschatology)

What will be perhaps most striking to contemporary readers is that the
dispute concerning the nature of the person between these two giants
of speculative philosophy, whose influence extends over the whole of
twentieth-century continental thought, is rooted in the Trinitarian debates
of the third century, a point which I can only touch on briefly here, reserv-
ing detailed discussion for the second book. If proof were needed that theology still determines secular theory, this is it. Hegel is clear enough that

the dialectic of recognition is a philosophical expansion of the orthodox notion of the Trinity: the I is one who stands recognised by a Thou, and the relation between them is not an accident but the necessary bond, the third, which eternally ties them together, as the Father is always with the Son in the unity of Spirit, according to the Nicene tradition (Hegel 1845: para. 377, *Zusatz*; para. 381, *Zusatz*). The subordinationist position, defeated at Nicaea, and represented by Arius, and before him, Origen, maintained that the relations between the persons of the Trinity were free relations: they need not be (Williams 1987: 97). No necessity, according to Arius, compels the Father into expressing his Word. The Spirit does not eternally bind the Father and the Son together in love. Love, for Schelling, does not bind, it unites two that need not be united. The procession of the persons from the Godhead is no logical emanation for Schelling. The Trinity is founded in the freedom of the Father.

The Arian doctrine of the primacy of the Father was reduced to a crude denial of the divinity of the Son by Athanasius and Augustine. The primacy of the Father can be construed otherwise, and this is precisely Schelling's contribution in the Philosophy of Revelation. The primacy of the Father can be understood as needed to render the relations among the three divine persons non-dialectical, that is, relations of love. God, having overcome necessity, having personalised, has decided for the Son, and so the Word is expressed. Similarly, the Son has overcome the necessity which is the fallen world, and decided for the Father in the Christ event, and the union of the two is a fact, all the more wondrous for not being necessary. Union, order, love need not be – that is why they are precious. That is why they are worth fighting for. Victory is never guaranteed. The history of the Trinity in Schelling is a 'theo-drama', to borrow Von Balthasar's phrase, a cosmic struggle between divinity and the non-divine, between freedom and necessity, which has in fact, in the course of history, turned in our favour. Christ has recapitulated the person-alising act of the Father and overcome necessity – this is the meaning of the cross. And we, in the Spirit, can hope to do the same.

Schelling recognises that Hegel thinks God as living subject, certainly. Hegel's error is not Spinoza's mistake of forgetting divine subjectivity and substantialising God; but the living subjectivity of God in Hegel is trapped in a necessary process, in an endless, and hence pointless, self-mediation through self-alienation. Hegel's God, as Schelling reads it, is compelled to lose and find Godself forever, without end, and so condemned to never really lose or find itself. Hegel's divine subject never attains personhood in Schelling's sense of the term: Hegel's God never overcomes necessity. Is it any wonder that Žižek, despite his penetrating understanding of the Freedom Essay (Žižek 1996) and his superb reading of *The Ages of the World* (Žižek 1997), prefers Hegel to Schelling? The God who must be mediated through the other, another who is nothing more than God in an alienated form, the person who only exists insofar as his or her identity is recognised by one who in turn depends upon his or her recognition – are these not figures for the Lacanian neurotic subject? We only avoid psychosis according to Žižek's Lacanianism by the deliberate and sustained maintenance of illusions about ourselves, which depend at every moment on the ideological assent of others. We cannot break free from this ideological circle into some more authentic position, since we are only subjects for ourselves insofar as we maintain, and continue to insist upon, a position in the neurotic/ideological circle, even when life, symptom, mental illness and its cure reveal, incessantly and with relentless consistency, the lie at the foundation of our identity. So too is Hegel's God described by Schelling as a neurotic who compulsively returns to the place where God is not Godself, to the real, which delimits God and so threatens God, because only in being so opposed and mediated is God God.

> The God did not throw himself into nature, but throws himself into it again and again, in order to set himself on top in the same way, again and again: the event is an eternal one, which is to say a continuous event, but, precisely because of that, is also no real event. In addition, however, the God is free to empty himself into nature, which is to say, he is free to sacrifice his freedom, for this act of free emptying is at the same time his freedom's grave: from now on, he is in the process or is himself the process; however, he is not the God who has nothing to do (as he would be if, as the real one, he were only the end), he is rather the God of eternal continuous doing, of unceasing unrest that never finds Sabbath, *he is the God who always does only what he has already done, and who therefore cannot create anything new*; his life is a circulation of forms in that he continuously empties himself so as to return again to himself, and always returns to himself in order to empty himself anew. (Schelling 1833: 160/159–60, translated in Kasper 1965: 125, italics mine)

At the bottom of Hegel's philosophy of religion is his denial of absolute transcendence. The other is never wholly other, it is always a hidden mediator of the same. The outside is posited by the inside for the sake of the inside:

> Through the development of the *human* spirit, through *its* progress to ever greater freedom, that is basically to ever greater negativity . . . through this progress alone [Hegel's] God will be realised, that is, so that outside human consciousness God does not exist at all, that man is really God, and God is only man, which one subsequently even designated as the incarnation of God, to which corresponds a becoming God of man. (Schelling 1842d: 154/198)

For Hegel, the externality of revelation is mere appearance, and the unmasking of its revealedness is one of the principal tasks of speculative philosophy. Schelling also takes revelation as the object of philosophy, but its externality is not to be logically overcome. Philosophy can never assume the subjectivity of the revealer. The 'of' in 'philosophy of revelation' is exclusively an objective genitive. The unprethinkable nature of revelation precludes the kind of transparency of the object enjoyed by the *Naturphilosoph*, who can logically assume the mind of nature in philosophising about natural things.

The strangeness of the revealed is destined to remain as a limit for thought until the end of time. Religion is therefore essentially eschatological for Schelling. The late Hegel's philosophy of religion, by contrast, is teleological. Religion for Hegel is 'the relation of the subject, of the subjective consciousness, to God, who is spirit'. More precisely, religion is 'spirit that realises itself in consciousness' (Hegel 1827: 104). Spirit does not 'realise itself' abstractly or subjectively, but concretely and objectively, in the history of religion and philosophy, which have the same content. All forms of historical religion for Hegel, like all forms of philosophy, are related to one another as moments in the single historical development of the consummate religion and its speculative counterpart, absolute philosophy: from natural religion, with its doctrine of divine immanence (Taoism, magic, and so on), through strict monotheism and its separation of spirit and nature (Judaism, Islam), to Christianity (the consummate religion), in which God is both immanent and transcendent.[75] Spirit leaves nothing behind in its progress through history but always brings us back to the beginning by actualising the potencies locked within it, a beginning that was cancelled by what followed it, but that is also preserved in the new form to which it gives rise.[76] Herein lies the nub of the conflict of interpretation that separates the two thinkers on the meaning of Christianity. Where Hegel is intent on folding Christian eschatology into Aristotelian teleology in pursuit of a synthesis of the two fundamental horizons of Western thought, Hebraic and Hellenic, Schelling (on this point, the more radically Lutheran thinker) reasserts the difference between the Jews and the Greeks. Schelling's distinction between negative and positive philosophy, which are separated by a chasm that cannot be traversed by logic, is intended to hold apart the Platonic-Aristotelian cosmos, on the one side, and the Pauline-Lutheran redemption, on the other.

The tension between Hegel's teleological reading of the history of theology and modern philosophy and Schelling's eschatological counter-reading of this same history comes to a focus in their two opposing approaches to the New Testament. For Hegel, the positivity of Christianity, its historical objectivity, is, however necessary to the dialectic of the consummate religion, still only a 'sensuous presentation' of a spiritual truth that is in need of a philosophical *Aufhebung*, which it receives in Hegel's absolute idealism. For Schelling, the historical positivity of revelation is the basic presupposition (in Collingwood's sense of the term) of the positive philosophy, one that is never cancelled, even in the philosophical religion to come. At the centre of the revealed stands an irreducible remainder, the positivity of the revelation, the truth that is not native to reason but willed by God, and that reminds us, and will remain forever a reminder, that we are creature and not creator.

Hegel certainly agrees with Schelling that Christianity is no myth (Hegel 1827: 157). The positivity of revealed religion is essential to the new conception of divinity that emerges from it. But philosophy, for Hegel, must not leave the positivity of Christianity as it finds it; on the contrary, philosophy strips historical Christianity of its sensuous and representational form to release its conceptual content, which is now taken up in a higher and purely secular key by speculative philosophy. The Hegelian philosophy of religion stands in relation to revealed religion in exactly the same way as that of the philosophy of spirit to the philosophy of nature. Like nature, revelation has a primarily negative role in the dialectic of spirit, and must in turn be negated so that its one-sidedness can be overcome and it can give way to a properly speculative truth. Revelation, like nature, is a vanishing mediator.[77] H. R. Mackintosh is surely correct when he writes of Hegel's philosophy of religion:

> While urging that everything affirmed in the Church's catechism about Christ fits perfectly into the system of autocratic and creative reason, with its aesthetic powers of unification, Hegel silently treats Jesus as, in the last resort, irrelevant. Christianity obtains rank as the absolute truth, but at the cost of its bond with history. (Mackintosh 1937: 109–10)

The positivity of Christianity is for Hegel an obstacle to be overcome: the New Testament is a picture-book version of the speculative truth that spirit is that which realises itself in its other. For Schelling, by contrast, the positivity of Christianity remains the *ground* of philosophical religion, even at the end of history. The point for Hegel is that the dead Jesus is only the risen Christ *spiritually*, through the mediation of the faith of the community. Thereby does the early Church grasp the truth of spirit itself: that its being is self-mediated. To put this in ordinary language (which is always something of a mistake, according to Hegelians): we do not believe Christianity because it is true; Christianity is true because and only because we believe it. Žižek summarises the point:

> The ultimate lesson to be learned from the divine Incarnation: the finite existence of moral humans is the only site of the Spirit, the site where Spirit achieves its actuality. What this means is that, in spite of all its grounding power, Spirit is a *virtual* entity in the sense that its status is that of a subjective presupposition: it exists only insofar as subjects *act as if* it exists. Its status is similar to that of an ideological cause like Communism or the Nation: it is the substance of the individuals who recognise themselves in it, the ground of their entire existence, the point of reference which provides the ultimate horizon of meaning to their lives; yet the only thing that really

exists are these individuals and their activity, so this substance is actual only insofar as individuals believe in it and act accordingly. (Žižek and Milbank 2009: 60)

Schelling, by contrast with Hegel, remains the objective idealist, the thinker of the objectivity of the ideal, even in his last lectures, which recapitulate in a qualified manner the Kantian critique of reason. Just as nature-philosophy begins with the assumption of objective reason – reason exists outside the rational subject as intelligible nature – so too does positive philosophy begin with the recognition of the objectivity, which means for Schelling the contingency, of revelation. This objective beginning is not epistemically founded, and so no violation of the Kantian limits on noumenal knowing is committed; it is volitionally initiated: the philosopher of revelation *asserts* the possibility of objective revelation and on the basis of the assertion probes the coherence and adequacy of the assertion and the evidence for or against it. The assertion is not secured by natural theology; it is not a knowing but a wanting that transitions from negative to positive philosophy. But neither is the assertion an act of faith – and here Schelling breaks with both mainstream Protestant and Catholic traditions. No divine intervention in our cognitive faculties is needed to explain it. The assertion that posits the objectivity of revelation is a decision of the philosopher who refuses to remain with the merely ideal and ventures to think the existential and the historical (two sides of the same coin).

That this move is the origin of pragmatic logic has been noted before.[78] The turn to the positive is fallibilist and exploratory rather than apodictic; it opens up lines of refutation as well as possibilities of new knowledge. Philosophical religion (which does not yet exist) will not simply leave revelation in its brute positivity. The end of religion (and here the agreement with Hegel is clear) is the philosophical appropriation of the revelation, the overcoming of its externality, so that it is no longer merely received on authority, and no longer divides the human community between those who have heard and believed and those who have not. But the end has not yet come, and we must not misjudge our times. One could be forgiven for mistaking Schelling's philosophy of religion for Hegel's absolute spirit deferred, as though Schelling's point is that Hegel is right but simply has the timing wrong. However, Schelling's philosophical religion is not the final immanentisation of the transcendent, because the otherness of God always remains the unassailable limit to thought. One could say that, for Schelling, the absolute never fully historicises. Post-Žižekian Hegelians will want to insist that Hegel does the same by installing the negative as the very motive of reason. Notice the difference, however: for Hegel, the irreducible remainder is 'the cunning of reason', the *necessary* negation, and therefore nothing other than reason itself in its endless, we might say neurotic, self-concealment. For Schelling, the irreducible remainder is pure contingency, the contingency of being as such, the contingency of the divine, and its irreducibility means there is always an outside to reason. Reason, for Schelling, is constitutively non-total (even if for that very reason impelled towards totality, and so always in need of critique). Philosophical religion will take over as its ground a foundation that it did not lay for itself and that must always, even at the end of time, remain strange to it. Like Heidegger's *Dasein*, which never exists *before* its ground and therefore never gains power over its ground but nevertheless is called to exist *as* this ground – to be identified with that which in the first place it is not – and like the self in Schelling's Freedom Essay who must *become* what he or she always already was – which means what he or she presently *is not* (Schelling 1809: 384–6/49–51) – philosophical religion must identity itself with that which it can never master, that which will in some basic way never be its own.[79]

In the end, for Schelling, the infinite and the finite remain other to one another – their relations are non-reciprocal – even in the hypostatic union. On these grounds, Hegelians will always be justified in arguing that Schelling fails to move from 'the understanding' to 'reason'. If the infinite 'becomes' finite in the incarnation, this can only mean that, for Schelling, the two orders of being, which were not clearly distinguished prior to the incarnation, become for the first time distinct by means of it. According to Schelling, the infinite finitises itself in the Christ event and in so doing absents itself, retreats into the non-actual, so that the Christ might genuinely exist. It is not as though two separate modes of being which precede the union are brought together; the union effects their separation. What occurs in incarnation is a repetition of what has occurred in creation: the *kenosis* of divinity into that which is not divine. The infinite negates itself in creation, contracts its being, as in the Kabbalistic account of *zimzum*, clearing the space of the nothing in which something other than the divine can come to be. Divine *kenosis* reaches its zenith in the infinite finitising itself in Christ. To say that this denies the real distinction between the infinite and finitude is entirely muddled: the distinction is exactly the outcome of the union of the two natures in Christ. In Christ, the human is first fully realised as human, and – equally – the divine is first fully realised as divine. The human becomes the predicate of the divine, which means distinct from it while identified with it, while the divine withdraws itself, becomes potency for the actuality of the human.[80]

This alternative to Hegel's dialectic of infinity and finitude (in which the finite is the negation of the infinite, a negation which must in turn be negated so as to realise that the infinite *is* the finite) will always appear to Hegelians as a retreat to the Kantian-Jacobian abstraction of infinity from finitude, a move which Hegel devoted his career to refuting. This is a superficial reading that misses what is essential in Schelling's thought. In the late Schelling, the infinite is reconciled with the finite but without ceasing to be infinite; on the contrary, the reconciliation *is* its infinitisation. Conversely, the redemption does not annul the finite but rather renders it fully finite, or other than the infinite. The reconciliation is not a work of speculation or the 'spiritual' act of a community 'acting as if' Jesus were God; it is the salvific work of the second person of the Trinity, 'the God outside God', the divine person whose freedom from the Father is as pronounced as the creature's distance from the creator. It is the *kenosis* of the Christ, not ours, his renunciation of a divine claim, his death, which unites (and thereby distinguishes) infinity and finitude.[81] Schelling, like Hegel, sees in the cross the moment of reconciliation of the infinite and the finite, but the two that are here reconciled are not cancelled in any sense, and neither is the tension between them preserved in some new form that renders their earlier forms null; God and creation are each restored to their proper dignity so that they can now be united in love – love which, Schelling says, does not abolish difference but brings the different into self-deferring and self-differentiating unity (Schelling 1809: 408/70). For Hegel, the human is God in alienation from Godself, and God is the human in alienation from itself; the Hegelian redemption is the realisation that what we have called other to ourselves is ourselves in another form. The contrast with Schelling could not be starker. The human for Schelling is creation become conscious of its divine origin; the redemption reverses the disavowal of this original knowledge of transcendence, that is, it reverses the refusal of this relationship which the tradition calls original sin. Evil is undone and love between God and the world is made possible. The redemption allows creation to be fully, genuinely, that is, religiously finite by freeing it for its relation with infinity. This love between God and humankind will be fully incarnate in the community of the future, in what Schelling calls the Church of St John (to succeed the medieval Catholic Church of St Peter and the modern Protestant Church of St Paul), which, unlike Hegel's godless collective that succeeds the age of religion, is a community of individuals capable of loving one another without encroaching upon each other's freedom, because all equally love God. Where, in Hegel's age of spirit, transcendence is abolished, in Schelling's third age of revelation transcendence is unveiled as the ground of love.[82]

Schelling's critique of Hegel anticipated (and perhaps influenced) Žižek's inverted Hegel, the Hegel who does not so much declare the triumph of reason as demonstrate over and over again that spirit is eternally out of joint. For Žižek, Hegel's dialectic does not overcome the negative; it makes it a permanent condition of rational life (Žižek 1996: 123). Schelling also sees that Hegel's teleology has no genuine resolution; it is a teleology without an end. His objection to it was key to his breakthrough to eschatological thinking. Schelling's critique of Hegel not only gave a certain definition to his later path of thinking, a definition that had eluded him in his earlier work; it inspired his turn to the positive. In sharp contrast to Schelling's early, proto-Hegelian identification of reason and truth,[83] reason in the late Schelling is free, which means, first of all, free *from* the truth, and therefore free *for* the truth. Reason is not *necessarily* answerable to the real (which means it can *decide* in favour of the truth). On the contrary, reason has, by virtue of the self-contained system of concepts it contains, every right to make itself into a totality, a whole without an outside, to let the real go hang itself, as it were. Far from being bound by necessity and the concrete, as Hegel imagined, the system of reason is a free play, a 'flight of thought', a 'poetic fiction', reason's poem composed to itself (Schelling 1841: 115).

The practice of infinity

It is tempting to read Schelling's distinction between negative and positive philosophy as constituting primarily a theoretical critique of idealism, and an elevation of revealed religion, and the positive philosophy consequent upon it, above idealism, as though positive philosophy were the truth and negative philosophy the false. This, however, would be more Hegelian than Schellingian, for it would subscribe, wittingly or not, to the Hegelian *Aufhebungsdialektik*, rather than holding the more difficult thought, the Schellingian alternative, characterised by Beach as an *Erzeugungsdialektik*. A positive philosophy which stands as the *logical* negation of the negative philosophy, which sets it aside as having in itself no truth, as being inadequate to its inchoate truth and so logically requiring the positive philosophy as supplement, is essentially Hegel's argument for the relationship of the historical forms of objective spirit (the family, society, the state) to the final forms of absolute spirit (art, religion and philosophy). The religious-philosophical coda of the odyssey of spirit is thus logically produced, and a necessary outcome of conceptual tensions inherent in every penultimate stage of spiritual life. Schelling, however, finds no incoherence in negative philosophy, and insists that there is no conceptual or logical necessity to move beyond it. No doubt positive philosophy, should one decide for it, displaces negative philosophy, renders it the past. A Schellingian negation or displacement does not not 'cancel and preserve' the truth of the displaced. It orders the displaced with respect to the emergent and so temporalises the truth of that which has emerged and is to be affirmed: the negated becomes antecedent, that which negates is consequent, and the law of the ground, which is the order of nature, applies. 'The antecedent has its actuality in the consequent in respect of which it is accordingly mere potency' (SW IX: 375f.). Or in Grant's words, 'what is antecedent has its actuality *qua antecedent* in its *having* consequents' (Grant 2013b: 9).

A positive philosophy which had *aufgehoben* the negative philosophy would be experienced as the truth of the negative, the truth that the negative has no truth in itself – everything that the negative intends would be achieved and surpassed in the positive – whereas Schelling argues exactly the opposite. The negative is in a certain way the truth of the positive, that is, it denominates the positive, for it knows how to name it, even if it knows nothing of its existence. The negative intends more than the positive gives, at least at this stage of history. Far from being cancelled, the negated is rendered determinative in the negation, but as potency, not act, insuperably subordinated to the consequent, which in turn is rendered constitutively dependent upon it. Negation does not de-realise the negated (here the meontology is crucial, for reality does not equal actuality), it does not annul it or render it nothing; it renders the displaced the past and the living ground of the present. If by contrast positive philosophy was an *Aufhebung* of negative philosophy, it would not install it as potency and ground but unmask it as so much appearance, as inadequate to its own notion, as bearing within it a logical inadequacy or contradiction.

A Hegelian reading of the relation of the positive to the negative would not only tie the two together in a bond of logical necessity, and so destroy the entire personal thrust of the Philosophy of Revelation – its foundation in irreducible freedom; it would also fail to recognise the truth proper to the negative; put more paradoxically, it would fail to recognise that which is irreducibly given *only* in the negative, and which is never to be annulled but which is destined to stand unto the end of history. The Hegelian-Schellingian, who misreads positive philosophy as an *Aufhebung* of the negative, fails to see the positive in the negative, and she does so because she exaggerates the superiority and independence of the positive. She sees in the positive a complete and absolute philosophy, and not, as Schelling says at many points, a partial philosophy that stands in need of illumination by the negative. She fails to acknowledge that something is still lacking to the positive.

That said, negative philosophy is not *already* positive philosophy, as some enthusiastic contemporary *Naturphilosophen* argue. Many efforts to bring the negative and the positive together on the basis of the undeniable presence of *naturphilosophischen* principles in the latter are motivated by a not so hidden rejection of the possibility of revelation. Of course, *naturphilosophischen* principles are at play in the positive philosophy, for they are the principles of reason itself. Revelation, if it has occurred, has not given us a new capacity for thinking, an new organ for truth (as Kierkegaard put it);[84] it has given us something new, radically new, unprethinkable, to think. The rush of Schellingian immanentists to find in Schelling's early philosophy all that which first appears in the latter philosophy fails to do justice to the proper power of negative philosophy. They loudly insist that *nature-philosophy* also knows the positive, is also a philosophy of contingency. One can get there without revelation, and so, by implication, one could be a philosopher of the positive in a purely immanentist key. The blurring of the Schellingian distinction between the negative and the positive, the ideal and the real, which is motivated by a desire to protect the dignity of the early Schellingian systems, has the opposite effect. By ascribing to negative philosophy what can only be affirmed in the positive philosophy, the defence neglects or underplays the distinctive role of the negative in the late Schelling. The ahistoricality of negative philosophy – its engagement with essence, identity, in abstraction from existence and history – can certainly be pitched as a weakness, but it is also its strength. Reason in negative philosophy achieves a degree of certainty in knowledge which is nothing less than absolute (but curiously limited nevertheless, for it is strictly conceptual absolutism), and this certainty is not to be taken from it.

> Reason is the self-knowledge of the eternal identity. With this proposition, we have simultaneously defeated forever all subjectivization of rational knowledge . . . In *reason* all subjectivity ceases, and this is precisely what our proposition argues. In reason, that eternal identity itself is at once the knower and the known – it is not *me who recognises this identity, but it recognises itself, and I am merely its organ*. (Schelling 1804a: 142–3/144)

Not to be missed here is the emancipatory note that Schelling strikes: negative thinking is an elevation above the merely subjective, above the petty concerns, obsessions and delusions of the finite mind, fixated as it is on its merely individual ends. We might even conceive of it – and I will in what follows – as an *enlightenment* of the egoic consciousness of everydayness.

It is nevertheless true that no negative philosophy floats freely of existence; every negative philosophy presupposes the existence of the philosopher who thinks it, however suspended or disavowed this existence might be. In this sense the negative philosophy is already rooted, at the very least unconsciously, in the positive. There is another sense in which a positivity lies at the heart of the negative philosophy. There is something unalterably true in the negative, something in its own way real and true, namely the experience of *essence*, which is co-given with reason itself. By essence I mean ideality, the intelligible structure of anything whatsoever, closely akin to what Husserl means by the term.[85] Schelling speaks of essence variously as the mirror of wisdom, the Kantian Ideal of reason, the *ens necessarium*, or

Spinoza's substance. The infinite is for Schelling, as it was for Kant, the concept of that which pre-contains all predicates, but in an absolute fashion, and without negation (the concept of an *omnitudo realitas* or an *ens realissimum*).[86] The point is also a neo-Platonic one: all forms of intelligibility, all ideas must ultimate converge on one master idea, one crystalline, infinite concept, the thought of which entails the thought of everything else. This experience of essence is the positive in the negative, it is what is given to negative philosophy, and as Jesus said of Mary, who neglected the housework to sit at the Lord's feet and contemplate his words (Luke 10:38–42), it is not to be taken from it.

And conversely, there is something undeniably negative in the positive, that is, something undeniably partial and lacking to positive philosophy, namely, a full and comprehensive explanation of the explanandum, which is history itself. This is, on the one hand, because history is not yet over, and so a total explanation is still outstanding. Uncertainty and ambiguity are inescapably part of historical knowledge, and are manifest at every turn, from the unanswerable question, which inaugurates the positive philosophy, Why is there something rather than nothing? to the impossibility of creating a science of revelation. Schelling must go further than this. Total and transparent knowledge of the real will elude reason, even beatified reason, because the real is grounded in divine freedom. In short, we will never comprehend the really existing God. We spoke of this as the first pillar of late Schellingian thought, the principle of absolute transcendence. And while Žižek likes to spin it cynically – because of the constitutively ideological fore-structure of subjectivity, the real must always slip from the subject's grasp, and so on and so on – the point can be affirmed otherwise, without Lacanian commitments to constitutive self-deception. The logical remainder at the core of the real (*der nie aufgehende Rest*), which renders closure and systematic knowledge of the real always elusive, is the mark of divine freedom as such.[87]

What more can we say positively about the negative or ideal experience of essence? We might say, for example, that it constitutes a perennial philosophy. It is found, Schelling says, everywhere there is reason. No human being is born without the idea of God; it is the innate content of reason (*notitia Dei insita* [Schelling 1842a: 76]). Descartes is correct to see that this idea is the presupposition of the cogito's idea of itself by which he endeavours to found science. Kant describes it more or less as the lynchpin of the architectonic of reason. Our tendency is to read essence as a purely theoretical structure, a merely regulative ideal, as Kant puts it. Here we can align Schelling with those twentieth-century advocates of a *philosophia perennis* – Aldous Huxley, Rudolf Steiner, Titus Burckhardt, René Guénon – as we can align him with ancient thinkers of the *logos* such as

Heraclitus, Socrates, Philo, Plotinus and Marcus Aurelius, as much as with Zhuang Zhou, Nagarjuna and Shankara, who use different terms of course (the Tao, the Buddha Nature, the Dharma), but who must, if Schelling is right, mean the same thing. An experience of infinity abides in the negative philosophy, and this knowledge is in itself not false, not a pseudo-knowledge. It can *become* a pseudo-knowledge when it is mistaken for an existential knowledge. On its own, the experience of essence which is reason's own is incontrovertibly true, or better, beyond truth and falsehood, as experience (*aesthesis*) in Aristotle is neither true nor false.[88] Essence in Schelling, like the primordial experience of truth in Heidegger (*aletheia*), has as its opposite not falsehood but non-appearance (Heidegger 1927a: ¶ 33). Here one either knows, or one is ignorant of what is eternally true. Nevertheless, demonstration is always possible. The experience of essence is the very substance of reason and can only be denied at the price of performative contradiction. It is not a knowledge that is corrected or supplemented by the positive philosophy. It remains reason's own, it is the light of reason, and upon it reason depends and always will.

The positive gives the negative an existential dimension; it presents that which is formally known in the negative as real, that is, it existentialises essence. The essential truth of the negative remains the essential truth of the positive, just as the existential truth of the positive is the existential truth of the negative, or will be revealed to be so, in the future. A circle of non-dialectical dependency holds the two together, and at the centre of the circle is the positive philosopher, deciding to relate them, that is, deciding to ecstatically empty his or her own reason before the real. Schelling says that the negative philosophy is the truth of idealism, idealism which he argued in 1809 is the soul of philosophy (Schelling 1809: 356/26). A Schellingian, therefore, can never be simply anti-idealist, as Kierkegaard is anti-idealist. Schelling affirms idealism as the true if not complete philosophy. If idealism, or the philosophy of essence, is also a perennial philosophy, it is found wherever reasoning occurs, and so is known by all people in all places. Schelling, for example, argues that the *essential* knowledge of the Trinity (as distinct from the historical knowledge of the Trinity, as God acting in history and revealed through the Jews), the natural knowledge of the three potencies, is expressed in various ways in all of the mythologies and religions of the world (Schelling 1854c: 313–14). Schelling points directly at the triad of Brahma, Shiva and Vishnu in Hinduism, but we could also point to Purusha, Prakriti and the psychic being that mediates them in Aurobindo's Integral Yoga (Aurobindo 2010: 185–99). There is no good Schellingian reason why we should not think of idealism, the philosophy of essence, otherwise known as negative philosophy, as the true content of the world's religions.

This path, however, is fraught with danger. Are we to think of Advaita Vedanta or the Madhyamaka school of Buddhism as instances of Schelling's negative philosophy? Would any Hindu Brahman or Mahayana Buddhist accept this? Or would such a view be rejected as so much condescension, just as Rahner's well-meaning bid to include non-Christian religions within the circle of revealed truth by calling them 'anonymously' Christian was rejected by even Christian theologians as paternalistic? On the other hand, this approach to the issue opens up whole domains of the negative which could and should be interpreted by the Schellingian philosopher of religion. If a Schellingian accepts the distinction between negative and positive philosophy, he or she ought to be ready to find expressions of the negative everywhere, and not solely in the history of Western philosophy. Negative philosophy, Schelling argues, is not dependent upon history at all. It is a philosophy that is not limited by history. It proceeds timelessly, and would be true if nothing existed. Perhaps we can approach this question of the universality of the experience of essence in a less condescending way. Perhaps we can speak of a negative *spirituality*, a practice of infinity, which is perennial and ubiquitous, and if not a way of salvation, certainly a way of truth. After all, negative philosophy is not only a theoretical philosophy, without any practical sense. To take it as such is an error in interpretation, however understandable.

The error proceeds as follows. Because positive philosophy is the philosophy of freedom, because positive philosophy is a philosophy contingent upon will, we are inclined to map on to the distinction between the negative and the positive in Schelling Kant's distinction between theoretical and practical reason. This would have the effect of saying that all ethical and political questions as well as all spiritual questions – anything related to the non-theoretical – are part of the positive, and that the negative has only a theoretical significance to human living. This is not the case. On the contrary, the negative and the positive in Schelling do not directly map on to the theoretical and the practical in Kant. The proof of this is that Schelling writes about morality, ethics and politics in the *Darstellung der reinrationalen Philosophie*, that is, as part and parcel of the purely rational philosophy. There is a purely rational ethics, as there is a purely rational theory of the State, and lecture 23 of the *Darstellung* is meant to outline it. So then, we are bound to admit a *practice* of the negative in Schelling, which is found wherever reason exists and struggles to order its living. What might the practice of the negative look like? What is the practical aspect of the negative philosophy? We know, more or less in outline, what the practical aspect of the *positive* philosophy looks like: it is personalist, politically messianic, egalitarian and emancipatory. When philosophical religion comes into existence, humanity will be liberated from the contradiction between freedom and equality which renders human life an unresolved longing for justice and the State a necessary evil. But this emancipation is reserved for the future. We must not misjudge our time: philosophical religion does not yet exist.

The practice of the negative, on the other hand, is a spirituality of the present and for the present, or better, it is an eternal spirituality, always and everywhere valid. It is a practice of interiority, an inner practice of the experience of infinity that lies just beneath the egoic consciousness of ordinary mind, and which can, through discipline and training, become a habitual state of mind. The practice of the negative is an interiorisation of infinity, a practice of transcendence, a disidentification with the finite, whether it be a concept of being, a sense of identity, a desire or a fear, and through that dissociation – productive, not destructive – an achievement of peace, humility and compassion.

Consider the following passages from great spiritual masters of the East and West in the light of Schelling's thesis that an experience of infinity is constitutive of consciousness. The first is from the pre-Socratic Greek philosopher Heraclitus, who has as good a claim to being the father of Western philosophy as does Socrates. The second is from the Heart Sutra, a seventh-century Chinese text of the Madhyamaka school of Buddhism and the root of all Mahayana practices (Tibetan, Zen, Shin). The third is from Shankara, the great ninth-century Hindu interpreter of the *Upanishads*, the foundational texts of philosophical Hinduism or Vedanta. The fourth is from Meister Eckhart, the Dominican preacher and Rhineland Scholastic who knew nothing of Vedanta, and could not have known anything even if he wanted to. The last is from Schelling's 1804 Würzburg Seminar.

1. It is wise to listen, not to me but to the Word, and to confess that all things are one. (Heraclitus, Fragment 50)
2. Form is emptiness; emptiness is form. Form is not different than emptiness; emptiness is not different than form. (The Heart Sutra)[89]
3. In the ocean of Absolute Bliss, what is there to be rejected or accepted, what else is there than the Self, what distinct from it? . . . [In that state] I neither see nor hear nor know anything. I am the Atman, Bliss Eternal . . . (Shankara, *Vivekacudamani*, in Torwesten 1991: 128)
4. The eye through which I see God is the same eye through which God sees me; my eye and God's eye are one eye, one seeing, one knowing, one love. (Eckhart 2009: Sermon 57, p. 298).
5. In truth there does not ever nor anywhere exist a subject, a self, or any object or non-self. To say: I know or I am knowing already [posits] the *proton pseudos*. I know *nothing*, or my knowledge, to the extent that it is *mine*, is no true knowledge. Not I know, but only totality *knows* in me, if the knowledge that I consider my own is to to be a real, true knowledge. Yet this One that knows is the only thing known . . . Now this one that knows and is known is necessarily the identical One in all possible situations of knowledge and being known;

> hence, there exists necessarily and everywhere only one knowledge and one
> known . . . the supreme knowledge . . . is that knowledge wherein the eternal
> self-awareness comes to recognise itself. (Schelling 1804a: 140–1/143)

It would be a gross generalisation to suggest that each of these texts is saying
precisely the same thing. Nevertheless, a formal hermeneutical convergence
can be noted. The proper interpretation of each requires a movement from
the dualisms of grammar (subject/object), logic (true/false), consciousness
(self/not-self), theology (creator/creature) and epistemology (appearance/
reality) to a non-dual level of thought that can only expressed in paradoxes.
Each of the above passages is a testimony, in a different cultural register, to
a non-dual experience of reality – non-dual, not monistic. The difference
between monism and non-dualism lies in this: where the monist affirms
only one thing, the non-dualist denies that there are two (or many) things.
Thus the non-dualist presupposes duality, where the monist does not. This
logical presupposition leads to the characteristically paradoxical claims of
non-dualism, such as the founding principle of the Madhyamaka school
of Buddhism, the Heart Sutra, cited above. The claim is not that there is
no emptiness and there is no form, but rather, that these two opposites
are not exclusive. The non-dualist needs the two, emptiness *and* form (self
and non-self, Purusha and Prakriti, enlightenment and delusion, eternity
and time, God and the soul) in order to make his or her point, that what
appears as two that exclude one another are both essential moments of
being. Monism denies logic, which presupposes duality (true/false, being/
nothing, 1/0); the non-dualist relies upon it, if only to transcend it. There
can be no transcending with nothing transcended.

> By relying on the mind only (*cittamatra*), know that external entities do not exist.
> And by relying on this system, know that no self at all exists, even in that. Therefore,
> due to *holding the reins of logic as one rides the chariots of the two systems*, one attains
> [the path of] the actual Mahayanist. (Santaraksita cited in Blumenthal 2004: 245,
> italics mine)

Heraclitus, Shankara, Eckhart, Santaraksita are no doubt speaking of *experiences* of non-duality; not logical conclusions, but experiences attendant
upon certain practices, meditation, contemplative prayer, yoga, and so
on. Schelling adds that the non-dual experience is not beyond reason but
presupposes it. 'This knowledge in which the eternal self-identity recognises itself is reason' (Schelling 1804a: 141/143). Nevertheless, I think
we misread the early Schelling if we reduce this claim to logic. Logic is
the necessary but not sufficient condition for the experience of the infinite. Reason at this stage in Schelling's thought is much more than mere
logic: it is *nature*. Reason is as outside us as it is inside us. Reason is reality, the absolute. We could say that reason in the identity-philosophy is

analogous to Buddha Nature in Zen. The non-dual conclusion of identity-philosophy is not merely a logical deduction, not even primarily a logical point (although logic is needed as a vehicle, as Santaraksita says). In identity-philosophy reason *experiences* the non-ultimacy of the dualism which it depends upon, that is, it experiences *itself* as non-dual: the reasoner knows himself or herself as simultaneously the subject and the object of the absolute. We might conclude, therefore, that an account of the negative as an experience of essence lends credibility to the experience of mystics and sages of all ages, and offers a certain explanatory framework for recognising the plausibility of transcendent states of consciousness, be they described as moksha, satori or the *unio mystica* of neo-Platonism (pagan, Jewish, Christian, Muslim).

And yet we should remain wary of a certain temptation attendant upon all forms of mysticism, something Schelling was only too cognisant of and spoke directly about in his later work. The mystic is vulnerable to mistaking an interior experience of essence, the experience of identity, of the *essential* oneness of things, for a personal knowledge of divine existence, and so inflating reason's innate sense of infinity into an experience of the existing God. While in the following passage, drawn from lecture 24 of the *Darstellung*, Schelling targets Christian mysticism (Schelling cites Fénelon [Schelling 1854c: 557]), there is no reason to confine his critique to that literature. On the contrary, Schelling's identification of mysticism with negative philosophy, and his insistence on the ahistorical universality of negative philosophy, requires that we extend his remarks to mystical experiences as discussed in other world religions, in Jewish Kabbalah as much as in Sufism, in Taoism and Hinduism, and in Mahayana Buddhism as well.

> Here is thus what the I can attain in its search to escape the unblessedness and to save itself in *its* world. The I indeed seems to have its satisfaction in the good attained through contemplation, for the God from whom the I had separated itself in practice has him once again in knowledge; the I has an ideal in God by which he rises above himself, emerges from himself. But he has only an *ideal* relation to this God, he can thus not have any other relation to him. For the contemplative science leads only to the God that is *end* [*telos*], and that is not the actual God. It leads only to he who is God in essence, not to God in actuality. (Schelling 1854a: 558–9, 566, translation Kyla Bruff)

In this move the contemplative shakes free of the bewitching attraction of the conceptual and acts as a person, one who is not satisfied with the *idea* of God, the universal being of reason, but seeks a God like himself, one who, as Schelling puts it, can love him in return ('person seeks person' – *person sucht person* [Schelling 1854a: 566]). Schelling's starkly critical assessment of mysticism is not widely enough recognised by

Schellingians, many of whom have mystical penchants themselves. There is no hiding from the master's pronouncement on this: the mystical ascent fails to reach the genuinely existing God. The contemplative, precisely by turning away from the world, from history, the ethical-political realm, will never find the living God. All that he or she enjoys in the *unio* is an individual, volitional union with the infinite potency. The inadequacy of the union is proven for Schelling by the fact that the contemplative cannot stay in ecstasy but must return to the fallen world, untransformed, even if the world has contracted to the compass of the cloister. He or she is not permanently changed by the experience, and nor is the world.[90]

Here Schelling's way swings off from perennial forms of contemplative practice towards revealed religion, and there is no getting around this. The contemplative is motivated by a genuine desire for infinity, but through practice only ever attains a negative or ideal infinity. The mystic has transcended negative philosophy in desire, but not in attainment. Mysticism cannot satisfy us, at least not now, at this penultimate stage of human history. The contemplative is circling around the ideal of reason as much as the idealist philosopher, only he or she is motivated by an expressly practical and existential desire for the real. The contemplative may succeed, however, in producing a momentary cessation of finite activity, a respite from 'the unblessedness' of the active life, which should not be underestimated, even if it cannot be sustained. Mysticism results in the production of treatises on the ideal God, God 'in essence' not in 'actuality', God as the final cause of all movement, but not as the efficient cause of human salvation. Schelling argues that the *via negativa* of mysticism, while it expresses the individual mystic's authentic desire for the real, and therefore, to some degree, also expresses the contemplative's realisation of the limitations of the ideal, is still for all that *negative* philosophy.[91]

Could we put this point more positively? Insofar as there is no method or path that leads to the actual God (should God in fact exist), the contemplative practice that points to God is the pinnacle of human religious experience. Schelling is not dismissing mysticism; he is affirming it as necessary, and within certain limits, true. At the same time, Schelling is calling to the mystic to remain conscious of their negativity, without slipping into the Hegelian error of assuming a logical incompleteness therein, which would make the positive philosophy a necessary correlate of the negative, and absolve the mystic of the need for the individuating decision. I would hazard to say that this difficult negotiation of the negative and the positive, since it is not and cannot be a work of conceptualisation, any more than it can be the result of a deduction (as though the negative philosophy discovered that it was merely a moment en route to the positive, as in Hegel, that it was inadequate to its own notion and harboured within itself a contradiction that rendered the move into the positive a necessary and logical one) – I would hazard to say that this remaining with the negative is a *practice*, not a theoretical assumption or a scientific result at all. As such, the mystic, while he or she may remain conceptually ensnared in the negative, has stepped into the positive; contemplative practice intensifies existence, almost to a breaking point, while never freeing the mystic from the negative. Mysticism as a propaedeutic to positive philosophy (and not, as it sometimes becomes, a return to impersonal unconsciousness and a flight from love)[92] is the paradoxical practice of the individual experiencing his or herself as essence, and as simultaneously existent, that is, knowing his or her own infinity, and yet in that knowledge remaining finite, that is, conscious of the negativity of the experience.

How would this work, a mystical practice of the negative that opens the practitioner to the positive? The interior infinity of the ground, the blissful liberation from a limited sense of mind, from egoic finitude, the experience of the non-dual origin of everything, would be experienced in an ecstatic death of the ego, and, at the same time, recognised as non-total, and not final, a way and not the end. A finger pointing at the moon is not the moon. Without necessarily expecting revelation, the practitioner of negative spirituality would remain, so to speak, within certain limits, that is, would resist the temptation, which is so marked in historical forms of negative philosophy and in mysticism, the temptation to expand a purely essential infinity into the existential, that is, to take the essential infinity of reason to be identical with the existential infinity of a really existing God. The negative mystic who acknowledges his or her own negativity can rightly pass for an atheist, for he or she knows no God above. The *practice* of the negative would be the practice of an essential and interiorised infinity. It would be a provisional liberation from the prison of the ego, an expansion of the mind into the blissful presence of the fullness of essential being, a compassion based on non-discrimination between self and other, and a transcendence of the small-minded neediness and distractedness which so dogs our ordinary mind. It would be the experience of the truth, the absolutely incontrovertible truth of what the Vedantist has been saying for as long as recorded history. 'The Infinite alone justifies the existence of the finite and the finite by itself has no entirely separate value or independent existence. Life, if it is not an illusion, is a divine Play, a manifestation of the glory of the Infinite' (Aurobindo in Mohanty 2012: 162). In this non-knowledge and dissolution of subjectivity, the practitioner of infinity remains as awake and vigilant as an early Christian, awaiting the day of the Lord, which will come upon us suddenly and unexpectedly, Paul says, like a thief in the night (1 Thess. 5:2).

Notes

1. 'The most severe misunderstanding it [identity-philosophy] could encounter was the charge that, on the analogy with other systems, it had a self-warranting *principle* from which the truth of other parts of the system could be derived. So right from the start it was demanded that the system demonstrate its principle. But it couldn't do this! *Originating in the Kantian critique*, it could claim truth as its principle only at the end of its work. At that point it would be the *freest philosophy*, the purest flight of *thought that was free even of truth*, and impelled only by its innate laws. Those who took it *as nothing but a poetic fiction* understood it better. *It was a poem composed by reason itself.* For *reason is bound to nothing, not even to truth*' (Schelling 1841: 115).

2. This is the gist of Horst Furhmans's widely disputed reading of Schelling. See Furhmans (1954).

3. See Peirce (1901; 1908).

4. There is an experience at the foundation of identity-philosophy, of course. It is the experience of intelligibility as such, or what I shall describe below as the experience of essence.

5. 'Considered in itself, nothing is finite' (Schelling 1804a: 161/143). On the Würzburg system, see Vater (2014). Vater argues that the Würzburg system is an effort to give nature-philosophy a more robustly logical foundation by anchoring it to a revised Spinozism. Vater describes the Würzburg system as Spinozism 'with an ultimate but discursively inaccessible self-founding and self-cognised absolute (Spinoza's substance) serving as ontological ground for parallel but mutually exclusive orders of phenomenal elaboration, viz., the subjective and the object (Spinoza's attributes)' (Vater 2014: 129). The absolute indifference posited as the ground of both the subjective and the objective is expressly not a personal God but a presupposition which would explain the merely quantitative differences between subjectivity and objectivity. Vater's conclusion: 'Schelling is [in 1804] still a transcendental Spinozist, and "nature" – as *natura naturans*, to be sure – can still be intersubstituted with God' (Vater 2014: 138).

6. Aquinas speaks of the passive potency for revelation as a *potentia obedientialis* of human nature for the act of grace that will perfect it. We do not possess an active potency for sanctifying grace, for that would place the supernatural within the teleological reach of the natural. But we possess a passive potency to respond to an act that would make us receptive to grace. See Aquinas, *Summa Theologica*, 3, q. 11, a. 1c.

7. In the *Denkmal* (Schelling 1812: 25), Schelling traces his distinction between ground and existence back to his 1801 *Darstellung meines System* (SW 4: 105–212). He cites the following key passage from the early text: 'We understand by nature absolute identity insofar as it is considered not as being [*seiend*], but as ground of its own being [*Sein*].' In the Freedom Essay, Schelling also refers to this text as his source. See Schelling (1809: 356/27).

8. See Tritten (2018). See also Beierwaltes (1972: 104–5, 154–87).

9. For the most relentless examination of the puzzle of relations, see Bradley (1897: Book I, chs. I–VIII).

10. Proclus (1992). In what follows I have learned much from Bullerwell (2020). In the Freedom Essay, Schelling uses a series of verbal examples to illustrate the problem. 'The body is blue'; 'the perfect is the imperfect'; 'good is evil' (Schelling 1809: 341/13). The symbol of A = B for identity in difference comes from the Würzburg seminars. See Schelling (1804a: 330). See also the translator's note 32 in Schelling (1809: English, 147–8).

11. 'All that is unparticipated produces out of itself the participated; and all participated substances are linked by upward tension to existences not participated' (Proclus 1992: prop. 23, p. 27).

12. We must take care at this point not to overlay the false dichotomy of nature and spirit on Schelling's distinction between necessity and freedom. Both necessity and freedom are spirit, although in different ways, and both are ultimately natural in the broadest sense of the term. Their opposition to one another is only possible because they belong together essentially.

13. *'All that is is, to the extent that it is, One*: namely, it is the eternally self-same identity, the One that alone exists, and that therefore is all that can be known . . . That whereby a *difference* is posited in general (that is, if something of that kind should exist) does not belong to the essence, to the *esse*, but rather to the *non-esse*, to the nonbeing of things, and is a mere determination of these, not to the extent that they are (for in that respect they are one) but to the extent that they are not. To the extent, then, that the absolute identity is the immediate expression of the absolute itself (for only the absolute affirms immediately the eternal and immutable self-sameness of subject and object by affirming itself), and to the extent that the *absolute identity* is the immediate expression of God or of the absolute in all existence, the proposition: "all that is has Being, to the extent that it is", should be phrased as follows: "To the extent that it has being, all that is, is God." Hence all *being* that is not the Being of God is no *Being* but much rather the negation of Being, and we can therefore claim the following with determination: (11) *There is everywhere only One Being, only One true Essence, identity, or God as the affirmation of the latter*' (Schelling 1804a: 156–7/153).

14. The return to Kant's practical philosophy is here obvious. See Hutter (1996).

15. See McGrath (2010; 2012: 179–89).

16. On Schelling's rediscovery of Boehme and the Speculative Pietism in which he was educated as a child, see McGrath (2012: 44–81) and Matthews (2011: 39–68).

17. It should be remembered that Schelling's earliest writings were on religious themes. See the 1792 student text, 'Antiquissimi de prima malorum humanorum origine' (SW 1: 1–40) and the 1793 'Über Mythen, historische Sagen und Philosopheme der ältesten Welt' (SW 1: 41–84). It should also be remembered that when Schelling edited the *Kritisches Journal* with Hegel (1802), he shared with Hegel an interest in a speculative interpretation of the Christian Trinity. See Harris (1989). Schelling outlines a broadly Hegelian theory of the history of creation, fall, and redemption as a history of the Trinity in the eighth lecture of 1803 lecture course *On University Studies*. See Schelling (1803: 285–95).

18. Herein opens a path towards a strict theology of revelation such as Barth's or Von Balthasar's. It is important to note that Schelling never considers this as a viable, scientific path. This, as I will argue at greater length in the second book, is a weakness in his late philosophy.

19. The law of the ground is stated by Iain Hamilton Grant as follows: 'What is antecedent has its actuality qua antecedent in its having consequents, or: nature is whatever behaves in accordance with a law of antecedence. The above formulation combines Schelling's statement of that law in the Freiheitsschrift, such that "no kind of combination can transform that which is derivative into that which is original"; with that in the *Darstellung der reinrationalen Philosophie*, drawn from Aristotle, and which states that "the antecedent has its actuality in the consequent in respect of which it is accordingly mere potency" (SW 9: 375f.). The former emphasises not only the irreversibility of the relation, but also that antecedence is, due to the irreversibility of the criterion,

insuperably antecedent with respect to any consequent, paradigmatically in the case of emergence. The latter by contrast emphasises the inactuality of the antecedent prior to its acquiring actuality in the consequent' (Grant 2013b: 9).

20. Schelling himself admitted that 'the beginning of the positive philosophy was in the *Denkmal an Jacobi* (1812)' (Schelling 1841: 138/90). The treatise, which is the last thing that Schelling published, was a critique of the last thing that Jacobi published, *Von den göttlichen Dingen und ihrer Offenbarung* (Jacobi 1811). See also Schelling (1842: 86/149).

21. See Jacobi's 1785 *Concerning the Doctrine of Spinoza in Letters to Herr Moses Mendelssohn* (Jacobi 1994: 173–252)

22. See 1 Cor. 15:28: 'When all things are subjected to him, then the Son himself will also be subjected to him who put all things in subjection under him, that God may be all in all [*panta en passin*].'

23. See Jacobi's *Vorrede* to the 2nd edition of his *David Hume über den Glauben* (1815: 3–126).

24. 'Whoever throws nature away in advance, as that which is absolutely devoid of spirit, thereby deprives himself even of the material in which and from which he could develop the spiritual' (Schelling 1833: 177/173).

25. This is the very point to which Jacobi objects: the basic assumption of most theories of evolution, that perfection should arise from imperfection. See Jacobi (1811) and Schelling's response (Schelling 1812: 63ff.). It should be clear that Schelling will later qualify this point: in terms of time and evolutionary history, possibility precedes actuality, but metaphysically, actuality (unprethinkable, eternal existence) precedes possibility. Primordial and pure act, however, is still not perfection, but the ground of perfection. In this regard, perfection is still subsequent to the imperfect, or rather, the non-perfect.

26. See Kasper (1965: 267–97).

27. See Schelling (1812: 65).

28. Schelling (1794). The meontological tradition is transmitted by Schelling to the Russians Soloviev, Bolgakov and Berdyaev, in Germany to Tillich and Moltmann, and in America to Peirce and, more recently, Ray Hart. It is a minority tradition that stands in the shadow of the much more influential Aristotelian-Hegelian approach to the question of being.

29. Amazingly, Boehme recreates the distinction independently of any Greek sources. See Boehme (1623).

30. See Schelling (1809: 356/26): 'The entire new European philosophy since its beginning (with Descartes) has the common defect that nature is not available for it and that it lacks a living ground.'

31. See Schelling (1812: 65): 'But that there is something in God that is pure power and strength cannot be denied, if only one does not claim that he alone is this and nothing else. Rather, the opposite must be denied. For how should the fear of God exist if there is no strength in him, and how should he himself, together with his wisdom and goodness, exist without strength, since strength is existence (*das Bestehen*) and all existence is strength. Where there is no strength, there is no character, no individuality, no true personality, but vain diffusion, as we see daily in characterless people. Furthermore, the old saying can be reversed, that without strength the highest goodness could never rise to majesty. It is not for nothing that the sacred Scriptures speak of God's power and the strength of his might.'

32. See McGrath (2012: 6–11).

33. See Aquinas, *Summa Theologica*, 1a, q. 15. See McGrath (2013a).
34. 'He [Schelling] wanted to recover the living, real God as opposed to all recently formulated abstractions of philosophy and theology. He already clearly recognized the connection that today repeatedly emerges between a worldless understanding of God and a godless understanding of the world. If God is moved higher and higher beyond the world, one is soon dealing with an unreal God and with a godless, secularised world' (Kasper 1965: 233).
35. See Benz (1955; 1983), Schneider (1938), Dierauer (1986), McGrath (2012: 44–8), Matthews (2011: 39–68) and O'Regan (2001).
36. Similar statements have been made concerning Hegel's *Logic*. See O'Regan (1994) and Magee (2001). One might want to also put Schelling's nature-philosophy into a genetic relation to theosophy, but this is a more tenuous, albeit intriguing, claim.
37. In his 1833 critique of Boehme, Schelling situates Boehme alongside Jacobi as a metaphysical empiricist. Both seek to ground revelation in experience, that is, in inner vision. But where Jacobi's 'feeling' has no speculative content, Boehme's mystical insight is advanced as grounds for a speculative theosophy. Boehme, unlike Jacobi, does not renege on science. However, because of the fall, our co-knowledge of creation, which is our birthright and Boehme's presupposition (as well as Schelling's in the period 1809–15), is not what it should be, and theosophy fails in its ambition to be a science of God. Boehme finds himself as incapable of sharing his vision as Jacobi is incapable of communicating his 'feeling'. See Schelling (1833: 184ff).
38. See Freud (1900: 382): 'In the best interpreted dreams we often have to leave one passage in obscurity because we observe during the interpretation that we have here a tangle of dream-thoughts which cannot be unravelled, and which furnishes no fresh contribution to the dream content. This, then, is the keystone of the dream, the point at which it ascends into the unknown.'
39. Cf. Schelling (1842: 166/132): 'We must assume an originary being of God that even precedes God himself.'
40. Gabriel has this, inexplicably, exactly wrong, and proceeds in one place to interpret first potency as though it were sheer determinacy, and second potency as though it were sheer determinability, when from the very passages of Schelling he cites it is the reverse that is explicitly the case. See Gabriel (2011: 68–9).
41. On the Lacanian subject, see Fink (1995).
42. See Heidegger (1927a: ¶ 9).
43. It is well known that Lacan drew on Heidegger, among other sources, for his reconceptualisation of Freud.
44. Peirce's categories of firstness, secondness, and thirdness appear to be modelled after Schelling's late doctrine of potencies (Bradley 2012: 169). Cf. Peirce (1903: 75ff.). Peirce referred to Schelling in several places in his collected works, but never directly to the late lectures on revelation. Nevertheless, the parallels are striking. See Franks (2015: 732–55). Peirce never concealed his admiration for Schelling, which makes it unlikely that he would not have read the later work – but unfortunately Peirce's references to Schelling are all references to the early Schelling, in which Schelling's theory of the three potencies is still under construction and not quite the triunity that Peirce insists upon. In short, Peirce's three categories manifestly do not map on to Schelling's early doctrine of potencies. And the late Schelling in fact frequently uses the language of firstness (*Einheit*), secondness (*Zweiheit*) and thirdness (*Dreiheit*) to name his three potencies, which are, like Peirce's categories, essentially sequential because they are the archetype of number, order and time itself.

45. The distinction between the speculative notion of being as an activity and the analytical notion of being as instantiation was James Bradley's seminal insight. See Bradley (1999; 2012), as well as the essay, 'What is Existence?' in Bradley (2021, forthcoming).

46. See Duque (2007: 60, n. 5): 'In Hegel – for whom "the wounds of Spirit are healed without scarring" (*Phenomenology* 9: 360) – the "loop of interaction" between subject and predicate is closed in *absolute* dialectical propositions. On the contrary, Schelling's logic of *domination* yields always an *irreducible* remainder – both when the predicate *returns* to the subject as *Grund* or basis (namely, as nature) and when the subject freely elaborates its *future* by intervening in the predicate. The "object" (namely, the world) of divine Spirit is never going to fully return to its maker. This is not only due to the Fall, but also due to the fact that the world was created *mediately*, in the *Ebenbild* of the *existing* subject. In this way, even if there had been no *peccatum originans*, the mediating *copula* remains *refractory*. Without such "resistance", how could the subject see himself reflected in the Image, and see things within the Image?' Cf. Hegel (1807: 38): 'The subject itself falls into the universal'; 'the subject is dissolved in the predicate'; (1807: 39): 'The predicate itself has been expressed as a subject, as *the* being or *essence* which exhausts the nature of the subject.'

47. According to Saitya Das, Schelling hereby disrupts Schmittian political theology which would see the highest being as the divine model for the exceptionalism of earthly sovereignty; the highest being, for Schelling, the pure act, is the most powerless of beings, the one that sets itself aside, that does not advance its own interests, but defers to the other. See Das (2016: 41–89).

48. The contingency of the eternal truths, the *a priori* principles of reason, is the central claim of Schelling's last public lecture, 'On the Eternal Truths'. See Schelling (1850).

49. Schelling's most important passages on Hegel are in the 1833 lecture course, *The History of Modern Philosophy* (Schelling 1833: 126–65/134–63); the 1841 *Paulus Nachschrift* (Schelling 1841: 121–39/70–91); and the 1842 *Grounding of the Positive Philosophy* (Schelling 1842d: 87–94/149–54).

50. To be sure, Schelling objects in 1833 and in 1841 to Hegel's positing 'being' as the first concept, rather than *Seinkönnen* or 'possibility' (Schelling 1841: 125). On closer inspection it is not at all clear that Hegel's first category and Schelling's first potency are different. This is not to underestimate the significance of the difference between Hegel's *Aufhebungsdialektik* and Schelling's *Erzeugungsdialektik*. The potencies in Schelling do not cancel and preserve each other; they displace each other, complement one another, but cannot substitute for each other. See Beach (1994: 84–91) and McGrath (2012: 143ff.).

51. 'Hegel cannot be denied the credit for having seen the merely *logical nature* of the philosophy which he intended to work on and promised to bring to its complete form. If he had stuck to that and if he had carried out this thought by strictly, decisively renouncing everything positive, then he would have brought about the decisive transition to the positive philosophy, for the Negative, the negative pole can never be there in pure form without immediately calling for the positive pole. But that withdrawal to pure thought, to the pure concept, was, as one can find stated on the very first pages of Hegel's *Logic*, linked to the claim that the concept was *everything* and left nothing outside itself' (Schelling 1833: 126/134).

52. Copleston (1965: 315, n. 36); Laughland (2007: 14, 89).

53. The critique of essentialism was a centrepiece of Etienne Gilson's work. See, for example, Gilson (1952).

54. See Gilson (1936: 42–83); Gilson (2002: 41–8); Maritain (1956).

55. See Aquinas (1949); for an excellent interpretation of Aquinas's *actus essendi*, see Norris Clarke (2001).

56. On Hegel's system as an elaboration of the ontological argument, see Schulz (1997: 166–72).

57. See Anselm, *Proslogion*; Aquinas, *Summa Theologica*, 1a, q. 2, a. 1, ad 2. Aquinas, like Schelling, assumes that Anselm is speaking of a *concept* of God, which reason possesses and from which we can deduce God's existence. There is a different reading of Anselm, however. In *Proslogion* XV and XVI, Anselm appears to deny not only that we have an adequate concept of God, but also that such a concept is even possible. He no longer refers to God only as 'that than which nothing greater can be thought' (*aliquid quo nihil maius cogitari possit*), but as 'something greater than can be thought' (*quiddam maius quam cogitarum possit*) (Anselm, *Proslogion*, XV). In a neo-Platonic vein, Anselm describes God as beyond all concepts: 'Therefore, O Lord, not only are You that than which a greater cannot be thought, but You are also something greater than can be thought' (Anselm, *Proslogion*, XV, in Charlesworth 1979). 'Something greater than can be thought' is close to Schelling's inverted idea. On this other reading of Anselm, see Marion (1992). Many thanks to Memorial University PhD candidate Gil Shalev for pointing this out to me.

58. See Schelling (SW 10: 260–1): 'God is not truly the in-itself [*an sich*], God is nothing but relation, pure relation, because God is only lord; everything else that we add to [our concept of] God renders God mere substance. God exists, so to speak, for nothing other than to be the lord of being. God is the only one not self-preoccupied, unattached to self and therefore God is the absolutely free nature. Everything substantial has to do with itself, it is self-absorbed and self-obsessed. God alone has nothing to do with self, God is *sui securus* (sure of Godself and therefore alone), and has only to do with other things. God is, one could say, completely outside self, that is, free of self, and thus also the one who liberates everything else. God is what limited and oppressed humanity seeks, when a people elevates above itself an individual who does not seek self, but exists purely and simply for them, and who is therefore a universal liberator.' See Tillich (1910: 60): 'If God were only being itself, then he would be bound to be, unfree before it, and unhappy, as is everything that bears the shackles of being.'

59. See Schelling (1842d: 161/202). The argument is also, of course, Descartes' in the Second Meditation. See Descartes (1641).

60. 'Since the infinite potency comports itself as the *prius* of what it generates in thinking through its transition into being, and since it corresponds to nothing less than *all* being, so then is reason, due to the fact that it possesses this potency from which everything real for it can emerge – and, indeed, possesses it as what has grown together with it and is thus its inseparable content – set into an *a priori* position vis-à-vis all being. One grasps, to this extent, how there is an *a priori* science, a science that determines *a priori* all of *what* is (not *that* it is). In this way, reason of itself, without somehow calling on experience for assistance, is put in the position to arrive at the *content* of everything that exists, and consequently to the content of all real being; not that it takes cognizance *a priori* of whether this or that thing really exists (for that is an entirely different matter), but rather that it only knows *a priori* what is or what can be, if something is, and determines *a priori* the concepts of every being' (Schelling 1842d: 66/134).

61. See Tritten (2017).

62. See Schelling (1809: 356/27).

63. See Hegel (2007: ¶ 248–50).

64. See Hegel (2007: ¶ 193): 'The being of nature does not correspond to its concept; its existing actuality therefore has no truth; its abstract essence is the negative, as the ancients conceived of matter in general as the *non-ens*.'

65. The connection of Schelling to Kierkegaard is clear on this point. 'Existence' for Kierkegaard is not objectively known, not a passive experience of the positivity of being, but the truth of subjectivity, that which is only disclosed under the duress of the existing subject's incommunicable, and thus infinite self-problematisation. See Kierkegaard (1846: 68–77).

66. On Schelling's and Hegel's contesting accounts of evil, see McGrath (2006b).

67. See Bowie (1993: 84): 'If the Absolute really is able to relate to the Other as to itself, it would already have to know that the Other is itself, before the reflexive relationship: I can only see myself in a mirror, as opposed to an object which may or may not be me, if I am already familiar with myself. This entails a necessary ground which precedes any movement of reflection, without which, as was evident in relation to Derrida, difference could not even be known as difference.' See Henrich (1982: 159–60) for the origin of this argument.

68. Schelling offers many metaphors to describe the necessity which once overcome becomes the ground of personal freedom. See, for example, the example of the eagle, in the Munich lectures on *The History of Modern Philosophy*. 'The power of the eagle in flight does not prove itself by the fact that the eagle does not feel *any* pull downwards, but by the fact that it overcomes this pull, indeed makes it into the *means* of its elevation' (Schelling 1833: 177/173).

69. This is a distinction Schelling himself makes in many places, perhaps most memorably in the Stuttgart Seminars: 'The most profound essence of the human spirit – *nota bene*: only when considered in separation from the soul and thus from God – is madness [*der Wahnsinn*]. Hence madness does not originate but merely surfaces when what is properly non-being (i.e., the irrational) becomes an actuality and seeks to attain an essence and existence. In short, it is the irrational itself that constitutes the very foundation of our understanding. Consequently, madness is a necessary element, albeit one that is not supposed to manifest itself or become an actuality. What we call the understanding, if it is to be an actual, living, and active understanding, is therefore properly nothing other than a coordinated madness [*geregelter Wahnsinn*]. The understanding can manifest itself and can become visible only in its opposite, that is, in the irrational. Human beings devoid of all madness have but an empty and barren understanding. Here we find the source for the inverted proverb: *nullum magnum ingenium sine quadam dementia* [attributed by Seneca to Aristotle: 'no great genius has ever existed without some touch of madness'], as well as for the divine madness alluded to by Plato and the poets. That is, when madness is dominated by the influence of the soul [*durch Einfluss der Seele beherrscht ist*], it is a truly divine madness, and it proves the foundation of enthusiasm and efficacy in general. More generally, the understanding, if only it is a vigorous, living one, is properly speaking but a controlled, restrained, and coordinated madness [*beherrschter, gehaltener, geordneter Wahnsinn*]. To be sure, there are instances when the understanding is no longer capable of controlling the madness that slumbers in the depth of our being. Thus the understanding proves unable to console us when we feel intense pain. In that case, when spirit and temperament exist without the gentle influence of the soul, this primordial, dark force [*das anfängliche dunkle Wesen*] surfaces and seizes the understanding (i.e., a non-being relative to the soul), and madness emerges as a terrifying sign of the will when separated from God' (Schelling 1810a: 470/233). See also Schelling (1815a: 338–9/103–4).

70. The line of influence runs from Hegel on this point through Feuerbach to Rosenzweig and Buber and the twentieth-century philosophers of dialogue (Edmund Husserl, Hans-Georg Gadamer, Jozef Tischner, Karol Wojtyla, etc.). Thus Hegel is the father of dialogical philosophy.

71. On Levinas's critique of dialogical philosophy, see Levinas (1961: Section 1.B) and Bernasconi (2004).

72. It should be noted here that according to Schelling's late Satanology, Satan is not a creature or a being but a principle that hungers for being. This does not render evil unreal. Nor is evil an eternal principle opposing the good. Evil is the ground becoming obscenely actual, which it never fully achieves (since it is not possible), hence a wilful refusal and a hovering between nothingness and being, the ground refusing to ground, and overthrowing the order of nature, or striving to break the law of the ground. In himself, Satan has no actuality. He only achieves it insofar as he succeeds in finding an accomplice in the human being. See Schelling (1831: 634–61; 1854c: 241–74). Ultimately, the decision for good and evil, insofar as it is a personal act of free self-actualisation, is originally a human act, not an inherited proclivity that compels us. I shall discuss Schelling's Satanology in detail in the second book. On the late Schelling's understanding of evil as the negation of nature (the refusal of ground), see Wirth (2020).

73. In his theological classic, *The Crucified God*, Jürgen Moltmann opposes 'the analogical principle of knowledge', whereby like is known only by like (*similis a simili cognoscitur*, attributable to Empedocles), which he describes as knowing as anamnesis or within a closed circle, with 'the dialectical principle of knowledge', which he traces back to Hippocrates and ancient medicine: *contraria contrariis curantur* (the opposite is cured with the opposite). Citing the above passage from Schelling (1809: 373), Moltmann comments: 'This means that God is only revealed as "God" in his opposite: godlessness and abandonment by God. In concrete terms, God is revealed in the cross of Christ who was abandoned by God . . . The deity of God is revealed in the paradox of the cross. This makes it easier to understand what Jesus did: it was not the devout, but the sinners, and not the righteous but the unrighteous who recognised him, because in them he revealed the divine righteousness of grace, and the kingdom. He revealed his identity amongst those who had lost their identity, amongst the lepers, sick, rejected, and despised, and was recognised as the Son of Man amongst those who had been deprived of their humanity' (Moltmann 1973: 27).

74. See McGrath (2006b).

75. On Hegel's philosophy of religion, see Fackenheim (1967).

76. See Hegel (1807: 2): 'The more conventional opinion gets fixated on the antithesis of truth and falsity, the more it tends to expect a given philosophical system to be either accepted or contradicted; and hence it finds only acceptance or rejection. It does not comprehend the diversity of philosophical systems as the progressive unfolding of truth, but rather sees in it simple disagreements. The bud disappears in the bursting-forth of the blossom, and one might say that the former is refuted by the latter; similarly, when the fruit appears, the blossom is shown up in its turn as a false manifestation of the plant, and the fruit now emerges as the truth of it instead. These forms are not just distinguished from one another, they also supplant one another as mutually incompatible. Yet at the same time their fluid nature makes them moments of an organic unity in which they not only do not conflict, but in which each is as necessary as the other; and this mutual necessity alone constitutes the life of the whole.' See also Hegel (1827: 107–8).

77. Cf. Hegel (1827: 472): 'As to the empirical mode of the appearance, and investigations concerning the conditions surrounding the appearance of Christ after his death, the church is right insofar as it refuses to acknowledge such investigations; for the latter proceed from a point of view implying that the real question concerns the sensible and historical elements in the appearance [of Christ], as though the confirmation of the

Spirit depended on narratives of this kind about something represented as historical, in historical fashion.' See also Hegel (1827: 468): 'The history of the resurrection and ascension of Christ to the right hand of God begins at the point where this history receives a spiritual interpretation.' And Hegel (1827: 468, n. 204): 'The Church cannot undertake an investigation of it [the history of Christ] in a sensible manner.' This is not to say that the historical claim of Christianity is inessential for Hegel; on the contrary, it is crucial to the dialectic of the infinite and the finite that the transcendent God enter history and become immanent. See Fackenheim (1967: 154–5).

78. See Franks (2015).

79. Cf. Heidegger (1927a: 330). See McGrath (2010).

80. On this crucial point, see Tritten (2014: 1): 'Christ [according to Schelling] is not human *and* divine, but *neither* human *nor* divine, at least not as such. Humanity and divinity are rather the two *termini* or *relata* united by the differentiating enactment of the *Logos* as the copula itself. Copulation only unites by differentiating. Thus, humanity and divinity are not pre-given data to be combined in the incarnation, but are rather both consequents. The *Logos* is neither God the Father as the subject-term proper, who would accept the form of – i.e., acquire as a predicate-nominative – human nature, nor is the subject term Jesus of Nazareth, who would be predicated with divinity. To say that Christ is both human and God is neither to say that God became human (which tends toward Docetism) nor that a human became God (which tends toward Arianism). It rather says that that which is God is the same as that which is human. That which is already a middle nature, the *Logos* as copula, becomes God precisely by becoming human (a sort of monophysitism or Eutychianism that does not begin with two distinct natures but nevertheless ends with two natures).'

81. This insistence on God's redemptive work, before which we can only be passive, is a Lutheran theme in Schelling. God, for Schelling as much as for Luther, is always subject, never object, and redemption is God's work, not ours.

82. What Charles Marsh says of the theology of Dietrich Bonhoeffer can also be said of Schelling: 'The finite contains the infinite without loss of the propriety of their distinction precisely because Jesus Christ comes out of the impenetrable mystery of God into the resplendent multiplicity of the world to bring the world home to God without collapsing the difference between the two. In the homecoming is redemption – not the identification of God and world but the recovery of the divinity of God and the humanity of the person . . . God . . . is for the world without being the world. God is neither totally other than nor identical to the world but is together with the world because God remains God and humanity remains human' (Marsh 1996: 97–8). The redemption, for Schelling as much as for Bonhoeffer, does not abolish or immanentise transcendence. Not all forms of transcendence are alienating.

83. See Schelling (1804a: 142–3/144): 'Reason is the self-knowledge of the eternal identity. With this proposition, we have simultaneously defeated forever all subjectivization of rational knowledge . . . In reason all subjectivity ceases, and this is precisely what our proposition argues. In reason, that eternal identity itself is at once the knower and the known – it is not me who recognizes this identity, but it recognizes itself, and I am merely its organ.'

84. Kierkegaard (1844: 9–22).

85. See Husserl (1913: para. 4).

86. See Kant (1787: A 576, B 604).

87. I take this point to be further evidence of Schelling's alignment with the Greek Fathers, not only controversial figures such as Arius and Origen, but also canonical figures such

as Gregory of Nyssa. See Nyssa's notion of *epektasis*, or endless evolution in beatitude, in Von Balthasar (1995: 103): 'The infinity of the created spirit is an infinity in the process of becoming. It is an infinity "of endless growth", "an infinity that, in all the eternities piled on eternities, draws near him . . . who is The-Always-Greater" [citations from Gregory of Nyssa, *In Cant.* 8; I, 941 B.]'

88. Aristotle, *Metaphysics*, Book 10, 1051b25.

89. Prajñāpāramitāhṛdaya Sutra in Cowell et al. (1894: 147–8).

90. See Tillich (1910: 101): 'If it could remain in the contemplative life, the ego might find refuge with this merely ideal God. "But the ego must be permitted to act . . . and with that the former despair returns, for its duality is not annulled (11:559f.)."'

91. That Schelling may have changed his view on mysticism in later years and become more pessimistic about its possibilities is a distinct possibility. See the Fragments to the first draft *Weltalter* for a more positive assessment (Schelling 1811: 214–15/196–8). Joseph Lawrence's introduction and translation of these texts underscores the religious nature of Schelling's thought at the time of his turn to the positive. See, in particular, Schelling's use of the Eckhartian term *Lauterkeit*, which Lawrence translates as 'lucid purity'. '*Lauterkeit* . . . is a word that will be familiar to readers of Meister Eckhart. It refers primarily to the sheer emptiness of eternity before time, that is, eternity so deeply conceived that it can be said neither to be, nor not to be. Secondarily, it refers to that place in the soul that is fully unified with the eternal. In his own commentary on the word [Schelling 1811: 214–15/196–7], Schelling emphasises that, to the degree that we know things through their qualities, *Lauterkeit* has to be regarded as unknowable, for in its naked purity it has no qualities. At the same time, it is knowable in a certain fashion, to the degree that a person can uncover his or her own purity, recalling, as it were, the condition of the soul before birth. This does not mean that it is knowable solely through an act of introspection, for one recognises it in the innocence of a child or in the honesty and integrity one occasionally encounters in others. It is because of such outward manifestations of *Lauterkeit* that I have described the purity it entails as "lucid" (a word, by the way, that shares an etymological root with the German *lauter*). Schelling even goes so far as to depict *Lauterkeit* as entailing a lucent luminosity that is too intense for mortals to withstand . . . More pristine than something that has been purified, its innermost being remains "untouched", even when it is held captive by the conflicting forces of reality. What he is referring to is something that has impressed mystics in every culture. There is a dimension within the soul that is so completely unified with the eternal that it remains untouched even when a person is subject to active torture' (Lawrence 2019: 49).

92. See Torwesten's summary of the Vedantic critique of the misuse of yoga in Torwesten (1991). Schelling does not appear to recognise the contemplative Christian distinction between meditation as a practice, an ascetic discipline, which is our responsibility and as such of non-ultimate significance (a 'work'), and contemplation as a gift of the personal God (a 'grace'), undeserved and always a surprise. Meditation is the mystic's practice of preparing the self for contemplation, the experience of union with God which is never an achievement and is always available. Maybe we cannot reach the living God through mystical practices, but God can reach us through mysticism. Schelling's early references to the experience of God (see above all the *Clara* and the Stuttgart Seminars) speak of an impersonal immersion in the absolute. Schelling does not appear to have much sympathy with what we might call non-dialectical personal mysticism, mystical union that is a free act of two who draw near to each other in contemplative experience. The Cistercian monk Thomas Merton wrote about little else. See, for example, Merton (2007).

Chapter 3

The Decision

'I want that which is above being.' Schelling, *Darstellung der reinrationalen Philosophie*

What for Hegel is a rational move, the transition from essence to existence, is for Schelling a moral imperative that neither logic nor phenomenology can decide for us. The move from negative philosophy to
positive philosophy, from essence to existence, which leads the philosopher to the truth of history, is an act of will (Schelling 1842d: 132/182;
1833: 165/166–7). The turn to the positive is contingent on the decision of the philosopher. While the turn is reasonable, there is nothing irrational about refusing the move, about deciding otherwise. As in
Schelling's earliest, Fichtian phase of philosophy, the path of thinking
one chooses rests on a practical judgement.[1] That said, Schelling II has
travelled miles beyond both Spinozism and transcendental philosophy.
The ontological difference between nature and God introduced in 1809
determines a fundamentally new assessment of the limits of reason.
Reason is not limited by the kind of data it can conceive; it is limited by
its relation to its origin. What lies beyond it is its beginning and its end.
Moreover, these limits need not be recognised; they are not demarcated
from within epistemology, logic or phenomenology. Reason is now conceived, not as the absolute, but as that which *could* be absolutised. If
there is no strictly rational passage from negative to positive philosophy, there is also no necessity to acknowledge the positive whatsoever.
From a psychoanalytical perspective the late Schelling is describing with
impressive accuracy the structure of a neurotic subjectivity whose identity is constituted by ideological disavowal. The symbolic is a place of
familiarity and comfort; the real can be so deeply disavowed, it hardly
registers.

Notwithstanding the early intuition of two paths of philosophy (a characteristic mantic moment in Schelling's development), it took three decades of false starts before Schelling struck on the true import of the decisional foundation of philosophy. Nature-philosophy could not of its own resources achieve the self-critical standpoint of positive philosophy, for it had rejected the starting point of the needed critique of the negative: finite subjectivity. In its healthy enthusiasm for the objective in an age of increasing subjectivism, for the being of things that actually, materially become, and in some sense undeniably are, nature-philosophy left the finite subject behind. What was needed, after Hegel, and in some sense after nature-philosophy, was a new post-Kantian account of subjectivity, which squarely reckoned with reason's self-absolutising pretensions, and a historical subject, not a transcendental subject, that is, a subject that *exists*, and that does not, therefore, need to climb out of itself to find the real. Nature-philosophy, in spite of its pregnant insights into the reality of the objective subject-object, could not of its own resources prevent the Hegelian mistake. As Hegel himself argued, Schellingian nature-philosophy is the presupposition of his system.[2] After Hegel, Schelling needed to rethink the whole question of nature and find a starting point for philosophy, which could secure itself against idealism by recognising both the finitude of subjectivity and the objectivity of reason, a new beginning which admitted the limits of reason while still affirming its exteriority as 'nature'.

To correct Hegel's error, Schelling needed to work in a different register, that of historical theology. Here he found exactly what he needed: a doctrine of finitude, constituted by a strong notion of history, and a new account of morality which sees in reason's tendency to deny its exteriority nothing less than the original sin of humankind. Just as in the biblical account, sin is more than a moral mistake – in the account of Genesis, it is the fall of nature as such, a cosmic event – so too is the solution to sin much more than a rational strategy. It is *redemption*, nothing that we could do for ourselves, but something that must be done, if it is to be done, for us. The turn to the positive is the existential, but still hypothetical, acceptance of redemption (herein lies the problem with the late Schelling that Kierkegaard will attack, and which I shall discuss in the second book). The one who works in a positive register lets himself be taken up into the overcoming of necessity effected by the Christ event. Everything thus comes together for Schelling in the positive philosophy, and one begins to grasp the reason for his unflagging enthusiasm for the project, sustained over four decades, despite the difficulties he faced in completing it: the freedom of philosophy, the spirituality of nature, the objectivity of reason, the transcendentality of the act of individuation, the reality of evil and the notion of personality as the overcoming of necessity. It all came together for him when he himself decided, sometime between 1804 and 1809, to consider seriously the possibility that the New Testament was true, not a series of uplifting metaphors, not a picture book of rational truths which philosophy must liberate from their representational husks, but a true account of *the* historical event, the Christ event, which singularly in the annals of religion and mythology reveals the meaning of history, and with it, that which is true in all religions.

Revelation as possibility

The first major pillar of the late Schelling's thought is the theorem of absolute transcendence, a thought which still eluded him in his middle period (the sea monster with which he struggled throughout the 1811–15 drafts of *The Ages of the World*), but which came into sharp focus for him in his Erlangen period (1820–27), when he first defined the idea of the ecstasy of reason (SW 9: 207–52, 303–52). Reason confronting the real is always ecstatic, outside itself, because the truth transcends it, leads it beyond itself, in a never ending ascent into divinity. The thought is essentially Platonic, and one sees Schelling toying with it at various points in his career, even if the full recognition of the finitude of reason in the face of the truth is a position restricted to his late work.[3] The theorem of absolute transcendence, reconstructed from a variety of Schellingian statements, runs thus. Any identifiable structure, any system of relations, any ordering of things whatsoever, such as the system of reason (the ordering of the three potencies), nature or the order of history, is always horizoned by an excess, an unnameable X which is at once recognised as the condition of the possibility of the structure, *and* as that which cannot appear as a term in the structure, as that which is not, as such, structured. In the middle period the theorem of absolute transcendence is broached under the theme of the indivisible remainder, but this phrase has been too often repeated, and is now too associated with Lacanian cynicism (after Žižek, who does not think of the Lacanian real when they hear it?), such that it would be advisable to proceed without it. That which transcends order is neither ordered nor disordered, neither good nor bad, neither desirable nor undesirable, neither pleasant nor horrifying. All of these terms are consequent to the transcendent, and none are therefore applicable to it. We cannot, therefore, conclude with Žižek that because of the indivisible remainder, subjectivity is a constitutive lie. We cannot, that is, conclude that the transcendent is the repressed in Freud's sense of the term, because we cannot decide *a priori* whether it threatens or enlivens us. We must risk a decision on this issue, and this is the axial decision that will divide thinkers into two broad camps, those who still hope in the ultimate, and those who have resigned themselves to the relative; but this decision is not a deduction, a certainty or a foundation. It is always a personal risk, a willing to be such and such a kind of person, who is such because he or she has decided to live in a certain kind of world.

The absolutely transcendent is not an impersonal first principle – a principle we might aspire to get behind. In this way Schelling breaks with what we might call the *philosophia mystica perennis*, from the Vedas to Eckhart, the mystical-speculative discourse that subordinates personal existence to the impersonal absolute. What transcends absolutely, according to Schelling, is the personal as such, for nothing is more free than personality. Knowledge of the personal, knowledge of what we do not and cannot through ordinary means know, is strictly speaking revelation. 'Revelation . . . is expressly conceived as something which presupposes an *Actus* outside of consciousness, and a relation which the most free cause, God, grants or has granted to the human consciousness not out of necessity but in complete freedom' (Schelling 1854c: 3). This sentence is probably the most important in the entirety of both volumes of the Philosophy of Revelation. Where the first part of the sentence could have been written by the early Schelling, the *Naturphilosoph*, the second part exceeds the scope of his early speculation. The self-manifestation of *natura naturans* in the forms of the nature we see, hear and feel certainly presupposes an *Actus* outside of consciousness, an intelligibly real, 'outside', transcendental subjectivity. It is for this reason that nature-philosophy finds transcendental philosophy incomplete and calls for its supplementation in a philosophy that begins in the objective subject-object. Fichte's mistake, to see nature as nothing more than the negative of spirit (without its own intrinsic logic), is perpetuated by Hegel for whom nature is external to logic or logic-poor (Schelling 1833: 152/153). Nature, broadly conceived as an infinite inhibition of infinite production by an infinity of finite natural products – that is, the universe itself – *is* a revelation in some sense, no doubt. In the Freedom Essay and the Stuttgart Seminars, Schelling calls Christianity a 'second revelation', nature is the 'First Testament' (Schelling 1809: 411/72; 1810a: 463/228). The last part of the above sentence – 'and a relation which the most free cause, God, grants or has granted to the human consciousness not out of necessity but in complete freedom' – this, at least, is no longer nature-philosophy. Between these two phrases of the sentence lies the whole problem. We must first of all recognise that the late Schelling comes to see matters differently than he presented them in 1799: although nature may be conceived as a self-manifesting, objective infinite, it is still less than the really existing and self-revealing God. In short, nature is revealed to be limited to the degree that it is recognised as horizoned by transcendence.

The way in which Schelling's views on the question of transcendence evolved rapidly in his middle period can be seen by comparing the 1809 Freedom Essay with the 1806 *Aphorisms*, a text which is replete with anticipations of positive philosophy but which is most notable for its difference from it. In 1806 Schelling writes, 'There is no revelation either in science, religion, or art higher than that of the divinity of the universe; indeed, they begin only with this revelation and have meaning solely through it' (Schelling 1806: n. 1). Schelling here appears to deny the very concept of personal, divine revelation which will be the basic assumption of the positive philosophy. While he will continue to maintain that revelation, which is properly understood as a free self-disclosure, not a necessary movement of becoming manifest, begins with the 'revelation' of the universe, and has meaning through that revelation (i.e., through objective reason), the genuinely divine revelation reveals precisely the opposite of the claim advanced in the *Aphorisms*, namely, that the universe is *not* God, and that the manifestation of the universe ('revelation' in a loose sense) is transcended by the self-disclosure of the Trinity. As a free act of a (divine) person, revelation is not a necessary natural occurrence, not a 'product' in the *naturphilosophische* sense of the term, but an act of will directed at another person, one who is invited to recognise it or not (Schelling 1854b: 3). The knowledge of God we have through revelation should therefore be clearly distinguished from knowledge of God through nature or through reason's reflection upon itself. 'There is a philosophical cognition that transcends nature' (Schelling 1854b: 192). Could Schelling be more explicit? We cannot, *a priori*, even reach a knowledge of the most humble bit of historically existing matter. History as such is entirely veiled to nature-philosophy. And yet in revelation, freedom is revealed, and the freedom of the will, which is in some confused way experienced everyday, is lit up, validated and rendered coherent by the revelation of divine freedom. With the revelation of freedom, history is revealed, positive existence is revealed, and the contingency of being, the non-identity of essence and existence, is revealed. Only with the theorem of absolute transcendence does the historical disclosure of a free creator become possible. Whether or not revelation must first occur in order for transcendence to become plausible, or the other way around, is a wrongheaded question. There is no logical order that initiates the positive philosophy. Everything depends upon the individual's free decision to ask the question about God, and to really mean it. The decision is not founded upon a knowledge of transcendence, as in traditional natural theology; the decision opens up the horizon of transcendence. It is only with this decision that the question of revelation as such becomes coherent.

Revealed religions presuppose the existence of a *personal* God, not the old man in the sky of children's catechisms, but the infinitely free will and intelligence that has created the universe. This God is not known through inferences on the basis of the things that God has made.* To attempt to come to know the personality of God by looking at the things God has made is as inconclusive as attempting to know something about the character of Rembrandt from his artworks. Like any person, God can only be known in God's self-expressive acts, acts that constitute history as such. All of history is believed to reveal the personal God, but special historical events, which are revealed events *sensus strictus*, reveal the revealedness of history as such. These revealed events are non-ordinary sources of knowledge that transcend reductively empirical and scientific methods of legitimation. Writing towards the middle of the nineteenth century, with historical-critical methodology developing around him simultaneously in multiple academic disciplines, Schelling is aware of a growing consensus of scientific resistance to the topic of revelation.[4] It would seem that the way to historically-critically investigate revealed religions is to study the practices and beliefs of believers in suspension of any religious truth claims. One should use social scientific methods to catalogue and analyse the texts of those religions as one would any other literature. This would mean refusing in advance any supernatural explanations of so-called revealed truths or stories recounting extraordinary events, such as the parting of the Red Sea or the resurrection of the Christ, while investigating the sociohistorical conditions attending the production of those texts. The most that scholars of religion who pursue this line can do is conclude that the first Christians, the writers of the New Testament texts, *believed* that Jesus was divine and had redeemed the world through his death and resurrection. Whether Jesus was divine or not could not be decided or even investigated.[5]

The problem with this apparently modest, scientific and open-minded approach, which Schelling tackles head on, is that such an attitude is anything but neutral; suspension of belief in revelation is not equally a suspension of disbelief: on the contrary it is at least implicitly a confession of disbelief, for it is a denial of the *possibility* of revelation. Moreover, disbelief distorts its object (another scientific violation), for the texts and their writers are not permitted to speak for themselves. An academic study of religion that is methodologically committed to suspending *any* positive judgement concerning the truth of revelation has pre-decided the matter in advance. The investigation cannot end in affirmation because it is grounded in an *a priori* denial. In opposition to this mounting scepticism, Schelling's Philosophy of Revelation proposes to test the plausibility of a *positive* affirmation of the revelation. He has not decided the outcome of the investigation in advance, and rejects any pre-judgement against the

---

*Cf. Rom 1:20.

possibility of revelation as basically unphilosophical, or better, unscientific, just as the theological pre-judgement for the reality of revelation is also unscientific. The philosopher of revelation *hypothesises* that a revealed text is what it purports to be, a revelation, and looks to see what explanatory power that hypothesis possesses. Schelling asks the question: If revelation were true, what puzzling historical and empirical facts would thereby find an explanation? He does not assume the truth of revelation and on the basis of that assumption elaborate a doctrine of God. That is the method of theology. He tests out the explicative power of the revelation on certain philosophical, empirical and historical data, and on the basis of the test, assents to the revelation. The assent or refusal is probabilistic and falsifiable and therefore genuinely scientific.

To grasp the sceptical quality of Schelling's approach to revelation it is enough to consider how it would have to be rejected by any proponent of the traditional theological view that faith is the condition of the possibility of assent to revelation. Theologians of revelation such as Hans Urs von Balthasar or Karl Barth, or, for that matter, Aquinas, would ultimately have to reject Schelling's Philosophy of Revelation for one simple reason: Schelling denies that a particular gift of faith is still the necessary presupposition for grasping, understanding and assenting to the revelation. They would see that to follow Schelling in this respect is to declare the end of the Church as the guardian and authoritative interpreter of revelation, and they would be correct.[6] Schelling agrees with the historical-critical researcher of religion that a faith-based approach to revelation can never be legitimate as science. So long as theology remains the special work of a group of thinkers who have been particularly gifted to carry it out, a revealed truth can never become a universal human truth, that is, it can never be a scientific truth. The theological claim that the assent to revelation presupposes faith is tantamount to saying that a certain kind of philosophy, that is, a general account of being based on a reasonable perspective, one that appeals to all reasoning people as such and asks of them no more than that they should reason well about these matters, is shut out from the discussion.

Alongside his opposition to theologies of revelation, we should also recognise Schelling's distance from any psychology of revelation, any ostensibly Christian philosophy or theology that translates faith into psychological terms by speaking of a *feeling* of conviction, an immediate *felt* certainty that ostensibly founds belief in revelation.[7] For Schelling, this psychologising of the revelation still leaves the knowledge of redemption cloistered in a community of the chosen. Moreover, it remains as philosophically indefensible as any assertion that refuses to move beyond immediate experience. The one who believes in the truth of revelation because he or she *feels* convinced of it is no better, no more reasonable, than the one who believes the opposite on the basis of an immediately felt conviction.

> One will demand from it [negative philosophy] the *actual* God, not the mere idea of God. How will it furnish this, which within its philosophy is left standing as something unknowable? To begin with, it will perhaps say: 'The God that is in reason is a mere idea, and must become real for us through feeling.' But then what? If one for whom this bankruptcy of reason is unacceptable – because it is acceptable for him to limit his thoughts to the sensible world – if this person uses the appeal to feeling to show that the real God is but a creation of our emotions and of the heart, of our power of imagination, and that he is altogether nothing objective – then will not only Christianity but also *every* religious idea have at the very most a psychological significance? (Schelling 1842d: 154/197–8)

From this passage, it is clear that revelation for Schelling is not a privileged experience of those granted faith or those gripped by an inexplicable feeling, but an extraordinary and communally witnessed case of an ordinary happening: the manifestation of a personality (albeit a divine personality, or even, as we shall see, *divine personalities*) through acts in time expressive of it. Every person is an abyssal font of freedom who reveals his or her character in acts in time, and who, to that degree, can never be anticipated or known *a priori*. The revealed God would be infinitely higher and superior to any human person, the maximal case of the being that can only be known *a posteriori*, the one whose self-revelation is carried out by means of the creation and redemption of the world. The revelation of this God in history no longer requires special categories to be interpreted: it has penetrated our thinking to the point that the separation of the history of philosophy from the history of theology is no longer tenable. The foundation of Schelling's Philosophy of Revelation is a philosophical cognition which makes revelation comprehensible by showing what can be comprehended by means of it. In this regard Schelling's late philosophy represents a rehabilitation of the pre-Nicene idea of Christian gnosis, which was never about esoteric or mystical knowledge, but about *revealed* knowledge.

Ever since Emmanuel Levinas and Michel Henry in France made it a phenomenological theme in the second half of the twentieth century, and Jean-Luc Marion made an industry of defending it against Dominique Janicault's critique of '*le tournant théologique*', revelation has become a problem for philosophy once again.[8] The phenomenological legitimacy of revelation has been variously defended by contemporary French philosophers: as a limit concept of phenomenality necessary if the latter is to be defined as such; as the visibility of the invisible; as the index of the non-representable, or as the inverse intention, which delimits transcendental subjectivity from within; and finally and perhaps most emphatically, as a 'saturated phenomenon'. All of these phenomenologies of revelation converge on the notion of revelation as that mode of givenness for which subjective constitution is not only lacking; transcendental subjectivity, if allowed to pre-decide the issue, becomes distortive of the revealed, and hence must let itself be overwhelmed by it, saturated, or at any rate put into question. What was fresh about the French turn is that it broke with Heidegger's phenomenological moratorium on theological themes and insisted, against Heidegger's arbitrary edict prohibiting God-talk, that revelation is also a philosophical problem.[9] To discuss revelation as the free self-disclosure of God is for Heidegger to overstep the boundaries of philosophy, which assumes atheism as a methodological principle, and to ingress on the proper work of theology, which works on an opposed assumption, and elaborates an ontic mode of being-in-the-world, the existentiell of faith. Levinas, Henry and later, Marion, all take exception to the Heideggerian effort to foreclose the range of philosophical questioning, and on decisively phenomenological grounds. The universal method of phenomenology, first defined by Husserl in his principle of principles, which no phenomenologist has totally rejected, stipulates that any pre-judged decision about what could or could not constitute a phenomenon will always be arbitrary, metaphysical or dogmatic (Husserl 1913: section 24).

It will be evident that the philosophy of religion of the late Schelling belongs to this discussion, both because of the similarity of content (revelation as possible), and because of the traceable influence of Schelling's Philosophy of Revelation on French thought through the translations of Marquette and Courtine (Schelling 1991). This is not the place for an extended discussion of the French reception of Schelling.[10] Let it suffice to briefly compare and contrast Schelling's philosophical approach to the question of revelation with Marion's. In *Being Given*, Marion states the issue clearly:

> The very concept of revelation belongs by right to phenomenality, and even to contest it, it is appropriate to see it. *Here*, I am not broaching revelation in its theological pretension to the truth, something faith alone can dare to do. I am outlining it as a possibility – the ultimate possibility, the paradox of paradoxes – of phenomenality, such that it is carried out in a possible saturated phenomenon. The hypothesis that there was historically no such revelation would change nothing in the phenomenological task of offering an account of the fact, itself incontestable, that it has been thinkable, discussable, and even describable. (Marion 2002: 5)

Marion is explicit: he is not talking about the *actuality* of revelation but of its *possibility*. Phenomenology, with its methodological commitment to givenness, cannot foreclose this ultimate possibility, because phenomenology is the science of possibilities. Insofar as it is thinkable as a possibility, revelation is given to phenomenology to think. Marion is not speaking of the *fact* of a divine revelation, or making a case for any particular revelation;

he is speaking of the possibility of an overwhelming of subjectivity by 'the thing itself', a 'saturation' of our expectations and our predetermined sense for what is or is not possible. The ultimate possibility would include, for example, the Sinai experience of Moses, the revelation given to Muhammad, and by implication other varieties of religious experience, for example the visions and locutions of saints and mystics, as well as non-religious phenomena, in particular aesthetic phenomena. Revelation belongs to the overarching category of saturated phenomena, in short the class of all phenomena in which subjectivity is experientially overwhelmed by the object.

The question of revelation for Marion, then, centres on the relation of the subject's transcendental horizon to a possible object. In Kant, as in Husserl's phenomenology, this has been conceived primarily as a unidirectedness, from the subject to the object. The subjective horizon makes the object possible. As in Kant, where the *a priori* forms of space and time make possible all spatial and temporal things, transcendental subjective horizons of possibility for Husserl set up fields of determinate experience, within which objects can appear. The object is the *noema* of a *noesis*, the *intentum* of an *intentio*.[11] Constitutive of what the I can experience is how the I experiences anything at all, and this how is not a determination of the object alone, it is a determination of the subject intending the object as the kind of object it is. I intend the object as, for example, spatial, or as purely internal, as a memory, or as a fiction. The *as* structure of intentionality sets up the situation within which the object is what it is. Hence there are no real surprises for intentional subjectivity. The key to the understanding of what appears is still hidden in subjectivity.

Marion's saturated phenomenon breaks this circle of intentional predetermination. Because the saturated phenomenon overwhelms the subjective conditions for a possible object, it appears as a non-appearance. 'The I cannot *not* see it, but it cannot look at it like an object either' (Marion, cited in Horner 2001: 144). Saturated phenomenality amounts to a reconceiving of the notion of intuition. No longer restricted to either the direct perceptual grasp of a sensible content, or to the direct grasp of an ideal object, intuition is expanded to include the non-perceptual and un-objectifiable. The sense of the intuition is not that the I grasps X, but that X gives itself to the I. In the giving, the conditions of the gift rest with the giving. Like a genuine gift, the given gives itself entirely on its own terms, without meeting or requiring any anticipation or reciprocation from the subject. Marion does not hereby deny the transcendental fore-structure of human subjectivity, intentionality and *a priori* horizonality. He denies that the transcendental fore-structure of subjectivity is absolute and unbreachable. Is it not possible, he asks, to imagine a phenomenon that is irreducible to whatever the subject is inclined to see in it, a phenomenon that constitutes the ego rather than being constituted by it, the possibility of a phenomenon in which intuition gives more than any act of consciousness could ever intend? In such a case a reversal would occur of common-law intentional experience. The revealed phenomenon is not determined by an *intentio*; the *intentio* is determined by the phenomenon. The subject in these instances is no longer the ground of what it experiences. He or she becomes a 'witness'.

Along such a line of argumentation Marion concludes that as a possibility, phenomenology must reckon with revelation. Phenomenology cannot, in the style of Heidegger, or even more emphatically in Janicaud, foreclose the question and remain faithful to the principle of principles, which is to let the given determine how it should be thematised. However, Marion has not broken entirely with the Heideggerian theological moratorium, and this is crucial for underscoring his difference from Schelling: as an *actuality*, revelation is a subject for theology alone; about it, Marion insists, philosophy can say nothing, positive or negative. The phenomenology of saturation supports rather than supplants the theology of revelation, much as the revised Aristotelianism of the Scholastics supported medieval theology. While the discussion of inversion and saturation are of direct relevance to the interpretation of Schelling's concept of the ecstasy of reason – Marion approximates the Schellingian idea of an *experiential* transition from negative to positive philosophy, of a positive experience within the limits of the negative (but crucially without the decision) – Schelling goes much further than merely affirming revelation as a *possibility*. He would question why Marion regards the act of considering revelation to be true as reserved for faith. Despite its promising thought experiments, Schelling would ultimately regard Marion's phenomenology as still only negative philosophy. Schelling is from the outset concerned with revelation as *fact*, revelation as *event*, not only possible, but actual. To think of revelation as merely a possibility of inverse intention, saturation or absolute givenness is not to think the Jewish-Christian revelation at all, and this, above all, is what Schelling purports to do. One cannot understand the Mosaic tradition or the New Testament without recognising that the writers of these traditions, as distinct from myth makers, were not *expressing* religious subjectivity but *narrating* objective historical events.

Anticipating the French turn, especially Levinas, Schelling argues that there is nothing irrational about the notion of revelation just as there is nothing indefensible about the existence of a personal, that is, self-revealing God. God may not necessarily exist, but God's existence is not *a priori* impossible. While God remains possible, revelation too remains possible, that is, thinkable. Going much further than Levinas and Marion, however, Schelling ventures into a historical-critical consideration of the possibility that revelation has in fact happened, and that this happening is the best explanation of history as such. The evidence for or against a factual revelation must be considered *a posteriori*, and not decided in advance. A genuinely scientific approach to revelation, according to Schelling, proceeds philosophically, for it takes seriously the possibility that revelation is true, and on the basis of that possibility gives an account of reality on the hypothesis that revelation has in fact occurred. This does not amount to an apodictic proof of the revelation. Neither is it confessional theology in the sense of an intra-ecclesial account without universal significance. The Philosophy of Revelation is hypothetical in the sense that as philosophy, it remains open to the possibility of falsification, while nevertheless demonstrating the explanatory power of revelation, which in turn counts for evidence in its favour. The Philosophy of Revelation is not a confessional explanation of the presuppositions of revealed religion (not *fides quaerens intellectum*); it is a universal and to that degree scientific reconstruction of the whole of history (natural and human) in the light of revelation. It takes the form: if revelation were true then certain facts would be made intelligible. But these facts are made intelligible by positing the truth of revelation. Therefore we have reasons for considering revelation as true, and therefore, reasons for reading revealed texts on their own terms.

Long before Henry, Levinas and Marion, Schelling broke with the widespread academic prejudice that revelation is not possible, and he did so on phenomenological or experiential grounds. His Philosophy of Revelation also challenges the phenomenological judgement, from Heidegger to Marion, that revelation as *actual* belongs outside the bounds of philosophy as such. One must recognise, in this regard, that Schelling is a speculative philosopher to the end, and while his work is replete with phenomenological insight, he is not afraid to risk logical deductions, explanations or a 'magnificent declaration' of what might be the case (Schelling 1842d: 183/133). A phenomenology of saturated phenomenality would never be enough for Schelling, for it leads ineluctably to a question that it cannot answer. Given that it is not impossible that God has revealed Godself, what evidence is there in history that God has *in fact* revealed Godself?

The inverted idea

Positive philosophy begins at the threshold between the negative and the positive, at the place of decision itself, with one foot in the negative and another tentatively stepping beyond it. The beginning is not a concept, but a non-concept, not an existent that exists thus and so, or an essence that can be conceived, but an act of existence dirempted of essence. We cannot think such a thing, we can only decide for it. The transition from the negative to the positive philosophy is an act of will that prefers the unknown and unknowable over the merely conceptual. We could say of this act of will that it is a letting go of control, a letting be (*Gelassenheit*). In the posthumous *Darstellung der reinrationalen Philosophie*, the act is willed by the reasoner who wants more than the negative and who wills a philosophy of being, not just of reason.

> I want the God beyond the idea . . . This wanting refers only to the transition [from the negative]. What positive philosophy itself begins with is A°, which is detached from its precondition and declared the prius; as the whole free of the idea, it is the pure that [*das rein Daß*]. (Schelling 1854a: 570)

The decision for the positive is the 'ecstasy of reason', first defined in Schelling's 1821 Erlangen lecture (Schelling SW 9: 230).[12] This act of will is the heart of Schelling's 1833 objection to Jacobi's doctrine of 'feeling'. Schelling approves of Jacobi's protest against absolute idealism, but he believes that it needs to lead to an act. He reformulates the Jacobian objection to idealism in striking language. 'I do not want this result. I find it revolting. It goes against my feeling . . . The first declaration of [positive] philosophy (which even precedes philosophy) *can* in fact only be the expression of a wanting' (Schelling 1833: 166–7/165). Even more existentially, Schelling adds, 'I do not *like* it, I do not want it, I cannot bring it into accord with myself' (Schelling 1833: 166/165). Where Jacobi was content to leave his feeling for the personal God on the level of protest and 'nonphilosophy', Schelling argues that this desire for the real God can found a new form of science when it leads to 'a real deed' (Schelling 1833: 167/165).

The desire is intentional, it has an object, even if its object is that which is not yet known, and cannot be pre-conceived. In 1842 Schelling calls the *intentum* of positive philosophy 'the inverted idea' (*die umgekehrte Idea*) and argues that it alone is the absolute *prius*. He distinguishes it from the relative *prius* (the *a priori*), which is a secure possession of reason. The relative *prius* is the triadic system of potencies, which cannot *not* be thought, for they structure all thinking itself. To deny the potencies is just as much a performative contradiction as to deny the principles of identity, noncontradiction and excluded middle (the logical expressions of the potencies). The absolute *prius*, however, is not a potency or an *a priori* truth, that is, not a being whose existence must be necessarily (logically) affirmed, even if its existence cannot be doubted *a posteriori*. The inverted idea or the absolute *prius* is not found within thought at all but is rather the presupposition of thought.

Kant is, for Schelling, an irreversible transformation of the trajectory of philosophy, the one who puts philosophy itself into question in a totally unprecedented way. In lectures three and four of *The Grounding of the*

Positive Philosophy, Schelling notes that the Kantian distinction between the *a priori* and the *a posteriori* is the origin of his distinction between the negative and the positive, and that it was Kant's great contribution to first ask how the two sources of knowledge are structurally related. Schelling recommended that the students who remained in the Berlin lecture hall in his second year of lecturing on the positive philosophy (1842) read Kant's *Critique of Pure Reason* as a background preparation for his lecture course on the Philosophy of Revelation (Schelling 1842d: 33/111). Schelling rethinks all of the major questions of philosophy, from ontology to ethics, from the philosophy of history to theology, in the light of Kant. Most curious of all is Schelling's insistence that, notwithstanding his denial of Kant's limitation of knowledge to the sensible, and the related Kantian refusal of metaphysics, Schelling believes that the positive philosophy does not contradict Kant. While he demolishes the old 'dogmatising' philosophy, Kant leaves open the possibility of a positive philosophy. Kant refuses the move from the *a priori* to the *a posteriori* (the mistake of the ontological argument), but he never refuses the move from the *a posteriori* to the *a priori* (the argument of positive philosophy). Kant's unmasking of rationalist and idealist metaphysics as purely negative says nothing about a realist metaphysics that begins with existence. Thus Schelling claims his project to be entirely in line with Kant (Schelling 1842d: 51f./124f.).

> The question, therefore had to arise whether after the breakdown of the old metaphysics the *other* positive element is completely destroyed or whether – on the contrary – after the negative philosophy had been beaten down into a pure rationalism, the positive philosophy, now free and independent from the negative, must configure itself into its own science. (Schelling 1842d: 83/147)

There is no going back to philosophy before Kant for Schelling; we can only go forward and beyond him. What Schelling believes he has added to Kant is a positive account of how the transition from essence to existence in fact occurs: it happens by means of assertions (*Behauptungen*), which are not as such deductions or concepts but acts of the will venturing a total explanation of being. Thus the one who asserts something is already outside the purely conceptual and so does not need to pass from concept or essence to actuality and existence. It is hard to miss the pragmatist note here: the move beyond both transcendental philosophy and dogmatic metaphysics is a practice of reasoning, a way of acting in the world. The new metaphysics after Kant will neither be Hegel's absolute idealism, nor a return to the old metaphysical realism, which simply assumed exteriority: it will be, rather, a practical metaphysics that begins and ends in existence, and passes through the negative, the conceptual, as though through a detour, en route to a fuller understanding of *historical* existence which is at first not understood at all.

Schelling is never more elusive than in his discussion of the absolute *prius*. From 1831 to the end of his career, he calls it by various names: unprethinkable being (*unvordenkliches Sein*), being without potency (for it is preceded by nothing but is itself the absolute first), the pure that (*das rein Daß*), the *actus purus*, the real existent A^0, the blind act of being, and the absolutely transcendent being, so transcendent that it transcends even the being of God. As the absolutely first, the absolute *prius* is not experienced, at least not directly or immediately, for to experience anything at all is to experience something, a *that* which is given as a *what*. The question concerning the *prius* is a question that interrogates the being of being, the existence that precedes all essence, or the absolute fact, that there is something rather than nothing. I will quote Schelling at some length here, for nowhere else in his corpus is his reasoning so close and inscrutable:

> The positive philosophy starts out just as little from something that occurs merely in thought (for then it would fall back into the negative philosophy) as it starts out from some being that is present in *experience*. If it does not start out from something that occurs in thought, and, thus, in no way from pure thought, then it will start out from that which is before and external to all thought, consequently from being, but not from an empirical being. For we have already excluded this, in that empirical being is external to thought only in the very relative sense, to the extent that *every* being that occurs in experience inherently carries with it the logical determinations of the understanding, without which it could never even be represented. If positive philosophy starts out from that which is external to all thought, it cannot begin with a being that is external to thought in a merely relative sense, but only with a being that is *absolutely* external to thought. The being that is external to all thought, however, is just as much beyond all experience as it is before all thought: positive philosophy begins with the *completely transcendent being* and it can no longer be just a relative *prius* like the potency that serves as the basis of the science of reason. For precisely as potency – as *nonbeing* – it has the necessity to pass over into being, and, thus, I call it the merely relative *prius*. If that being from which positive philosophy proceeds were also merely relative then the *necessity* of passing over into being would inhere with its principle. Thus, through this principle, that being would be subordinated to the thought of a necessary movement and, consequently, the positive philosophy would fall back into the negative. If, therefore, the relative *prius* cannot be the beginning of the positive philosophy, then it must be the absolute *prius*, which has no necessity to move itself into being. If it passes over into being, then this can only be the consequence of a free act, of an act that can only be something purely empirical, that can be fully apprehended only *a posteriori*, just as every act is incapable of being comprehended *a priori* and is only capable of being known *a posteriori*. (Schelling 1842d: 126–7/178–9)

One of the many challenges in interpreting the above paragraph is that Schelling moves between two senses of being and does not always specify when he does so. He sometimes means being as essence (*quidditas* or *Washeit*), and at other times, being as existence (*quodditas* or *Dasheit*).

'Some being (*Seyende*) that is present in experience' is an essence (*quidditas*) given as existent. 'Being' (*Seyn*) 'which is before and external to all thought' is existence (*quodditas*) without essence – not that *an existent* can exist without essence but that *existence* as such is the presupposition for positing any essence, for to assert otherwise, to assert the primacy of essence over existence, is to fall into contradiction, to say that *something* (some essence) *is* and that that same something *is not* (does not exist) in the same respect at the same time. The potency that is a relative *prius* is 'non-being' in the sense of non-existent, essence that is not yet determined as existing, or as a possible being. To think being as non-existent is not to fall into contradiction because being is here thought as the *possibility* of existing in some way or another. The relative *prius* (here meant as −A, or first potency, determinability) 'has the necessity to pass over into being', not in the sense of the necessity to exist (for that way lies the ontological argument), but rather as the necessity to be a possible *something*. −A cannot be posited alone but only in conjunction with +A, that is, −A (determinability) *is* as the possibility to be *determined* (+A). But the absolute *prius* has no necessity to be a possible something because there is no possible being available to it which it could be: as absolutely first it is preceded by no possibilities by which it could be determined. Thus it exists without prior determination; in other words, it is absolute necessity. Hence it can only be known *a posteriori*, or more exactly, *per posterius* (through or by means of the posterior, its consequence).

We can only think of the absolute *prius* as *being itself*, as sheer existence, being that is always presupposed in any line of thinking. The first potency (−A) can only be because something else is, which is not a potency or a thought, but is rather the fact of being itself. The absolutely *prius* is existence as really distinct from essence, and as the presupposition of all essences. To single it out in this way, by remotion as it were – for we do not posit unprethinkable being or define it as we do a thing, we isolate it as that which remains when we deny all predicates of it – is not to say anything determinate about it at all. It is rather to negate determinacy and determinability, to say that it is prior to anything else. It is neither possible nor impossible, not because it exists necessarily, but because it is the presupposition of our own thinking about it.

Nothingness is in a certain way the horizon of unprethinkable being, and 'it' shows itself in the question, Why is there something rather than nothing? Nothingness cannot be posited or affirmed, for it is not a being; but neither can it be denied.[13] In this recognition of the nothing which profiles being, we grasp something of the facticity of being itself, its somehow or other being posited outside the nothing, its dependency on something which it does not command, pre-think or understand; reason is ecstatic, entirely outside itself. It points beyond all concepts to that which is not a concept but which must *be* somehow if any concepts are. Reason is stunned into silence before it, literally speechless or astonished (*erstaunt*):

> That which just – that which only – exists is precisely that which crushes everything that may derive from thought, before which thought becomes silent, and before which reason bows down; for thought is only concerned with possibility and potency; thus where these are excluded, thought has no authority. That which infinitely exists is precisely for this reason – because it is this – also positioned securely against thought and all doubt . . . thus, indubitably exists – that which can never perish, abiding and necessary, which above all endures, come what may and regardless of what happens. (Schelling 1842d: 161–2/202–3)

Luigi Pareyson notes how, in such passages, Schelling reverses the Platonic-Aristotelian thesis that wonder is the beginning of philosophy (Pareyson 2010: 481–540). For Schelling, wonder is not the beginning but the end of the positive philosophy. The beginning is not wonder, questioning, and so on, but silence, the 'stupor' of reason, its speechlessness before the incomprehensible and unprethinkable. Rendered mute by the unprethinkable, reason ceases its inner monologue and beholds with an intellect lacking any categories by which to determine or anticipate the phenomenon, that which is entirely excessive of reason. 'In positing this it becomes motionless, paralysed, *quasi attonita*, it is paralysed by that being which overpowers everything' (Schelling 1842d: 165/206). The purely existent being, the *actus purus*, existence without potency, which means without conceptual access, can only be approached via a reversal of the ordinary trajectory of thought, from possibility to actuality. With his departure from the Greek paradigm, Pareyson sees Schelling align with the Jewish alternative of the *mirabilis Deus* of Psalm 67, which finds its modern expression in Luther's concept of the 'astonishing God' (*der wundersamer Gott*) (Pareyson 2010: 498, n. 2). Rather than Greek *theoria*, which contemplates an order of things that confirms reason's innate categories, Jewish thinking stands astonished before the miraculous, and discovers the absolute freedom of God, manifest in His creation, which appears, not as emanation or necessity but as 'play'. Just so Schelling's positive philosophy begins with reason's speechless astonishment before the unexpected and initially inexplicable sheer existent.

> Going out of itself, it [reason] is guided by its own expectations, and by the time it attains its end, it is already too late. Setting out into unknown territory, it finds the area already occupied by a solitary and strange presence, that of the pure existent, which has nothing to do with the conceptual and which is itself the opposite of an idea; and faced with this, it stops, astounded and lost, paralysed and speechless, struck as much by its own failure as by this novel and unanticipated being. This is the moment of stupor, because reason cannot . . . find the power to return and resume its

path . . . from that moment, it habituates itself to the pure existent, to the point of giving it a name and recognizing it . . . [as] the Lord of being. (Pareyson 2010: 488)

In this ecstasy of reason Schelling finds the solution to the problem of modern philosophy, which is the problem of the narcissism of reason, or idealism. It is not a logical solution but an ethical one, for on the level of logic, idealism is entirely consistent. One must *engage* one's own existence and *decide* to put oneself into question in order to step outside the circle of the *a priori*. This existential engagement indicates the decision, the act of will, which undergirds the argument and places it on the terrain of the ethical. We can reconstruct Schelling's line of thinking here as a reversal of Descartes' ontological proof for the existence of God (Meditation Five). Schelling's argument is compressed into the following passage:

> That which just is [*das bloß Seyende*] is being [*das Seyn*] from which properly speaking, every idea, that is, every potency is excluded. We will, thus, only be able to call it the inverted idea [*die umgekehrte Idee*], the idea in which reason is set *outside* itself. Reason can posit being in which there is still nothing of a concept, of a whatness, only as something that is absolutely *outside itself* (of course only in order to acquire it thereafter, *a posteriori*, as its content, and in this way to return to itself as the same time). In this posting, reason is therefore set outside itself, absolutely ecstatic. (Schelling 1842d: 162–3/203)

In Cartesian terms, this amounts to a reversal of the *cogito ergo sum*, thus an anti-*cogito*. Descartes doubts everything outside his own thinking and endeavours to proceed from within thought itself to the establishment of an outside. Schelling doubts thinking itself, and proceeds from that which is absolutely outside thought. He does not commit the error of assuming that thought does not exist, he rather attempts to think how thought need not exist. He attempts to think the contingency of thinking, the miracle that there is thinking at all, when there need not be. Descartes discovers within reason a rich world of possibilities, innate ideas, which he assumes he has produced himself. The ontological argument is then used to build a bridge between the innate idea of the infinite to the exterior, to bring about the transition from essence to existence on the level of essence – the move from the negative to the positive – without ever leaving the negative. In the Third Meditation Descartes sees that he, the thinker, could not have produced the idea of infinity, since as a thinker who doubts and is vulnerable to deception, he is manifestly finite, and there cannot be more 'objective reality' in the effect than there is 'formal reality' in the cause. At this point, the thinker knows that there is something outside reason, even if he does not know that God exists: he knows that there is an external cause of the idea of infinity which he cannot deny exists in him. In effect, Schelling returns to this pivotal moment in modern philosophy, this decisive place where a possibility of realism occurs but is not pursued by Descartes. Descartes decides to reassert the threatened sovereignty of reason by remaining within the brackets of radical doubt and deducing the existence and nature of God through the ontological argument of Meditation Five. Schelling returns to this place of decision and says No to the temptation to idealise God. Schelling decides, first, that being is primary to thought (since it manifestly is [see Tillich 1910: 60: 'Doubt always presupposes true being']), and, second, that thought think this real being and not substitute for it its own innate ideas. We will not discuss in detail here Levinas's important observation that already in Meditation Three Descartes discovers that his epoché is an impossibility because the *existence* of the idea of the infinite present within his thinking is already an indication that he did not produce himself but depends upon an exterior.[14] Descartes *decides* to become the father of idealism, the one who proves that reason is sovereign over itself and apparently contains within itself all that it needs to begin, the whole world of ideas, as its own immediate content. What Schelling demonstrates is Descartes' disavowal of being in this move, the deliberate forgetting of the *sum* in his argument *cogito ergo sum*. Thinking may be given and self-productive in the *cogito*, but *the being* of the thinking – this is not produced by thinking, but is rather the presupposition of thought. Positive philosophy does not begin in idea, essence, whatness and possibility, as does Descartes, but in facticity, existence, thatness and reality, traces of which are already present to Descartes.

Let us try to reconstruct Schelling's inversion of the ideal in terms of an alternative Cartesian meditation. I do not need to climb through the ideal to find the real (which is in any case impossible). I am already in the real insofar as I regard myself not merely as abstract reason, as disembodied thinking, but as that which exists, that is, as a will (*Ursein ist Wollen, nicht Denken*). Now I posit, that is, I intend (or better, *I will*) that I am what I am, not that upon which all depends, the infinite being, but nothing more than the finite being which I experience myself as, one who wants and wills because he does not possess the fullness of the real. The presupposition of this act of will is the possibility, which I habitually actualise, but now will not to, the possibility of mistaking myself as sufficient unto being, as infinite and first. Instead of making the I the foundation of being, the Schellingian meditator posits the self as that which depends on something that is not self, as the I which depends on being in order to be able to say 'I am as that which has come to be.' This positing of the finite self is not a logical movement but a decision, that is, it is not a process that occurs logically in thinking but an act of willing. I could posit myself otherwise. By abstracting from my existence, I could posit myself as reason itself, as pure possibility, for I am also a reasoning being, not merely a willing being, and insofar as I am a reasoning being, I possess the idea of being as my own content. If I did so, that is, if I followed modern idealism, then I would remain in negative philosophy, but not in negative philosophy that knows itself as such; rather in a negative philosophy that disavows its own negativity, chooses not to know that reason is always the reasoning of a finite, willing existent. To know negative philosophy as negative is only possible for one who has already posited the positive; thus while negative philosophy has a logical priority to positive philosophy, positive philosophy has an existential priority to negative philosophy. Since it would still be I, the really existent finite being that I am, that would, with Descartes, posit itself as reason as such, negative philosophy's disavowal of its own negativity can only be an epoché of the real – which it is in Descartes – a suspension of not only the spontaneous and everyday judgement that things *are* and that they exist outside myself, but also a more primordial judgement, that 'something' is, and it is not me.

Since I now do not suspend the real but posit myself as real, which means since I *will* and know myself in my willing, I am already in the real. My very capacity for decision, for a free act, proves that I am more than thought: 'A free action is something more than what allows itself to be discerned in mere *thought*' (Schelling 1842d: 114/168). But how precisely do I posit myself *as finite*, that is, how do I posit myself without at the same time absolutising myself, without intending myself as the first being? How do I empty myself and thus stay in the act of willing *on the outside*, resisting the siren call of reason to enfold itself in itself and become absorbed in its own inner world? I do this, not by positing myself as real as such, that is, not by asserting myself, willing myself and insisting *I am*, but rather by willing another, and thereby negating myself, saying, 'It alone is, I am as though I were nothing.' To get to this moment of *kenosis* Schelling introduces an intermediate step, no less ecstatic than the recognition of the truly existing God, but not yet asserting the latter as such. I do not posit myself directly, but only indirectly, performatively, by deciding, acting and judging, not that *I am*, but that *that being*, which is not me, and upon which I depend, truly *is* and cannot not be (because it factically is). Not that being exists as modally necessary, but that being exists factically and indubitably, for if it was not, neither would I be. I posit, not the I but the sheer reality of being upon which the I depends for its existence, the being that has no priority in concept: the unprethinkable being which Descartes in Meditation Three briefly but clearly recognises as the extra-mental source of his idea of infinity. I posit this being purely negatively at first, as that which I am not, insofar as I can conceive myself and so have an *a priori* notion of myself. I posit being as that which has no apriority in thinking, which is the *prius* absolutely, and in that sense the groundless being, which I presuppose in any assertion of my own being.

Notice that it is not an *experience* of being that starts the positive philosophy: I do not *experience* sheer existence, the pure *that*; I *posit* it as that which is without any prior potency determining it. If it were an experience, sheer existence would be in part conceived, since nothing can be experienced without some degree of conceptualisation. And if it is in part conceived, then the being that is so conceived is not the unprethinkable being, the being that is wholly outside of reason, but rather a being that has an *a priori* concept adequate to it in reason. The pure *that* is in a way the *intentum* of an *intentio*, but a very peculiar intention, one that renounces *a priori* any possession of its *intentum*, thus the intention of the non-conceptual, and to that degree, an inverse intention (the inversion of intentionality).[15] This intention lets be rather than assigns a sense to what is. Reason in this act empties itself and gestures to that which it does not and cannot contain in itself, that is, it gestures to the factical condition of its own possibility. In the ecstasy of reason, thinking thinks itself as product, not producer, by endeavouring to think that which cannot be thought. In this decision, reason experiences itself as inadequate to the real, which is to say, reason experiences itself *as real*, that is, as existing by means of an act which is not its own.

The next question is somewhat inevitable, but no more logically compelled than was the decision to think the unprethinkable ground of determinate being. Does the absolute *prius* in fact hold sway as God?

What would it mean for eternal existence to be the ground of the personal God? At this point, it is necessary to speak in some detail of Schelling's various 'deductions' about how God might emerge from eternal existence (see Schelling 1830: 21–5; 1831: 32–8; 1841: 160–76; 1854a: 464f.; and the 1841 *Andere Deduktion der Prinzipien der positiven Philosophie*, SW 14: 335–67). We have seen how Schelling takes the Scholastic trope of *ens necessarium* and turns it upside down, to show that the exclusion of possibility from the *actus purus* means that it first exists without plan or design, and must be thought of as initially less than divine, as both absolutely necessary and radically contingent. How does Schelling propose to move from eternal, blind, existentially necessary and primordially contingent, unconscious existence to the free and personal God? According to 'the law of the world' (*das Weltgestz*), one of the late Schelling's most understated and yet most fundamental principles, which he calls in one place 'the only law' of pure reason,[16] eternal existence 'finds' itself confronted by the possibility of its other, the possibility of a being that *can be*, a being that could be, if it so wills, 'lord of being', that is, the possible God. 'It [the possible God] finds itself in the first [eternal existence] without its doing' (Schelling 1841: 162/127; cf. 1854b: 291ff.). The verb 'find' is key, and the nub of the difficulties associated with the idea. Eternal existence is not God and does not itself, indeed cannot, will that another shall be possible. In itself it lacks the consciousness needed to will anything. It is only through its other that primal being receives the consciousness to will and to act. 'The highest law of all being, which wants nothing to remain untried, and everything to be open, clear, and decided' (Schelling 1841: 168/135), requires that a cission occur in the night of unprethinkable existence, and the other to blind being appear as a possibility, as something that could be desired. The primal 'other' to blind being can only be deliberative being, intelligent and self-determining being, in a word, personal being, being 'as the ability to be' (*das Andere / Seynkönnende*; Schelling 1841: 169/136).

Schelling's justification for this move is a tangle of logic, Hebrew theology and Western esotericism,[17] and it is not clear which of these three has the upper hand. In any case, Schelling needs a mediator between eternal existence and God if he is to preserve divine freedom, a 'means' (*das Mittel*), whereby 'God frees Godself from unprethinkable existence' (*sich von dem unvordenklichen Sein zu befreien*) (Schelling 1841: 168/135). Eternal existence cannot will to be God because it is without will.[18] And since God cannot pre-exist God's decision to be God, there must be a mediator; 'something' or 'someone', a non-divine potency, must reveal all the possibilities available to being if it is to become the ground of God. Enter Sophia, the Hebrew personification of divine wisdom, the child who is with God from the beginning but is not identical to God (Prov. 8:22; Schelling 1841: 185/157). It falls to her to hold up a mirror to being, in which all possibilities are revealed.[19] In a particularly dense overlay of mythic associations, Schelling aligns Sophia with Fortuna Primigenia, the Roman goddess of luck, with Maya, the temptress in Eastern mythologies, with 'the wet nurse of the world', with the divine mother, and with matter in general.[20] We are here on well-mapped gnostic terrain; in particular, we are in the domain of the divine feminine. The way in which 'she' takes the lead in Schelling's theogony from the masculine 'lord of being' is worthy of note. She gives infinity something to will if it should decide to will at all, or perhaps we should say, she transforms desire into will and demands a decision.[21] In the *Urfassung*, the role of bringing the hidden to light and driving the undecided into decision is the prerogative of Satan, who is compared with the goddess Nemesis; Satan is not in himself evil, but compels others to decide between good and evil (Schelling 1831: 622).

Mythology aside, Schelling believes himself to be resolving a logical dilemma. If eternal existence is simply God from eternity, God is not free. But if, on the other hand, God is a *causa sui*, then God precedes God's own existence, which Schelling rejects as a contradiction (Schelling 1841: 166). Schelling's solution is to render God's necessity 'contingent' on God's own decision to be God. But the decision is itself preceded by the possibility of God being God, which God does not decide for *as possibility*, but which is 'legislated' by the law of the world, or more mytho-poetically, which is revealed by Sophia. In a way she precedes God, for she is the condition of God's decision. But there is no temporal succession in eternity. It is not that, at one time, eternal existence is alone, at a second moment with Sophia, and in a third moment transformed into the ground of God. With the Sophianic showing of possibility, the event of grounding has already occurred. Schelling does not speak of a birth of God in 1841, but birth is certainly implied by the primacy of the feminine, the notion of the material substratum (*hypokeimenon*) of divinity, and the decidedly esoteric approach to the figure of the mother of God. Schelling wishes to steer clear of the theosophical language that caused him no end of trouble in the Freedom Essay and *The Ages of the World*, and instead only insists that God is not enslaved by God's own law. 'He' is not dominated by Sophia, but free to assent to the vision she unveils, or not. God thus remains free from existence and free for being. Nonetheless, it is Sophia who makes God free by giving God something to decide.

The upshot is that God is the first existential subject who faces existence as a task into which God is 'thrown', a project of being. Schelling's contingent God is the clear forerunner of Heidegger's concept of Dasein. The existential subject, human or divine, can decline the offer, but cannot undo the offer itself. Should God in fact will to be, eternal existence shall immediately be transformed into God's ground, and the law of the world shall obtain, the law that realises all possibilities and orders them by compelling a decision among them. Presumably, God could will otherwise; God could will that nothing should be, including the law of the world, and an endless night of cancelled possibility would prevail (Tritten 2017: 150). All of this remains on the level of thought: whether eternal existence actually holds sway as God cannot in this way be decided. The point of the 1841 theogony – and this is a significant development from 1809 – is to prepare the ground for positive, historical evidence in support of the fallibilist assertion of the existence of a personal God. In this way, the speculative construct of the *a priori* theogony becomes a concrete, philosophical hypothesis, a practice of reason in the world, a 'magnificent declaration', which is no mere theoretical gamble, but a programmatic investment of the one who declares in a certain vision of the self and its purpose in the world. If Schelling hypothesises that God has in some unimaginable sense decided for order, personality and love, it is for the sake of enjoining the same decision on the positive philosopher.[22]

The search for the living God

The aim of the positive philosophy is to write a philosophy that engages history on history's own terms. Nevertheless, history is not to be accepted simply as it presents itself to the 'unprejudiced' academic eye; rather history is to be interpreted according to a heuristic, a theory of the whole, which Schelling insists that he both *finds* in history and *brings* to history. Schelling's first presupposition is that the engine of history is religion, and not, say, the material conditions of civilisations. More decisively, the doctrine of the potencies determines everything Schelling says about history, a doctrine which, as we have seen, is fully explicable *a priori*. Thus the philosophy of history is preceded by a metaphysics of reason. The positive philosophy, however, is not another idealist philosophy of history, whereby history is cut to fit logic. The doctrine of the potencies is to be demonstrated *per posterius* (through experience) as the consequent 'logic' of history, a demonstration that remains fallibilist and exploratory.

In the *Darstellung der reinrationalen Philosophie*, Schelling models his method of metaphysical empiricism on Plato's dialectic (referencing *Republic* 6.511B) (Schelling 1854a: 295ff.). He describes the method as setting out in pure thought to arrive at first principles 'inductively'. The method is inductive because it begins hypothetically and on the basis of a certain kind of experience. But the experience with which it begins is thought itself, and the possibilities are purely conceptual. Nevertheless, the method is a kind of empiricism because 'thought is also experience' (Schelling 1854a: 326). It is 'not demonstrative but persuasive' (Schelling 1854a: 330), for in the end each will have to decide for themselves whether they are satisfied with the argument. The premises are not assumed but sought through a process of trial and error, the criterion for which is not the real and the unreal, but possibility and impossibility (Schelling 1854a: 325). The method proceeds not from antecedent to consequent, as does deduction, but from consequent to antecedent.

The method Schelling invents to achieve this curious balancing act of the *a priori* and the *a posteriori* has come to be known as 'abductive', after C. S. Peirce perfected it (Peirce 1901; 1903a; 1908; Bradley 2009).[23] While there are disputes among Schellingians and Peirceans about how it works, the basic logic of the method is clear: it is neither purely deductive nor purely inductive, that is, the method neither works purely with an *a priori* logic, nor is it empirical in the crude sense, presuming to say only that which could be extracted from the evidence of the senses. The abduction *steps back* (*ab-ducts*) from experience, which means that in some sense it begins with experience, with some 'surprising fact' (Peirce 1908: 441), but having surveyed the data to be explained, it steps back and conceives, in an *a priori* fashion, an explanation that could make *complete* sense of the data.

To make comprehensive sense of the data the explanation must go beyond the data and include the ontology that makes the data possible. The scope and sense of the explanation is not to be restricted by that which is simply given: rather a complete account of the whole is sought, within which the data to be explained will also find its meaning. Imagination, memory, even the unconscious, are deployed in an effort that Peirce called 'musement on the whole',[24] a playful, non-systematic experimentation with possible explanations on the assumption that no source of understanding should be ruled out *a priori* in a genuinely scientific approach. Peirce described abduction, somewhat prosaically, as the basic pattern of hypothesis formation. His point is to underscore the undisciplined nature of scientific thinking, the wild creativity of scientific genius. Against reductionist views of induction, Peirce argued that the hypothesising thinker legitimately draws on *any* source available to them in the construction of their hypothesis, be it empirical, logical, or even intuitive. The process of hypothesis formation can be as undisciplined as it needs to be because hypothesising itself (as distinct from proving a hypothesis) does not depend upon a method; the hypothesis stands or falls on its success in explaining the data to be explained. Risk and imagination play as important a role in science as method and deductive thinking.[25] The controls are applied after thought has taken flight, not before. The one engaged in abduction does not think in the strict terms of that which is given; he or she thinks that which is not given. The move goes, not from premises to a certain conclusion, but from a conclusion to the premises which are not as such given, as Peirce puts it, 'reasoning from consequent to antecedent' (Peirce 1908: 441). If something remains unexplained, if something obtrudes on the explanation as still unaccounted for, then the hypothesis is proven inadequate and the process must start again.

Abduction shares with *a posteriori* induction the limitation that it can never claim the certainty and finality of deduction; as Peirce would put it, an abduction is a reasonable 'guess' at the truth, one which stands to be challenged by equally reasonable guesses or by counter-examples. Unlike induction, abduction does not deny the apriority of the process of forming a hypothesis. The guess is the product of an *a priori* reasoning process which seeks to conceive an explanatory whole that would be adequate to certain empirical experiences. The difference from rationalist methods is that the conception of the whole does not precede experience. The empirical determination of the course of thought is decisive: the conception is produced, validated or falsified by means of experience; if the explanation is proven at any point to be inadequate to some dimension of experience, then the conception falls. The difference from empiricist methods, on the other hand, is that the explanation, however constructed on the basis of experience, is not *reducible* to the data; it is not *derived* solely from experience, but derived from a creative fusion of the empirical and the extra-empirical, the *a priori* in its widest sense (not just innate ideas, but intuitions, creative leaps of the imagination, and so on) and *applied* to experience.

It has been noted before that the late Schelling does not seem to be speaking of mere hypothesis formation.[26] He is aiming at the true metaphysics and the true philosophy of history, which reason, he believes, can construct by judiciously applying its own native resources, its own immediate content, to the data of history. Nevertheless, the test of the truth of the explanation is its explanatory power, and this gives the thesis of the positive philosophy, that history is the personalisation of the Triune God, the structure of a grand hypothesis. The thesis is falsifiable and is falsified to the degree that it leaves out some fact that needs to be explained. What makes Schelling's method different from common-law science is that the *explanandum* is the existence of order itself (whether we call it the fact of reason or the world), and the *explanans* is the existence of a personal, that is, a free God. To be explained is not this or that fact but the very fact of existence itself. The specification of Schelling's method as abductive helps us situate his position more precisely in the history of modern philosophy. German idealism is generally considered the next step after Descartes, Spinoza and Leibniz, on the rationalist side, and Locke, Berkeley and Hume, on the empiricist side. As such it is read as a systematic attempt to heal the split between rationalism and empiricism, subjectivity and sensibility. This characterisation, although somewhat facile, does shed some light on Schelling's approach to history. It is neither deductive and rationalist nor inductive and reductively empirical, but speculative and empirical at the same time. The data of history is the matter to be thought, but the form of thought, how that matter is to be explained, is not induced from history; it is in that sense *a priori*.

Schelling first experimented with abductive reasoning in his early nature-philosophy, which was expressly intended as 'speculative physics'. By this term he envisioned a philosophy that constructed comprehensive explanatory accounts of the universe which could make sense of the results of the natural sciences as well as the conclusions of transcendental philosophy. The explanations were to be both *a priori* and *a posteriori* at the same time. On the one hand, nature-philosophy was spontaneously the product of reason; as Iain Hamilton Grant, the world's authority on the topic, has argued, nature-philosophy rejects epistemology, for its starting point is the assumption that the subject and the object share a common, if mysterious, source (Grant 2006). The epistemological presupposition that thoughts and theories need to first prove that they are more than mere fantasies of the brain by *corresponding* to things is dismissed as not only arbitrary, but laden with metaphysical assumptions that determine the outcome in advance. Reason theorising is an event *within* nature; it thus can be trusted to express the same patterns of being that we experience in the physical world. A thoroughgoing idealism, then, would also be a realism. The method of nature-philosophy was to construct a comprehensive theory that satisfied all rational criteria, including coherence and even aesthetic criteria, while at the same time being verifiable and to a certain degree falsifiable by experience. Nevertheless, however much it longed for the real, nature-philosophy never truly broke free from the circle of reason, as I have discussed at length above: its *explanandum* remained ideal, not real entities. The possibility of nature and natural entities was explained, not the existence of nature itself. In this regard nature-philosophy remained negative philosophy, and 'would be true even if nothing existed' (Schelling 1841: 118).

Positive philosophy, by contrast, is concerned with singular events, which cannot be reduced to universal patterns, structures or ideas. Positive philosophy depends upon experience for its soundness. 'It enters into experience itself and grows, as it were, together with it' (Schelling 1842d: 128/180). Positive philosophy will prove the *a priori* possibility of certain experienced facts: thus it will derive experience from the *a priori*. But the *a priori* with which it starts is not simply *before* all experience but *above* all experience: it is that which can never be experienced but which must be if anything at all is to be experienced. It is the *prius* as such, the absolute presupposition of all reasoning and questioning. This *prius* is not identified *a priori* with the innate notion of God, the *ens necessarium*, which is the immediate content of reason and the result of the negative philosophy. If the *prius* is to be identified with contingently necessary being, that is, if the *prius* is to be called God, this will be done *per posterius*, that is, through experience. The positive philosophy does not take up the notion of *ens necessarium* from the negative philosophy as its first principle, but as something to be proven to be real, as a task and a demand (*Aufgabe*) (Schelling 1842d: 93/154):

> *From this prius*, positive philosophy derives in a free thought and in an evidentiary sequence that which is *a posteriori* or that which occurs in experience, not as what is possible, as in the negative philosophy, but as what is real. It derives it as what is real, for only as such does it have the meaning and the force of proof. (Schelling 1842d: 129/180)

A system of history in the traditional sense of the term 'system', a complete and self-sufficient totality in which every part is derivable from the whole, will always elude positive philosophy. 'Positive philosophy . . . can never be called a system because it is never absolutely closed' (Schelling 1854b: 133). A system in the Reinholdian sense is a whole that derives all of its parts, *a priori*, from a first, self-evident principle. The world, unfolding as it does in unprethinkable events, acts of human freedom, that is, history, could only be a system *sensus strictus* at the end of time. Nevertheless, positive philosophy will be systematic, and will aim towards a system, even if the final system must necessarily elude it. Schelling had spoken in the past about 'a living system'; now he imagines a system that is not a comprehended whole but is a venture at a comprehension of a whole which has not yet fully emerged, a comprehension which is open to correction and falsification, but which is yet secure enough to serve as maxim of action and belief: 'a totality of knowledge that serves as the basis for a magnificent declaration' (Schelling 1842d: 183/133). One should not miss the aesthetic dimension of this argument. The theory to be ventured will have something 'magnificent' about it, daring to think history, not as a tragedy, a series of unfortunate events, but as a comedy, as what Tolkien described as a 'eucatastrophe' (Tolkien 1942: 75), an astonishing befalling of a joyous resolution, apparently random events converging upon a final consequence that could never have been guessed and exceeds our wildest hopes. History, if it is meaningful, is revelation, the unveiling of the design of providence. It is neither a series of accidents nor a representation of rational ideas. History is no picture book of rational truths that reason already possesses, but that only needed to be represented for it so that it could thereafter properly express them.

> The content of revelation is first of all a historical content, but not in the vulgar or temporal sense. It is a content that is *revealed* at a determinate time, that is, intervenes in worldly phenomena. Yet according to its subject matter it is nonetheless veiled and hidden, as it was present and prepared 'before laying the foundation of the world' [John 17:24], before the foundation of the world had been laid, whose origin and proper understanding thereof leads back to that which is beyond this world. (Schelling 1842d: 142–3/189)

Schelling's first explicit articulation of positive philosophical method as abductive, or in more Schellingian terms, metaphysically inductive, is in his 1812 *Denkmal*. In defence against Jacobi's attack on *Naturphilosophie* as inadequate to both ethics and theology, Schelling describes a method which starts with the empirical, the irregular, the novel and then risks the most speculative explanation for why such things would exist.[27] In his polemic against all *naturphilosophische* approaches to the question of God, Jacobi had argued that the higher cannot be explained through what is lower, but only the other way around.

> A ground of proof [*Beweisgrund*] must always and necessarily be above that which is to be proven by means of it; it comprehends under itself that which is to be proven; from the ground of proof, truth and certainty flow to those things that are

to be proven by means of it; from it, they borrow their reality. (Jacobi 1811: 136, translated in Franks 2015: 750)

This is hardly a revolutionary claim. Jacobi sides with Spinoza on this: natural things are to be explained deductively on the basis of an *a priori* concept of divinity or substance.[28] Ever since 1804, Schelling had insisted that on the basis of a deductive system that begins with the concept of the infinite, not only can natural things not be known in their singularity and diversity, but novelty as such is impossible. Schelling therefore offers the following alternative to Jacobi: 'A ground of development must always and necessarily be below that which is to be developed; it posits above itself that which is to be developed from it, knows it as higher and, after the development has been accomplished, subordinates itself to it as matter, organ and condition' (Schelling 1812: 59, translated in Franks 2015: 750). Paul Franks correctly sees this as a first, roughed-out model of abductive logic: rather than starting with premises and deducing conclusions with iron-clad certainty, abduction begins with the conclusion as something to be explained and attempts to derive the premises from it, which it can only do probabilistically. God is not the premise from which nature is to be deduced; nature is the conclusion, the given, the premises for which are lacking. Nature is the *explanandum* and our concept of God, the *explanans*, but in order to be such, the concept of God must be adequate to what it explains. It cannot leave anything out that needs explaining. The old concept of God as the timelessly perfect leaves the irregularity and imperfection of nature unexplained. What must God be such that nature as we know it is possible?[29]

Notice how Schelling introduces the idea of religious naturalism in the opening paragraph of the *Denkmal*:

The first person who, in his soul, leapt out of the way of purely rational research considered as a solution to the great problem of thought, to the idea that a personal being could be the originator and governing principle of the world – that person was unquestionably left as if struck by a miracle and filled with the greatest wonder. It was not simply an audacious idea, but absolutely the most audacious idea ever. Since, thanks to that idea, everything for the first time received a human significance, the first one to discover it (provided such a person did exist) certainly had an entirely human conception of that personal being. He surely did not just stand there with his arms hanging by his sides, but went out under the open skies and asked all of nature, the stones and the mountains, the plants and the animals, whether they could impart to him some facts concerning the unique, concealed and hidden God; or, he travelled to distant lands, amidst unknown people, tribes and folk, seeking signs or historical traces of that being. But even he, who was led to this thought by scientific research, needed to recognise as clearly as possible that the perfectly justified understanding of the existence of that being could only be the final product of the most accomplished science. (Schelling 1812: 54)

Religious naturalism does not begin with a concept of God, it ends with it, as 'the most audacious idea ever', through which 'everything for the first time received a human significance'. The concept of God is rendered adequate to the surprising facts of nature, not deduced but constructed on the basis of the wildest speculative romp imaginable, an inquiry that proceeds 'under the open skies', that interrogates 'the stones and the mountains, the plants and the animals', and travels 'to distant lands, amidst unknown people, tribes and folk, seeking signs or historical traces of that being'. Abductive natural theology begins with the wonders, the irregularities, the strangeness of nature, that is, with facts; above all, the strangest fact of all, why is there something and not rather nothing? And it proceeds from there to the most comprehensive explanation that could justify such oddities, an explanation that will be higher than the *explananda*. It does not begin from above, with certain premises, and deductively proceed from what is better known to what is unknown; it begins from below, with certain strange, barely comprehended facts, and proceeds from there to develop a concept of that which could account for the facts. Because abductive natural theology proceeds this way, the certainty which is the hallmark of deduction eludes it, but it never becomes lost in a world of pure concepts, for always calling to it, demanding to be explained, are the facts.

Revelation moves Schelling's abductive project into a yet a more aggressive key. The *explanandum* now is the whole of human history, the *explanans*, the self-revealing God of the Bible. Positive philosophy will attempt to prove that being *in fact* exists as the biblical God, that A^0 is, through the unfathomable act of its own freedom, $\pm A$, in other words, that being, *das reine Daß*, holds sway as God. What grounds positive philosophy, as presented in 1842, is not the authority of revelation but a philosophical cognition, 'a running proof' for God's existence, which remains open until the end of history, and progressively makes historical experience itself comprehensible (Schelling 1842d: 130–1/181). In lecture eight of *The Grounding of the Positive Philosophy*, Schelling sketches what could be called his abductive argument for the existence of God. Following Kant, Schelling regards the ontological argument as not one argument among others but as the spontaneous product of reason, the expression of reason's own reflection on itself. In this regard he is quite close to Hegel: of all the traditional proofs for the existence of God, the ontological proof is of the utmost importance (Hegel 1827: 181–9). It is the most rational of proofs, and the proof that most displays the spontaneity and necessity of the idea of the infinite. For Schelling, as for Hegel, the ontological argument only makes explicit the relative infinity of reason – reason in abstraction from existence finds no limits which it cannot transcend – but this infinity for Schelling is only a virtual, not a real infinity, only an apparent sublation of all limits. The point of the ontological argument is the demonstration of the identity of thought and being: a thoroughgoing thinking of being as infinite leads ineluctably to the affirmation of the existence of the infinite. What this means, Schelling argues, is not *that* God exists, but that the only adequate concept of God is *necessary being*. But whether this necessary being exists, that is, whether a being is to be found whose being is not the product of a cause or a process of becoming, but rather that which exists as a result of its own will – that is an open question. Like Aquinas and Kant, Schelling argues for a categorical distinction between essence and existence: there is no direct passage from the one to the other. Therefore the question of the existence of infinite essence is to be settled, Schelling argues, *a posteriori* – not through a cosmological argument, but, to use Peirce's term again, abductively.

In its barest form, here is Schelling's running proof for the existence of God:

> That which necessarily exists (that is, that which simply and necessarily exists) *is* – not necessarily, but rather *factically* the necessarily necessary existing being [*Wesen*], or God. This is proved *a posteriori* in the manner already indicated, namely, in that one says: 'If that which necessarily exists is *God*, then this and that consequence – we want to say, then *a*, *b*, *c*, and so on – become *possible*; but if according to our experience *a*, *b*, *c*, and so on, really exist, then the necessary conclusion is that that which necessarily exists is *really* God. (Schelling 1842d: 169/208)

If this argument is truly abductive, then the conclusion is falsifiable. If a further experience, say *d*, emerges which contradicts the explanation, in this case the necessarily necessary existing being, the explanation fails. Schelling's proof of God's existence follows neither in the footsteps of the Scholastics nor the moderns; it is neither cosmological, a proof of the necessary being based on the contingency of events, nor ontological, derived from the innate idea of the infinite. Both methods were demolished by Kant, who showed that they illegitimately hypostasised the idea of the infinite or unconditioned, which Kant argues is merely regulative, or in Schelling's language, negative. Against the cosmological argument, Schelling agrees with Kant that one does not *deduce* the existence of the infinite, one presupposes it. Against the ontological argument, Schelling insists that there is no logical movement from essence to existence, from the concept of the infinite to its extra-conceptual reality. The cosmological argument makes the mistake of presuming the possibility of a purely *a posteriori* access to the infinite; the ontological argument makes the mistake of presuming the possibility of a purely *a priori* access to the infinite.

What is proved by Schelling's running proof? The argument allows us to name the absolute *prius*, unprethinkable being, God. But God is not proven directly; rather, the divinity of the act of being is indirectly proven as the assumption that makes possible certain real facts. 'These [consequences] must be *factually* proved, and only thereby do we prove the divinity of that *prius* – that it is God, and that *God* therefore exists' (Schelling 1842d: 129/180). Notice that Schelling sees no contradiction between the philosophical idea of God as necessary being and the theological idea of God as personal creator. He follows Aquinas in this regard. If the infinite is a personal creator – and this, for Schelling, is alone worthy of the name 'God' – then certain consequences are possible, for example, order in nature, the existence and history of spirit, and the fact of love. It is not necessary that these things be, for they are contingent facts. But these things, if they in fact exist, require an explanation. The personal God explains them: that is, if the creator God exists, such things become possible.

> This consequence [order, or spirit, or love], however, really exists (*this* proposition is one founded now in experience: the existence of such a consequence is a datum, a fact of experience). This datum, thus, shows us – the *existence* of such a consequence shows us – that the *prius* itself also *exists in the way* we have *conceived* it, that is, that God exists. You see that in this manner of argumentation the *prius* is always the point of departure, that is, it always remains the *prius*. The *prius* will be known from its consequences, but not in such a way that the consequences had *preceded* it. (Schelling 1854c: 129/180)

Schelling distances himself both from the rationalists who derive the world from the innate idea of the infinite, and the empiricists who refuse to see anything in reason other than what is given in sense data. If the former base their claim on the ideal or the *a priori*, and the latter, on the real or the *a posteriori*, Schelling advocates a lively *coincidentia oppositorum* of the irreducibly ideal and the irreducibly real, a marriage of thought and existence, if you will, which can only conjoin and become one because they are originally two. The conception of the divine nature of the fact of being is *a priori*, a hypothesis, to be confirmed or falsified in experience. 'The preposition "a" in "*a posteriori*" does not in this instance signify the *terminus a quo*; in this context "*a posteriori*" means "*per posterius*": through its consequence the *prius* is known' (Schelling 1842d: 129/180).[30]

The decisive question is, What experiences are to furnish the positive philosophy with the data it needs to name that which is above and therefore prior to all experience? Not raw sense data, but the world as a whole, such as the philosopher finds it – this alone is the adequate basis for Schelling's running proof. 'The experience towards which positive philosophy proceeds is not just of a *particular kind* but is the entirety of all experience from beginning to end. What contributes to the proof is not a part of experience but all experience [*die ganze Erfahrung*] from beginning to end' (Schelling 1842d: 130–1/181). It should be clear from this, and other statements, that Schelling, as much as Hegel and the British idealists (above all, F. H. Bradley) and the American pragmatists (James, Peirce), breaks with the atomistic empiricism which would reduce experience to discrete bits of data that have, à la Locke and Hume, been built up into complex ideas. In experiencing anything whatsoever, according to Schelling and this tradition of transcendental empiricism, we do not deal with the synthesis of discrete bits of a sensible manifold, nor with conventions of speech masquerading as givens, but rather with that which is always already world, what Heidegger calls a totality of references that has the existing subject as its ground. In thinking about experience, we muse, to paraphrase Peirce, not on the part but on the whole.

But whose world? It can only be the world of the philosopher who ventures the explanation. This is the most radical aspect of this extraordinary argument, Schelling's insistence that experience is at one and the same time perspectival, that is, finite (we are no longer speaking of the absolute subject of transcendental philosophy), and transcendent, an experience of the whole. The world appears to me to be thus and so, says the abductive philosopher; any explanation that I will find reasonable will have to be adequate to the world as I experience it. If something of the world remains unexplained by the explanation, and if that something strikes me as undeniably real, then the explanation is to be rejected or modified. In the transcendental empiricist tradition that followed Schelling, especially in Whitehead, this comes to be known as the criterion of adequacy: it is not enough to produce a coherent account, one that harmonises with itself, for it might refer to nothing outside itself. Nor is it enough to produce an account that corresponds with certain facts, for there might be other facts to which it does not correspond. The account must be adequate to the whole of experience.[31]

Who decides the parameters of the whole of experience that is to be normative for the argument? Who is to say such and such a fact must be included (or can be safely ignored) in the whole because it is to be affirmed as real, or denied as unreal? No convention or tradition can decide this: the only one who can is the one who ventures the explanation. Herein lies the origin of existentialism in Schelling's late philosophy. The argument does not deny the contingency of every explanation, or its dependence on the selection, or even construction, of an *explanandum* that must in the end be the personal decision of a philosopher. On the contrary, Schelling's argument explicitly affirms the decisional quality of the argument. Hence the running proof is open (new experiences might lead us to modify our explanation) and controvertible (other configurations of the whole of experience are possible, which would lead to different explanations). It was this quality of Schelling's argument which the pragmatists took up: here truth is put to work, or a truth is taken as true because it works and it is only to be taken as true to the degree that it continues to work, that is, that it continues to explicate whatever it is that needs to be explained. The proof is open because experience is not closed, but fundamentally historical and futural:

> This is nothing other than the progressive, strengthening with every step, and continually growing proof of the actually existing God. Because the realm of reality in which this proof moves is not finished and complete – for even if nature is not at its end and stands still, there is, nonetheless, still the unrelenting advance and movement of history – because insofar as the realm of reality is not complete, but is a realm perpetually nearing its consummation, the proof is therefore also *never* finished. (Schelling 1842d: 131/181)

To say that the proof is open is to say that the argument is controvertible, because its foundation is the decision of a philosopher to regard this and that as real and in need of explanation. Schelling's proof for the existence of God is not compelled by logical necessity, not a deduction, but demanded by the thinker who refuses to rest content with a world that just happens to make sense, the world that a large majority of contemporary thinkers seem to have resigned themselves to, one that is only accidentally ordered (Schelling 1842d: 132/182).

We know from Schelling's 1853 Literary Testament that he was not happy with the lectures of *The Grounding of the Positive Philosophy*, and came to see that they were not an adequate introduction to the Philosophy of Revelation.[32] The posthumously published work, *Darstellung der reinrationalen Philosophie*, was intended in part to replace it. The *Darstellung* shows us Schelling's final revision of the negative philosophy and its place in history, and his last word on the turn to the positive. It was assembled from lectures, notes, and fragments by Schelling's son and editor, K.F.A, and by both father and son intended as a new, philosophical introduction to the Philosophy of Mythology, and a sequel to *The Historical-Critical Introduction to the Philosophy of Mythology* (Schelling 1842a). Both the philosophical and the historical-critical introductions would serve as the prolegomena to the complete positive philosophy, inclusive of both the Philosophy of Mythology and the Philosophy of Revelation. The Philosophy of Revelation would no longer have its own separate introduction. Instead the monotheism treatise, a standalone set of lectures that went through a variety of revisions and was originally a part of the Philosophy of Revelation (Schelling 1842b), would serve as the transitional text between the two introductions and the Philosophy of Mythology proper. The implication seems to be that there is no direct transition from negative philosophy to the Philosophy of Revelation.

The transition is a transcendental empiricist detour through the history of religions, on the lookout for evidence of the personal God. Furthermore, the Philosophy of Mythology in Schelling's final plan passes directly into the Philosophy of Revelation without a break, underscoring Schelling's assumption that revealed religion is continuous with natural religion or mythology.

The *Darstellung* notably contains no abductive proof for the existence of God. Instead, we are left in the final lecture with the passionate call of the individual for a *personal* God, the cry of one who cannot remain content with a God who is only an idea. The negative philosophy as revised in the *Darstellung* culminates in the pain of the person who longs for a love that is at once proportionate to the human self and, in its sovereignty and power to heal and save, infinitely beyond the human. The person finds no satisfaction in the system of reason, and is driven to look into the history of religion, first in mythology, then in revelation, for that which he or she longs. Schelling's conclusion could not be more bleak: purely rational philosophy leaves us as existing individuals bereft of a genuinely divine God. What we seek when we ask the question concerning God, and really mean it, is not a metaphysical principle, not a cosmic foundation of the intelligible order of things, and certainly more than the lynchpin of the architectonic of reason, which is all Kant has to offer us; we seek a God who is alive as we are alive, and who can give sense and purpose to our living and dying. We seek, Schelling says, beatitude (*Glückseligkeit*). Our search for beatitude, for the salvation that can only be accomplished by a living God, is not a movement of thought but an act of will: in it we express ourselves not merely as rational beings but as existing, suffering and acting individuals. The person needs the healing touch of a God who is also personal, and will be content with nothing less. The turn to the positive in the *Darstellung* is a cry of the heart of one who understands that everything may in fact be rationally ordered, as it appears to be in the world as it is understood by reason, and nevertheless the whole may remain absurd. The closing paragraphs of the *Darstellung* are among the most poignant of all Schelling's writings.

> The need for the I to possess God outside of reason (and not only God in thought or in the idea) is born out of the practical. This willing is not contingent, it is a willing of spirit that, by internal necessity and in the aspiration of its own freedom, cannot remain enclosed in thought. As this demand cannot come from thought, it is thus also not a postulate of practical reason. It is not the latter, as Kant would have it, but only the individual that is driven to God. For it is not the universal in the human which demands beatitude, but the individual. If the human is obliged (by moral consciousness or practical reason) to regulate his relation to other individuals according to the intelligible mode [*wie es in der Ideenwelt war*], this can only satisfy the universal in him – reason – and not the individual himself. Only the individual can aspire to beatitude . . . the I which, as personality itself, demands a personality,

calls for a person that would be outside the world and above the universal, that can hear him, a heart that would be the same as his own. (Schelling 1854a: 569–70)

In place of the theoretical approach of the running proof of the *Grounding*, Schelling closes the negative philosophy of the *Darstellung* on a Kierkegaardian note. The whole tone of this passage is reminiscent of the indignation of the religious heart in the face of the bloodless constructs of rational theology which Schelling expressed in his 1833 review of Jacobi. 'I do not want this result. I find it revolting. It goes against my feeling . . . I cannot bring it into accord with myself' (Schelling 1833: 166/165). The infinite has become more than a thought; it is now a passion, an infinite longing that intensifies the loneliness and lostness of existence. On the basis of this existential thought, Schelling makes what Kierkegaard would regard as a regressive move: he turns to the philosophy of history for an answer to the question of existence. Thus even if the departure point of the positive philosophy in the *Darstellung* is no longer the theoretical move of an abductive proof, the consequence is the same. The turn to the positive is a turn to history, but not in a vague aesthetico-speculative key: history is to be questioned in a specific way. Is there any evidence in history that my feeling for God, the longing of my heart, is not absurd?

That said, in his Literary Testament, Schelling envisioned not the Philosophy of Revelation but the monotheism treatise followed by the Philosophy of Mythology, coming directly after the existential aporia of these closing pages of the *Darstellung* (Schelling 1853). The existential questioner is offered a transcendental-empirical investigation of the historical and systematic relations existing among the three competing philosophical doctrines of God which emerge from a survey of the history of religion: theism, pantheism and monotheism. What are we to make of this change of strategy? It seems that in 1853 Schelling was concerned above all with avoiding foundationalism, and *The Grounding of the Positive Philosophy*, with its running proof for the existence of God, smells like foundationalism. I have, I hope, demonstrated that the proof is not foundationalist, but a pragmatic 'guess at the riddle', to borrow a Peircean phrase. Nevertheless, it seems that Schelling worried that the review of the history of negative philosophy which culminates in the running proof could lead one to the fatal misjudgement that the transition from general positive philosophy (the Philosophy of Mythology) to the Philosophy of Revelation is a logical transition.

In the Literary Testament, the beginning of the positive philosophy is stipulated as *The Historical-Critical Introduction to the Philosophy of Mythology* (Schelling 1842a), and the Philosophy of Revelation as such is to remain without an introduction. In this way, Schelling distinguishes negative and positive philosophy even more sharply. Negative philosophy begins and ends with the *a priori*, positive philosophy begins and ends with the *a posteriori*. Negative and positive philosophy become, therefore, two parallel lines that do not meet at any *logical* point: only the decision of the philosopher connects them. The *Historical-Critical Introduction*, Schelling stipulates in 1853, is to be followed by the revised negative philosophy (the *Darstellung der reinrationalen Philosophie*), to which the 1850 lecture, 'On the Source of the Eternal Truths', is to be appended (Schelling 1854a: 572; Schelling 1850). The latter demonstrates the contingency of the eternal truths, the laws of reason, on the will of the divine. After this detour through negative philosophy, the narrative is to begin directly with the monotheism treatise, which offers an interpretation of monotheism as 'esoteric' pantheism (Schelling 1842b: 93n4; cf. 1804: 67/53), on the basis of an historical fact, which is the result of the *Historical-Critical Introduction*, the fact of a theogony in the religious consciousness of ancient peoples, or polytheism as 'diverged monotheism' (Schelling 1842a: 91/66).[33]

Since he regarded this as his last word on the subject, something must be said about 'On the Source of Eternal Truths'. The lecture defends a qualified voluntarism derived from Descartes, who made the truths of reason contingent on the will of God. Schelling presents Descartes' voluntarism as an improvement on the essentialism of the Scholastics, who made God dependent on the eternal truths, the essences of things, the divine ideas, which were held to be co-eternal with God. Is God free of the ideas, which would mean that reason is without reason? Or is God Godself answerable to reason, in which case God is not free but bound to something that coexists with God? Schelling's solution to this ancient debate (it is a version of Plato's Euthyphro dilemma) is to argue that the divine ideas depend on the will of God for their *existence*, as consequent depends upon antecedent, but God depends on the ideas for God's *essence*, without which God could not exist, for to exist is to exist *as* something. The law of ground applies to God as well (and this is the strongest evidence for reading Schelling as a defender of *univocatio entis*): God's antecedent being (God's will) depends for its actuality as antecedent on its having a consequent (God's essence, which contains the ideas). The point can be taken to be a metaphysical refinement of the theogonic account offered in 1841 (and perhaps Schelling's final effort to extract his thought from theosophy), but hardly a change of view on the question of the contingency of God.[34]

However we are to begin, we are still on the look out for the living God. There is only one place to look: history, in particular, the history of the development of absolute monotheism (Trinitarianism) from polytheism. An early sketch of the monotheism treatise appears in the *Urfassung* (Schelling 1831: 140–9), and is repeated in the first Berlin lectures (Schelling 1841:

189–98). A much more elaborated version was published as the first book of the Philosophy of Mythology (SW 12: 3–132). Common to all three versions is Schelling's distinction between theism and pantheism as competing conceptions of the infinity of God, and his argument for absolute monotheism (Trinitarianism) as the resolution of the opposition between the two. Both theism and pantheism are correct in recognising that God is the one without another. God is being itself, the *ens universalis*, or infinite essence. This notion of being itself as infinite is not yet knowledge of God (herein lies the mistake to which Spinoza falls prey); it is only the conceptual presupposition of the full knowledge of God, which is the experience of God as personal, God as one who, having overcome necessity, is capable of personal relations. The God who has overcome something in Godself which is not God is a divinity that includes diversity. As I shall explore in greater detail in the second book, this divine diversity is revealed in history as the ground of the Trinitarian relations that constitute the full and complete monotheistic concept of God. Thus the cry of the heart that closes the negative philosophy leads to a reconsideration of the notion of the personal God as it emerges from historical monotheism (chiefly Judaism and early Christianity, although Islam and certain forms of Hinduism are also implied). Personality, even in an infinite mode, requires internal diversity, and thus something in Judaism pushes inexorably towards the Christian Trinity. A being that excludes all diversity is an impersonal substance, as Spinoza rightly concludes, and such a God will not satisfy the cry of the heart, Schelling says. Lacking the duality of subject and object, it cannot be considered self-conscious or the ground of agency and knowledge, and thus can be in no sense personal or related to us as persons. An impersonal substance, however infinite, leaves the person unredeemed. My life has no meaning in it, and hence pantheistic thinkers such as Spinoza always urge us to give up on finding a sense to life. 'Only being itself can be God, but being itself is not as such God. The concept of universal being must receive a further determination in order to be God. Being itself is the material of divinity but not divinity as such' (Schelling 1842b: 25).

Schelling's thesis that absolute monotheism is essentially personal and Trinitarian is a direct answer to both modern deism and certain modern versions of pantheism, mystical theology and negative theology. Aren't we settling for less than we need, Schelling asks us, when we resign ourselves to an impersonal divine substance, to the one without another, to a field of divine energy, or a continuum of eternal and impersonal being from which we have all emerged and to which we shall all return? Isn't the metaphor from Vedanta of the soul's relation to the divine (Atman's relation to Brahman) as that of a drop to the ocean, which is not essentially different from the neo-Platonic *henosis*, isn't it somehow a refusal of the deepest experience of personality? This part of your being, the personal core of the self, the heart or *Gemüth*, such speculative mystical theologies are saying, is not real and must evaporate like mist before the rising sun. Schelling argues exactly the opposite. What is most religious in us, and most real, is that which is most personal in us, and which longs, not for dissolution in the absolute, but for perfect relation. We long for love and will not find it in Spinoza's infinite substance, any more than we could find it in Plotinus' One, or the non-dual experience of Brahman in Advaita Vedanta. The longing for a personal relation with the divine, for love, which simultaneously justifies our personal existence even as it transforms it by ending our isolation and existential loneliness, leads not to Spinoza or Vedanta, but to the New Testament.

The monotheism treatise tracks the crucial move, which takes place in history in a variety of registers, from the idea of divine substance, the one God, whose infinity precludes a diversity of gods, or more philosophically conceived, the notion of the absolutely simple infinite which contains no diversity because it excludes all potency (*das Einzige*), to the idea of the God who is all (*das All-Eine*), who excludes other gods by including divine diversity within Godself. *Das Einzige* is not yet personal. With the later idea of *das All-Eine*, which is Christianity's great contribution, we see a recognition of the partial truth of pantheism: God is all, but is diversified internally, according to the ordering of the three potencies. As such, God can be thought of as personal in some superlative sense, as super-personal, and the archetype of personality. Theism goes no further than the notion of the one God without another; pantheism in a sense goes beyond it by identifying the divine with being as such. Both conceptions stalemate in the impersonalism of their respective notions of divine unity, and so neither break through to divine personality, which is the demand of the negative philosophy and the presupposition of the Philosophy of Revelation. The one-sided insights of theism and pantheism are taken up in genuine monotheism, which is, in its full iteration, Trinitarianism, the notion of the personal God, who must, as personal, contain an internal diversity, a diversity which is ordered, and a necessity or internal otherness, which is mastered.

> God is Lord only as Lord of the three potencies which he holds together in unbreakable unity. The three causes are enclosed with him, outside of which there is nothing, except the transcendent absolute cause, in which the all is confirmed and effective. The creator is not the absolutely simple, but, insofar as this plurality is an enclosed totality, the all-one [*das All-Eine*]. And so are we led to the concept of monotheism, which constitutes the transition from the general positive philosophy to the philosophy of revelation. (Schelling 1841: 189)

The creator God is the all-in-one, the God who contains within Godself all possibilities, ordered as the subordination of −A to +A in ±A, and sets each of the potencies free to personalise themselves in history and so achieve not only divine unity, but divine community. The pure act of being, Spinoza's infinite substance, is properly conceived by theists and pantheists alike as without equal because being without potency cannot share being with another, or stand opposed to another of its kind. And yet such a being, Schelling says, is not yet an actual God, for to be actual is not merely to be without potency, but to have overcome and mastered potency (*ein actu Seiendes is nur das, durch dessen Sein eine entgegenstehende Potenz überwunden wird* [Schelling 1841: 190]). To be actual as a person is thus to have traversed an internal diversity and to remain one. Infinite substance is the *matter* of divinity, the opposing potency which gives form something to work on, but God's personality is the true form of the divine. A God who is only infinite essence is a God who is non-actual, and merely another name for reality, which is understood in a negative and timeless way, as Kant demonstrated. Such a God is the *ens perfectissimum*, the sum of all perfections, of which nothing can be denied, but from which nothing real can be concluded.[35] Spinoza, like all pantheists, still knows nothing of the God who acts; that is, Spinoza knows nothing of the personalising God, the creator of finite being and author of history. Spinoza's God is 'pure object' (Schelling 1842b: 38).

> The true God is the living God. The living God is only he who steps out of his unprethinkable being, renders it a moment in his being, so as to free himself from his essence and posit himself as Spirit, in which is given him at the same time the possibility to be a creator, through which he posits another being out of his unprethinkable being. (Schelling 1841: 191)[36]

To be sure, Spinoza has made an advance towards existence with his notion of God as substance, but he has not begun to think from out of existence itself. Spinoza's error is not that he identifies God and being, for the God who is all includes being within Godself. Spinoza's error, rather, lies in his absolutisation of the formal concept of divine being to the point where personality is denied as a possibility of God. God then becomes, for Spinoza, 'blind, substance without will' (*blinden willenlosen Substanz*), hence the exact opposite of what is revealed as the true God (Schelling 1842b: 38).

While the differences between the two beginnings of the Philosophy of Revelation are significant, the conclusion of both is the same: what is to be proven, either metaphysically or historical-critically, is that God personalises Godself and so is the God of revelation, the lord of being, the subject of history. In the monotheism treatise, the personality of God is defended as a historical finding, one which is alone adequate to the legitimate claims of theism ('God is one') and pantheism ('God is all'). In any event, philosophical monotheism, either metaphysically or historical-critically grounded, is not yet Philosophy of Revelation. The presupposition of the Philosophy of Revelation is to think God positively, that is, in relation to existing things, and neither negative philosophy nor the Philosophy of Mythology bring us there, for negative philosophy knows nothing of existing things, and mythology is a tissue of illusions. The philosophical recognition of the actuality of the living God is no more a conclusion of the philosophy of history than it is a deduction of the negative philosophy; it still requires the *decision*, which will move the philosopher from the negative to the positive. Only in the light of this decision is mythology shown to be the propaedeutic to revelation. The one who does not so decide will not see it. Reason can and does lead elsewhere. Pantheism, which is a fully rational and coherent conclusion, 'can only be overcome through positive knowledge' (Schelling 1841: 193). Neither in 1842 nor in 1853 is there a direct proof of the revealed God, but only the ad hoc convergence of several lines of probability: negative philosophy, failed and inconclusive proofs for God, mythology, historical-critical biblical studies – a confluence of facts and theories, requiring first of all recognition (the preliminary decision: these are to be explained), and then, on the ground of the cry of the heart for a divine person who could redeem a world which is not what it ought to be, the founding decision, the turn to the positive as such, the magnificent declaration that could make sense of it all.

What does faith have to do with it?

One of the most curious features of Schelling's positive philosophy is that it inverts the Augustinian formula of faith seeking understanding (*fides quarens intellectum*), which was more or less accepted by Patristic, Scholastic and Reformed theologians alike as the foundation of theology. On the traditional view, the understanding of revelation presupposes faith in its revealedness, faith conceived either as an act of grace that enables the ascent of the will to divine truth in the absence of clear reasons, or a blind leap. For Schelling, the fullness of faith is the *end* of revelation, the *terminus ad quem* of revelation, not its presupposition or *terminus a quo*. Faith is where revelation leads, it is the 'not-knowing' in which reason finds its 'rest' (*die Ruhe des Wissens* [Schelling 1831: 412]). Schelling's theorem of absolute transcendence is at play in this unique position on the relation of faith and reason. Where the tradition has generally seen certainty and the secure position of the truth as the end of reason's long quest, which begins in faith and through progressive attainment of understanding leads to knowledge, Schelling argues that reason's search for God culminates not in the security of possession but in silent astonishment (*Erstaunen*) before the fact of God's existence. The path begins with fallible judgements concerning the evidence of history. Closure only comes through the decision, with all of the risk that such an act entails. The decision is not based on a grace-enabled act of faith. The turn to the positive is a free act: it is compelled neither by grace, nor by irrefutable proof. Consequently, something inscrutable and doubtful about revelation always remains, as the negated opposite of faith. 'It is not possible to make the fact of revelation understandable; only the revelation that has occurred can become understandable, or, as Schelling said more carefully, "partly understandable, partly understandable in the essential parts of its implementation" [SW 14: 12]' (Kasper 1965: 195). Faith comes once reason has stepped outside of itself and allowed itself to be expanded by revelation. 'All the human being has to do in this respect is to enlarge the narrowness and smallness of his thoughts to the greatness of the divine ones' (Schelling 1854c: 12).

Schelling's positive philosophy raises many questions concerning the relation of faith and reason, not all of which he clearly provides an answer for. The problem is that the old distinction between theology in the Jewish and Christian traditions, the understanding of revelation that presupposes the grace of faith, and philosophy, which concerns the truths of reason alone, is no longer tenable for Schelling.[37] It was once the case that revelation was received and interpreted by the community of faith (the Church), but with the birth of the modern, it no longer is so contained. Revelation, having occurred at a specific time and place, has now penetrated all strata of existence and is found everywhere, in the structure of our institutions, in the constitutions of our governments, as much as in our everyday assumptions concerning ourselves (Schelling 1842d: 135/184). However secular a critique of faith-based science Schelling defends, he does not swing over into the opposite extreme and reduce revelation to truths of reason in mythic form. Negative philosophy allows us to discern the outlines of the possibility of revelation, but revelation itself cannot be deduced. To be sure, Schelling's thinking evolved on this issue. Schelling II rejects all idealist attempts to subsume revelation into a philosophy of reason, where Schelling I briefly entertained the possibility.[38] If what reason encounters in revelation merely dramatises what reason already knows *a priori*, then revelation would have merely a negative value: it would simply negate the abstract universality of reason and historically concretise its concepts. Revelation, for Schelling II, is positive knowledge.

Does revelation, then, allow us to discern the truth of negative philosophy? Is the reception of revelation therefore the condition of the possibility of ontology? This would mean that negative philosophy lies dormant and unconscious in reason until external events allow us to recollect its structure. This option Schelling also rejects. It is too dogmatically theological for Schelling, for it amounts to saying that it is only on the basis of Christian faith in historical revelation that we are able to understand the structure of reason itself, when clearly Plato and Aristotle understood something of the triadic structure of being in independence from revelation. What then is the answer? Does revelation contradict or confirm the innate content of reason? This way of putting the question will not work for Schelling. In a certain way revelation surprises and corrects reason. In another way, revelation confirms and concretises reason. Schelling may not be Hegel, but neither is he Kierkegaard. Negative philosophy may be *a priori* but it does not exist independent of history, and so we must speak of negative philosophy in a historical frame if we are to understand its relationship to the positive. In this regard we could call Schelling a hermeneutical thinker: reason has a history and this history determines and makes possible whatever we can think and know at any given time. Negative philosophy in the age prior to revelation is quite different from negative philosophy in the age of revelation, just as the negative philosophy of the Middle Ages is different from the negative philosophy of the modern age. The essence of negative philosophy remains the same – the doctrine of the potencies – but its outward form and manner of expression changes.

Could we produce a true philosophy of history without the doctrine of the potencies? Do we not need the potencies clarified first, so that we can then decide, for example, that Dionysus is the second potency in his Greek disguise, and so on? Schelling would appear to be promoting a doctrine of hermeneutical circularity: that which is presupposed (potencies) makes the explanation (of history) possible, but that which is explained (history) makes the presupposition (potencies) possible. This problem is not easily solved, and while Schelling everywhere writes as though there is no problem here, careful readers might not be so easily convinced. The one thing that is clear is that the negative and the positive play off each other in history: the relation between reason and revelation is not static but is in constant movement, and in every moment of the history of philosophy and religion one or the other gains prominence at the expense of its opposite. Thus in the age of myth, the positive is latent and the sense for real history is wanting. In the age of revelation (the European Middle Ages and early modernity), when the positive is manifest and thinking is through and through historicised, negative philosophy is put into crisis and gives way to fideism and empiricism, that is, philosophies which fail to recognise the truths of reason. However, the negative is never for Schelling the last word (even if it is the first word): reason begins in the positive, in existence (for only an existing reasoner can reason), and takes a detour through the negative in order to arrive at a richer notion of the positive. And the reason that recognises its own positivity is not strange to faith; on the contrary, it has already taken the first step towards it. It believes and trusts in being.

Thus the faith that crowns the Philosophy of Revelation is preceeded by a far more common faith which is part and parcel of practical life. Schelling distinguishes two kinds of faith, a faith in existence, in the reality of the real, which is universally required of anyone who would move beyond negative philosophy, and which is an average and everyday affair of ordinary living; and the faith in revelation, which only comes at the end of a process of reasoning about the meaning of history. The first kind of faith is better described as an act of trust in the intelligibility of existence. It goes beyond the merely intelligible, and so moves into the positive and deals directly with the factical, the existent as such. But it also goes beyond the sheer positivity of the existent in that it sees the existent as something that could be understood, even if it is at first not understood. This is faith as Aristotelian 'wonder', the questioning, seeking, hypothesising reasoning, which would not take a single step forward if it did not first assume that that which it questions is potentially understandable. Schelling's point, which has been made by other Aristotelian thinkers, is that the scientific impulse, to ask after the reason for anything whatsoever, is an implicit faith in the reasonableness of the whole nexus of causes without which the thing asked about would not be what it is. More prosaically, faith in its first moment is submission to reality, and we express it when we recognise and accept that things are what they are, regardless of how we might want to think them to be.[39]

Faith in the second sense is properly religious (if still not theological in a traditional sense): it is faith in the existence of God as personal, as one who reveals Godself, as all persons do, in deeds, except that the deeds in question constitute history as such (creation, redemption and the end of history, or sanctification). Such faith is not ordinary or everyday, but is the fruit of a long and patient search for the meaning of existence, a search which culminates in the astonishing thought that being is God's act of self-revelation. In short, faith is the discovery that history is meaningful, and this discovery does not begin the Philosophy of Revelation; it crowns it, and brings philosophy as such to an end. In this second act of faith, existence, which is accepted as a fact in a first move into the real, is taken as God's own act of being, God's willing to be as God. The necessity to which we submit in our faith in the real is in the final act of faith recognised as that which God wills so that God might be God. 'Thus the bottomless nothing is overcome, and precisely in reason giving itself up is there reasonableness and the meaning of life and of history is maintained' (Kasper

1965: 207). But even this full expression of faith is not rational certainty: it is still faith, not knowledge in the idealist sense of that which could not be conceived otherwise. Its opposite, the meaninglessness of everything, is still plausible. The fool who says in his heart, 'There is no God' (Ps. 14:1), is not falling into a contradiction: the atheist thinks a thought that can indeed be thought. Schelling's Philosophy of Revelation is also a justification of atheism insofar as it concedes to the atheist the plausibility, the reasonableness, of the atheist conclusion.

The theologian of revelation will have to ask whether Schelling so domesticates revelation in the process of transforming the *a posteriori* into the *per posterius* as to render revelation innocuous, non-confrontational, no longer a No to the logic of the fallen world. Does Schelling not subsume revelation under the class of personal self-manifestation, for example? Is he not therefore guilty of the error often attributed to Levinas, of making the revelation of God an everyday instance of a commonplace disruption of thinking, a break with what Levinas calls 'sameness' or 'totality', which is not in essence different from the ordinary experience of another human being?[40] Is Schelling guilty of making every other wholly other, and so dispensing with God, the absolutely transcendent other, altogether? I will argue no; Schelling remains a *metaphysical* thinker of transcendence, and hence insists, in the end, on the absolute difference between the creator and the creature, even if the revelation of the former can ultimately be recognised by reason (if, however, only through the mediation of history). Schelling abandons the faith-condition of traditional theology in anticipation of the third age of revelation, in which theology gives way to philosophical religion. But this is not to deny the glory of faith and its necessity for a previous age of revelation. It is to posit the age of faith as past.

It is certainly true that Schelling draws an analogy between the manifestation of the character of another person and the revelation of God in history. Both are free acts of a person: in neither case is understanding the product of intentionality, anticipated meaning or the *a priori*, and both disrupt the sameness which is reason's primary *modus operandi*. With regard to the experience of the other as other, Schelling sharply distinguishes his 'metaphysical empiricism' from epistemological empiricism (Hume, Locke, etc.). He argues that the experience which is so decisive for positive philosophy is not reducible to sense experience, particularly where the sensible is understood atomistically, as discrete bits of data synthesised into complex ideas by the subject. There is much which can only be known *a posteriori* which is not reducible to sense experience, for example, knowledge of the character of another person. We can only know the character of the other through the sensibly manifest acts of the person, but the character itself which is revealed in those sensible manifestations is not itself a sensible manifestation (Schelling 1842d: 18/113). Von Balthasar has made similar arguments, that self-revelation, which comes to its apogee in the revelation of a personal God, is the nature of all being, from the smallest atom to the Trinity.[41] Schelling's argument is an apologia for both the reality of the personal and the possibility of the supernatural revelation of a personal God, for the empiricist objection that denies the one also denies the other on the basis of the same reductionist notion of experience.

What of the Derridean critique of Levinas, that if every other is wholly other, nothing is wholly other (*tout autre est tout autre*)?[42] Could this critique not also be directed at Schelling? Granted that every person is an abyssal font of freedom who reveals their character in their acts in time, and who, to that degree, can never be anticipated or known *a priori*, the God whose revelation is to be the content of philosophical religion is infinitely higher and superior to any human other. God is the maximal case of the being that can only be known *a posteriori*, the one whose self-revelation is carried out by means of the creation of the world. We might say that the *a priori* always plays a role in the understanding of a human other: we anticipate the meanings of the statements of the other on the basis of our own concepts and statements; we receive their acts, at least initially, as acts of one who is like us. Even granting the Levinasian argument that all of these preconceptions and anticipations must be corrected and dropped in the face of the other, still, do we not deal here with what Husserl calls the 'alter ego', not one who is so totally different from us that we can form no pre-concept of him or her at all, but one with whom we are intentionally 'paired'?[43] Schelling draws on traditional concepts of transcendence and *creatio ex nihilo* in order to distinguish the being of the divine creator from the being of everything that he creates. There is no necessity that God either create or reveal Godself, hence nothing of history can be known *a priori*. Further, God precedes the intelligible order God makes possible. Hence no concept exists that could be adequate to a personal knowledge of God.

Schelling argues that, just as we know other people through their acts in time, so we know the creator God through God's acts in history, and, at this late point in the history of Christianity, we no longer require a special alteration of our cognitive powers to see those acts as expressions of will. The point concerns the historicity of reason: what was once an object of faith becomes in the course of history something known. Traditionally, theologians have argued that God's existence as a first cause of being can be deduced on the basis of experience. Moreover, because God is the first cause, we can also deduce that God is infinite since God depends on nothing outside of Godself to exist. But beyond that we cannot say much on a purely philosophical basis alone, that is, we cannot say that God loves us and acts in history to save us from ourselves.[44] Philosophy in the mainstream theological traditions can affirm God's existence but cannot affirm that the God who exists is a *personal* God, for the first cause, insofar as reason can recognise it on the basis of experience, could coherently be interpreted as the deist's God, or the unmoved mover of Aristotle, an impersonal first principle of being and becoming. Hence the traditional theological argument holds that knowledge of God as personal exceeds natural reason: it presupposes an alteration or elevation of reason, the supernatural virtue of faith.[45] Only because of the grace of God which elevates the understanding and will of the believer beyond the compass of his or her natural abilities is the believer able to understand and believe in God's actions in history.[46] It is this theological notion of faith as a particular grace that Schelling challenges, for not unlike Hegel, and contrary to Kierkegaard, Schelling envisions the Jewish-Christian revelation becoming the content of a purely philosophical science, and anticipates Church Christianity being superseded by philosophical religion. In this regard, the positive philosophy might be regarded as another system that collapses Christianity into culture, sending Kierkegaard storming out of the hall. We would do well to remember, however, that Schelling's 'secularism' is messianic and deferred; it is as much a Christianisation of culture as an enculturation of Christianity. The total extension of revelation to the compass of the human as such, the universalisation of revelation, Schelling believes, is the end of Christianity predicted in the New Testament.

Given Schelling's novel conception of faith as 'the rest of reason', the *terminus ad quem* of knowledge, and not, as it is more conventionally understood, the graced act of belief or trust that precedes understanding or the *terminus a quo* of theological insight, we can conclude that faith is not superseded by reason in philosophical religion. Paul writes that 'when the perfect comes, the partial passes away' (1 Cor. 13:9). Where 'the partial' in this Scriptural passage is traditionally understood to be faith, Schelling reverses the sense of Paul's claim: 'the partial' is now speculative reason, and the perfect, faith. As an orientation of the will, Schellingian faith remains essential to the life of reason, and insofar as reason is not annulled in the end – it is fulfilled, not destroyed, by revelation – faith can be anticipated as enlivening reason without end. Reason will find the answers to its ultimate questions in revelation, and will come to rest in an orientation of the will that no longer doubts but believes. Schelling's problem, however, with theology as a faith-founded science is that it could never be legitimate as philosophy, which means it is not genuine science, and will pass away, as Paul says (1 Cor. 13). Even more important for distinguishing the age of faith from the age of philosophical religion is the argument concerning access. As long as theology remains the special work of a group of thinkers who have been particularly gifted by God to carry it out, the universalisation of revelation predicted by Paul has not yet happened. The Philosophy of Revelation is not a faith-based science; it has left that beyond with a previous age of the spirit; even philosophical religion still lies ahead of it.

One could imagine a cursory reading of Schelling confusing the act of will, the decision which inaugurates the turn to the positive, with the proverbial blind leap of faith. It is not the same thing at all. Schelling is no fideist, either at the beginning or at the end of his career. The problem of fideism was a central concern of Schelling's since his dispute with Jacobi in 1812. It is major theme in his 1833 retrospective on Jacobi's place in the history of modern philosophy (Schelling 1833: 165–85/164–92). In his justified objection to rationalism, Jacobi endeavours to ground Christianity in a leap of faith, a *salto mortale*, and according to Schelling, psychologises the revelation. Schelling's 1833 treatment of Jacobi is the culmination of a course on the history of philosophy. The course itself is not just a survey, but is crafted as a prolegomenon to the Philosophy of Mythology and Revelation. Jacobi and theosophy are the final subjects of the course. They are both treated as types of theological or metaphysical empiricism. It perhaps does not need to be said that the kind of empiricism at issue in Jacobi and Boehme (or in the late Schelling for that matter) is not Lockean or Humean atomistic empiricism, which having broken experience into atomic bits can never recover even ordinary human experience, let alone the experience of God. At issue here is the knowledge of God through a non-reductive account of experience as encompassing both knowledge of the self, of creation, and of the personal.

Schelling opens the 1833 discussion of Jacobi by clarifying that what is of most interest in theological or metaphysical empiricism is the experiential grounds for justifying an ostensible revelation of God. It becomes clear in the course of the discussion why knowledge of the living and personal God could only be a revealed knowledge – in short because knowledge of a person, human or divine, is always mediated through that person's self-disclosing deeds and speech. Revelation is uncontroversially defined by Schelling as knowledge by authority, albeit on the authority of Godself. Schelling distinguishes two possible responses to an authoritative divine self-revelation: on the one hand, 'blind submission', which renounces philosophy and the scientific project of knowing God, and on the other hand, a philosophical effort to justify revelation on independent grounds.[47] It is with the second approach, the philosophical approach to revelation, that Schelling is most concerned in this lecture; the effort to rationally justify revelation on grounds that are independent of the revelation itself, that is, the reception of revelation 'supported by grounds of reason of whatever kind they may be' (Schelling 1833: 165/164). Such an external justification can proceed via an appeal to immediate, inner experience, and it is precisely this notion of experience that most interests Schelling.

There are two ways to justify a knowledge of the revealed God by appeal to inner experience: one, taken by Jacobi, is subjective, the other, taken by Boehme and theosophy, is objective. Jacobi's notion of faith as feeling (later, the immediate knowledge of reason) is subjective because it renounces all effort at scientific elaboration, whereas theosophy is not without content, and endeavours to found a scientific project. It is not only incommunicable, it is also without speculative content, and its only weapon against rationalism is scepticism. Herein lies Schelling's ultimate problem with Jacobi's philosophy of religion, and his problem with all forms of fideism: Jacobi rightly objects to rationalism, but has nothing to offer in its place save the bald assertion that his faith 'knows' better. For Schelling, the incommunicability of Jacobian feeling undercuts its philosophical worth. As a proponent of non-knowledge, Jacobi has nothing to teach philosophy.

Already in the 1812 *Denkmal*, Schelling argues against Jacobi's fideism that a true knowledge of nature not only can, but also must be the starting point for a knowledge of God. Schelling's defence of 'naturalism' as a propaedeutic to 'theism' is no reactionary return to onto-theology. In the most formal sense, Schelling defends natural theology, understood in its broadest outlines as the correlation of a revealed knowledge of God with general knowledge of nature. There is no question of reviving the foundationalist natural theology that Kant had proven invalid. But what is totally indefensible for Schelling, and a dead end for both naturalism and theism, is Jacobi's exclusive dualism which would posit nature and the divine as two things standing in accidental relation to each other. A nature that is only accidentally related to the divine is a Godless nature; a divinity that is only accidentally related to nature is an unnatural God. It may be that God in fact does not exist – Schelling never presumes certainty on this issue, either in 1812 or in 1833 – but if God exists, God does not exist as a being that is separate from the things which he causes to be. Traditional theism, anxious lest God be pantheistically implicated in creation, has always foundered on the question of the intelligibility of nature. The naturalism that Schelling pursues in 1809, and later as well, assumes that if God exists, God is the principle of the intelligibility of all things that exist through and in God. Whatever we truly know of nature is in some obscure way disclosive of divine being. Schelling's naturalism is a theophanic naturalism, not an onto-theological naturalism, and if it finds analogues in traditional Jewish, Christian and Muslim mystical theology, his departure point is Boehme. For Boehme, we do not 'naturalise' or 'anthropomorphise' God by attributing natural processes to God; we recognise that natural processes reveal divine processes, even if the latter are not exhausted by the former.

In his 1833 retrospective on Jacobi, Schelling returns to the question of naturalism, but now with a much greater appreciation for how Jacobi's notion of feeling had opened a way towards positive philosophy, even if Jacobi himself had not taken the path. 'Of all modern philosophers', Jacobi 'had in the most lively way discovered the need for historical philosophy (in our sense)' (Schelling 1833: 168/166). That said, Schelling draws a clear distinction between the early Jacobi, who defended faith as a feeling for the living God of the Bible, and the later Jacobi, who in Schelling's view confused the feeling for the divine with an immediate knowledge of reason.[48] The early Jacobi had correctly grasped how felt experience always outstrips reason, and how access to the positive, the personal and the historical must be based on feeling, or more generally, experience, and can never be *a priori* or purely deductive. But when the later Jacobi argued for an immediate knowledge of the personal God, he confused everything. Reason for the late Schelling, who follows Kant closely in this regard, is the faculty of totality, of limitation, of the ideal and the essential; it only ever knows the *ens necessarium*, Descartes' *idea substantiae infinitae*, which Kant regarded as an ideal necessary to the proper functioning of the mind, but which must never be inflated into genuine knowledge of divinity. If one wishes to know something of the existing God, Schelling argues, one must proceed via experience and the understanding, which opens on to the unknown and widens the mind to the new. One sees in these remarks the late Schelling's assumption that his method of positive philosophy does not contradict Kant, for the Kantian critique of onto-theology precluded only an *a priori* knowledge of God, not a *per posterius* knowledge of God; that is, Kant, at least in Schelling's reading of him, did not preclude a probabilistic knowledge of God that is achieved by means of experience. Jacobi, however, showed himself to be the true rationalist by conflating a knowledge of the true God with the immediate content of reason. Earlier Jacobi had prematurely surrendered science to the rationalist and too hastily conceded defeat; later he unwittingly identified himself with the rationalist project. 'No other philosopher had conceded so *much* to pure rationality . . . as Jacobi. He really laid down his arms before it' (Schelling 1833: 167/166).

From a strictly theological perspective, faith is a direct act of God's grace elevating the intellect and strengthening the will.[49] But can philosophy affirm such a thing? Is the claim not tantamount to saying that philosophy as such, that is, a general account of being, based on a reasonable perspective, one that appeals to all reasoning people as such and asks of them no more than that they should reason well about these matters, is shut out from theological understanding? If the Christian philosopher is gifted with faith, then he or she affirms the revelation, not on the basis of reason and experience, that is, not by means of philosophy as such, but by means of an extra-philosophical act, a miracle that has transformed his or her intellect and will, while leaving the intellect and will of others in the dark. The philosopher might maintain this scandal of particularity as fully reasonable, but he or she could no longer coherently try to convince others by means of philosophy alone, nor hold others accountable for their lack of insight. On the other hand, if faith is a condition that is given in principle to all in the revelation, if the human intellect as such has been illuminated, then we no longer need to delimit philosophy from theology. Reason would thereby become a pre-eminently historical phenomenon: it has a history prior to the revelation, in which it is in the dark about the true God, and a history after the revelation, in which it is given the means to affirm God.

Something like Schelling's conception of revelation as a general illumination of humanity seems also to have been the inspiration of the pre-Nicene Fathers, particularly of the Alexandrian school, who spoke with Clement of a Christian *gnosis* to displace the pseudo-*gnosis*, the illumination reserved for the elite, of the Valentinian gnostics. Schelling's Philosophy of Revelation is a revitalisation of this ancient approach to gnosis, which is still recognised as legitimate by some Eastern Orthodox theologians.[50] If there is any substance to the oft-repeated claim that Schelling is a gnostic, it is in this sense of *gnosis* as the general illumination of human reason by divine revelation. Schelling's thought has nothing in common with Valentinian gnosticism. Philosophical religion has nothing to do with the liberating of the 'divine sparks' from the bodies of those elite souls trapped in the botched creation of an idiot demiurge. Valentinian gnosticism is elitist, particularist and exclusive; philosophical religion is egalitarian, universalist and inclusive. The end of Christianity, the *eschaton*, which will both bring historical, revealed religion to its end and fulfil its promise of the fullness of divine knowledge, is the third age of revelation. Christ will be all in all (*panta en passin*). Pantheism will have become true: no one, no creature, nothing, will be left out.

Theologia crucis

The standard reading of the history of German idealism sees Schelling as the most irrational and 'mystical' of the post-Kantian philosophers. I hope it has become clear from the foregoing that nothing could be further from the truth. No German idealist is more committed to the principle of reason than Schelling. His insistence on a somewhat conventional understanding of the principle very likely alienated the Berlin Hegelians from the late

Schelling. They no doubt saw in Schelling's talk of adequate explanation, falsifiability and non-contradiction an abstract, truncated philosophy that could not move beyond the understanding. It is also worth remembering that Hegel is much more positive about the philosophical value of mysticism than Schelling is. It was Hegel who called Boehme the 'first German philosopher', while Schelling was not so sure that Boehme was a philosopher at all.[51] Hegel sees in medieval mystical theology the dialectic of infinite and finitude truly articulated, while Schelling sees it as a form of negative philosophy beating against its cage.[52] As we have seen, according to the late Schelling, the mystic, who attempts to climb up to the divine via a negation of all creaturely concepts, does not in fact break through to the real God.

Schelling's late critique of mysticism reasserts the basic point of Luther's theology of the cross.[53] Luther rejected Scholastic theology as systemic unbelief. The Scholastic reordering of created knowledge in the uncreated light, which the medieval mystic presumes to have accessed in the interior depths of his or her soul, is a merely aesthetic speculative achievement, a *theologia gloriae*, a presumptive revelling in the resplendent shining of the divine in all things. The medieval theologian of glory insists on remaining the lord of all he surveys, and so is no better than an unbeliever, one who refuses to stay with the conceptual darkness of faith but is confirmed in the certainty and clarity of an inner knowledge.[54] By turning away from the historical towards the timeless realm of essence, the theologian of glory does not stay with the uncertainty and obscurity of the *Deus absconditus* revealed in the cross, for he or she does not need to. The theologian of glory presumes to possess the key to a deeper understanding of the mysteries revealed. These are the ones Luther derides as pseudo-theologians, those who, inflated by their own distorted sense of their abilities, presume to have transcended the obscurity of the divine revealed in the abjection of the crucified. Schelling, in his reading of the *kenosis* hymn of Phil. 2:5–11 as the Son's paradigmatic renunciation of sovereignty before the Father, in his denial of the finality of proofs for the existence of God, and above all in his distinction of negative and positive philosophy, is clearly a thinker of the *theologia crucis*.[55]

Schelling's distinction between negative and positive philosophy unmistakably echoes Luther's distinction between *theologia gloriae* and *theologia crucis*. Like the *theologia gloriae*, negative philosophy is a metaphysical distraction from the submission to the real God who transcends reason, and can shut the reasoner off from receiving the revelation. Like the *theologia crucis*, positive philosophy draws reason down to earth, to the contingency and uncertainty of history, and the revelation of a God who descends into it, to be revealed not in glory and majesty but in the humiliation and obscurity of the crucified messiah. Like the *theologia crucis*, the revelation of the really existing God for the late Schelling is as much a revelation of God's essential hiddenness to fallen human reason as it is an unveiling of divinity in the Christ. For Luther as much as for Schelling, revelation is unprethinkable (*unvordenklich*), for reason possesses no *a priori* category by which to anticipate it.

But what if the *theologia gloriae* were somehow necessary? What if it had a necessary role to play in the preparation of the ground for the reception of the mystery of the cross – not a logical propaedeutic, but an ethical one, as a temptation to be resisted and an original sin, to take oneself for God, to be reversed? Reason, according to Schelling (and here the way swings off from a certain reading of Luther), is capable of *learning* to partially understand the revelation in the cross. What else, Schelling asks, is the purpose of revelation other than to instruct the human intellect in the divine wisdom?[56]

Schelling's position, therefore, is opposed to neo-Lutheran revelational positivism. The revelational positivist denies that reason possesses any innate capacity for understanding the revelation; revelation can only be received on the condition that reason is fundamentally altered by faith.[57] As we have seen above, reason's innate idea of God is not in itself false. It is reason's spontaneous knowledge of the mode of being of the divine, reason's innate concept of infinity, which (as Schelling does not disagree with Descartes) is a trace of the real God in creation.[58] Even if it corresponds to no experiential object, the concept of God cannot be entirely disavowed, for reason requires the ideal of the unconditioned, understood prosaically along Kantian lines as the totality of predicates, as a presupposition to systematise its concepts. The forgetting of the distinction between an idea of God and knowledge of a really existing God, between essence and existence, is the root mistake of the ontological argument, for Schelling as for Kant, and this error dominates modern philosophy and renders it for the most part idealism, that is, forgetfulness of being. But Schelling goes much further than Luther in his assessment of the value of the theology of glory, or more prosaically, natural theology. Without the idea of the *ens necessarium* which drives the theology of glory, reason could not receive the revelation, even if the idea is not enough to anticipate or deduce the revelation. As we have said, the negative philosophy *is* the presupposition of the positive philosophy, even if the negative can only be properly understood in the light of the positive. We must not mistake this point and misjudge Schelling as a foundationalist: it is not that the idea of God gives us a heuristic means to approach the existing God, as it does for the modern Thomist Bernard Lonergan.[59] Rather, the manifest ideality of the innate concept of God shows us that we lack existential knowledge of the divine. Without the failure of the ideal, the human being would never fully understand the degree to which he or she needs a mediator. We only know truth in its contrast to the false, and error in the light of truth. Schelling sees in negative philosophy, as in mythology (or the theology of glory for that matter), a crucible of illusion through which any consciousness that would know the truth must pass. This ordering of the negative to the positive is the pivotal move in the integration of human experience, and a recognition of the role of not only philosophy, but also paganism and natural religion in the hearing of the Word.

But what, more precisely, is the relation of Schelling's positive philosophy to Luther's theology of the cross? Luther's distinction between *theologia gloriae* and *theologia crucis* is expressed in a few key theses from the *Disputatio Heidelbergae*:

> That person is not rightly called a theologian who looks upon the invisible things of God as though they were clearly perceptible through things that have actually happened (Thesis 19).
>
> He deserves to be called a theologian, however, who understands the visible and manifest things of God seen through suffering and the Cross (Thesis 20).
>
> A theology of glory calls evil good and good evil. A theology of the Cross calls the thing what it actually is (Thesis 21).
>
> That wisdom which sees the invisible things of God in works as perceived by man is completely puffed up, blinded, and hardened (Thesis 22). (Luther 1955–86; vol. 31, 39–40)

Luther's point is that one who already possesses God in reason does not need the cross. It is in this way that the cross becomes a No to human philosophy and religion, the refusal of direct access; 'the foolishness of God', which is 'wiser than human wisdom', and 'the weakness of God', which is 'stronger than human strength' (1 Cor. 1:25). And yet, Schelling would counter, the *theologia gloriae* presupposes *something*, a rational tendency, which is constitutively a part of human thinking, an anticipation of divine things, to be renounced as genuine knowledge to be sure, but first of all to be acknowledged as a sense for how things fit together, which can be frustrated precisely because it is always and everywhere operative. In itself the innate 'ideal of reason' is not untrue. It is only when merely human wisdom is elevated above the God revealed in the cross that theology capitulates to unbelief. Properly ordered, human knowledge, science and natural religion, which is mythological religion, have their place. Natural religion and mysticism, Schelling urges, if interpreted correctly, can serve as a propaedeutic to the reception of revelation. That, at least, is Schelling's strategy in distinguishing negative from positive theology, and mythology from revelation. The problem with medieval natural theology is that the medieval theologian is tempted to glory in it, rather than see it for what it is, a means, not an end.

But perhaps Luther can be read through Schelling on this point. One notices that Luther's critique focuses on the *attitude* of the theologian of glory, not on the content of his or her theology. The theologian of glory 'looks upon' the things of God as 'though they were clearly perceptible through the things that have actually happened', that is, as though revelational history were an open book, written for the theologian's speculative aesthetic enjoyment. It is not the proposition, that God's wisdom is revealed in the world, which stands in the way of the truth; it is the theologian's attitude that is the difficulty. The theologian glories in his presumption of possessing this wisdom; he is 'puffed up' and needs to be humiliated, like the dinner guest at the Lord's banquet in the Gospel of Luke, who assumes the best seat at the table only to be embarrassed by the host who moves him to the lower seat assigned to him (Luke 14:7–11). Only he who first assumes the lowest seat can be elevated to the best seat at the table. If he assumes the best seat first, he can only be demoted. This purification of the speculative narcissism that presumes to possess as absolute knowledge that which is only known in part, obscurely, 'as though through a glass, darkly' (1 Cor. 13:12), and that boasts certainty where at best probability is offered to reason – this is precisely the path from negative to positive philosophy according to Schelling, a path that is opened up not by means of logic, but by means of the decision for the real. The philosopher who awakens to the contingency of reason, its dependence upon the good will of God to reveal Godself or not, can no longer pretend; the illusion has to be traversed. Reason, discovering its poverty, empties itself. This reversal of attitude is the ecstasy of reason, which I have already discussed, the act whereby reason turns itself inside out, and emerges from the ideal realm, in which it deals only with its own content, into the real, the contingent and the historical. Only an encounter with the real can reveal the virtuality of the ideal, but everything depends upon the attitude, the openness and the vulnerability of the thinker to reality.

The humiliation of reason before the real, Schelling argues, has already occurred. It is nothing less than the history of Christianity, which is far more deeply entwined with Western rationality than most philosophers have recognised. It is to be conceded that the productive enmeshing of Western philosophy with Christian theology was also Hegel's insight. We would do well to draw Schelling and Hegel together on this point, if only to better understand where they part ways. Hegel presumes to *possess* that which is irreducibly external to reason, to *command* that which is always a gift (with the conditions of the giving always remaining in the hand of the giver). Schelling's Philosophy of Revelation, as distinct from Hegel's absolute idealism, never completely internalises the revealed; reason never fully negates the externality of the divine; the indivisible remainder always stands between finite reason and infinity, indicating reason's dependency, its groundedness upon that which it does not control or command. But there is still something decisive for us to do, and upon this fundamentally free act everything depends. The move to the positive philosophy, as we have seen, is a free act of the philosopher deciding for the real. If Schelling can be read as following Luther on the critique of natural theology, he swings to the Catholic side and argues for a role for the reasoner in the reception of the revelation. Here, too, caution is required, for Schelling, to repeat, is not a foundationalist: the free act is not deduced as necessary, not even as reasonable, on the basis of the results of the negative philosophy; it is willed by the philosopher who wants more than the negative philosophy, and who wills a philosophy of *being*, not just of reason. The negative philosophy ends and the positive begins when the philosopher says, 'I want that which is above being, that which is not merely being [*das bloße Seyende*], but rather what is more than this, the lord of being [*der Herr des Seyns*]' (Schelling 1842d: 93/154). The Philosophy of Revelation need not be, but if it be, it will be only by virtue of a decision of the philosopher to acknowledge the nature and extent of his or her desire for the living God (Schelling 1842d: 133/182).

Here we see Schelling's admittedly non-Lutheran antidote to the *theologia gloriae*. And while I call it non-Lutheran, the positive philosophy is not onto-theological either; it does not slide back into *theologia gloriae*. It is not natural theology or rational evidence that compels the decision that inaugurates the positive philosophy. It is not a logical solution but an ethical one, for on the level of logic, negative philosophy (the *theologia gloriae*, if we use Luther's term) is entirely consistent. One must *engage* one's own existence and *decide* to put oneself into question in order to step outside the circle of necessity, the domain of essence, of *eidoi*, of that which gives itself to be mastered *a priori*, into the domain of the real.

The theologian of the cross chooses finitude over self-delusion. In following the crucified, he or she becomes nothing more than what he or she already is. Similarly, in moving into the positive, the philosopher of revelation disidentifies from that upon which all depends, the infinite being, and becomes nothing more than the finite being that he or she is, one who wants and wills because he or she does not possess the fullness of the real. The presupposition of this finite act of will is the possibility – Luther would say, the temptation – which the philosopher of revelation will not actualise, to disavow finitude and mistake oneself as sufficient unto being, as infinite and first. The move into the positive presupposes the actuality of sin, that is, the historical efficacy of the primal temptation, to refuse the sovereignty of God and take the self for the infinite. The beginning of positive philosophy is an act of the human being seeking to be free of illusion and to know the truly divine God. The positive philosopher cannot satisfy this desire, but can begin to habituate him or herself to the contingent realm, to the real, in which alone a satisfaction is possible. He or she does not anticipate revelation, but by means of setting oneself outside of reason, the positive philospher is ready for it. The reason that empties itself before the real is open to hear the Word, that is, it has a capacity to receive revelation. God remains the revealer and the revelation remains in God's hand. 'Freedom' here applies both to the revealer and the receiver of the revelation. God need not reveal Godself and so is free in God's revelation; the human being need not receive the revelation, and so is free in their reception of it. The free reception is a surrender of mastery, of control over the revealed. The turn to the positive is not an act whereby reason negates its finitude and so *infinitises* itself; it is not a project of self-overcoming or self-divinisation that is here described. According to Schelling's strict definition of revelation, cited above, we are not assumed to possess a potency for divine truth, but only a capacity to be so affected by the divine as to be rendered able to receive the truth. In Thomistic terms, we have no natural or active potency for divine knowledge, but only, by virtue of being created, a *potentia obedientialis*, a potency to be acted upon by the divine in such a way as to be rendered *capax Dei*.[60]

Notes

1. See SW 1: 243: 'The first postulate of all philosophy is to act freely from within oneself.' See Fichte (1797: 20): 'The kind of philosophy one chooses depends on the kind of person one is.' See also Kasper (1965: 63–9). Not only the decisional beginning of the positive philosophy, but also the content of the two alternatives of negative and positive philosophy represent a striking return to Schelling's early thought: dogmatism is Spinozism or the philosophy of necessity, negative philosophy is idealism, and just as *a priori* as Spinozism. Criticism is the philosophy of freedom, or transcendental philosophy, positive philosophy is the philosophy of history, that is, the philosophy of free and unanticipatable events. The difference between the dogmatism/criticism alternative and the relation of negative to positive philosophy is that after the decision the negative philosophy serves as the support and presupposition of the positive philosophy, whereas dogmatism and criticism run side by side like two parallel lines that never meet.
2. See Hegel (1801).
3. The theorem of absolute transcendence is the key to understanding the elusive 'formula of the world' of the *Ages* and the Stuttgart Seminars. 'B' in the formula is the transcendent as such, that which is never encompassed by a formula, never comprehended, but always required for that which is in fact formulated and comprehended. See McGrath (2012: 149–51).
4. Schelling was not alone in attempting to craft a modern philosophical defence of revelation in the face of such criticism. Schelling's Philosophy of Revelation belongs to a forgotten philosophical literature on the topic centred around the work of his Catholic contemporaries: Johann Sebastian Drey, Franz Xaver Staudenmaier, Friedrich Pilgram, Martin Deutinger and Franz von Baader. See Kasper (1965: 190).

5. This was the position of historical-critical biblical scholarship in the early twentieth century, and is still widespread. Barth's theology of revelation was immensely influential in this regard. See, for example, Bornkamm (1960: 180): 'The event of Christ's resurrection from the dead, his life and his eternal reign, are things removed from historical scholarship. History cannot ascertain and establish conclusively the facts about them as it can with other events of the past. The last historical fact available to them is the Easter faith of the first disciples.' N. T. Wright contests this view directly, and adopts Schelling's line, that there is no *a priori* reason why the resurrection could not be the object of historical study. See Wright (1992).

6. This is the heart of Kasper's critique of Schelling. Schelling is held to have sidelined the revealed word in favour of the revelatory deed, and thus allegedly becomes 'gnostic'. Kasper (1965: 208–11). This strikes me as inaccurate insofar as scripture remains the primary source for knowledge of revelatory deeds, at least until the advent of philosophical religion. What Schelling has sidelined is the need for the hierarchy of the Church as the authoritative interpreter of scripture, and this is what Kasper truly objects to, which he must, as a faithful Catholic, future bishop, and now cardinal of the Roman Catholic Church.

7. Schleiermacher comes to mind, and his many followers in the nineteenth and twentieth centuries. See Schleiermacher (1799; 1830). It is crucial to remember, however, that Schleiermacher was no foundationalist. The feeling of conviction which founds knowledge of revelation is a specifically Christian form of consciousness. See Wishart (2019).

8. See Levinas (1974: 142ff.) and Henry (1963). Both Levinas and Henry laid the groundwork for Marion (2002). On the critique of revelation as phenomenology, see Janicaud (1991).

9. In the 1927 lecture, 'Phenomenology and Theology', Heidegger more or less forbade phenomenology from discussing religious revelation, even though his own retrieval of the Greek experience of truth as originally *aletheia* or 'unconcealment' seemed to recommend a primal connection between theology and philosophy. See Heidegger (1927b).

10. On the French reception of the late Schelling, see the contributions in Courtine (2010).

11. See Husserl (1931: para. 8).

12. See Schelling (SW 9: 228–9): 'But philosophy is not demonstrative science, philosophy is, in a word a free spiritual act [*freie Geistesthat*]; its first step is not knowledge, but rather not-knowing, a giving up of all human knowledge. So long as man desires knowledge, the absolute subject will become an object for him, and he will not know it in itself. In so far as he says, I as subject cannot know, I *will not* to know, insofar as he takes recourse to knowledge, he makes room for that which is knowledge, namely, for the absolute subject, who shows itself to be knowledge itself.'

13. This Heideggerian theme is plainly Schellingian in origin. See, in particular, Heidegger (1929).

14. According to Levinas, it is undeniable that Descartes discovers already in Meditation Three that a suspension of all existence claims is not in fact possible. See Levinas (1998: 64): 'The placing in us of an unencompassable idea overturns this presence of self which is consciousness . . . It is thus an idea signifying within a significance prior to presence, to all presence, prior to every origin in consciousness, and so an-archic, accessible only in its trace.' See also Levinas (1998: 66): 'The Infinite affects thought by simultaneously devastating it and calling it; through a "putting it in its place", the Infinite puts thought in place. It wakes thought up.'

15. See Levinas (1961: 67).

16. See Schelling (1854a: 492): 'The science which we now pursue knows no other law than that every possibility must be fulfilled, none can be suppressed.'

17. While I have Boehme in mind here, the Kabbalistic idea of *zimzum* or the contraction of infinity which makes room for something other than the infinite hovers over all of this – over Boehme's notion of the splitting of the unground, Schelling's 1809 narrative of the 'birth of God' and his 1831 trope of 'the law of the world'. We don't know how much of the Kabbalah Boehme was exposed to. But the late Schelling's Kabbalistic research and his interaction with the Frankfurt Kabbalist J. F. Molitor is well known. See Sandkühler (1968: 182ff.)

18. In the *Urfassung* Schelling distinguishes the divine essence from eternal existence in terms of the relation of willing (*willen*) to desiring (*wollen*). Eternal existence is desire without will because it has nothing before it which it could will, *Wollen ohne Willen* (Schelling 1831: 43). With great psychological insight, Schelling understands primordial being to be nothing other than pure desire, which, like Lacan's drive, subsists without a determinate object. The divine essence, God before creating the world and becoming personalised as an actual Trinity, is the opposite: God is essentially will without desire (*Willen ohne Wollen*), quiescent, *gelassene* will, *der nicht wollende Wille* (Schelling 1831: 43). The transition from the desire without will to will without desire is the transition from unconscious infinity ('blind' being) to self-conscious and potentially personal infinity (deliberative being).

19. See Prov. 8: 22–31; Wis. 7:25–30. See Schelling (1841: 160ff.; 1854b: 294). Cf. Boehme (1623: 1). On Boehme's notion of the mirror of wisdom, see Koyré (1929: 206ff.) and McGrath (2012: 66–71). Boehme's development of the Old Testament figure of Sophia was a centrepiece of the Freedom Essay (Schelling 1809: 359/29–30). It plainly remains decisive for his positive philosophy. See especially Schelling (1841: 168/135). '"The Lord possessed me at the beginning of his way," i.e., when he moved out of the unforethinkable Being; before his deeds.—This line demonstrates that it is about something that is not an act of God. That originary potency [Sophia] is not brought forth by God. While it is not before him as a potency of Being, it is there as he is; it presents itself to him as something he can either desire or not desire. The original other is "with" God and shows God what God might be . . . It is not some power alien to God . . . it is only his [God's] idea which he submits to if he takes up the possibility [of existing]; for the law forbids anything from remaining in doubt.'

20. 'Fortuna was celebrated as the wet nurse of the world. *Mater* [mother] and *materia* [matter] are factually related; for [*Fortuna*] is the ὑποκείμενον of the future Creation. She is the Maya (related to power, possibility, potence [*Macht, Möglichkeit, Potenz*]), which spread the web of (mere) semblance before the Creator in order to trap him and impel him toward the actual Creation' (Schelling 1841: 185/157).

21. The Boehmian idea of a primal event of division in infinity remains plainly influential here. Recall that in Boehme's unground, which is undivided nothingness, a desire for *something*, specifically for manifestation, arises, and therefore a desire for another emerges, for one to whom infinity could be manifest. But the unground is preceded by nothing and so has nothing to desire. Sophia, 'the mirror of wisdom', the 'eye of his seeing', shows the infinite 'all powers, colours, wonders and beings . . . in equal weight and measure' (Boehme 1623: 1.9), and so the unground or 'first will' gives rise to a 'second will', 'an apprehensible will', which 'is the first will's eternal feeling and finding' (Boehme 1623: 1.5). It seems to me beyond dispute that from Boehme, Schelling derived all of the essential moves of his theogony, both in its 1809 historically immanentist form, and in its 1831 monotheist form. These moves are three: 1) the positing of an unconscious infinity (pure desire without an object); 2) the deduction of the

necessity of dividing the infinite into two contesting wills if a will for creation should arise; and 3) the deduction of the need for a mediator who is neither the unconscious infinite nor the self-conscious and actually willing infinite, but the one who offers the divine the possibility of being self-diversified and productive of a world.

22. The law of the world has a New Testament theological root in Luke 8:17 and Rev. 20:11–15, 'the second death', which I shall discuss in the second book. The law of the world not only requires that all possibilities be rendered conceptually distinct and logically ordered, it also demands that a decision be made among them, for good or evil.

23. Abduction is the logic of discovery and can be seen at work wherever human beings had to invent something radically new in order to achieve a desired consequence. Where deduction begins with sound premises and deduces valid or unshakeable conclusions therefrom (arguing from antecedent to consequent), abduction begins with conclusions ('surprising facts' needing explanations), or desired outcomes, and postulates the premises that could produce such results, arguing in effect from consequent to antecedent. When early humans needed to invent a way to take down a mammoth from a distance with a projectile weapon, they invented the spear launcher, a thing that had never before existed. They began with the 'conclusion' or the consequent – spearing a mammoth from a distance – and on the basis of that, proceeded to 'dream up' something absolutely novel. Peirce calls this move 'musement' (Peirce 1908: 436). I owe this example to Professor Dietrich Dörner at Bamberg University.

24. See Peirce (1908: 436): 'There is a certain agreeable occupation of mind which, from its having no distinctive name, I infer is not as commonly practised as it deserves to be; for indulged in moderately – say through some five to six per cent of one's waking time, perhaps during a stroll – it is refreshing enough more than to repay the expenditure. Because it involves no purpose save that of casting aside all serious purpose, I have sometimes been half-inclined to call it reverie, with some qualification; but for a frame of mind so antipodal to vacancy and dreaminess such a designation would be too excruciating a misfit. In fact, it is Pure Play. Now, Play, we all know, is a lively exercise of one's powers. Pure Play has no rules, except this very law of liberty. It bloweth where it listeth. It has no purpose, unless recreation. The particular occupation I mean – a *petite bouchée* with the Universes – may take either the form of esthetic contemplation, or that of distant castle-building (whether in Spain or within one's own moral training), or that of considering some wonder in one of the Universes, or some connection between two of the three, with speculation concerning its cause. It is this last kind – I will call it "Musement" on the whole – that I particularly recommend, because it will in time flower into the N.A. [the so-called neglected argument for the existence of God, which is in fact a version of Schelling's running proof]. One who sits down with the purpose of becoming convinced of the truth of religion is plainly not inquiring in scientific singleness of heart, and must always suspect himself of reasoning unfairly. So he can never attain the entirety even of a physicist's belief in electrons, although this is avowedly but provisional. But let religious meditation be allowed to grow up spontaneously out of Pure Play without any breach of continuity, and the Muser will retain the perfect candour proper to Musement.'

25. 'Retroduction does not afford security' (Peirce 1908: 441).

26. 'Abduction for Peirce posits a problematic hypothesis in order to account for a surprising observation. Schelling's astonishing observation, for which one cannot account through rational explanation, is the fact that there is something rather than nothing or that there is sense (*Sinn*) rather than chaos (*Wahnsinn*), reason rather than unreason. Any attempt to explain *this* fact must make recourse to that which is not merely

rational, be it sub- or hyper-rational. In other words, only a "rogue" explanation is in order' (Tritten 2012a: 49). Tritten's point, as far as natural science is concerned, is well taken. A natural scientific explanation rests on certain presuppositions which it cannot question from within natural science, for example that matter is real and is basically intelligible. However, Peirce uses abduction on a much larger scale than this. In his 'Neglected Argument for the Existence of God', he more or less reproduces Schelling's running proof: the world is ordered, full of beauty and personal meaning, and it need not be. If God existed such an order would be expected. Therefore we have reasons to believe that God exists. See Peirce (1908).

27. On what follows, see Franks (2015).

28. The method of proof, Jacobi argues, must proceed from antecedent to consequent, resulting in an incontrovertible conclusion. To be clear, Jacobi is not interested in such a proof for God's existence. His point is that this is the *only* way to proceed, and that Kant has justly demolished the whole proofs industry.

29. Abductive reasoning offers philosophy the capacity to deal with novelty. Franks comments: 'Peirce also rejects the tradition of explaining the heterogeneous in terms of the homogeneous, mainly in what he takes to be its contemporary version, which starts not with divine aseity but rather with exceptionless natural law. The necessitarian, as Peirce dubs his opponent, does not think that irregularity can or should be explained, and his ultimate explanatory factor – universal law – "is a hard, ultimate, unintelligible fact". Consequently, there can be no explanation of many features of the universe – namely, those that are irregular. Yet this includes increasing complexity and diversity – in short, novelty, which is observed wherever there is development in both the natural and historical realms. General regularity explains particular regularities, but general regularity itself remains a brute fact. In contrast, just as Schelling begins with a brute act of arbitrary divine will, Peirce begins with bruteness itself, understood as chance; and, just as Schelling seeks to find a general developmental pattern for the emergence of novelty within a single life that includes the possibility of disease and evil, so Peirce comprehends novelty and irregularity as features of the life of the cosmos itself' (Franks 2015: 749).

30. See Burbridge (1992: 66): 'The positive philosopher asks: Within experience itself does one encounter the features specified in reason's hypothesis? This is not strictly an argument *a posteriori*. One does not move from the particulars of experience to an inductive generalisation. Schelling calls it a proof *per posterius*. The consequent of a hypothetical statement is experienced as true. *A priori* reasoning has already shown that one or other of two contraries is necessarily implied by the one condition that is in question. That condition had in fact been in doubt because both contraries could have been false. The fact that one has been experienced as true thus establishes the truth of that condition. "Through its results is the *a priori* known." At each stage in the positive philosophy, then, the following logical pattern occurs. Two givens that have a definite logical order are acknowledged. The first principle plus whatever has already been derived from it *per posterius* has a logical priority; it is a possible condition. The task is to find a middle term which is both the immediate consequent of the condition and sufficiently determinate to entail a difference in the actual world. When that difference is found independently to hold true in the world, the truth of the middle term is confirmed, and it can then be added to the set of logically prior terms.'

31. See Whitehead (1929: 3–17). Cf. F. H. Bradley on satisfaction as criterion of truth (Bradley 1914: 317): 'The truth for any man is that which at the time satisfies his theoretical want, and "more or less true" means more less of such satisfaction. The want is

a special one. We do not of course know beforehand what it is and what can satisfy it. We only at first feel that there is something special that we miss or gain, and we go on to discover the nature of the want and its object by trial, failure and success.'

32. See Schelling (1853); Buchheim (2020).

33. On this point, see Buchheim (2020). Buchheim sees this as a significant change in Schelling's position. I am not so sure. In any case, Schelling's late insistence on the primacy of the historical-critical entry into the Philosophy of Revelation does not invalidate the earlier deductive method; it only underscores the contingency of both approaches on the decision of the philosopher.

34. In insisting on the distinction between God's existence and God's essence in 'Eternal Truths', Schelling calls to his defence both Plato and Aristotle. Schelling interprets Socrates' argument that the Good is 'beyond being' in *Republic* 6 as indicating a distinction between being as existence (that which is beyond *ousia*) and being as essence (*ousia*), which depends upon it. Aristotle's *hylomorphism* is perhaps a less disputable source, for Aristotle insists that what primarily exists is the individual, and the universal is its attribute, and is, as such, dependent upon it. Both authorities for Schelling confirm his point that being (as existence or pure act) precedes thinking, even in God, and that God's existence grounds God's essence. See Schelling (1850: 587/65): 'This, which is the absolute individual [*das absolute Einzelwesen*], is the universal essence [i.e., eternal existence actually exists *as* the divine being]. Since he is it not by willing [*nicht wollend*], and also not in consequence of his *essence* or self – for the latter, as the most singular [*Absonderlichste*] [*to malista choriston*], i.e., as the most individual, is rather that from which nothing universal follows – therefore he can be the *all*-comprehending only in consequence of a necessity extending beyond himself. But what necessity? Let us attempt it in the following manner. Let us say that the latter necessity is that of the unitary-being [*Eins-sein*] of thought and being – that *this* is the highest law, the significance of which is that whatever *is* must also have a relation to the *concept*, and that what is *nothing*, i.e., what has no relation to thought, also *truly is not*. God contains in himself nothing except the pure *thatness* [*Daß*] of his own being [*Sein*]; but this, that he *is*, would be no *truth*, if he were not *something* [*Etwas*] – something, to be sure, not in the sense of a [determinate] being [*ein Seiendes*], but in the sense of the [determinate] all-being [*das alles Seiende*] – if he did not have a relation to thought, a relation not to a *concept* but to the *concept of all concepts*, to the *idea*.'

35. See Schelling (1842b: 39–40): 'Present-day theologians are so terrified of pantheism that, instead of abolishing it in its principle, rather try to ignore it, denying to it even the possibility of manifesting. But to be actually abolished [*aufgehoben*], to be negated at its root, this principle must manifest in an actual way, and must be recognized at least as existing [*daseyend*], as impossible to exclude. It cannot just be silently put to the side. Simply ignoring it is not to overcome it. It must be explicitly contradicted. It is a concept that, by nature, cannot be excluded – a concept that must be addressed. Because they close their eyes to this principle, their whole theology remains vacillating: this principle must therefore be satisfied. [The claim] that only being is with God, and consequently, that every being is only God's being, this idea cannot be denied to either reason or feeling. It alone is the idea that makes all hearts beat. Even Spinoza's rigid and lifeless philosophy owes the power which it has always exerted over hearts – and not the most superficial among them, but especially the religious ones – it owes this entire power only to the fundamental idea that can no longer be found anywhere else. By rejecting the principle of pantheism (apparently because they do not dare to conjure it), theologians deprive themselves of the means to achieve true monotheism. For

true monotheism is perhaps nothing other than the overcoming of pantheism' (trans. Fakhoury).

36. Cf. Schelling (1809: 348–50/19–21).

37. Cf. Aquinas, *Summa Theologica*, 1a, q. 1, a. 1.

38. See Schelling's 1803 *On University Studies* (SW 5: 286–95).

39. See Schelling (1854c: 15): 'Every beginning is really faith in the end.' For a similar point from a Thomistic perspective, cf. Lonergan (1957). See Kasper (1965: 204): 'This faith differs from real faith because it is still only urging on to knowledge and shows itself in knowledge, "so that the one who believes the most is the one who knows the most, and conversely, the one who trusts most in knowledge is the most believing" [SW 14: 15]. At the beginning is a primeval faith, a primeval trust in the ultimate meaning of being. Only such a primeval trust makes it possible to explain why human beings start out on the path of seeking knowledge.'

40. See Levinas (1961: 35–40).

41. See Von Balthasar (2000: 80–107).

42. See Derrida (1996: 84): 'If every human being is wholly other, if everyone else, or every other one, is every bit other, then one can no longer distinguish between a claimed generality of ethics that would need to be sacrificed in sacrifice, and the faith that turns towards God alone, as wholly other, turning away from human duty.'

43. Husserl (1931: para 51). The difference for Schelling is that the pairing is not logical but ethical. That is, the I need not recognise the Thou, and need not be in relation to another; evil is a logical possibility for a free self. This is the essence of Schelling's non-dialectical personalism.

44. For a representative of this traditional distinction between philosophical theology and revealed theology, see Lonergan (1957: 740–51). On the move from the concept of a first cause to the notion of infinity, see Scotus's *De Primo Principio*.

45. Lonergan deduces God's being personal on the basis of his being infinite, but this is, as far as I know, not typical of Scholastic thought. See Lonegan (1957: 668): 'In the twenty-sixth place, God is personal.'

46. See *Dei Verbum, the Dogmatic Constitution on Divine Revelation* ¶ 5 (Flannery 1988: 750–65).

47. It is telling that Schelling has nothing much to say about the 'blind submission' option, and never considers the possibility of a theology of revelation, a reception of revelation that also receives from the revealer the cognitive conditions for understanding the revelation itself. Such a reception need not be blind, nor need it renounce the scientific project of constructing a theology on that basis. Here is the late Schelling's greatest oversight, one which Kierkegaard would exploit. Schelling does not, it seems, have any desire to understand a properly theological method in theology. Cf. Kierkegaard (1844: 9ff.).

48. See Schelling (1833: 175/172): 'When Jacobi later substituted reason for feeling in order to make his peace with rationalism, his philosophy also lost the truth which it had previously had. Feeling expresses a personal relationship. But now an immediate relationship to the *personal* God was to be attributed to impersonal reason, which is completely unthinkable. Jacobi has the clearest insight into the fact that rational systems do not really explain anything in the last analysis.'

49. See Aquinas, *Summa Theologica*, 1a2ae, q. 62, a. 3, ad 1.

50. See Kasper (1965: 190).

51. Hegel (1896b: 188) and Schelling (1842d: 119–22/173–5).

52. See Hegel (1827: 333–4/192–3) and Schelling (1854a: 558–9).

53. Mysticism is ultimately inadequate, for Luther and Schelling, because it underesti-
    mates what Luther calls the conflict between the Law and the Gospel. See Schelling
    (1854a: 554): 'But here it comes to light what the I has gotten itself into in getting
    away from God. Separated from God, it is held captive under the law as if under a dis-
    tinct power of God. It can neither go beyond this power, because it is completely bent
    under it, nor can it escape it, for the law is, so to speak, intertwined with the will of the
    I and engraved into it. Nor is the I happy with itself under the law. Aversion for and
    antipathy toward the law is its first and natural feeling, and so the more natural, the
    more harsh and unmerciful, the law appears to it. [Footnote]: "Therefore, the more the
    law dictates what he cannot do, the more hostile the human is towards it," says Luther
    in the preface to Paul's Letter to the Romans' (trans. Bruff).
54. A distinction between the cataphatic and apophatic mysticism of the Middle Ages is
    no doubt required here, but Luther does not draw the distinction, although we know
    he had a sympathy for certain forms of the *via negativa*, for example, the *Theologia
    Deutsch*.
55. Erich Przywara argued that the late Schelling's philosophy was in essence a creative
    appropriation of Luther's theology of the cross. See Przywara (1952: 376) and Kasper
    (1965: 206). See also Buchheim (2017). Cf. Loewenich (1976: 155–6): 'Since the God
    of the theology of the Cross is the God of historical revelation, he is always an acting
    God, he remains person, for he never becomes an "abyss", a "nothing" in which the
    soul can be submerged . . . Viewed from their center, mysticism and the theology of the
    Cross form the harshest kind of antithesis.'
56. It goes without saying that the late Schelling thinks of reason historically. The reason
    that European Christendom deploys in the nineteenth century has been changed by
    the 1900 years of reflecting upon the revelation that have elapsed since the events
    recounted in the New Testament. God's wisdom has already penetrated human institu-
    tions and attitudes to the degree that the so-called secular world is largely determined
    by Christian concepts. See Schelling (1854b: 136–7).
57. The early Barth and Kierkegaard are the most vocal proponents of this, originally
    Patristic, view.
58. On this, as on many other points, Schelling is a follower of Scotus rather than Aqui-
    nas. Where the latter argues, against Anselm, that we do not know the nature of God,
    Scotus holds that the foundation of human thinking is an *a priori* concept of being,
    which has two clearly defined modalities, finite and infinite. It is on the basis of our
    knowledge of infinite being that we can speak truthfully about God.
59. See Lonergan (1957: ch. XIX).
60. See Aquinas, *De Veritatis*, 29.3 ad 3. See also Rahner (1941: 1–9).

Chapter 4

The Real

Just as we feel we first know someone when we become acquainted with the expressions of his heart, so does God first become truly personal in revelation.

Schelling, *Philosophy of Revelation*

Revelation as actuality

Revelation as a technical term in Christian theology is no longer widely understood. Revelation, for Schelling as for mainstream theology, is not mystical or private in any sense. On the contrary, it is rational and collective. It is the historical happening, the fact of Christianity and its historical aftermath in thought, ritual, theology, science and politics. 'The content of revelation is nothing other than a higher history, reaching from the beginning to the end of things' (Schelling 1854c: 30). Revelation concerns the highest things – the origin of being, the nature of God and the destiny of the human race. It spans human religious history, comes to an epochal manifestation in the Christ event, and points ahead to the *eschaton*, when God shall be all in all. But revelation is more than simply data or information: it is the disclosure of a personal divinity; more precisely, it is the understanding of history itself as a personal, divine disclosure. 'A divine revelation is a real relation of God to human consciousness' (Schelling 1842a: 81/60). The opposite of a revealed relation to God is an ideal relation to God, such as the relation of consciousness to the ideal of reason in negative philosophy. Between the two, the negative and the positive, revealed relation to God, lies the mythological relation to God, which is more than ideal, but less than a direct relation to the existing God. In mythology, human beings are collectively enmeshed in various distorted relations of fallen subjectivity to the real God.

Schelling, along with Schleiermacher, Jung and Tillich, is an advocate of instinctive religiosity. We are 'the God positing beings' and have to do with God, even when we are most deeply alienated from him (Schelling 1842a: 185/129). Schelling is careful to distinguish this theory of natural religiosity from similar theories among his contemporaries. He is speaking neither of a natural knowledge of God, nor a feeling of absolute dependence, nor an intuition of divinity, but in far starker, even psychoanalytical terms, of an emptiness at the heart of the human being, an obsession with divinity, which cannot rest with any form of the divine but continually presses on in search of the absolutely divine. Schelling is concerned that he not be misunderstood on this point as Romantic or mystical. There is no monotheism of human understanding – we can, it seems, believe any number of things concerning the ultimate, or nothing at all – but only a monotheism of human nature. Whatever we believe will become God for us. The desire for God, which posits God as an absence, a need, is

> not a monotheism of the human understanding, but rather of human nature, because man has in his original essence no other meaning but to be the God-positing creature – thus not the nature which is for itself, but rather the one that is devoted to God, as it were enraptured in God. For I gladly need everywhere the most proper and characteristic terms, and do not fear that one, for example, says here that that is a fanatical teaching. For indeed the talk is not about that which man now is, or also only about that which he can be, since there lies in the middle of his primordial being and his current being the whole large, eventful history. Indeed, the teaching that maintained that man only is in order to posit God would be fanatical. The teaching of the immediate positing of God by man would be fanatical if one – after man has made the greater step into reality – wanted to make this positing of God into the exclusive rule of his current life, as happens with the mediators, the Yogis of India or the Persian Sufis, who, internally torn apart by the contradictions of their faith in the gods, or weary in general of being and thinking subordinated to becoming, practically want to strive back to that disappearance into God – that is, like the mystics of all ages find only the way backward, not however forward into the true knowledge. (Schelling 1842a: 185–6/129–30)

All of human knowledge, all of human religious history, is saturated with the divine, but none of this natural religion is comprehensible except in the light of revelation. And none of it leads with any surety to the true God. Mysticism ('the Yogis of India or the Persian Sufis') retreats from revelation, from history and the political, into unconscious religiosity (non-duality), but this is a flight from reality. Only in the light of revelation can we properly interpret the myths which express the historically unfolding, partially unconscious experience of divinity, which is an inalienable part of the human psyche, just as it is only in the light of revelation that we properly understand the triadic structure of being. But the revelation itself is neither mythic nor mystical.

The Philosophy of Revelation does not leave revelation as it finds it in scripture and tradition; rather, it transforms what is revealed in history and mediated on the authority of those to whom it has been revealed into properly philosophical knowledge. This is not a quickly accomplished task. It is something that has already begun, with the modern emancipation of reason from religious authority, and will continue until it comes to its fruition at some indefinite point in the future. Schelling humbly situates his work in the trajectory of this historical stream of the secularisation of revelation and the sacralisation of the secular, which begins with Descartes and will end in the promised enlightenment of all humankind (1 Cor. 15:28). While he is critical of the lack of sensitivity for the positive in early modern thinkers, Schelling insists, with Descartes, Spinoza, Leibniz and Kant, on the autonomy of philosophy. Reason has become dependent on something external to it in the age of revelation, it is true. However, in the Philosophy of Revelation, philosophy does not surrender its freedom nor capitulate before faith or mysticism, but realises a higher modality of reason. This higher mode of rationality, as I have discussed above, Schelling calls 'the ecstasy of reason'. A philosophically religious reason does not remain ecstatic, outside itself, but returns to itself, for the explanatory power of the historical revelation is for philosophy to demonstrate. The work of philosophising the revelation is nothing short of a progressive demonstration of the existence of that which alone is worthy of being called God, that is, a God who is personal yet infinite, or infinitely personal, and who can therefore satisfy the deepest desire of the human heart. The demonstration is inevitably fallible, incomplete and prospective, and will only be finished when history itself comes to an end.

The technical term for the Philosophy of Mythology and Revelation is 'positive philosophy' because both mythology and revelation begin and end with historical facts. As we have seen, the method for both is a blend of the *a posteriori* and the *a priori*. Schelling describes positive philosophical method as 'metaphysical empiricism', 'the empiricism of what is *a priori* insofar as it proves that the *prius per posterius* exists as God' (Schelling 1842d: 130/181). Apriorism, or negative philosophy, characterises the alternative method of most of the history of modern philosophy in Schelling's view. Its persistent power is due to reason's secure possession of certain truths, which it could only deny by performatively contradicting itself. These truths are negative in the sense that they say nothing about the positive, about that which exists outside of reason (really existing things, historical facts and freely acting persons) – something which negative philosophy is continually forgetting. In his account of history as divine personalisation, Schelling emphatically decentres human reason, leading to the enthusiasm of postmoderns for the late Schelling in the 1990s. If in the nature-philosophy humans were caught up in natural history, which was not reducible to their intentions and which they could never master, in the positive philosophy they are caught up in divine history, which equally exceeds their control.

Negative philosophy concerns conceptual relations in abstraction from existence, possibilities, not concrete beings. Conceptual relations negatively determine what a being *might be*, how it can be conceived, but they cannot tell us whether or not it exists. As Spinoza put it, in a phrase made famous by Hegel, determination is negation (*determinatio negatio est* [Wolf 1966: letter L]). Negative philosophy comes to its clearest expression in early modern rationalism and achieves its highest point in German idealism. It is not refuted by positive philosophy; on the contrary, without negative philosophy, there is no knowledge of positive philosophy, for two reasons. First, the positive can only be acknowledged as positive insofar as it is profiled against the negative. Without knowledge of the apriority of the conceptual, the aposteriority of the positive is missed altogether. For this reason, the Philosophy of Revelation presumes Kant's critique of knowledge and refuses to go back to a metaphysics that preceded it. Secondly, the only means philosophy possesses for thinking the positive are the principles and categories given with reason itself. Positive philosophy does not change the structure of reason but gives it something real, that is, existent, to think. Where negative philosophy concerns necessary truths (the principles of reason), positive philosophy engages contingent truths, and the contingency of being itself. Negative philosophy understands the essences of things, the *quidditas* of whatever it is that can be thought, and does so with surety and conclusiveness, for its arena of operation is *a priori*; positive philosophy is concerned with the contingent existence of things, the *quodditas* of that which is *given* thought to think. Here reason can only proceed fallibilistically, for nothing that is historically or factically given is necessary. But the positive is not only a philosophy of the contingent; it is above all a philosophy of freedom. It investigates the manifestation of acts of will in history.

The beginning of positive philosophy is the metaphysical question, Why is there something rather than nothing? In the citation that stands as the epigraph to Chapter 2 of this book, Schelling recasts the Leibnizian question in a far more existential key than is typical. Far from the mere expression of human wonder, a speculative, aesthetic venturing forth into relatively innocuous metaphysical possibilities, the question is a cry of the heart, the desperate demand for an explanation from one who recognises that the world is only partially ordered, and only partially good. One can even hear the cry of Job in the way Schelling puts the question. 'Why was I not hidden away in the ground like a stillborn child, like an infant who never saw the light of day?' (Job 3:16). The burden of being human is experienced in the question, the burden of one who, unlike the non-rational animals, suffers the senselessness of suffering, the non-coincidence of existence and essence, the contradiction of being and thought. Being human is experienced as a surd in the question, which 'drives' the questioner to the 'belief in the wretchedness of all being' (Schelling 1842d: 7/94).

The philosopher of revelation does not stay with the absurd. He or she passes through it, like a crucible of doubt, and eventually comes to grasp the reality of the fall of creation, which is the centrepiece in the Jewish-Christian revelation, and sees that Moses, Job, Ecclesiastes and Paul are all right: things are out of joint. Being is not what it ought to be. Nihilism is a reasonable conclusion from the existential crisis of meaning, of which the metaphysical question is but one symptom, but it is not the only conclusion. With this question, not only does philosophy expose the contingency of being – for in the question itself being is shown to be possible, not necessary (the questionability is only possible on the assumption that being need not have been) – philosophy also exposes the vulnerability, the exposure, the contingency of reason itself. The question includes the questioner. However necessary the principles of reason are, none of them need be, for reason itself need not be. Schelling deepens the metaphysical question first articulated by Leibniz by exposing the disturbing experience that underlies it: Why is there reason and not rather un-reason? (Schelling 1842d: 7/94; 1833: 143). This incapacity of reason to explain itself is not a justification for scepticism or a reinstatement of the Kantian limits of reason. Reason *does* possess a world of its own which it can and in the past has inflated into a false absolute. The poverty of reason consists not only in its inability to think the truly divine God but in its perennial susceptibility to substitute its self-generated fiction for the divine. Contrary to his earliest assumption, the late Schelling discovers that reason cannot think the genuinely divine and so cannot fulfil itself. The impotence of idealism leads Schelling to realism, but of a curious and convoluted sort: the real is not directly affirmed in a simple common-sense recognition of the outside. Reason only recognises its dependence on an outside and the need for positive philosophy by failing in its effort to idealise everything.

That reason is finite for Schelling means that it is historical: it need not exist, and the necessity which determines its concepts is first and last a merely logical necessity, with at best a questionable relation to contingent reality. It is on these grounds that Schelling can be said to have returned to Kant and reasserted the limits of reason, albeit in a radically different way than Kant had. Where the Kantian limits of reason are demarcated *a priori*, from within as it were, the Schellingian limits are demarcated *a posteriori* – from without. It is not some arbitrary definition of knowledge as an *a priori* category filled out by sensible intuition that delimits reason; the Kantian principles of knowledge remain as problematic for the late Schelling as they were for the early Schelling, confusedly bifurcating reality into two incommensurable domains, that of the phenomenal and the noumenal. For the late Schelling, what delimits reason are not 'things' but history. Reason can only grasp *a priori* an act which is preceded by potency, a real that is determined by a concept. History, however, is an order that emerges out of unprethinkable events, acts that are not preceded by potency but which emerge literally out of nothing.

The revelation at issue for Schelling is, in the broadest sense, history itself. Schelling is far closer to Hegel in this regard than most Schellingians would care to admit.[1] Revelation is not a subjective experience of God enjoyed at one time by a privileged few. Revelation is objective; it concerns historical events, witnessed by a community and more or less reliably recorded in historical documents. For Schelling history is not essentially the record of battles and the rise and fall of earthly kingdoms; it is the history of humanity's relationship to its divine origin and end, or religious history. This religious history, the history of revelation, begins in the pre-historical, mythic past of the human race, which Schelling endeavours to speculatively reconstruct on the hypothesis that the three potencies, which fore-structure reason and can be demonstrated logically, have been experienced by mythological consciousness as a history of the gods. Mythological consciousness is disrupted by the experience of the Jewish revelation of the one God of the universe, and the history of revelation proper begins. What was experienced as an external plurality of gods is revealed to be an internal plurality of divine persons in the Christ event: polytheism and monotheism are reconciled in absolute or Trinitarian monotheism. Revelation, then, broadly speaking, encompasses the whole history of the human race, but more narrowly conceived, it concerns what is known as the Christian revelation.

We come up, then, against the first of many unpopular claims made by the late Schelling, which could be misinterpreted as an all-too-familiar Christian triumphalism. It is no doubt true that Schelling regards Christianity as the culmination of human history and the key to understanding that history, and in this regard 'higher' than any other religion. But this is not the triumph of the Church over other forms of culture, and should not be used to justify it, for none of the institutions of the Church, Schelling argues, are adequate to the revelation, and all are destined to pass away. Nor is this the triumph of a certain *conception* of God over other conceptions of God. The Christ revealed in the New Testament and to some degree defined in the Nicene and Chalcedonian formulae is the revelation of the truth of all genuine experiences of God, even as he is also the singular and unique union of the human and the divine natures. And the religion which Christ's appearance inaugurates is, in Marcel Gauchet's sense, a 'religion for departing from religion' (Gauchet 1985: 101), for it sets into motion a historical trajectory that can only end in the complete secularisation of the world and the total emancipation of the individual from mythic and historical religions. Christianity reveals *freedom* even as it frees revelation from religion and emancipates the human conscience and will from sin.

The *Naturphilosoph* can create nature by philosophising about it (Schelling 1799a: 78/14) because he or she assumes the standpoint of nature. Nature is both subject and object of nature-philosophy. Such a transparency of thinking to its object is denied the philosopher of revelation by virtue of the quality of the revealed object: a free and unprethinkable revelation of a personal God is never mine to possess, any more than the free expressions of the other can be reduced to my anticipations of their meaning. To presume a revealed philosophy (philosophy of revelation in the subjective genitive sense) is to lapse back into theosophy and negative philosophy, and to never genuinely penetrate through the veil of reason to the really existing God. The Philosophy of Revelation is not a *revealed* philosophy, not a Christian philosophy in the substantive sense that one might encounter in the history of theosophy. It is a philosophy that takes revelation as its object, that is, philosophy that endeavours to think salvation history. The knowledge of history far transcends the narrow confines of empiricism for Schelling: a philosophical understanding of history (revelation) requires the speculative deployment of all of reason's native resources consequent upon the decision of the thinker.

That said, the Philosophy of Revelation is much more than a philosophy of history, for it is simultaneously an ontology (founded, as all ontology must be, on logic) and an ethics, which is, for Schelling, inseparable from ontology. In the Philosophy of Revelation, philosophy endeavours to understand the Christian revelation, not beholden to any orthodoxy or ecclesial authority, on the reasoned assumption that this revelation is exactly what it says it is, the unveiling of truths that 'eye hath not seen, nor ear heard, neither have entered into the heart of man' (1 Cor. 2:9). In sum, the Philosophy of Revelation is the philosophical appropriation, interpretation and elaboration of the singular divine revelation which is the event of Trinitarian redemption. This appropriation, interpretation and elaboration is not at the price of the autonomy, universality and rationality of philosophy. 'This combination of philosophy and revelation does not occur at the cost either of philosophy or of revelation . . . neither component will relinquish anything nor suffer any violence' (Schelling 1842d: 142/189). The point is worth dwelling upon, since the late Schelling could easily be misread as privileging theology over philosophy. The reception of revelation by philosophy (i.e., positive philosophy) in no way compromises the rationality or independence of philosophy, because revelation is not a faith-presupposition for positive philosophy: it is a demonstrable, if still falsifiable, conclusion of historical analysis. Revelation requires no special categories to be interpreted, and philosophy does not cease to be philosophical in receiving it, nor does philosophy become religiously qualified in the late Schelling. Positive philosophy interprets the whole of nature and history in the light of the Philosophy of Revelation, but it is not for that reason *revealed* philosophy. Neither faith nor mystical experience is its presupposition, but rather rigorously self-critical reason.

The revelation is Christianity itself, Christianity, which for Schelling is the sum and substance of Western history. Philosophical religion will go beyond Christianity in a sense, but will continue always to depend upon it, as the ground it did not lay for itself. While Schelling insists against many of his predecessors on the continuity of pagan mythology and revelation, nothing essential to Christianity could have been deduced from pre-Christian pagan philosophy: it had to be revealed in history. In this historical sense, then, the Philosophy of Revelation is a Christian philosophy: it starts from the unfathomable event of Christ's redemption of fallen being and remains grounded in it. It then proceeds to show how the ontology, anthropology, ethics and politics of redemption have penetrated the secular to the point where it becomes difficult, if not impossible, to separate Christianity and modern European culture. The Trinitarian redemption is no longer a topic exclusive to theology and presuming faith to be understood.

> One could I contend, in order to show that a positive philosophy is nonetheless *necessarily* a Christian philosophy, point to the material dependence of all modern philosophy on Christianity. For as one would say, philosophy of its own accord *would have never* come across these subjects and, still less, across this perspective toward these subjects without the preceding light of revelation. (Schelling 1842d: 135/184)

The late Schelling anticipates Max Weber and unmasks the causal connection between Christian religion and certain foundational modern concepts. He does not specify what concepts he has in mind, but we can with some certainty amplify his point and speak of, first of all, the notion of freedom itself, and its allied concept, the notion of the person. It is hard to deny that the Gospel and the Gospel alone in the ancient world granted the individual the freedom and dignity of personhood.[2] Without this elevation of the individual, or to be more precise, the person, above the universal, the reality of history – history which is not a cyclical return of archetypes but a linear series of unprecedented and unrepeatable events that are the product of free decisions – would have never become an object of investigation. And finally, and perhaps most decisively for Schelling's political eschatology, the notion of history itself, of meaning that progressively unfolds through time, is inextricably intertwined with Jewish-Christian eschatology.[3]

The secularisation of theological concepts is not something to be reversed, for it is not a deterioration of dogma, but the destiny of Christianity, which, for Schelling as much as for Weber and Gauchet, is the self-secularising religion. Hence the Philosophy of Revelation is not a Christian philosophy in the sense that here philosophy is possessed by Christianity – a philosophy by and for Christians alone. It is a Christian philosophy in the sense that this is the philosophy that emerges out of Christianity, the philosophy that owes its content and its explanatory power to Christianity, but it is no less a philosophy for all that. The Philosophy of Revelation philosophises Christianity and it does so in a way that is made possible by the rational assumption of the truth of the Christian revelation. But the destiny of Christianity is not merely to become the final form of philosophy; its destiny is to become the light of the world.

To be sure, others had made similar claims. Even Kant's philosophy is in a general sense 'Christian'. On the one hand, Kant brings to explicit thematisation the Christian discovery of subjectivity.[4] On the other hand, and perhaps more obviously, Kant thematises and defends the rationality of Christian ethics. Schelling will have nothing of the move, common in his day, of reducing Christianity to a general system of meaning, an instantiation in pictorial form of the general truths of reason. In defence of his approach to a philosophy of Christianity, Schelling speaks of certain truths which are fully rational, and now completely available to reason, which, however, would never have been known without revelation. 'Philosophy would not have known some things without revelation, or at least it would not have discerned them as it has' (Schelling 1842d: 138/186).[5] He illustrates the point with an example from astronomy: certain stars and planets could not be seen with the naked eye until they were first revealed by the invention of the telescope. Once so revealed, they can be discerned with the naked eye (Schelling 1842d: 138/186). The point is that philosophy itself is *historical*: even when it is thoroughly dependent upon the *a priori*, it is itself still a contingent product of history, which means that philosophy is not everywhere the same. Philosophical truths are not always and everywhere accessible. History changes reason, for it changes the kinds of things reason can conceive and know. Revelation – redemption and its historical aftermath – have irreversibly changed reason.

Church-based Christianity is to be succeeded by what Schelling calls 'philosophical religion'. Schelling anticipates the restoration of the unity of the human race by means of this new form of secularism (religious secularism), a unity that allows to each and all the dignity and freedom of their own ethnic and religious origins, even as it restores to humanity the unity it lost with the advent of religious consciousness (the descent into polytheism) and the ethnic and national diversity that polytheism produced.

Where the original unity of the human race was by virtue of a lack of distinction, the unity to come will be *by means of* ethnic, national and historical diversity. Philosophical religion is secular and, in a certain way, pluralist. 'Having no external authority, this Church will exist because everyone will come to it by his own volition and belong to it through his own conviction, for in it each spirit will have found a home' (Schelling 1854c: 328, trans. Hayes 1995: 334).

The story of the triune God becoming a trinity of persons united in love through the drama of creation, fall and redemption, which Schelling reconstructs over the course of the seven books of the positive philosophy, can be told in a couple of paragraphs, even if it will take a second book to explain Schelling's unique, and in some cases, heterodox, approach to classical problems in Christian theology. The short answer to the question, What exactly has been revealed? is this: Revelation reveals that 'God is love' (1 John 4:8). What does this mean? Schelling's concept of love, which is the central, if often overlooked, theme of the Freedom Essay, is neither vague nor sentimental. Schelling has a very precise, even formal understanding of what love is. Love is union, but not the union of ontological or dialectical indiscernibles, not the union of two that only appear to be distinct, but which are revealed to be the same. Schelling understands love to be a *free* union, that is, a union of two who are ontologically and morally individuated, and thus who could decide to exist apart but have *in fact* decided otherwise, two who have already decided for each other, whose decision for each other grounds an internal relation, and so now can no longer be conceived apart from one another. Towards the end of the Freedom Essay, Schelling gives the answer to the question, Why is there something rather than nothing?, formulated in terms of the problematic of the identity-philosophy: Why are there many things rather than only one? The answer:

> The non-ground divides itself into the two exactly equal beginnings, only so that the two, which could not exist simultaneously or be one in it as the non-ground, become one through love, that is, it divides itself only so that there may be life and love and personal existence. For love is neither in indifference, nor where opposites are linked which require linkage for [their] being, but rather . . . this is the secret of love, that it links such things of which each could exist for itself, yet does not and cannot exist without the other. (Schelling 1809: 409/70)

Love is only possible in freedom, that is, it is only possible where two find each other in a space of freedom which leaves both independent of one another. The relation of love is in every way non-necessary.[6] One thinks, naturally, of a good marriage. After many years, the married couple are not less but more individuated, more than even at the time of marriage, and yet somehow entirely dependent on one another such that their friends and relations cannot imagine them apart. The archetypal lovers, for Schelling, are not a romantic pair, but God and nature in the history of creation, fall and redemption. God is personalised in the relation as the Father; creation is personalised as the Son. They are in the beginning of time two. The Father and the Son do not share the same being in the beginning of creation, but only in its end. The God who is revealed as love is not merely the good that all things desire, moving the world from without, as in Aristotle (although he is that for Schelling as well), nor is God the intelligent designer of early modernity, an intellect untroubled by time and desire. Such immobile transcendence, if it is not qualified by more dynamic and voluntarist conceptions of personality, would be for Schelling something less than divine. God is, as the ancient Jews experienced him, a will, *the* will to personality, the primordial source of all movement, desire and agency, which creates something in place of nothing so that personal relations, ultimately so that love, might come to be.

Why does the Father will the world in the light of the evil that obviously besets all of life? This leads to the long answer. Love is only possible where there are two, where the ground has been set loose from its subordinate position in the divine nature, and grounds something which exists for itself, which stands out from the nothing and can in independence love the Father in return – or not. In creation, the dyad of God and nature supplants the divine infinity-without-another, and makes love, the unity of difference, possible. In order to create anything at all, the infinite and all-sufficient divinity needs to make room for it, to clear the space for something other than Godself, for infinity as such exhausts possibility (the Lurianic-Kabbalistic *zimzum*, which decisively influenced Schelling's philosophy of religion). This clearing is the original negation of God, which formally creates the possibility of evil. Only with God's creative self-negation of infinity, God's productive dissociation, does evil (the perverse destructive dissociation) become possible. In its first moments of being, creation falls and evil is actualised. If creation is to be redeemed and love is to conquer hate, God's Word, the potency for otherness within God, which is eternally with God, must become flesh (John 1:14), and through his earthly career, and the mediation of Spirit, reunite nature and return it to the Father. For this to occur, the Word must dwell among us, must evolve in an order of being that is other than God (*das außergöttliche Seyn*).

The essential point is that for love to be, something must first come to be that is *not* divine. Nature for Schelling, as for Isaac of Luria and Jacob Boehme, is a negation of infinity, a contraction (*zimzum*) of the divine being, which leaves the space, the meontic nothingness, in which something other than God can come to be. Nature, however, also needs a positive ground of being upon which to develop, and this is granted it from God, who lays, as the basis of the emergent creation, that in God which is not Godself (God's ground), but which in God is always subordinated to divinity. The dark ground of spirit, that in God which is not God, is let loose and something comes into being, which in a strict sense ought not to be (something that is logically unnecessary): a being outside of God. This renders nature formally equivalent to evil, but formal equivalence is not sameness. It is by its fruit that the moral significance of a contingent being is known: the ground is let loose by God, not in order to produce evil, but for the sake of love. Nature is intended by God to become a free partner to God, another to God, which can be united with God in love, that is, which can be contingently, freely and knowingly united with its divine origin. This union of love, in which God becomes known, can only occur if God runs the risk of evil.

The fall is the first historical effect of God positing being outside of Godself. Creation, to be clear, does not fall because of weakness. The fall is as non-necessary as the creation. The being posited outside of God by God so that it might freely return to God rebels, and in that inversion of order destabilises creation. Evil is not only a possibility, it is a historical actuality, and burdens creation with demonic forces, needless suffering and self-willed destruction. Spirit after the fall is in fact shackled by necessity, but a necessity which it has brought upon itself, as in Augustine's account of the loss of freedom in sin: sin is a chain, every link of which spirit forged for itself, and which it is no longer free to break.[7] The dark principle, which ought not to be, and which is eternally subordinated to spirit in God, has been aroused into actuality. For this to have happened, however, the crown of creation, nature become conscious of itself, the human being, intended by God to be God's beloved, had to have rejected love and decided for hate instead, choosing not to know God and erecting idols to worship in God's place, thereby corrupting not only its own being, but all of nature.

In the Christ event, God intervenes and rescues the fallen order of being by incarnating in it, raising up from within humanity itself one capable of doing what the first humans failed to do: Jesus, who rejects the temptation to be God, that is, who *decides* for the authentically divine God, wills to know this God as his God and the God of the universe, and so unites his will with the will of the Father. Schelling is with Paul and Luther on the question of the atonement: Christ takes our place. He dies for us. Christ's overcoming of sin is accomplished in his surrender to death on the cross, which is, as Paul describes it, a 'self-emptying' (*kenosis*), an ultimate and world-changing act of humility, deference and relinquishing of power (Phil. 2:5–11). In a quasi-Arian move, Schelling describes the Christ as not originally 'one in being with the Father' as the Nicene creed would have it, but as possessing the 'form of God' (Phil. 2:6), meaning the capacity for dominion, which he renounces, and in this self-emptying becomes one with the Father. In acknowledgement of his sacrifice, the Father raises the Christ from the dead, and elevates him above all others as the mediator, the one who restores the order of nature by reversing the decision of the first humans to be above God (Rom. 4:24–5). Much of the world in the era of the historical churches still rejects the Christ, but it is destined, according to the revelation, to come to recognise the crucified and risen Christ as the God become man, the saviour. In that recognition, human beings, who have competed and warred with each other since the fall because they have lost the unity which they possessed with one another in God, will be at peace once again. The conversion of the world will be the restoration of creation, which Schelling thinks of in terms similar to those of Irenaeus, who, commenting on Paul, spoke of *anakephalaiosis*, the recapitulation of all things in Christ.[8] Christ will sum up all things and restore the order of being while adding to it something that did not exist in the beginning: namely, restorative love.* This is, of course, a historical and Christian variation on the *exitus/reditus* theme of neo-Platonism, and the *Shevirat/ Tikka* of the Kabbalah: what has emerged from the divine and descended into otherness, into Godforsaken denial of the divine, shall return to the divine, but freely, not under compulsion. In this free return of a fallen and redeemed nature, human beings will become undeservedly blessed, united in peace with one another and with nature, and identified with the Father through the Son by the power of the Spirit.

While much of this is traditional and Patristic, if taking a heterodox swerve towards subordinationism (towards Arius, Origen and Antiochene Christianity),[9] Schelling's account of redemption exceptionally includes the whole history of paganism, as he clumsily but painstakingly endeavours to reconstruct it in the Philosophy of Mythology. The *Logos*, the second potency, which is not yet the Christ, is incarnated at the beginning of creation, and wanders through the pagan world, where he is recognised by other names (above all, for Schelling, as Dionysus), and becomes explicitly revealed as the Christ in the events recounted in the New Testament. The *Logos* is the divine personality who comes to be outside of God (*die aussergöttliche göttliche Persönlichkeit* [Schelling 1842c: 249; 1854b: 371]). The fracturing of divinity in the incarnation and death of the Son is possible because of the plurality that eternally exists in God, which the Patristic tradition defines as the immanent Trinity, and which Schelling speculatively explicates in his doctrine of the three potencies. Thereby does Schelling maintain the doctrine of the Trinity as a universal, rational, if *a posteriori*, account of the God who is not only one (*das Einzige*), but is all-in-one (*das All-Eine*).

---

* 'An act of saving and restorative love is the absolutely greatest miracle, a greater one than the act of creation itself' (Baader, 4, 282, cited in Betanzos 1998: 125). 'Restored love is deeper than untested love' (Betanzos 1998: 125).

The union of the Son with the Father in the act of redemption is as contingent and free as the fall of the first humans, and so can bring about the end intended by God: love, which conquers all by freely eliciting love from all. But Christ's redemption is only the second act. The third act, yet to come, will occur when Christ will have succeeded in winning the free allegiance of all of humanity, and thereby return God's rebellious creation, contingently and freely, to the Father. In redemption, Christ overcomes necessity and personalises the second potency. In the sanctification of the world, the Spirit overcomes the evil that resists the Christ and personalises the third potency. In the free act of restoring the sovereignty of God through the mediation of the human being, creation as such will become one with the Father, and God will be *panta en passin* as Paul prophesied (1 Cor. 15:28). This will come to pass, if it comes to pass (since we are in the second act, the drama is not yet finished, and the final act is contingent on human freedom), at the end of history.

This is a lot to accept as a reasonable guess at the riddle. Is it any wonder that Schelling's Philosophy of Revelation stands largely unreceived in contemporary continental philosophy? Schelling asks more of philosophy than even Hegel did. His Philosophy of Revelation risks everything on a speculative reading of the Christian scriptures, which your average continental philosopher can only be persuaded to look into if they have been edited for them by a deconstructive atheist such as Agamben, Nancy or Žižek. Things fare no better for Schelling on the theological side. Reopening questions long considered closed by a series of creeds, Church councils, and patriarchal and papal pronouncements, Schelling asks theology to rethink the whole story from the beginning, and dares to rehabilitate positions long since anathematised: Arianism, Origenism, subordinationism, monophysitism, pelagianism – practically no stone is left unturned. Theology might have to reject this, but it must at least take it seriously and offer an alternative which is equally capable of interpreting the Gospel in a post-Christendom age.

The end of mythology

This is not the book in which to reconstruct Schelling's sprawling, three-volume Philosophy of Mythology.[10] Neither is it the place to offer a critical, philosophical interpretation of it. I am concerned here with mythology only insofar as it is the historical predecessor to revelation according to Schelling, both the ground of revelation and that which revelation succeeds and replaces (what he calls 'natural' as distinct from 'revealed' religion). Revelation brings the mythological age to an end. It reveals the truth of mythology and, at the same time, shows us how all mythology is an indirect and distorted experience of divinity which is only preparatory for a more direct experience of God. Mythology does not deal with revelation, with a free, personal act of divine self-disclosure, which is received in freedom, but with certain necessary determinations of consciousness by the divine under conditions of alienation – of people from each other, and of all people from God. In mythic experience, people encounter the divine under the guise of various symbolic figures: Demeter, Dionysus, Krishna. These experiences are genuine religious experiences, but they are not revealed experiences of God's personality. The divine, we could say, is anthropomorphised in mythology, but not personalised. In mythology the diversity of the divine is external; not unordered – mythology is a progressive theogony of the second potency – but unmastered, represented in a pantheon of symbolic figures, who are conceptually and historically related to one another, and succeed each other in human history. Revelation, by contrast to mythology, reveals God as one who has overcome necessity, one who has personalised and is hence free for personal relations because God has mastered within Godself the diversity experienced mythologically in polytheism.

It is only in contrast to Schelling's notion of revelation that his theory of mythology becomes coherent – a point routinely overlooked in recent, English Schelling scholarship. The Philosophy of Mythology, although it precedes it in the order of demonstration, presupposes the Philosophy of Revelation in the order of discovery. Without the revelation, mythology could not be known for what it is. The poverty of mythology, its lack of a personal relation to the real God, only becomes manifest after the fact, once the revelation has occurred, just as a dream will generally go unrecognised as a dream until the dreamer awakens. Prior to the revelation, mythology does not and cannot know itself as such. Knowing no better, mythological people are bound to take their limited experience of divinity for the whole truth. With revelation, the revelation of the personalising divine, first as Jehovah, then as the Christ, and finally as the Spirit, humankind awakens from myth, as the one who traverses the Lacanian fantasy in the course of analysis awakens from the ideology constitutive of his or her psychic identity. This does not mean that revelation 'sublates' (cancels and preserves) mythology. Revelation *displaces* mythology, renders it the past, where it continues to function as ground of the present and the future.

Mythology deals with events 'in consciousness', which are historical insofar as they determine the experience of a particular people at a particular time. Nevertheless, mythological events are no less real for being determinations of consciousness. The history of mythology recounts 'a succession of ideas through which consciousness has actually passed' (Schelling 1842a: 126/90). Original monotheism (pre-lapsarian God-consciousness), lost through the fall, gives rise to polytheism on the one hand, and relative monotheism (the religion of ancient Israel) on the other, which sets the stage for absolute or

Trinitarian monotheism – the synthesis of the two. The mythologies of the world, according to Schelling's reading of what he knew of them, describe a threefold theogony which prefigures in broad outlines the history of the economic Trinity, but as an external succession of diverse and competing gods. A^1 (the Father God) is aroused into actuality as B, under various names, only to be pacified and returned to potency by A^2 (sometimes the Mother Goddess, sometimes the divine child), in anticipation of a coming God who can reconcile the two conflicting powers (the Spirit). The plot of the story, in whatever form it is told (Schelling refers to Persian, Babylonian, Arabian, Canaanite, Phoenician, Phrygian, Thracian, Egyptian, Indian and Greek myth cycles), is ostensibly the same: mythology recounts the progressive reunification of the three potencies, who were originally united in consciousness but were sundered in the fall, and the consequent diversification of peoples. Thus the presupposition of all myths is the fall, the original, tragic and world-historical loss of God-consciousness, and with it the loss of the primal unity of the human community.

It is crucial to the interpretation of the late Schelling that we keep his distinction between mythology and revelation clear – no small task today, when theological illiteracy and prejudice against Christianity predominates in academia. Myths recount the ways in which the divine becomes determinate for various people at various periods of history: they reflect the religious psychologies of the peoples who recount them. Revelation is a divine disclosure, akin to a personal speech act or deed. It is more than merely natural knowledge or mythic experience. Since this point is bound to be unpopular, even among Schellingians, it is worth being completely explicit about it. As I have repeated throughout this book, revelation in the late Schelling never means the general unveiling of being, Heideggerian *aletheia*, or the experience of the absolute disclosed in nature, such as the young Schelling elaborated in his early philosophy; it refers to what theologians from Aquinas to Calvin call 'special revelation'.[11] Specifically, revelation means the Jewish-Christian encounter with the God of history, which begins with the call of Abraham and culminates in the crucifixion and resurrection of the Christ at Jerusalem.[12] History, then, can be divided into two eras, prior to and posterior to revelation in this strict sense. That does not mean, however, that the line between the two eras of history is easily drawn. While the appearance of the Christ in history is localisable at a precise point in space and time, prior to the birth of Jesus the *Logos* accompanies humanity, unknown and generally unacknowledged, on a long sojourn through the mythological age. Nor does revelation for Schelling come to an end at Pentecost, as it does for some Christian thinkers; rather, these historical events, two thousand years ago in Jerusalem, point to the final moment of history, when revelation will have become knowledge. One need not be a believer to acknowledge the irreversible historical impact of the Christ event. It was the *conviction* of Christendom, that the divine was now fully human (hypostatically united with human nature), that effected the decisive transformations in the basic social, political and ontological assumptions of medieval Europe and the near East, a metamorphosis of values without which, as many have argued (Nietzsche, Weber and Gauchet), modernity as such would never have occurred.

A basic principle governing Schelling's positive philosophy is the tension between a religious consciousness compelled by an internal necessity to acknowledge the divine under a certain determinate form – mythological consciousness – and a free religious consciousness, that is, a religiosity that *decides* for the divine, or religion as the product of freedom. Revealed religion is the first iteration of such a free religiousness, but the divinity to which it relates, although free in its relations to us (God freely reveals God-self, and we freely acknowledge the revealedness of the revelation, which means we are free to reject it as such), remains external, positive and historical. Revealed religion is destined to become philosophical religion, in which revelation has been totally internalised. The more consciousness is dominated by religious *experiences*, the less free it is. Schelling's distance from supernaturalist accounts of the origins of religion in mystical or supernatural experience could not be more evident. The development of free religious consciousness moves from that form of consciousness which is compelled by an interior necessity to worship, to that consciousness which is free to worship or not to worship, which we can call secular consciousness. The freedom not to worship is also the freedom to freely believe. In a certain sense, the 'irreligious' consciousness is the freest of all, free to receive a revelation of a free God. Schelling's account of revelation as a free act of self-communication that presupposes a free reception of the act is a qualified endorsement of secularism – not the naive secularism that presumes to have vanquished religion as the lingering superstition of undeveloped peoples, but a religious secularism, which finds its freedom precisely in its freedom from and for a divinity who is freedom personified.

Mythology was the earliest form of historical, religious consciousness, the most bound form of religion, and for that very reason the lowest form. It was determined by extraordinary experiences of gods that left the subjects of those experiences overwhelmed by divinity. 'In the mythological process, man is not dealing with things at all, but with powers that rise up in the depths of consciousness – powers by which consciousness is moved' (Schelling 1842a: 207, trans. Hayes 1995: 115). At the same time mythological consciousness gave acute expression to the universal human sense of decline and loss. The first humans, Schelling speculates, lost God and entered history at the same moment; they became conscious of themselves in the very moment that they lost their immediate consciousness of God. God-positing consciousness remained constitutive of human being in the mythological age, but in the absence of the immediate knowledge of divinity, which determined our earliest condition, a fantastic plurality of experiences of divinity arose. Fallen humans worshipped what they did not know. As the God image became more determinate in a variety of forms of religious experience that precipitated the sundering of peoples into nations, a descent into deeper ideological religion followed, an even deeper forgetting of the one divinity, which caused the one human community to splinter into multiple competing communities. The lack of freedom of human beings under myth is the predominant theme of Schelling's Philosophy of Mythology. Mythological consciousness was dominated by divinity, repressed in development by a spiritual power 'which prevented every divergently striving development' and 'kept humanity . . . at the level of complete, absolute uniformity' (Schelling 1842a: 103/75).

No doubt, Schelling's Philosophy of Mythology is rife with problems. A first problem concerns its adequacy to its subject matter. When it comes to the details of Schelling's Philosophy of Mythology, his knowledge of the myths of the Greeks, Romans, Egyptians, Hindus, and so on, it is plain to see that he has an inadequate grasp of the material. His knowledge of Greek myth is impeccable, but it is not clear that he has the erudition needed, or even could have had the erudition at that time, to make some of the claims he makes about Indian mythology or Chinese mythology. There are whole mythologies of which he knows nothing and could know nothing (Native American mythology, for example). Surely all of this information is not irrelevant to his project. If the *Logos* wanders, unnamed or named otherwise, through the history of the world in the form of mythic gods and goddesses, then it would be important to fill in these gaps, to supplement Schelling's flawed history of world mythology with a more adequate one.

A second and more serious problem with the content of Schelling's Philosophy of Mythology is his undisguised racism. His hateful remarks about indigenous South Americans is now widely known (South Americans are, ostensibly, not quite human and so lack a genuine, mythological experience of divinity [Schelling 1842a: 40/32]). Schelling openly argues for the superiority of the Greek mind over that of all other ancient peoples, for example the Indian mind, which ostensibly abandons 'the religious principle' entirely (i.e., A^2), inviting the compensatory and purely negative movement of Vedanta (Schelling 1842a: 90/65). Schelling, it must be remembered, believes that the diversity of races is a remainder of a diversity of phases through which the human race progresses, from maximal fragmentation towards the recapitulation of its lost unity. Thus the black race, according to Schelling, in one of his more distasteful digressions, contains within itself a great diversity because it is not one race but the whole human species retarded in a certain, more primitive stage of its evolution (Schelling 1854a: 490–515). Schelling even tries to justify slavery on the basis of this argument. It is hard to imagine why anyone would want to preserve anything of this. If it is not to be preserved, the question must be asked, what is the relation of this racism to the formal structure of Schelling's late thought? Is it accidental to his thinking, and can it therefore be removed? Or is there something inherently racist in Schelling's Philosophy of Mythology? I think the answer is fairly obvious. Schelling believes deeply in the dignity of every individual as *imago Dei* and the ultimate equality of all before God: these Christian humanist principles are essential to his Philosophy of Revelation and to his political eschatology. His sketchy anthropology and racist attitudes are not.

Most importantly, Schelling's affirmation of revelation and its secular destiny is not a condemnation of paganism, but its vindication. Mythology grounds revelation, as paganism grounds Christianity, in every sense of the word 'ground': it supports revelation, makes it possible, and continues to nourish it, even in the present age, but as potency, not actuality. Mythology is the past of the human race, revelation is its present and future. 'The originality, even temerity, of Schelling consists in his rendering paganism, even more than Judaism, the precursor of Christ' (Tilliette 1999: 307).[13] Justin Martyr declared in the second century that Christianity was 'the true philosophy', the consummate philosophy, to which Greek philosophy had led by virtue of the *Logos* which guided it immanently, and Clement among other Alexandrian thinkers concurred. Greek philosophers such as Socrates and Plato were 'Christians before Christ' (Bell 2007: 45). But neither Justin nor Clement regarded mythology as a precursor to revelation; they saw the harbingers of Christianity in philosophy, which had an ambivalent if not antagonistic relationship to mythology. According to Justin, one of the indications that Socrates had been on the right path was his critique of mythic polytheism. Justin is the first in a line of Church Fathers who explained ancient Greek religion as demon-worship.[14] Schelling is with Justin in acknowledging that the sources of mythology are genuine, historic experiences of supernatural beings.[15] He is also with Justin in insisting that we must reason about the meanings of these events. But he contradicts Justin in finding in mythology, too, evidence of the *Logos*. The gods are not demons; they are powers that in various ways maintain the precarious but essential relation to divinity among human beings. Schelling's apologetic claim goes much further than Justin's, then. The plurality of divinities in mythology is indicative of a legitimate, if confused, experience of plurality within the genuinely divine, an experience of what Schelling identifies as the potencies, fragmentary and distorted to be sure, but nonetheless true as far as it went. In the light of the revelation of the *Logos* as the Christ we can now interpret mythology differently, and understand it better than the myth makers understood it themselves.

Schelling goes to great efforts to identify the concrete symbols and narratives in which the *Logos*, who will be the Christ, can be seen at work in paganism. Schelling means this quite literally: before the *Logos* becomes the person, Jesus, he is among the pagans, not personally but like a light shining in the darkness (Schelling 1841: 276–7). With brilliant arguments and a mastery of historical-critical method, Schelling refutes all deflationary and deconstructive accounts of mythology, such as the view, already widespread in his time, that mythology is allegorical, systems of symbols representative of something other than what they appear to be about. Myths on the allegorical account are tales of historical personages or natural phenomena symbolised by the gods. For Schelling, mythological symbols are 'tautegorical', not allegorical: they say what they mean and they mean what they say.[16]

Perhaps the most striking claim in Schelling's Philosophy of Mythology is his argument, against revisionists and historical critics, that human consciousness once genuinely experienced the universe as peopled by gods. Myths do not look back to experiences of the gods, which they represent in story form; they are themselves this experience of gods. The myth maker is responding authentically to a real, collective determination of consciousness by the divine.

> Both peoples and individuals are mere instruments in this process; they cannot transcend it . . . The representations do not come to them from outside; they are in them without them knowing how or why, for they come out of the depths of consciousness itself, and present themselves to consciousness with a necessity which leaves no doubt as to their truth. (Schelling 1842a: 194, trans. Hayes 1995: 112)

The collectivity of the mythological determination is crucial: Schelling has not retreated from his early, intense distrust of subjectivism. The collective determination of consciousness by gods is not in any one person's head; it is, rather, the substance of the myth maker's spiritual and ethnic identity, for it constitutes his or her language and culture. Mythological religion is a collective experience of divinity, remembered and recounted in symbol and narrative, which determines the consciousness of a people.

What, by contrast, does a free relation to divinity entail? It entails the possibility of rational unbelief. As I have argued above, Schelling's Philosophy of Revelation is, in a back-handed way, a defence of the reasonableness, the plausibility, of atheism. Because it is a free act received by freedom, revelation may be rationally rejected. It does not *determine* consciousness; it confronts us in person, so to speak, and demands of us a decision. A necessary process gives us nothing to decide. Myth makers in some basic sense do not know what they are saying, even if they unwittingly say true things about the structure of the divine potencies. The unconscious is religious, possessed by a primordial, pre-reflective and immediate monotheism (*ein Monotheismus des Urbewußtseyns* [Schelling 1842a: 187/130]). Note that this claim does not entail the affirmation of a natural knowledge of God; it is a psychological claim: human consciousness is constituted by a sense for a divine and infinite origin of all that is, a unity that by means of an internal dynamic pluralises and disseminates itself throughout human cultures. The innateness of our mythological ideas of the divine (which are representations of the potencies) does not render them subjective in the narrow sense. Mythology concretises and symbolises collective *ideas* of divinity, not divinity itself. In the light of Schelling's distinction between mythological and revealed religion, his claim concerning the natural religiosity of the human being should be put into alignment with Kant and Lacan rather than Augustine and Aquinas: we do not by nature *know* a true divinity, but we are constitutively oriented to the absence of God. For the late Schelling, as for Kant and Lacan, the ideal and the real do not necessarily converge: this natural trace of God (Kant's ideal of reason, Lacan's Big Other) may correspond to nothing real; it may be purely ideological, but it is nonetheless a psychological fact. Human being is in essence the God-positing being, and is never without a religious consciousness; but religious *consciousness* is not the same as religious *knowledge*.

Schelling explains mythology, as Jung did later, as symbolic narratives that emerge spontaneously from the collective (un)consciousness of humankind. The mythologies of the world resonate with one another and circle around common themes. The universality of certain mythic symbols, Schelling argues, cannot be explained on the basis of historical contact, but is indicative of the common origin and destiny of consciousness. Mythology, on the one hand, separates people from one another, for myths consolidate certain natural, ethnic connections of people with one another, and over against others. On the other hand, mythology unites all people through shared, recurring mythic symbols, which are expressive of the common religious instinct of humankind. 'We have to consider the mythologies of the various peoples as in fact only so many moments of a single and identical process which passes though and affects the whole of mankind' (Schelling 1842a: 211, trans. Hayes 1995: 117). Therefore, in any mythology whatsoever, we should be able to identify collective elements or analogies that show not only the deep unity of the mythological process and the persistence of a single human identity even in conditions of maximal diversification, but also glimpses of the true, triune God.[17]

The pre-mythological age of human consciousness, prior to the fall and the emergence of polytheism, consists in an all-absorbing, grounding, non-reflective experience of God. Before humanity is conscious of itself – before it has a self to be conscious of – it is conscious of God. 'He [the first human] does not possess this consciousness, he is it, and it is precisely in his non-act, his immobility, that he is the one who posits the true God' (Schelling 1842a: 187, trans. Hayes 1995: 109). The first humans live in undifferentiated unity with one another and with the divine. They are one in a timeless and unconscious pre-Oedipal unity with the origin. God was too near the human for the human to be free at this stage, and so Schelling describes this primordial God-consciousness as domineering and repressive of diversity, a 'spiritual power' which 'prevented every divergently striving development' and 'kept humanity . . . at the level of complete, absolute uniformity' (Schelling 1842a: 103/75). This is strictly speaking a pre-historical period, and it is as such timeless and immeasurable. In this state there is 'no actual time', for it is a 'period in which nothing happens' (Schelling 1842a: 103/75). The psychological point here is unmissable. As in the birth of the ego from the resolution of the Oedipus complex, Schelling maintains that self-consciousness only came about through dissociation from God-consciousness. The Genesis account of the expulsion from Eden means that humankind could not both possess God in immediate and impersonal consciousness and at the same time possess consciousness of itself; the one excluded the other. As in Lacan's forced choice – your being or your subjectivity (Lacan 1998: 211) – immediate God-consciousness and self-consciousness are mutually exclusive: an immediate experience of God is at the expense of one's sense of oneself as an individual, and vice versa.[18] The primitive presence of God to the unconscious is not a personal relationship to God; for such a relationship, humankind must first be dissociated from God, that is, it must *have* an idea of God and not simply be it, and to that extent it must become in some way *Godforsaken*.[19] One who *has* an idea of God can also conceive the possibility of there being no God. With this dissociation, subjectivity comes into its own: it knows itself as not-God and thus knows itself truly for the first time.

The cataclysmic loss of the immediate presence of God which is the result of the fall lifted consciousness out of the unconscious and inaugurated time. With the dissociation arose the human being's sense of having come into being (the past), along with a sense for the present and an anticipation of the future, and a consciousness of the fullness of being still lacking to it as a being underway, the sense of time of a being whose being is still not complete. Consciousness in its primitive unitive state was not only pre-personal; it was also unhistorical – time literally did not exist for it – because primitive humankind had not yet separated itself from God or from itself, and thus constituted itself as one with a past. If humanity was to exist not only *in* itself but also *for* itself, it had to defect from the primordial bliss of undifferentiated unity with the absolute: it had to transcend the religious idealism that was its native possession and enter into a difficult and historically incomplete revelational realism. The first movement towards self-consciousness, and the beginning of historical time as such, therefore, was the fall, a self-imposed exile from God, which in one way was the greatest calamity, but in another way the 'happy fault' that gave birth to personal, morally accountable consciousness and the departure from 'blind monotheism' (Schelling 1842a: 187/130).[20] The descent into polytheism and the diverse myths of those who possess consciousness of themselves as distinct historical peoples was both a growing alienation from the origin and an increase in consciousness. The divine did not abandon us completely in the mythological age but accompanied us through history until consciousness had achieved sufficient freedom to be able to receive a revelation of the true God.

From a psychoanalytical perspective, what is constitutively repressed according to Schelling is not the relation to the mother, or the trauma of separation from her, but the relation to God and the trauma of our collective loss of the relation. I will discuss the fall in the second book in the context of divine creation, since the explanation of what happened at the beginning of time requires an account of the inversion of the potencies in the creation of the world. An experience of the fall is also, however, a deposit of mythological consciousness, according to Schelling. Mythology bears witness in a diversity of stories and symbols to a spiritual calamity that lies at the very origin of human civilisation, a lost unity, a golden age, a lost experience of unimaginable blessing and nearness with divinity.[21] Ancient peoples are haunted by the memory of 'an original whole, of a body of an unprethinkable human knowledge, which gradually declined or was struck by a sudden devastation, a knowledge that with its debris – which no single people but only all together completely possess – has covered the whole earth' (Schelling 1842a: 89/65). Originally, all human beings spoke a common language, Schelling speculates, and were not separated into nations. A 'spiritual crisis' must have occurred if the plurality of languages and the diversity of forms of consciousness which they determine is to be accounted for, 'a tremoring of consciousness itself' that shook 'consciousness in its principle, in its foundation [Grund]' (Schelling 1842a: 100/73, 103/75), and fractured not only the unity of the divine with the divine origin but also the unity of the human family. The Mosaic account of the fall in Genesis, Schelling argues (in one of his breathtaking endorsements of traditional knowledge), is based on 'actual memory', and evidence for it is found in other cultures as well (Schelling 1842a: 102/74). Something cataclysmic happened to us, and mythology testifies to it, just as surely as the geological record testifies to the KT extinction event. The confusion of languages, the story of which is recounted in the tale of the Tower of Babel (Gen. 11:1–9), is not the cause of the fall, but its effect: it is a symbolic account of the historical fragmentation of a universal experience of the divine into competing experiences of divinities, the decay of human religious consciousness into 'diverged monotheism' (Schelling 1842a: 105/76).

In the nationalist and possessive devotion to local gods which ensued, humanity under myth remained haunted by loss, dogged by a sense that however great its particular gods and its priests, kings and queens, it was not whole and not the whole. Humanity was driven apart under 'the impulse of inner agitation', and in this antagonism knew itself to be guilty.

> The feeling not to be the entire humanity, but rather only a part of it; and no longer to belong to the ultimate one, but rather to have fallen prey to a particular god or particular gods: it is this feeling that drove them from land to land, from coast to coast, until each saw itself alone and separated from all the foreign peoples and had found the place proper and destined for them. (Schelling 1842a: 111/80)

Fear in the face of total fragmentation bound each of the sundered communities closer together and set each over and against the other groups: 'Horror before the loss of consciousness of unity, held together those who remained united and drove them to maintain at least a partial unity, in order to persist, if not as humanity, then at least as a people' (Schelling 1842a: 115/82). Civic institutions – above all the State – first arose as a means to stave off the forces of disintegration, to save what could be saved against further disintegration.

The Jews stood out among ancient, mythic cultures, as a people without a myth, a non-people. The memory of the revelatory acts of Jehovah – the call of Abraham, the parting of the Red Sea, the burning bush – are qualitatively different from the religious experiences at the root of mythology. The same divine power which caused the dispersion of human beings into competing forms of polytheism raised one elect group towards true religion. The ancient Jews were distinct by virtue of their homelessness and lack of national identity, but this was only symptomatic of the uniqueness of their non-mythological relation to God (Schelling 1842a: 144–74/103–22). Schelling singles out the Jews for possessing an uncommon degree of religious consciousness, which on the one hand 'disenchanted' them – they had no national gods, no magic identification with any particular land and its local deities – and on the other hand rendered them suspect to all others, and regularly despised. Only polytheists, Schelling argues, build nations, because without an ideological attachment to the gods of land and family, one cannot construct a national identity. The mythological age, then, the age of humankind under compulsive ideology or 'natural religion', reaches its end (both *eschaton* and *telos*) in 'revealed religion', which begins with the revelation of the one God to the Jews. This is the inception of the age of a free relation to divinity, the end of which will be the unification of the human race – not the restoration of the primordial unity from which we emerged, but rather the dawning of a new unity, an at-oneness, under the religion still to come (philosophical religion). The Jews were called not only by the God of Israel but above all by the God of the universe, 'the maker of heaven and earth', that is, the true God of all peoples.

To be sure, the Jews did not start there. Their knowledge of the true God began with a quasi-mythological experience of 'the relative one', whom they named *Elohim*, which, as Schelling notes, is significantly a plural word. This oldest of Jewish names for God indicates for Schelling a 'God who is still exposed to the solicitations of multiplicity' (Schelling 1842a: 162/114), a God who is the greatest and therefore not yet understood as the only one. Only later do the Jews learn his true name, Jehovah, the one and only one.[22] Jehovah and Elohim often competed together, Schelling says, as particular and generic experience of divinity. Elohim commanded Abraham to sacrifice Isaac; Jehovah stayed his hand. What made the Jews unique is that they alone among ancient peoples came to know the true, personal God; they learned his name. But their relation to him was historically contingent and precarious and pointed to a future in which the particular will become universal: the special relationship of the Jews to Jehovah will become the relationship of all people to the one God. Ancient Judaism remained caught in 'relative monotheism' – the monotheism which knows God as the one God, but not yet the only God – for most of its history, and hence pointed beyond itself, especially in the teachings of the prophets, to a religion of the future, an absolute monotheism, which would be adequate to the religious experiences of all peoples. In the name of God revealed to Moses, Jehovah says of himself, *'ehyeh 'ašer 'ehyeh* (Exod. 3:14). Typically translated as 'I am who I am', Schelling notes that the Hebrew is in a future tense, and indicates a divine process that is still to come. The Tetragrammaton could and perhaps should be translated as 'I will be who I will be.' Jehovah, Schelling concludes, is 'the name of one who is becoming . . . of he who is in the future, of he who now is only becoming, who *will* be in the future, and all his promises are directed at the future' (Schelling 1842a: 172/120).[23] What is promised to Abraham, a promise repeated to Moses, is not only a Jewish religion but a religion of all humankind. 'The Mosaic religious law is also pregnant with the future, to which it points mutely – like a picture' (Schelling 1842a: 174/121), to the time when the cult of Jehovah will no longer be 'the mere religion of Israel, but rather of all peoples or nations' (Schelling 1842a: 174/122). In the history of Israel, as it progresses from the worship of the indistinct Elohim to the cult of Yahweh, the God of Israel becomes 'severe, exclusive, jealous of his unity' (Schelling

1842a: 173/121).[24] This character of exclusivity, of the most severe, negative singularity, can only come from the relative one, Schelling argues, and indicates that Israel, for all of its pre-eminence among the peoples of the ancient world, was not yet absolutely monotheist. Religious freedom was still limited: Yahweh drew the Jews into his own unity by denying to them every movement (Schelling 1842a: 104/75). The true, the absolute God is not one in any exclusive way, for the God which excludes nothing is also threatened by nothing.

The beginning of the end of the mythological age was the moment when a part of the human community, the early Christians, came to *know* that neither relative monotheism nor polytheism were adequate to the divine. The one God is internally multiple, enclosing within his infinity the mythic plurality of gods of the pre-Christian world, ordered according to the three potencies. In short, Christian revelation modified the idea of God constitutive of human consciousness: for the God revealed was not one but three. Without the revelation we would still know the three potencies of being, either as mythological entities or as principles of logic, but we would not know the Trinity, nor we would be in a position to recognise the logical or ideal basis of mythology, and would remain, without choice, *in* the mythological. At Pentecost, 'Christianity, destined again to link the whole human species to the unity through the knowledge of the *one* true God, begins its great path' (Schelling 1842a: 108–9/78). Pentecost (Acts 2:1–31) was the inverted Babel and united that which was severed by means of that which severed it: language. Still, even in early Trinitarianism, the intimacy of the original relation was not recovered, and the fullness of human freedom in the divine was not yet actual. The Christian God was known externally by the early Church as including diversity within Godself, but the Trinity was not yet internal, not yet a knowledge that had taken root in the depths of consciousness. Revelation was still a knowledge of God in an alienated form, knowledge of God as the *Logos* of history, but not yet an experience of God as the *Logos* of humanity.

The future human will be God-conscious, God-knowing and religiously free. Future humans will not return to the oceanic unity of the first humans, for they will retain their hard-won consciousness and so remain individuated, and as free in the relation as God is free. Schelling does not look backwards to an event in the first century of the Common Era, but forward to the genuine singularity, the moment when humanity will become adequate to the divine subjectivity that lives in it. The final form of human community, the Church of St John, will be a community of genuine freedom and equality that will render obsolete all previous forms of the Church as it will the State, along with all forms of religion as we have known it. Philosophical religion transcends Christianity, as it does all historical forms of religion: it alone will show the genetic and systematic relationship between negative and positive philosophy, and between paganism and Christianity. Historical forms of Christianity stood in oppositional relation to paganism; they all lacked the perspective, the transcendent position of the third, from which to judge the true relation between paganism and Christianity.

Mythology ends with revelation; it has no logical or historical justification to persist in the current age of the world, at least not as an actual and living form of religion. Nature is no longer full of gods; the re-enchantment of the world is just not on for Schelling. Schelling thus provides us with resources for a critique of two of the principal forms that religious ideology takes today. First, Schelling offers us resources for a critique of the re-enchantment industry, from the folksy New Age movement of the 1970s, to the massive wellness movement of today and the more sophisticated forms of New Age religion, for example neo-Advaita, to the eco-spirituality of many well-meaning environmentalists, who are desperately trying to convince us (and themselves) that they still inhabit a normative cosmos, that nature is still full of gods.[25] The second form of contemporary religious ideology to which Schellingian philosophy is opposed is the somewhat darker and increasingly more institutionally entrenched resurgence of mythic forms of nationalism in contemporary, populist politics.[26] Both forms of religious ideology futilely seek to escape the disenchantment of the world, the death of the universe of meaning, 'the great step into reality' (Schelling 1842a: 186/129), which cannot be undone, even if it is not, for Schelling, the end of history.

Populism is an ideological effort to re-mythologise the world. It is a reaction and resistance to the technological unification of all people in the secular age into one, involuntary community, by means of a misguided effort to reactualise local deities and the ethnic and national bonds which they provide. A Schellingian view would have the involuntary community of globalised communication and exchange succeeded by voluntary internationalism, not by a return to sectarianism. Populism retreats from the demands of history, from the integrated planetary politics that must come if our civilisation is to have a future, to the more familiar theo-political terrain of religious ideology. From a Schellingian perspective, populism is untimely mythology. Mythology in a pre-Christian or non-Christian context is the spontaneous expression of natural religious consciousness. In a situation determined by revelation, such as the modern global situation, myth can only be ideology in the strongest sense of the word, that is, a disavowal of the truth of history, deliberate self-deception or false consciousness. A return to mythological consciousness at this stage in human history, when two thousand years of internalising the revelation has produced a society founded upon the ideal of individual freedom, can only be an ideological regression. This is no biblical endorsement of liberal individualism: freedom for Schelling is certainly 'individual', since a person is in some fundamental way the author of his or her own self, yet this self-determination is not unrelational or atomistic, nor is it merely negative or a justification of the neoliberal politics of self-maximisation. The transformation of our society, should it occur, will not be a return to old forms of mythological consciousness, but a transition to an unprecedented form of secular society, a genuinely religious form of secularism.

Because mythology creates the social and political consciousness of a people, it can in all of its traditional forms be called ideological in a weak sense of the term: mythology expresses a system of beliefs constitutive of a community's historical identity, a system that is not necessarily thematised but more often runs in the background of ordinary life, serving as the substance of a people, governing their language, values and religious aspirations. In another sense of the term 'ideology', the strong sense of the term, which we can trace back to Marx, mythology in Schelling's account is sometimes ideological, sometimes not. Mythology does not always deploy the collective imagination of a people for the sake of preserving a certain set of power relations, while disguising that it is doing so; mythology is not always an expression of false consciousness, but sometimes it is. Mythology becomes ideological in the strong sense of the term when it is no longer the *spontaneous* expression of a differentiation of collective consciousness, but is rather *used as means of retreat from consciousness*, and a defection from the universal ascent of human beings into more just relations with one another, and with all of nature, and freer relations with the divine. The rise of populism and the re-mythologisation of national identity in our times is just such an ideological deployment of mythology. Populism is untimely mythology, the return to mythic forms of consciousness when myth is no longer a *necessary* expression of consciousness, but the product of a *decision* taken in bad faith to distort the real situation in which we find ourselves.

Whether in the weak or strong sense of the term, ideology is not chosen. You do not choose ideology, as though shopping for a world-view; ideology chooses you. This is the reason ideology is so difficult to eradicate: it constitutes the very essence of the self of the one who is gripped by it. Ideology in the strong sense is marked by constitutive and yet culpable ignorance, for the ideologue is actively involved in its perpetuation. As Žižek puts it, what Jesus said of those who crucified him can legitimately be said of all who succumb to ideology: 'They know not what they do' – where the 'know' should be understood in an active and voluntaristic sense – they refuse to know what they are doing (Žižek 1991).

Populism seeks to assert the mythic identity of a people over and against other peoples in a time of accelerating ethnic, cultural and technological unification. If it does not speak of gods, populism nonetheless asserts 'the spirit' of the people, 'the greatness' of the people over and against any larger international unity – the social cohesion of a particular community bound together not only by common ethnic heritage and shared traditions, but also by opposition to others. As mythological, populism is ideological in the strong sense of the term because it is not driven by necessity but by the free decision of a democracy to stay with comforting and familiar fictions rather than accepting disturbing new realities. Populism is what I have described elsewhere as a destructive dissociation, as distinct from the productive dissociation which is the source of life: a dissociation from the dissociation that life is demanding of us (McGrath 2014a).

In an article in the neoconservative journal *First Things*, the editor, R. R. Reno, defends American populism as an ultimately laudable if politically clumsy effort to re-sacralise public life after the vacuity of postmodernist relativism. 'In our present circumstances', Reno writes, 'we should support the populist call for the return of something worth loving and serving – and we should tutor it as best we can' (Reno 2017). After running through the demise of liberalism from Weber's disenchantment thesis to the institutionalisation of postmodern relativism, Reno describes the populism transforming Western democracies as a return of 'the strong gods' to public life. Reno's argument unwittingly confirms Schelling's thesis concerning the political function of mythology: a people's identity is constituted by its experience of gods, that is, by a specific determination of religious consciousness. And yet where Schelling sees the determination of consciousness by national gods as the *past* of human civilisation, a determination by the potencies prior to the emancipation of the human being by revelation, the conservative Catholic Reno assumes that we are still largely determined by *mythos*, not *logos*. The mythic consciousness of the human being cannot stand its constant humiliation before the levelling forces of relativism and secularism, Reno argues. It yearns for a return of the limiting bonds of a legitimate moral authority to cleanse public life of the deterioration wrought by a century of relativism, scepticism and cynicism. Like many conservatives, Reno regards 'secular' as a pejorative term. Rather than an emancipation from mythology and authoritarian forms of religious life, secularism gives us false gods to worship. 'In the place of the strong gods of traditional culture, the globalised future will be governed by the hearth gods of health, wealth, and pleasure. Our high priests will be medical experts, central bankers, and celebrity chefs' (Reno 2017). We must worship gods, it seems.

Reno notes how the populism manifest in the Trump election or in the Brexit vote perplexes political analysis, for it does not conform to tradition models of left vs right. Trump's victory was the product of a fusion of left and right, united by a common enemy: 'the pattern of weakening' eviscerating our families, churches, workforces and societies. The backlash from the secular liberals only confirms in Reno's mind the moral force of the critique:

> The postwar consensus marshals cultural and political power to condemn the return of the strong gods in the strongest possible terms – racist, xenophobic, fascist, bigoted. Political correctness has many forms, but they are united in a shared repudiation of anything solid and substantial in public life, whether in the form of nationalism or strong affirmations of constraints that human nature places on any healthy society, constraints that get articulated by all forms of traditional morality. (Reno 2017)

In the end, Reno argues, populism is to be cautiously commended for desiring to reinstall the sacred at the centre of public life: the sacredness of family, of civil society, especially the covenants expressed in fidelity to heterosexual marriage, to local organisations, to schools, to volunteer organisations.

> It is a sign of health that our societies wish to reclaim, however haltingly, the nation, which is an important form of solidarity. Populism rebels against the fluidity and weightlessness of life. This impulse, however disruptive it becomes for our political institutions, reflects a sane desire for metaphysical density. Our goal should be to educate this desire in the proper order of love rather than allowing ourselves to be conscripted into the increasingly frantic efforts to sustain the postwar era by administering yet another round of the chemotherapy of disenchantment. (Reno 2017)

As we shall see, Schelling defends a theory of a strong and morally authoritative State as a product of spirit, something that in the best of circumstances ought not to be necessary, but given the degenerate state of the human being, is destined to last until the full emancipation of the human being. And yet, for Schelling, the State is not to be supported by recourse to mythology, but by democratic process, rational argument and free expressions of religion or irreligion (Schelling 1854a: 534ff.). Secularisation is the future of human society. Mythic consciousness, determination by strong gods in Reno's language, is the consciousness of the past. The disenchantment of the world is the natural if not logical trajectory of Christendom passing from the legalism of the Petrine Church (Roman Catholicism), through the ecstatic interiority of the Pauline Church (Protestantism), until it frees itself from all need for an external or internal regulator of the spiritual life in the age of freedom to come.

It is important to note that in Schelling's theory of history, the past is never cancelled and replaced with a better version of what was one-sidedly coming forward in it, as in Hegel's logic of *Aufhebung*. When the new is produced, that which preceded it and made it possible recedes from actuality but nonetheless meontically persists as the ground. This subtle difference from Hegel has dramatic implications for the philosophy of history. In a Hegelian doctrine of secularisation, our historical traditions are rendered null by the advent of the new and more adequate forms of spirit which have 'cancelled and preserved' them. To persist in maintaining these traditions on mythological terms is to resist the times and become a reactionary or Romantic. For Schelling, something of the past is never entirely replaced by the present; hence preservation and cultural memory are healthy and even necessary measures against the onslaught of time. Most importantly, the cultural differences distinguishing the various forms of the human community called to the Church of St John remain the ground of revelation. The one who preserves the memory of a past tradition is not to mistake preservation with reactualisation; it is one thing to know where we come from, quite another to resist history.

Schelling's Church of St John is a vision of a future planetary civilisation that is pluralistically grounded in a fully secular appropriation of the revelation. The internalisation of the Christ event will bring human communities together, even as it fulfils and so validates the varieties of religious traditions that led each of them there. To resist the move into the new, for Schelling, to insist on the actuality of that which is and ought to remain in potency, where it can serve as the ground of something new, is to dissociate from the dissociation that life is demanding of us. The return of mythical identities in Western populism is a flight from the real situation of consciousness, in which the unification of the human community under a set of shared if banal and even vulgar ideals is the historical outcome of the evolution of liberal democracies. Reno speaks of the weak 'hearth gods of health, wealth, and pleasure', but he distorts the situation: these are not gods so much as a base common denominator of goods we can all agree are genuinely good and should in principle be equitably and universally distributed among all, even if the actual situation remains scandalously otherwise. Disenchantment – the retreat of the gods – is irreversible, and in my reading of Schelling, the destiny of modernity; it desacralises the public sphere, no doubt, but for the sake of the emancipation of the person for genuine post-mythological religious life.

No one was more affirmative of mythology than Schelling. Mythology is first philosophy, but the first is not the highest stage in a developmental process; it is the lowest. The point of the Philosophy of Revelation is to free oneself from mythology. Those who do not emerge from mythology and set it behind themselves as the past do not have a mythology. Reno is surely right, there is something mythical about twenty-first-century populism, but he mistakenly thinks this to be a good thing, as though thereby something of the sense of the sacred imperilled by twentieth-century atomistic liberalism and postmodern relativism has been restored to the political scene.

The return of 'the strong gods' at this stage in human history can only be a pathological regression and retreat from that towards which we are truly called: not more nationalism, but ecological universalism; not more sectarianism and protectionism, but greater trust, and reverence for our common home. Liberalism has certainly eroded our communities, and alienated us from our livelihoods and traditions, but the healing cannot be by means of turning our backs on the world to look after our own. It was one thing to be under the *mythos* in ancient Greece or Rome; it is something altogether different to be under the *mythos* on an interconnected globe, where we can no longer avoid each other, as the 2020 pandemic made painfully evident.

No doubt Schelling's Philosophy of Revelation raises the spectre of colonial Christo-triumphalism. But before we too loudly trumpet the superiority of any confessional form of Christianity over other world religions, it is worth remembering that revelation according to Schelling is not the *possession* of any institutional form of Christianity; it is not even bound to faith or confession. Revelation is God's work, and it disseminates itself freely and universally throughout history. Revelation now inextricably permeates modernity and makes it difficult to distinguish the sacred from the secular. Revelation has as much to do with the hard-won political and religious freedom of the individual as it does with historical confessions of faith in the Christ. The enthusiastic twentieth-century Catholic interpreters of the late Schelling (Furhmans, Kasper, Hemmerle) found that they could not go all the way with Schelling because of his somewhat devastating critique of the Roman Catholic Church. For Schelling, Catholicism is a Church of the past, one that was crucial to the medieval reception of revelation, the closure of the ancient world and the mediation of modernity, but which is limited in a fundamental respect. For Catholics, revelation remains external to reason, something that must be promulgated and interpreted by ecclesiastical authority and received on faith. In short, the Catholic relation to revelation is not a free one according to Schelling (who, despite his years in Bavaria, remains the son of a Protestant pastor in this respect), and the Reformation needed to happen to correct this. But even the Reformation failed to achieve the freedom of religion requisite to the genuine reception of revelation, and regressed to authoritarian proclamations and legalistic interpretations of the Christian's relationship to the truth.[27]

One could say that the death of God, interpreted as the death of Christendom, needed to happen in order for the second age of revelation, the Pauline age, to become fully actual. The Pauline Church has the advantage over the Petrine Church of having actualised an internal relation to revelation: the individual is free in this relation and not compelled to believe by external authority. Even this internalised revelation under Protestantism remains too limited, however, too exclusively bound to the historical form of the Christ. The Johannine Church will realise an *inclusive* internalisation of the revelation, one which does not impose the Christ on the world so much as find the world in the Christ and the Christ in all of the diverse forms of religiosity in the world.[28] In the final age of revelation, the religiously secular age to come, a completely free reception of revelation will occur, one that does not divide people from each other according to conflicting interpretations, but one that will unite all under the one God. Where the first unity of humanity (pre-lapsarian) was undifferentiated and at the expense of diversity, the unity to come will be *by means of* diversity. The sundered human communities will be gathered together under a common experience of true divinity, which will not exclude plurality (and therefore will not exclude social and political diversity), but include it within itself as the condition of its possibility. To use Jürgen Moltmann's language, the human race will not so much be *unified* in the Church of St John as *united*.[29]

Political eschatology

Any effort to reconstruct Schelling's late political thinking on the basis of his slim but profound treatments of the subject of the relation of the State to the Church, on the one hand, and the relation of the State to the person, on the other, must keep in mind the essential distinction between utopian eschatological politics and political eschatology.[30] Comte and Marx belong in the first category; Joachim and the late Schelling in the second. Both utopian thinking and eschatological thinking break with teleological time; both understand the future rather than the past to be the determining factor in historical development. On the basis of this future orientation, both may think eventful time, the meaningfulness of singular events, which are not meaningful because they conform to a recurring or eternal archetype (they don't), but because they hasten the coming transformation of history. Where utopian eschatology arrogates to the human being the means to bring about the desired end, either political or technical, political eschatology trusts in the still unfulfilled promise of the beginning and anticipates a transformation, the origin and end of which transcends the human, even as it fulfils the human being's innermost drive for justice and freedom.[31] Coming of age at the time of the French Revolution, and ending his career amid the clamour of a new generation of utopian political thinkers (Bakunin, Engels, Marx), Schelling discovered the political eschatology of the New Testament somewhat late in the game, but once he struck upon it, he built his whole positive philosophy around it.

I have already drawn my line in the sand of contemporary Schelling interpretation and argued that there are really two Schellings: an early Schelling whose central preoccupation is an impersonal, pantheist philosophy of nature, which culminates in a system of objective reason (the identity-philosophy), and a later Schelling who has problematised and supplemented this philosophy of objective reason/nature with a philosophy of religion that has as its central theme the history of the fall and redemption of humanity. The point of divergence of Schelling I and Schelling II can be variously interpreted. I have pointed to the later Schelling's new appreciation for the reality of historical time, for existence and for the limits of reason. What changes first, however, is Schelling's assessment of human moral and political possibilities. It is not that Schelling turns to the positive and then constructs a philosophy of religion and a political philosophy adequate to it; it is rather that sometime between 1804 and 1809 he turns to an ethico-political question – Why is there evil? Why is history a record of decline? – and then constructs a positive philosophy to answer it, or at least to frame a possible answer.[32] Schelling I does not significantly challenge the Enlightenment optimism in the self-perfectibility of humanity. As even a cursory reading of *The System of Transcendental Idealism* shows, the early Schelling subscribes, quite uncritically, to the Enlightenment's master narrative of progress and cultural evolution, which comes to its apogee in the modern, European nation-state. Schelling's early idealist model of the State is given its most unequivocal definition in the 1804 Würzburg lectures: the State is 'that in which science, religion, and art are in a living way thoroughly one and in their unity have become objective' (SW 6: 575). The later Schelling, by contrast, sees the human being as ontologically changed by a history of self-inflicted evil, and this change has rendered its social-political options, to say the least, limited. History becomes an account, not of progress, but of ineluctable and ongoing decline.[33] The State is now understood as a punishment for sin, something which ideally ought not be necessary, but factically is and must remain so until the great transformation awaited at the end of history (Schelling 1810: 461/227; 1854a: 533). We must not tear the two Schellings apart: they are related as negative is to positive philosophy. So too are the two conceptions of the State related, the early idea of the state as human society perfected, and the later idea of the State as punishment. The State as punishment for sin *is* the intelligible order made objective. What was previously regarded as the full and complete manifestation of the ideal in the real is now imposed on the human being as an external necessity.

The late Schelling's negative view of human possibility entailed a reappraisal of the tragic nature of life, and a return to a theme which had preoccupied him since his student years.[34] What is new in Schelling II is the double insight that, on the one hand, the tragic gives the lie to the progress narrative, and on the other, that it gives new significance to the Gospels, especially to the letters of Paul. 'The way of the world and human-ity is naturally tragic, and everything tragic that occurs in the course of the world is only a variation of a great theme, which continually renews itself' (Schelling 1854a: 485–6). This return to ancient pessimism does not render Schelling II a cynic. On the contrary, it occasions Schelling's rediscovery of the reasonableness of Christianity. The presupposition of the Pauline redemption is the tragic and hopeless nature of humanity prior to the Christ event. What Paul adds to the ancient discussion of tragedy is the Jewish insight that the calamity of existence is not merely something that befalls humanity; it is something that humanity brings upon itself, something for which we are in the most profound sense *responsible*.[35] The fall is no longer conceived, as it was in 1804, neo-Platonically as an onto-logical diminishment of the absolute, a non-moral descent of being into materiality and multiplicity; it is now conceived Kabbalistically as '*that catastrophe through which the dark power that was conquered in nature arose* and took possession of human consciousness as contrary to the divine will' (Schelling 1841: 252). In original sin, the first human being, Adam Kadmon, awakens the principle that should not be, and with it, the indig-nation of God. But the end of this story is not tragic, it is comic. For we have reason to hope that in the genius of the divine mystery, the break in nature, the falling asunder of things that should be together, shall be for the sake of an achievement of an even great unity than has ever existed, a greater joy than could have been possible in an unalloyed eternity. In short, we have reason to hope that God takes our self-inflicted disaster and makes something beautiful out of it.[36]

The new appreciation for the fact of evil leads Schelling II into what is for him a new conception of time as eschatological. This notion of time as a series of disruptions of eternity – being thrown towards an end, which will not return to the beginning but inaugurate the radically new – the time of history, can be read between the lines of the Freedom Essay, and becomes an explicit theme in the Stuttgart Seminars and the three drafts of *The Ages of the World* – while it is notably absent prior to 1809. Where Schelling I is at home with a Platonic conception of time as a moving picture of eter-nity, time in which nothing *really* happens, and in which differences are only quantitative, Schelling II see the world as hurled towards a singularity, which renders every moment of decisive, ethical significance. Eschatologi-cal time does not contradict Platonic time in Schelling any more than posi-tive philosophy contradicts negative philosophy. Eschatology supplements eternity, or better, renders it past, displaces it with an order of being that in time gives rise to the new, the unprecedented, the irreducibly spontaneous, rather than cycling through a stable order of forms, as in Plato's *Timaeus* myth. Plato's conception of time is how reason must think time, in abstraction from history. Eschatological time is the time of the positive, the time of events, and could never be deduced.[37]

In his breakthrough study, *The Political Theology of Schelling*, Saitya Das has argued that for political eschatology to be truly disruptive of the logic of the world, the *eschaton* cannot be a historical occurrence. The *eschaton* must be conceived as *beyond* history – not an event in the order of things that have occurred or are occurring, but *the* event that brings that order to an end and inaugurates something fundamentally new (Das 2016: 90–131). The *eschaton* is not a grammatical part of the sentence of history, but the period that brings the sentence to a close. To conceive of the *eschaton* otherwise, as an intra-historical event, as historically immanent, is, according to Das, to fall into Schmittian political theology. Schelling, on Das's reading, refuses this kind of political theology and therefore insists that the *eschaton* will not apotheosise any political form of this world, and so cannot be anticipated in any terms familiar to us; the *eschaton* is radically discontinuous with time as we know it and resists all calculation. Das shows how political eschatology is not eschatological politics, for it is not strictly speaking a participation in politics as we know it. He writes:

> To come closer to Heidegger, it is a question of 'perdurance' (*Austrag*), which is not a lengthening of qualitatively indifferent time, but a matter of epochal breaks, without precedence. An ecstasy of interruption, this event of time is pregnant with eternity at each instance of its apparition, for it arises out of the gift of eternity itself. Schelling thought this exuberance eschatologically: the eschaton as difference that separates and sets itself apart from the *Koinon* (from the world-historical movement of quantitative, homogeneous and empty time). With this, Schelling's thought expresses its eschatological reserve toward any absolutisation of that which is only passing away: the divine event of redemption thus does not have, strictly speaking, a 'political meaning' (in the way that the state of the visible Church has). The unconditional event of coming does not coincide with any given historical presence; it bears neither any empirical historical 'date' nor any meanings as fate or destiny. The empirical-historical categories cannot congeal the originary event of decision. In that sense, the event of the eschaton is beyond history. In his Berlin lectures on mythology, Schelling elaborates on this idea of the excessive event of de-cision (*Ent-Scheidung*) which, as though in an *a priori* manner ('always already'), makes the historical possible for the first time, and which, as such, cannot be grasped in the categorical codification of the concept. Being not a 'presently given entity', it eludes the law of the concept. It does not become reconciled in speculative-dialectical mediation with the worldly regimes of the earthly order; rather, it radically puts into question the law of the worldly and opens up the futurity of the event from the heart of the finite world, that is, from the heart of the transient realm of history. (Das 2016: 59)

As Das presents it, political eschatology is not a move from within any pre-existing form of politics, but transcendence of the political itself. This absolutely transgressive feature of political eschatology is easily missed, and Das is right that it is crucial for understanding the political thinking of the late Schelling: the 'political' in political eschatology should be conceived as a means which is always inadequate to its end.[38] In a return to the thought tersely expressed in *The Earliest System of German Idealism* (Behler 2002), the late Schelling regards the State as something tragic, but with the wisdom of age he comes to see this tragedy as a necessary evil, something which factically now is, and must remain, as he tells his young, revolutionarily inclined Berlin audience, until the end of history (Schelling 1841: 91–2; 1854a: 534–53). As in the early critique, so in the latter: the State is criticised for treating the individual impersonally, and it cannot do otherwise. But unlike the Romantic revolutionary call of the *Earliest System* ('For every state must treat free human beings as if they were cogs in a machine; but that it should not do; therefore it should cease to exist' [Behler, 2002]), the late Schelling declares that the State must not be overthrown: it must abide until the end, even if it should remain as minimal as possible. As the *ground* of moral life, the State will always have a tendency to arrogate to itself tasks and responsibilities that must be reserved for persons, whose spiritual destinies transcend the State. Reform of the State is always needed, but revolution is to be avoided, for revolution falls prey to a false, modern assumption, that justice is a political rather than a religious outcome. The State is inadequate to the human imperative towards justice, to be sure, but the political as such cannot bring about that which is desired (the perfect synthesis of individual freedom and equality); it is only a necessary stopgap and the keeper of peace among a human community that is at war with itself. Even the modern political imperatives of political freedom and equality fail to satisfy the longing of the person for the good. In the best possible State, Schelling argues, in true conservative fashion, citizens shall be left free to pursue individual ends that, if not incompatible with their coexistence with others, nevertheless exceed the bounds of the political. If the State is vulnerable to the misconception that it is responsible for the moral lives of its citizens (the progressive's recurring error), the politically motivated citizen, inevitably dissatisfied with the State, is vulnerable to the false presumption that the people possess the means to bring about the good.

The argument might be conservative but it is also deeply Pauline. In Rom. 13:1, Paul argues for obedience to the law, but his intention is to point beyond the political. 'Let everyone be subject to the governing authorities', he writes, and we can conclude that there is no place for law breaking or revolt against legitimate political authority in the first Christian community. The lord of the universe is also the lord of every earthly authority and providentially guides the political governance of the world. But the next part of this oft-cited passage from Paul underscores the politically subversive edge of Christian obedience – 'for there is no authority except that which God has established'. If the authority of the State is only legitimate on the basis of its having been established by God, then there is no earthly sovereign who could demand the kind of absolute allegiance commanded by the emperors who arrogated to themselves the divine title, *Kyrios*.

Das follows contemporary French philosophy in his rejection of all language of sovereignty, but he goes beyond the late Schelling in this regard, who speaks repeatedly of 'lordship' – the lordship of the one God, the lordship of 'the lord of being' – and in the end argues in favour of constitutional monarchy as the most adequate form of government, for it reflects the personal nature of the sovereignty of God (Schelling 1854a: 569, n. 2, 570, n. 1). The late Schelling's prescription for the governance of the Christian State (and we should remember that he had the ear of the Prussian king) is self-negating sovereignty, the sovereignty of service.[39] 'The one who is most sovereign is the one who most serves' [*derjenige herrscht am meisten, der am meisten dient*] (Schelling 1854a: 529).

Among all of the pages of the late Schelling, these last remarks on the political are the most difficult, not only because they have been heavily reconstructed by Schelling's editor, nor because they confront the largely progressive contemporary Schelling readership with the master's undisguised conservatism. In these last fragments, which he did not live long enough to assemble into a text (his son, K. F. A Schelling, should be regarded as the co-author of lecture 24), Schelling's thought is still nascent, and it is a testimony to the fertility of his genius that even at the end of a long career he was still *in via*, pushing beyond previously secured terrain into new conceptions and lines of argument. A vision of modern human society is only sketched here, and the interpreter must construct what is only implicit or not stated at all. One thing is clear: against the young revolutionaries who clamoured for the overthrow of the religious and cultural institutions that they believed entrenched injustice and inequality – private property, family, monarchy – and in accordance with his king, Friedrich Wilhelm IV, who brought him to Berlin to do exactly this, Schelling defends the State and the political stability of constitutional monarchy. His presuppositions are fundamentally the same as the principles of early nineteenth-century European conservatism. First, the human being is fallen, languishing outside the centre; the human is not where it should be and could be, and therefore cannot attain what it most desires – a perfect society of freedom and equality. Second, the State exists to protect humanity from itself and to maintain a modicum of justice in a human society which, because of the fall, is inevitably stratified and unequal. Third, the State must not overstep its bounds and arrogate to itself that which is ultimately the responsibility of the person alone, the cultivation of virtue. The State is necessary but must be kept as small as possible; its role is to serve as the ground of a society of politically free individuals, each of whom must take up his or her own task of becoming persons, that is, the burden of becoming moral beings. The State's role is to make this moral development possible by supporting society, and leaving the individual free to cultivate virtue and pursue cultural and religious ends that exceed the purview of the political. Fourth, the perfection of both the individual and of society is not found in the domain of the political but in religion, which it is above all the State's sacred duty to support until neither State nor religious institutions are needed any more, that is, until the end of history itself. Schelling's conservatism bears little resemblance to contemporary American republicanism, free-marketeerism or neoconservatism, but has much in common with Edmund Burke's response to the French Revolution. Burke's reaction to the revolution, seldom read today, is the very inception of conservative thought, which progressives tend to forget is an originally modern position (conservatism does not pre-date the age of revolutions). Here I want only to flag what is most essential to Schelling's politics in the early 1840s and 1850s.

First, there is the defence of monarchy. It is based on what we could call Schelling's practical theology, which I discussed above, the claim that the pinnacle of the religious life is not the *via negativa* and the associated *unio mystica* but the existential cry of the heart, which might lead one to contemplative life, but might also lead one out of it, for the desire expressed is for a personal experience of a God who is not absolutely above us, nor within the depth of the soul, but a living, acting person like we are. We find no such person among us, at least not until we encounter the Christ, and even this encounter is still partial and promissory, an anticipation of the full presence of the personal God who is still to come. In the absence of our heart's desire, we turn to the political, and require of our society, first, support for our philosophical and religious pursuits, and second, a form of governance that reflects this deepest need of human beings, for personal encounter with the divine.

> The search for the [divine] person is that which drives the State to monarchy. Monarchy makes possible that which is impossible by law. For because the laws, for example, which are valid in the State, are not valid for the State, and there must be responsibility, it is necessary that a person exists who would be responsible (in front of a higher tribunal than that of the law), the king, who offers himself in sacrifice for the people. Furthermore, reason and law cannot love, only the person can love; but, in the State, this personality can only be the king, before whom everyone is equal. (Schelling 1854a: 569, n. 2)

There are several noteworthy points about this brief defence of monarchy. First, it is, not unlike Schmitt's political theology, a theological justification of sovereignty. But what the sovereign brings is not arbitrary power to declare the exception, but rather 1) responsibility for the whole society before God, and 2) equality of all before the throne. Further, the sovereign 'offers himself in sacrifice for the people'. He or she gives up the leisure and freedom of ordinary human life that the State makes possible, for the sake of serving the whole – that at any rate appears to be how Schelling thought of monarchy. We might interpret Schelling on this point by reading his political remarks in conjunction with his account of the Trinity, a subject that will occupy us more directly in the second book. We could conclude that the only legitimate, Christian form of earthly sovereign for Schelling is the sovereignty of one who, as in Schelling's interpretation of the *kenosis* of the second person of the Trinity, renounces any claim to domination, one who in ruling lowers his or herself beneath the ruled and becomes the servant of all. In Schelling's reading of Phil. 2:5–7 (Schelling 1854c: 36–7), the Son 'does not deem equality with God a thing to be grasped', because he decides otherwise. He lays down his life, empties himself of any claim to divinity that he might have, and thereby confirms the sovereign divinity of the Father. Divine sovereignty is essentially kenotic. The Son can only so decide because he stands before an option, the rejected alternative (which the first humans opted for), to refuse the sovereignty of the Father and claim for himself the divine status which is God's alone. When he empties himself, the Father 'raises him up' and proclaims the Son divine, precisely because the Son repeats the divine act of self-emptying, an act which is henceforth the divine archetype for any genuine form of sovereignty. We can conclude that for Schelling all genuine sovereignty, all genuine lordship, is self-emptying. Legitimate earthly rulers do not raise themselves above the human community and place themselves in the position of God, demanding worship; they rather lower themselves and identify with the least among those they rule.

The good monarch is an index of transcendence; he or she does not incarnate the divine but only points towards it. The monarch is a symbol that points beyond the earthly throne to the true ruler of heaven and earth, whose kingdom is still to come. Schelling's pessimistic assessment of human moral and political possibilities, and his support for the embattled traditions of political representationalism and constitutional monarchy, are essentially rooted in his political eschatology. Inequalities are the result of 'an intelligible order that is older than humanity' (Schelling 1854a: 528). In alignment with Plato, the Vedas and innumerable other ancient sources, Schelling sees human inequality as natural and necessary, the order of things, since the manifestation of spirit in time, whether this be conceived as the moving picture of eternity, Samsara or the fallen order (different accounts, to be sure), requires that every grade of perfection, from the lowest to the highest, be realised. With reference to Aristotle, he writes, 'there can be no type of order of possible or real things, in which one is not distanced from the other from birth in the way that one rules, the other is ruled' (Schelling 1854a: 529–30). And yet natural inequalities are in tension with every human being's call to personality, to love, to union with divinity. The personal nature of this union implies an equality of all with the divine, and of each with each other. The tension between the natural order of inequality and the religious longing for a personal relation to God requires a new kind of politics, a politics that, while acknowledging the necessity of inequality, overcomes it through religion. We must not confuse Schelling with the more familiar conservative who protects the status quo as good enough because it has been particularly good to him, while leaving a great majority behind in wage-slavery, if not poverty.

It should be clear from the foregoing that the core of Schelling's late political thought is theological, or better, religious. Because the State is punishment for sin, and not the final realisation of the teleology of Spirit, the individual cannot help but feel its rule as force, even as violence; in any case as something not wanted. 'The State is not established to cater to or reward the I, but rather for its punishment: what it demands, we owe it, i.e., it is a debt which we thereby repay or clear' (Schelling 1854a: 547). Schelling recognises the legitimacy of the individual's feeling of oppression by even a just State; given who we are and our sociopolitical situation pen-ultimate to the final emancipation, we cannot but want to be free of the State. But to attempt to overthrow the State is to produce a worse situation, an abomination, a rule-less society, Hobbes's 'state of nature' in which the individual, bereft of the conditions necessary for moral development, sinks back into a subhuman condition. The drive for a better world must, to some degree, be internalised; not externalised into anarchic revolution and political violence, but directed within, while attending to the ever-present need to constantly reform the State.

> We have recognised as justified and necessary a striving of the human to overcome the pressure of the State. But this overcoming must be understood as internal. With the application of an old word, we could say: first seek this inner realm, then the inevitable pressure of the lawful external order will no longer be present for you. (Schelling 1854a: 548)

Schelling is not advocating an apolitical contemplative retreat, but the cul-tivation of a genuinely civil society in which cultural and religious activi-ties can be freely pursued. The individual is called to master the obdurate necessity at the basis of his or her existence, the dark ground within the self which is inescapably a private affair, and to begin to lead a genuinely moral and religious, common life, through the mediation of society, which is made possible by the State. To seek to abolish the State amounts to wishing to live without society, since society, Schelling agrees with Hobbes, is not possible outside the State (Schelling 1854a: 536); more, it is a denial of necessity, which is a diabolic gesture, a refusal of grounding and a disavowal of the conditions that limit us in the fallen order.

Schelling conceptualises the relation of the State to society and the person in terms of the metaphysics of ground, and this is key to understanding his late politics. As the ground of society, and through society the support of moral and religious life, the State must persist, but always held in check by due political process, as the necessary antecedent to personal life, and never permitted to overstep its bounds (which it will inevitably try to do). The ground must not usurp the grounded – it must remain antecedent, meontic, potency for an actuality that is other than it; but neither must the grounded disavow its groundedness, its dependency on that which antecedes it. So too must the person be left free by the State to self-actualise, but this freedom should not become inflated into an anarchic denial of the person's dependency on the State.

> The State itself is the support structure [*das Stabile (Abgethanes)*], that which should remain in its place, which allows only reform (not revolution), like nature, which can be embellished, but cannot be made otherwise than it is, and which must remain as long as this world exists. To make oneself impassive, as nature is impassive, to grant the individual rest and leisure, to be the means and the impetus to the attainment of the higher goal: that is what the State should do; in this alone lies its perfectibility. The task is therefore: to provide the individual with the greatest possible freedom (autarchy), freedom, namely, that rises above and, as it were, beyond the State, but which does not react back on the State or in the State. (Schelling 1854a: 551)

The State is 'like nature', of the order of necessity, objective, immovable and less than divine. As the means to social and religious life, the State cannot be an end, and therefore cannot be the goal of history: 'There is just as little a perfect State as there is (in the same line) a last human' (Schelling 1854a: 551). In what he no doubt understands as an objection to both left and right Hegelianism, the former seeking to overthrow the State, the latter, to apotheosise it, Schelling sounds an emphatically Pauline, eschatological note: 'The present order is not an end, it is only to be negated; it is thus not this order itself that is the goal, but the goal is the order that is determined to take its place' (Schelling 1854a: 552).

What passes beyond the State is the individual, more precisely the person. But what of the person's duties to the society that makes his or her life possible? Schelling is no 'rugged individualist', and rejects contractarianism for its failure to recognise that society is the condition of the possibility of freedom, not the result of a free act of association. 'It is the first effect of a factual rational order and furthermore of the State, that it raises the individual to the person. Before and outside this order, there would be individuals, but no persons. The person is the subject whose actions are imputable' (Schelling 1854a: 536). It is society that first makes us persons, and as such positively free or at least capable of freedom.[40] Therefore we cannot be held to have contractually entered into it. Schelling's language on this crucial point of the relation of the individual to society is schematic and rough, but it is not difficult to reconstruct his thought, particularly insofar as it resonates with other, analogous conservative religious thinking.[41] The basis of his view is the distinction, cited above, between the individual and the person. All persons are actual individuals but not all individuals are actual persons. Individuals are not born as fully personalised; they are potential persons who become actualised through a difficult moral process of overcoming internal necessity. Hence, the human being in relation to society must be considered in two ways. As an individual, the human being is a part of the whole, a member of a community to the common good of which individual desires are justly subordinated. As a person, or one who is personalising, the human being is an end in itself, never a means, and one who, in his or her moral and spiritual destiny, transcends the community. Here Schelling disagrees with Kant. The moral law might be necessary, but it is not sufficient, and in its generality and abstractness it is experienced as a burden on the individual, as Luther so vividly testified (Schelling 1854a: 555–6). The law cannot create a heart equal to the law (Schelling 1854a: 555). The person yearns for more than morality – for personality, for love, for union with the divine, and this yearning is the beginning of the positive philosophy. We are no more happy under the universal moral law, which requires us to sacrifice individual desires to social duty, than we are with the God of reason, the essence of essences, or *ens necessarium*. Kant's ethics, like Kant's onto-theology, is still negative philosophy. Kant's results are not to be denied, but neither are they the end of the story. The results of the negative philosophy become the beginning of the positive philosophy when the philosopher decides to question further. The moral question for the individual (Can I be happy?) and the religious question to the tradition (Does God exist?) converge on the philosopher's question concerning the positive. Is history providentially ruled? The move, on both the moral and religious level, is a move from essence to existence, or as Kierkegaard put it, an intensification of subjective existence (Kierkegaard 1846: 159–251). We

> drive the existent to the point where it proves itself to be the active (existing) Lord of Being (of the world), the personal, acting God; with this, at the same moment, all other being is also explained in its *existence* as derived from this first *that*, and thus finds itself established in a positive system, i.e., actuality. (Schelling 1854a: 564)

If God *is*, everything is explained, and my hope for myself is not in vain. If God is not, nothing is explicable, and I have no reason to hope.

Schelling's eschatology is thus resolutely political, and his Christianity this-worldly, even ecological. What Nietzsche alleges of the earth-hating, neo-Platonising Christians misses its mark with regard to Schelling. Schelling is not holding out for another world; he is looking towards this world transformed and rendered suitable for human and non-human flourishing. The real-world focus of Schelling's eschatology also explains his historical realism with regard to revelation. Just as he posits a real-world end of history, Schelling does not shy away from insisting (as does Hegel, to a lesser degree) on the historical facticity of the Christ event. These two thoughts, then, are essentially connected in the late Schelling: real-world political eschatological anticipation and a historically realist Christology. This puts Schelling in tension with two main streams of twentieth-century theology: existential theology, founded by Rudolf Bultmann, and neo-orthodoxy, whose central figure is Karl Barth. Both Bultmann and Barth, in different ways, questioned or even suspended the secular political-historical significance of eschatology at the same time that they suspended historical-critical investigations of the Christ event. The search for the historical Jesus infects theology with the scepticism and presumption of unbelief. The thinker who looks for independent and objective evidence of the redemption raises himself above the theological conditions of that revelation, and in effect subjects revelation to the tribunal of unbelief.[42] Bultmann, who is, on many questions, opposed to Barth, retreats from a historical proof of the Christ just as much as Barth does, but for a different reason. For Bultmann, influenced as he is by Heidegger, the search for historical evidence for the Christ event denigrates the ontological transformation effected by faith in Christ to the level of the ontic. History cannot prove for us the divinity of the Christ; it can at best prove for us the conviction of the first Christians, that Jesus was divine. This, according to Bultmann, is no disaster for Christian theology; what matters, what is truly at stake in 'primitive Christianity', is the believer's inner relation to the Christ event, not its historical objectivity or lack thereof.[43] Bultmann, as much as Barth, retreats from a political reading of eschatology. Where Barth opted for a more familiar Protestant emphasis on a 'strange' new world to come, Bultmann existentialised and psychologised the *eschaton*. The end proclaimed by Jesus is the death each of us anticipates: eschatology is to be realised in the resolute, faithful being-in-the-world of the ordinary Christian.

Schelling's approach to eschatology, by contrast to that of Barth and Bultmann, neither renounces the task of a historical-critical reconstruction of the Christ event, nor retreats from its political-eschatological consequences. If eschatological time has an existential significance for Schelling (which it undoubtedly does), he has little to say about it, as he is more concerned with the objective narration of the history of revelation than he is with the psychology of the believer. The historical-critical reconstruction of the Christ event is of deep interest to Schelling. One cannot help wondering whether it was Schelling's dogged insistence on an objective approach to matters of faith that so alienated the much more introverted Kierkegaard, who otherwise agrees with the older philosopher on many points.[44] While everything Schelling has to say about history remains, as it must, probabilistic, fallibilist and open-ended, his main thesis is that the turning point of universal history is the crucifixion and resurrection of the Christ, which thrusts us towards the anticipation in hope of an objective, eschatological end to human alienation.

Schelling confronts us today with an unpopular claim, that the history of humanity is *one* history, not, as poststructuralists would prefer it, a multiplicity of non-convergent lines that can be narrated in an infinity of ways. This thought is perhaps the most distasteful of Schellingian themes for the Deleuze-inspired immanentists who have, for various reasons, taken up Schelling. Many insist, against the text, and in flagrant disregard of the Philosophy of Revelation, on a Schelling whose positive philosophy unleashes a dysteleological pluralism of random beginnings and ends, a 'rhizomatic' rather than 'arborescent' Schelling, and much of the effort to reduce Schelling's later work to nature-philosophy by other means is motivated by just such a dysteleological reading. Such a reading of the *early* Schelling may be plausible – although even in Schelling's *Naturphilosophie* it is hard to root out all finality, for 'unconditioned nature' is directed towards at least one end, manifestation, and on more than one occasion Schelling argues that it only achieves this end in human consciousness.[45] However, it falls flat in the Philosophy of Revelation. The late Schelling is a believer in at least one 'meta-narrative', and it is not one that he invents but one that he receives from Paul, from John the Evangelist and from the Book of Revelation. The Philosophy of Mythology and Revelation is held together by Schelling's late conviction that all past human history converges on a single point, the redemption of the world in the Christ event, which points ahead to the final end of the human odyssey, the sanctification of the earth.

In short, the late Schelling is a Christian philosopher. That said, it is not frequently enough recognised that in an age of idealist theology, the late Schelling mounted an argument for the reasonableness of atheism. The ontological argument, which Hegel takes to be formally true, an expression of the infinity of reason (Hegel 1827: 324–9/181–8), is in Schelling's view a deceit, and the cosmological arguments rest on shaky premises. It *may* be the case that God does *not* exist, that is, that history is without meaning. The question remains open. As we have seen, it is the task of positive philosophy to explore the historical evidence for (and against) God's existence and to elaborate a method suitable for such an investigation. Humanity is doubtless haunted by a sense of a lost divinity, but without any guarantee of its recovery. In this situation of religious alienation, freedom settles into becoming merely negative, freedom from others, without any compelling insight into what freedom might be positively for. Nature, for Schelling II, is no longer the absolute becoming ever manifest; it is the site of a disaster, the site of the historical enslavement of humanity to necessity. 'The whole Earth is one great ruin' (Schelling 1810b: 25). The pessimistic conclusion becomes inescapable: humanity is so incapacitated by the historical-ontological legacy of sin that freedom is rendered impotent. We can only look to that which is beyond us, in eschatological hope of transformation. If reason itself is fallen, then it cannot reach its *telos* unaided by divinity. Humanity lacks the practical means to mend society. We need to be transformed in our very essence. What Heidegger said in the infamous 1966 *Spiegel* interview, 'Only a God can save us' (*Nur ein Gott kann uns retten*), Schelling said in so many words in 1809.

Schelling's mid-life pessimism, however, did not lead him to atheism or nihilism. It led him to esoteric Judaism. In the Kabbalah he discovered the thesis that love is born of an original negation of identity, a contraction of infinity, and a division of being and nothingness. Love is not first, but last. We know from Habermas (1954) and Sandkühler (1968) that the Kabbalah was a considerably influence on Schelling's turn to the positive. We know, for example, that Schelling was engaged in a lively correspondence with the Frankfurt Kabbalist Franz Joseph Molitor between 1806 and 1853. Among the topics discussed were Molitor's critique of the early Schelling's lack of a practical philosophy, that is, the lack, or impossibility, of a philosophy of history in both nature-philosophy and identity-philosophy. Molitor also took exception to Schelling's non-moral account of the fall in the 1804 *Philosophy and Religion*. There the fall is described as simply a cosmic occurrence and not the consequence of an act of freedom or evil by a creature who rebelled against the divinely constituted order of being. According to Sandkühler, it is Schelling's appropriation of the Kabbalistic notion of the moral-cosmological fall of Adam Kadmon, the shattering of the vessels (*Shevirat ha-Kelim*), that underwrites his turn to conservative politics and his pessimism regarding the possibility of the just State.[46] If, *contra* the Enlightenment, we are ontologically fallen beings, constitutively perverse, in the grip of radical evil as Kant put it, then there is no *political* solution to the intractable social problems of our age (war, inequality, intolerance). If there is a solution at all, it will only be a religious one, a 'religious regeneration of the historical domain of freedom, that is, of the social relation' (Sandkühler 1968: 209).

Such gloomy thoughts compelled Schelling to turn back to his Speculative Pietist roots, and to take seriously the idea that a solution to human misery lies not in progressive politics, but in revelation. Justice and a flourishing human civilisation will only be achieved via a universal experience of the redeeming God – this is the social-political upshot of the Philosophy of Revelation. The solution to the social problems driving Europe into revolution – class struggle, economic inequality, capitalist wage-slavery – will only be found in a transcendence of politics through the internalisation of the *objective* revelation of the redeeming God, that is, a transcultural appropriation of the historical occurrence of God among us, a mystery which was originally entrusted to the Christian Churches, but is now, according to Schelling, in the process of being secularised and distributed to all people.

The secret of history, that which Paul refers to in Colossians, 'the mystery which hath been hid from ages and from generations, but now is made manifest' (Col. 1:26), is the central theme of the Philosophy of Revelation. Paul means the messiahship of Jesus. Schelling interprets Paul yet more esoterically. The secret is that love is in a sense higher than God; it is that which God, in choosing to be God, serves. God becomes God so that love might be. In the light of Schelling's theory of the copula as differentiating for the sake of identifying (Schelling 1809: 346/17), John's statement, 'God is love' (1 John 4:8), well known to the point of being worn out, takes on a new significance. The 'is' is transitive and has an accusative object: God grounds love. God is the *antecedens*, love is the *consequens*. God *loves*. God divides Godself from being, decides to exist as God, creates the world as God's other, and lets it fall so that it might freely rise again, all for one superb purpose, which is the stroke of the divine genius: that love might be. This is not a truth that is other than the Gospel: the fullness of love – the essence of revelation itself – is the Christ, crucified, resurrected and triumphant over history, at the end of which he 'will be made subject to him who put everything under him, so that God may be all in all' (1 Cor. 15:28). In the lyric and often overlooked conclusion of the Freedom Essay, Schelling paraphrases this passage from Paul and describes the culmination of the revelation begun with the crucified messiah as the Christ become the spirit of the perfected human community. We have reason to hope, Schelling writes in 1809, that history is moving towards such a perfect socio-personal unity, 'a general unity that is the same for all and yet gripped by nothing, that is free from all and yet a beneficence acting in all, in a word, love, which is all in all' (Schelling 1809: 409/70).

Notes

1. The similarities between Schelling and Hegel on Christianity come out most clearly in Fackenheim's reading of Hegel's philosophy of religion (Fackenheim 1967).

2. See Lossky (2005: 53): 'Our ideas of human personality, of that personal quality which makes every human being unique, to be expressed only in terms of itself: this idea of person comes to us from Christian theology. The philosophy of antiquity knew only human individuals.'

3. This is an argument first made by the Romantics and given definitive form by Wilhelm Dilthey, but which is now most associated with Löwith (1949). For a summary of the argument, see McGrath (2006a: 190–7).

4. On the Christian discovery of the irreducibility and essential historicity of the human subject, an Augustinian theme first taken up by Dilthey which proved foundational for the early Heidegger, see McGrath (2006a: 187ff.).

5. This is a point that was also made repeatedly by Etienne Gilson with respect to the Thomist solution to the problem of the relation of philosophy to theology. See Gilson (1936: 1–19). Cf. the notion of 'revelabilia' in Gilson (Maurer 1993: xv).

6. The non-dialectical nature of love is a recurring theme of Kierkegaard's, who very likely got it from hearing Schelling's Berlin lectures. See the parable of the king and the peasant in Kierkegaard (1844: 26–36). My thanks to McGill PhD candidate in Religious Studies Jason Blakeburn for this insight.

7. See Augustine (1991).

8. Irenaeus, *Against the Heresies* 1.10; 5.22.

9. I will discuss the relationship of Schelling's Trinitarianism and Christology to the pre-Nicene Church Fathers in detail in the second book.

10. See Beach (1994).

11. For an early glimmer of Schelling's growing sense that revelation is more than simply the manifestation of the absolute in nature, see Schelling (1809: 411–12/72–3).

12. Schelling is conspicuously silent on Islam. We can conclude that he interpreted it, as did medieval theologians, as a reaction to the Trinity and a regression to theism after the experience of absolute (Trinitarian) monotheism.

13. The idea of the continuity of mythology with Christianity predates the Philosophy of Revelation. One can see Schelling entertaining this thought as a hypothesis already in the 1815 lecture 'The Deities of Samothrace'. See Schelling (1815b: 362–3/25): 'What if already in Greek mythology (not to mention Indian and other oriental mythologies) there emerged the remains of a knowledge, indeed even a scientific system, which goes far beyond the circle drawn by the oldest revelation known through scriptural evidences? What if after all this, [scriptural revelation] has not so much opened up a new system of knowledge, but rather had taken that which had already been opened up earlier and confined it to a riverbed, more narrow but therefore leading onward more steadily? What if, after a decline had set in and an unpreventable deterioration into polytheism, it [scripture] had with the most prudent restriction retained only a portion of that original system, but yet those very features which could lead back again to a great and comprehensive whole?' This hypothesis of original traces of the divine in mythology, which have dropped from the historical trajectory that leads from mythology to revelation, is what drew Schelling's attention to the Kabiri, the oldest of gods, predating even India and Egypt.

14. 'In old times evil demons manifested themselves, seducing women, corrupting boys, and showing terrifying sights to men – so that those who did not judge these occurrences rationally were filled with awe. Taken captive by fear and not understanding that these were evil demons, they called them gods and gave each of them the name which each of the demons had chosen for themselves. When Socrates tried by true reason and with due inquiry to make these thing clear and to draw men away from the demons, they, working

through men who delighted in wickedness, managed to have him put to death as godless and impious.' *The First Apology of Justin, the Martyr,* 5, in Richardson (1953: 244).

15. Schelling is in fact closer to Justin in this regard than he is to his contemporaries, who held the pagan gods to be fictions or allegories. Justin at least recognised something real in polytheism, something against which the Church opposed itself, a dark force which revelation had to struggle to overcome. See Schelling (1842a: 247/172): 'Christianity presents itself as the liberation from the blind power of heathendom, and the reality of a liberation is measured according to the reality and power of that from which it frees itself. Were heathendom nothing actual, then also Christianity could be nothing actual.'

16. The term 'tautegory' was coined by Samuel Taylor Coleridge, an early disciple of Schelling's. See Schelling (1842a: 196/136).

17. I have written more extensively of the depth-psychological significance of Schelling's Philosophy of Mythology in McGrath (2012: 161–3).

18. This could go some distance towards making sense of the more extreme statements of non-dualist mysticism, for example, Eckhart's condemned propositions, or Shankara's Advaita Vedanta.

19. To be Godforsaken is not the same thing as being Godless. On this distinction, see McGrath (2006a: 11).

20. The 'happy fault' refers to the 'necessary sin of Adam', spoken of in the Easter Exultet, one of the oldest prayers in the Christian liturgy. 'Necessary' here does not mean logically necessary, but rather historically necessary, that is, without Adam's sin, Christ would not have been incarnated, hence sin was necessary to the Incarnation. Scotus famously disagreed.

21. The theme of a golden age of immediacy with the divine, sundered by an act of freedom, to be reconciled in a future age, could be the oldest of Schelling's ideas. Kasper traces it back to Schelling's student writings, 'Antiquissimi de prima malorum humanorum origine' 1792 (SW 1: 1–40), and 'Über Mythen, historische Sagen und Philosopheme der ältesten Welt' (SW 1: 41–84). Kasper summarises their contents as follows. 'These discuss the opposition between sensuality and reason, between the individual and the generally valid, and thus between the historical description of truth, for example, in the myths, and philosophical description. These oppositions cannot be united, they are for the human being the basis of all evils. These oppositions are broken open by the first act of freedom. In the beginning of history is the golden age in which human beings do nothing but follow nature. The first free act of self-determination led to the renunciation of nature. It is the goal of history to abolish this conflict and to bring about a higher unity of nature and freedom' (Kasper 1965: 79).

22. Von Rad concurs 'that Jehovah was not manifested to his elect from the beginning, but that the revelation of his name only took place in the time of Moses' (Von Rad 1962: 179).

23. Schelling's interpretation of the divine name revealed in Exodus anticipates Richard Kearney's doctrine of the possible God. Kearney refers to Rosenzweig and Buber's translation of the Bible as his source. This raises the question as to whether Rosenzweig and Buber were in fact influenced by Schelling's interpretation of the Hebrew passage. See Kearney (2001: 27).

24. Ringgren confirms Schelling's interpretation of the various stages in Israelite religion. Exod. 20:3, Deut. 5:7, 'You shall have no other gods before me', presupposes a plurality of gods (Ringgren 1966: 66). 'The religion of Israel, then, was originally not monotheistic in the sense of denying the existence of other gods . . . One of the distinguishing characteristics of the Israelite religion is the belief that there are not several gods of Israel, but one, Yahweh, who claims exclusive devotion' (Ringgren 1966: 67). Over time, this sense of the one God becomes more differentiated as sense for the

transcendence of the one God. 'The universal prohibition of images (Ex 20:4) places the strictest possible limitation upon anthropomorphism. Even if it was not always obeyed by everyone, this prohibition plainly expresses the transcendence of God to a degree not found in any other ancient religion' (Ringgren 1966: 80).

25. I offered an extended ecological critique of the re-enchantment industry in my recent book, *Thinking Nature: An Essay in Negative Ecology* (McGrath 2019).

26. I published a more developed version of the following critique of populism in McGrath (2017b).

27. On this crucial point, see the first lecture of the *Darstellung der reinrationalen Philosophie* (Schelling 1842d: 255–77).

28. See Lawrence (1989: 196): 'Die wahrhaft allgemeine Kirche wird nicht auf der Verallgemeinerung einer besonderen Gestalt beruhen, sondern auf der Befreiung von jeder Gestalt, einer Befreiung, die zugleich die Offenheit für jede Gestalt bedeutet.'

29. The unity of 'fellowship', not 'the identity of a single subject'. See Moltmann (1980: 95).

30. The primary political texts of the late Schelling are the Stuttgart Seminars (Schelling 1810a: 460ff.), the concluding lectures, on ecclesiology, of the Philosophy of Revelation (1831: 672–710; 1841: 314–21; SW 14: 292–335) and the last three lectures of the *Darstellung der reinrationalen Philosophie* (1854a: 516–73).

31. Hegel cannot simply be consigned to the utopian camp, for, on one reading of his philosophy of religion, he affirms that the spirit moving in history is the third person of the Trinity. See Hegel (1827: 470–89). The positive transformations in society which have led to the emancipation of peoples from slavery and which explain the forward thrust of modern science and technology are not purely the result of human ingenuity. For Hegel, the finite spirit of the human being is cancelled and preserved by the infinite spirit moving through history, which is representationally depicted in the Pentecost event. Thus Hegel would reject the either/or in the distinction I have drawn between utopian eschatology and theologico-political eschatology. As in every other matter, Hegel insists on the both/and. The divine spirit uses human hands. It is both the spirit of humanity and the spirit of God. See Fackenheim (1967: 206–15).

32. See Schelling's letter to Windischmann, cited in Chapter 1 note 15 above.

33. See Schulz (1977: 36–7): 'Der frühe Schelling hat, so kann man sagen, immer nur das Positive in der Natur gesehen. Das heißt konkret: er hat das Harmonische als Prinzip der Selbstgestaltung, etwa in den Bildungen der Kristalle oder den Phänomenen des Organismus, einseitig in den Vordergrund gerückt. Die von ihm beschriebene Natur ist gleichsam die paradiesische Natur. Jetzt wandelt sich seine Einstellung zur Natur wesentlich. Diese Wandlung vollzieht sich jedoch nicht auf einmal, sondern in Übergängen. Konkret: Wenn Schelling sagt, daß die Natur sich verkehrt habe, dann meint er zunächst nur die Natur im Menschen, d. h. dessen natürliche Bedürfnisse und seine Geschlechtigkeit. Nachdem Schelling aber im Menschen entdeckt hat, daß die Natur eine zerstörende Macht sein kann, sucht er das Wesen der Natur überhaupt neu zu fassen. Er erklärt, daß Natur eigentlich ihrer Struktur nach Trieb, Sucht und Begierde sei. Das heißt nicht, daß die Natur böse sei. Das Böse ersteht erst und allein durch den Menschen, der die Natur gegen den Geist zum Prinzip erhebt. Die Natur an sich ist also durchaus nicht böse ... Schelling behauptet, daß die ganze Unordnung und Unvernunft in der außermenschlichen Natur auf das Schuldkonto des Menschen gehe.'

34. See Schelling (SW 1: 1–84). See also Schelling's discussion of Greek tragedy in the 1803 *Philosophy of Art* (SW 5: 694–710).

35. Michael Vater comments: 'The result of creation shows us something ultimately unprethinkable as an actuality, even if it was foreseeable as a possibility: that humanity would fall because it tries to be like God. But since humanity cannot be the Lord of

being, in the very attempt at instituting itself as God-like, being obtains free rein over us. Consequently, natural, law-like processes, like those initially active in creation, now repeat themselves at the level of human consciousness' (footnote comment to Vater's unpublished translation of Schelling 1841, used with permission of the author).

36. See Schelling (1841: 257, Vater trans., slightly altered): 'God demonstrates his artistic character in that he seeks after the infinite and brings everything into the most intelligible and most finite form. What is limited in Christianity is, for him, its very purpose. One can see the divine folly in the following consideration: that God was not satisfied with merely contemplating a world that was, for him, possible. One can see the weakness of God in his weakness towards man. In creation God shows his spirit, in redemption his heart. The more powerful spirit is, the more impersonal it becomes. God's most personal deed is revelation. At that moment, God became, in the highest sense, the most personal to man.'

37. Schelling was not alone in discovering in eschatology a new conception of time, a concept of time which has shaped modernity and changed how we think of persons. See Heidegger (1920–21), Löwith (1949), Benz (1983) and Grant (1960; 1971).

38. I outline the late Schelling's political philosophy here only for the sake of underscoring its eschatological presuppositions. A more detailed account of the political thought of the late Schelling will follow in the second book in the context of its necessary correlate: Schelling's ecclesiology.

39. I have relied on Memorial University PhD candidate Kyla Bruff for her excellent translation of these lectures. See Bruff (2020).

40. Political freedom is consequent freedom, freedom for the good. There is also a more primordial, pre-political, antecedent freedom, the freedom that authors and grounds the self as such, which is described in the Freedom Essay (Schelling 1809: 382–6/49–51). This distinction between two senses of freedom is never explicitly articulated by Schelling, but it follows from everything he says. For a more explicit distinction between two stages of freedom, which is an ontological predecessor to Isaiah Berlin's ontic distinction between negative and positive freedom, see Berdyaev (1926: 148ff.).

41. On what follows, see Maritain (1945: 45–70).

42. See Barth (1959: 67).

43. See Bultmann (1948).

44. It might be useful to consider Kierkegaard's *Concluding Unscientific Postscript* as a reversal of Schelling's Philosophy of Revelation in a certain way: while conceding Schelling's basic principles – the distinction between essence and existence, the limits of speculative thought, the impossibility of a system of reality, the inconclusiveness and uncertainty of historical knowledge – Kierkegaard doubles down on the incommunicability of faith, which instead of offering universal foundations for a new human community, singularises the believer, and instead of asymptotically approaching the truth, absolutises the individual's relation to it.

45. See Schelling (1800: 6): 'The dead and unconscious products of nature are merely abortive attempts that she makes to reflect herself; inanimate nature so-called is actually as such an immature intelligence, so that in her phenomena the still unwitting character of intelligence is already peeping through. – Nature's highest goal, to become wholly an object to herself, is achieved only through the last and highest order of reflection, which is none other than man; or more generally, it is what we call reason, whereby nature first completely returns into herself.'

46. See Sandkühler (1968: 209ff.).

Chapter 5

Conclusion

Schelling's positive philosophy stakes out a middle ground between idealism and realism. With the idealists, the *a priori* is made essential to cognition. With the realists, the truth is held to be irreducible to innate ideas. Revelation is a disruption of the *a priori* by the *a posteriori* (which is no longer identified simply with sense data): it is an encounter with the real, not a deduction of it. This is to some degree a concession to Jacobi, who had tirelessly insisted, against Spinoza, Fichte, the young Schelling and Hegel, on the irreducibility of revelation. According to Jacobi the acknowledgement of the otherness of truth is the most reasonable thing the human knower can do (Jacobi 1803). Schelling goes much further than affirming with orthodoxy the trans-rational reality of the revelation. The late Schelling holds that revelation, received *a posteriori*, shall become the foundation for a new mode of philosophy when its truths are appropriated by reason. Such an appropriation lays the ground for a genuine philosophy of history, a metaphysical empiricism, which leaves the revelational positivism of Judaism behind and strikes a decidedly Hellenistic note. Philosophical religion will fulfil the dream of philosophy as a science.

The turn to the positive is the free decision of the philosopher who renounces rationalism, and the godless self-inflation to which it inevitably gives rise, along with its shadow, ideological mythology and the political conflicts it engenders. The decision is a repetition of what Christ does in Schelling's interpretation of Paul's *kenosis* hymn (Phil. 3:7), which is itself a repetition of what the Father does in creating the world.[1] The turn is a turning outward, a turning of oneself inside out, a self-emptying. It is in every way, then, a moral and theological matter. God empties Godself into existence; the Son empties himself of divinity before the Father; the positive philosopher empties his or herself of concepts. In each case, a possible form of being, which retreats from the demands of the real, is freely renounced. In each case, a necessity is overcome. Only because Christ has a genuine claim to an alternative divinity, only because he *could* be God in the place of the Father, only thus could he empty himself before the true and actual God and take on 'the form of a slave'. The divine pattern of self-emptying, of voluntarily lowering oneself below a level that is rightfully one's own to claim – which is nothing short of the essence of divinity – is repeated in reason's most reasonable act of recognising the real. In each case the *kenosis* produces freedom. *Creatio* sets matter free to exist in its own right, Christ sets the human being free from the bonds of the law and the historical effects of sin, and the turn to the positive sets the real free, allows it to exist as fully, mind-independent being.

The argument I have made in this book is that the affirmation of the revealedness of the revealed enacts the same pattern performed in the turn to the real. It is continuous with it, even if revelation intensifies the risk and uncertainty involved. Once affirmed, however, the revealed can become reason's *adopted* content. Having lowered itself and taken on 'the form of a slave', reason is raised up again. Revelation does not leave reason in the dark; it gives us knowledge and satisfies reason's infinite hunger for cognition.

Schelling's figure of ecstatic rationality, which sounds vaguely post-modern, is entirely biblical. It describes the mind of a creature who could make itself into its own God because it is made in the image of its creator, who possesses anarchic freedom, but who decides not to. In the ecstasy of reason, the human being renounces his or her pseudo self-sufficiency and wills the truth. Because no logical necessity binds negative and posi-tive philosophy together, they can be related to one another ethically. The only link between them is the philosopher who freely decides to turn to the positive. Still, there is no move into the positive without a move away from the negative, and in this sense the negative *is* the presupposition of the positive. Only one who speaks can be silenced.[2] Only one who pos-sesses something, or at least *could* lay claim to possession of something, can empty themselves. Reason in the late Schelling is only truly itself when it empties itself, renounces its own interior world as sufficient to itself and takes on the form of its opposite, one that possesses nothing but depends entirely on another. Just as it is crucial to understand Christ as renouncing a real possibility for self-divinisation and freely assuming the form of the anti-divine, so is it crucial for Schelling's metaphysical empiricism to recog-nise that absolute idealism is not simply a mistake; it is a logically coherent possibility for thought. Schelling in effect admits that absolute idealism can logically stand up as a pseudo-metaphysics, an ersatz philosophy of being. Reason can set up such an idol because reason is not, as in Locke's empiricism, a *tabula rasa*, but contains an *a priori* idea of being. Idealism is therefore unavoidable. Only one who possesses something, or at least *could* lay claim to possession, can empty themselves. A *tabula rasa* cannot empty itself before the real.

Every religion has some essential truth which can only be misunderstood when surveyed from the outside, some secret which requires total immersion and religious commitment to be understood. In the Mahayana traditions of Buddhism, the secret is *sunyata*. From the outside, to the non-Buddhist, *sunyata* appears to be nihilism. Then one meets genuine practitioners and one sees that one has misunderstood it: *sunyata* is a way of affirmation. In Islam, the secret is the Qu'ran. From outside, the Qu'ran appears to be a great work of literature, a masterpiece of the Arabic language, but hardly the direct and final expression of God to humanity, worth reciting day and night. And then one meets devout Muslims, and one sees how wrong one is, that the Qu'ran is much more than literature, and the devotion to every sentence of it is the source of the power and persistence of Islam. In Christianity, the secret is the personal relationship of the Christian to Jesus Christ. From outside, the personal relation of the Christian to Christ appears as anthropomorphic, infantilising, wishful thinking as Freud put it, the apotheosis of the unresolved Oedipus complex. Then one meets real Christians and sees how wrong one is. Or if one cannot find a real Christian (they are getting rare), one reads Augustine, Aquinas, Eckhart, and realises that this personal relation can hardly be dismissed as Oedipal illusion. Or, more recently, one reads Thomas Merton. In his journal entry for 26 June 1965, the Feast of the Sacred Heart, Merton writes:

> There is one thing more – I may be interested in Oriental religions, etc., but there can be no obscuring the essential difference – this personal communion with Christ at the centre and heart of all reality as a source of grace and life. 'God is love' may perhaps be clarified if one says that 'God is void' and if in the void one finds absolute indetermination and hence absolute freedom. (With freedom, the void becomes fullness and $0 = \infty$.) All that is 'interesting', but none of it touches on the mystery of personality in God. His personal love for me. Again, I am void too – and I have freedom, or *am* a kind of freedom, meaningless unless oriented to Him. (Merton 1999: 250)

This insight into what Merton calls 'the mystery of personality in God' was Schelling's mid-life breakthough, and remains that which most distinguishes Schelling I from Schelling II.[3] The young Schelling, inflated by his extraordinary abilities and early academic accomplishments, threw himself into transcendental and speculative philosophy, and constructed thought world after thought world, occasionally glancing back at the religion of his upbringing, but preferring instead his conceptual dedication to an impersonal absolute, a principle of identity in difference, 'nature naturing', perhaps believing with Spinoza that personality is beneath the divine. The older Schelling, whose career as an author crashed as quickly as it took off, coming to an end with the 1812 *Denkmal* (when he was still only 37 years old), deprived of his muse and soulmate, his beloved Caroline Schlegel, who died tragically two years earlier – the older Schelling discovers that personality is the highest. If personality is not to be found in divinity, then there is no God.

Schelling is clear that revealed religion is not the end of humanity's ascent to God; it is the middle act of a three-part drama. It brings the unconsciousness and compulsion of natural religion (mythology) to an end, and creates the condition for modernity and the freedom from God requisite for a personal relationship to God. But revealed religion in turn awaits its own de-actualisation, when it will become the ground for the truly free religion of humankind, the actualisation of a positive freedom for God, which Schelling calls 'philosophical religion'. What is received externally in revealed religion, as an unveiling of the secret of God, proclaimed by authorities who witnessed it, and preserved in sacred scriptures, shall become an inner experience common to all human beings, when the *Wirkungsgeschichte* of revelation has run its course and finally and irreversibly emancipated humanity from religious ideology. The secret of God will become the truth of reason, and humankind's religious odyssey, along with the sociopolitical fragmentation that attended it from the beginning, shall come to an end. Philosophical religion is nothing less than the Kingdom of God realised, as Christ prays that it will be, 'on earth as it is in heaven' (Matt. 6:10).

We shall have to say a great deal more about this most innovative and least understood aspect of the late Schelling's philosophy of religion. But for the moment, let this be said. As with all other major moves in the Philosophy of Revelation, Schelling's argument here is not without precedent. There is of course the largely forgotten history of millenarianism from Montanus to Joachim of Fiore, the radical Franciscans, Thomas Müntzer, Protestant esoteric universalism (Weigel to Oetinger), and so on.[4] But I have in mind a more profoundly lost tradition, older than the formal definitions of the Trinity, as old as the prologue to the Gospel of John: the tradition of Christian *gnosis*. *Pace* Jacobi, Christianity is for Schelling not non-knowledge; it offers a higher knowledge which reveals worldly or natural knowledge to be darkness, as *nous* reveals *dianoia* to be darkness for Plato (Schelling 1854a: 266). Christianity gives us something to know, not only something to believe; it grasps the essential mystery of things. But the achievement of Christian *gnosis* depends upon the historical emancipation of reason from unconscious religiosity. This begins but does not end with revealed religion. Key to the development of philosophical religion is the Protestant separation of reason and revelation, culminating in the immanentisation of the idea of God as a merely regulative principle of reason in modern philosophy. While the tradition remains, on the one hand, naive about the natural capacity of reason to know God (the Catholic error), and on the other hand, with a merely confrontational relation to revelation as something external to reason (the Protestant error), the actualisation of Christian *gnosis* cannot happen. We are still languishing in the homogeneous time that succeeds the divine immanentisation. We are all disenchanted Protestants and casualties of the death of God.

Christian *gnosis*, therefore, is still to come, and Schelling's positive philosophy is meant as its preparation. But the anticipated *gnosis* is still what it was defined as in the first century, direct knowledge of God through Christ crucified and resurrected, 'the true Light, which lighteth every man that cometh into the world' (John 1:9). The core of Christian *gnosis* is for Schelling what it was for Clement of Alexandria, who openly challenged the Valentinian gnostics, on the one side, and the pagan neo-Platonists, on the other, with what he declared to be the the true *knowledge* of God. *Gnosis*, for Clement (as for Schelling), is the effect of the revelation of the Christ as the *Logos*. The Christ shows us the Father, whom we could not otherwise know (John 1:18). 'The Father brings us from faith to knowledge by means of the Son, and knowledge of the Son and the Father which follows the Gnostic Rule – the rule of the genuine "Gnostic" is an intuition and apprehension of the truth though "the Truth"'.[5] For Clement, the Father is in himself unknowable,[6] but the Son, who makes the Father known, is the principle of knowledge itself, the *Logos* incarnate, the light of the world, the light of pagans as well as Christians, a principle of science as well as of religion. In Schelling's language the Father is unprethinkable: his existence cannot be known *a priori*. But the impossibility of an *a priori* or deductive access to the divine does not mean that the divine is unknowable, any more for Schelling than for Clement. The Father is made known *a posteriori* through the Son. Herein lies the core argument for the Philosophy of Revelation: Kant shows us that God cannot be known through purely rational means; Christianity shows us that God can only be known *a posteriori* through the incarnation. The two positions, in Schelling's view, are entirely consistent with one another, even if the former does not imply the latter. Christologically mediated knowledge of the divine, for Schelling as much as for Clement, is genuine human knowledge, that is, it is scientific – if not in origin, it can be rendered so – and universal. 'God is indemonstrable and therefore is not an object of knowledge. But the Son is Wisdom and Knowledge and Truth and all that is akin to these, and he admits of demonstration and explanation.'[7]

The Scholastic tradition, in its justified opposition to Valentinianism, and to its resurgence in Catharism, dropped the language of Christian *gnosis*. Thomas Aquinas introduced a set of sharp distinctions in order to keep philosophy and theology separate, to keep that which can be naturally known distinct but related to that which can only be supernaturally known, that is, through faith. It could be the late Schelling's most important (and most theologically questionable) contribution to Christian theology to have declared this Scholastic 'separation of powers' over. After two millennia, reason has been changed by the revelation, according to Schelling. Reason has been christened by the historical reception of Trinitarian thought, by wrestling with it for 1800 years.[8]

This Christological centre-point of the positive philosophy is completely misunderstood by those who take it to be a confessional turn in Schelling; it is far more a methodological move than a confession of religious belief. If, as Kant had shown, a categorical knowledge of divinity was not possible, if negative philosophy could no more know the existence of God than it could know the existence of anything *a priori*, then an *a posteriori* way had to be found. The Christ event, with its 'cloud of witnesses' (Heb. 12:1), is Schelling's departure point for a post-Kantian metaphysics. Schelling replaces natural theology with a speculative, historically-critically grounded Christology, not in order to prop up the dying Church, but in order to advance the project of metaphysics after Kant.

With the turn to the positive clarified, we are now in a position to discuss the specifically *theological* content of the late Schelling's Philosophy of Revelation. Schelling's regular annual lectures on Christian revelation, which begin in Munich in 1827 (with a run-up in the 1820–27 lectures of the Erlangen period) and end in Berlin in 1844, are built around revisionary interpretations of *the* two fundamental Christian dogmas: the doctrine of the Trinity, debated widely in the second and third centuries by the Greek and Roman Fathers of the Church, and defined at the Council of Nicaea in 325; and the doctrine of the hypostatic union of divine and human natures in the Christ, defined at the Council of Chalcedon in 451. Schelling interprets both doctrines so as to reconsider positions condemned as heretical at these ecumenical councils. On the Trinity, Schelling approximates, if not endorses, Arian and Origenan subordinationism, and on Christology, Eutychian monophysitism. Schelling reopens these debates in the spirit of constructing a *speculative* philosophy of revelation for our time: he is looking for the best, non-reductive explanation of the revealed mysteries of the triune God and the Christ, and he recognises that every such explanation, including his own, is provisional and falsifiable. His intention is not to destroy the theological tradition but to revive it, by thinking it forward into a new age of the Church, an age in which Christian doctrine no longer needs the mediation and protection of an ecclesiastical hierarchy. What is of most interest to theology in the late Schelling is not the question of which category of heresy he appears to best fit, but rather the reasons why he would have us reconsider the heretical positions of Arius and Origen on the Trinity, or Eutyches on Christology. If Schelling is guilty of anything from an orthodox theological perspective, it is of refusing to regard the questions of the Trinity and Christology as finally settled at Nicaea and Chalcedon.

Whatever the theological problems that remain unresolved in Schelling's Philosophy of Revelation, I consider the reactualisation of certain still open questions concerning Christian dogma in a secular, post-Christendom age to be vitally important for the embattled and declining academic discipline of theology. That Schelling is compelled to reopen the canon not out of confessional allegiance but on philosophical grounds only adds to the argument of this study, that Schelling's Philosophy of Revelation is still the strongest position on Christian philosophy ever taken in the modern age. And yet the late Schelling lies largely unread and unreceived, while 'new atheists', 'speculative realists' and 'new realists' run roughshod over the biblical traditions upon which not only the Jewish, Christian and Muslim religion depend, but also many of our most cherished democratic and civic institutions. With these Christian and democratic institutions decaying from within, it is time to give the late Schelling the careful reading he so richly deserves.

Notes

1. See Schelling (1854: 36–7).
2. Cf. Heidegger (1927a: 208): 'To be able to keep silent, Dasein must have something to say – that is, it must have at its disposal an authentic and rich disclosedness of itself.'
3. 'How much nearer I am than one might imagine to that silencing of science (that *Verstummen der Wissenschaft*), which necessarily ensues, once we recognize how infinitely *personal* everything is . . .' (Schelling: 1811: 103/164).
4. On this history, which should be of immense interest to anyone interested in Schelling's concept of philosophical religion, see Benz (1968).
5. Clement, *Stromateis*, v. i, 1, in Bettenson (1956: 235–6).
6. 'He [the Father] cannot be comprehended by knowledge, which is based on previously known truths, whereas nothing can precede what is self-existent' (Clement, *Stromateis*, v. xii, 82, 4, in Bettenson [1956: 233]).
7. Clement, *Stromateis*, iv, xxv, 156, 1, in Bettenson (1956: 234).
8. In this regard Schelling finds an ally in R. G. Collingwood, who argued in the early twentieth century that the Trinity has now become a basic presupposition of Western rationality, the influence of which is everywhere, in ethics, in metaphysics, even in science (Collingwood 1940). See James Bradley, 'A Key to Collingwood's Metaphysics of Absolute Presuppositions: The Trinitarian Creed', in Bradley (2021).

Bibliography

Agamben, Giorgio. 1998. *Homo Sacer. Sovereign Power and Bare Life*. Stanford: Stanford University Press.

— . 2005. *The Time that Remains. A Commentary on the Letter to the Romans*. Trans. Patricia Dailey. Stanford: Stanford University Press.

Altizer, Thomas J. 1997. 'Apocalypticism and Modern Thinking'. *Journal for Christian Theological Research* 2.2. <https://www.religion-online.org/article/apocalypticism-and-modern-thinking/> (accessed 1 July 2020).

Anselm, Saint. 1996. *Monologion and Proslogion: With the Replies of Gaunilo and Anselm*. Trans. Thomas Williams. Indianapolis: Hackett.

Aquinas, Thomas. 1948. *Summa Theologica*. Trans. Fathers of the English Dominican Province. New York: Benzinger Brothers.

— . 1949. *On Being and Essence*. Trans. Armand Maurer. Toronto: Pontifical Institute of Medieval Studies.

Augustine. 1991. *Confessions*. Trans. Henry Chadwick. New York: Penguin.

Aurobindo, Sri. 2010. *The Life Divine*. Pondichery, India: Sri Aurobindo Ashram.

Badiou, Alain. 2003. *Saint Paul: The Foundation of Universalism*. Trans. Ray Brassier. Stanford: Stanford University Press.

Barth, Karl. 1933. *The Epistle to the Romans*. Ed. Edwyn C. Hoskyns. London: Oxford University Press, 1972.

— . 1959. *Dogmatics in Outline*. Trans. G. T. Thompson. New York: Harper and Row.

— . 1960. *Anselm: Fides Quaerens Intellectum: Anselm's Proof of the Existence of God in the Context of his Theological Scheme*. London: SCM Press.

— . 1975. *The Doctrine of the Word of God. Church Dogmatics*. Vol. 1, Part 1. Trans. G. W. Bromiley. Edinburgh: T & T Clark.

Beach, Edward Allen. 1990. 'The Later Schelling's Conception of Dialectical Method, in Contradistinction to Hegel's'. *The Owl of Minerva*, 22:1, 35–54.

— . 1994. *The Potencies of God(s): Schelling's Philosophy of Mythology*. Albany: State University of New York Press.

— . 2020. Unpublished MS.

Becker, Matthew. 2014. *Fundamental Theology: A Protestant Perspective*. London: Bloomsbury.

Behler, Diana I., trans. 2002. 'The Oldest Systematic Program of German Idealism'. In *Philosophy of German Idealism*, pp. 161–2. Ed. Ernst Behler. New York: Continuum.

Beierwaltes, Werner. 1972. *Platonismus und Idealismus*. Frankfurt: Klostermann.

—. 2002. 'The Legacy of Neoplatonism in F. W. J. Schelling's Thought'. *International Journal of Philosophical Studies*, 10:4, 393–428.

Bell, David N. 2007. *A Cloud of Witnesses: An Introduction to the Development of Christian Doctrine to AD 500*. Collegeville, MN: Cistercian Publications.

Benjamin, Walter. 1985. 'Theses on the Philosophy of History'. In *Illuminations*, pp. 245–55. Ed. Hannah Arendt. Trans. Harry Zohn. New York: Schocken Books.

—. 1996. *Critique of Violence*. In *Walter Benjamin: Selected Writings*, Vol. 1: *1913–1926*, pp. 236–52. Ed. Marcus Bullock and Michael Jennings. Cambridge, MA: The Belknap Press of Harvard University Press.

Benz, Ernst. 1955. *Schellings theologische Geistesahnen*. Wiesbaden: Akademie der Wissenschaften und der Literatur.

—. 1968. *Evolution and Christian Hope: Man's Concept of the Future from the Early Fathers to Teilhard de Chardin*. Trans. Heinz G. Frank. Garden City, NY: Doubleday.

—. 1983. *The Mystical Sources of German Romantic Philosophy*. Allison Park, PA: Pickwick Publications.

Berdyaev, Nicholas. 1926. *The Meaning of the Creative Act*. Trans. Donald A. Lowrie. 2nd edn. London: Victor Gollancz, 1955.

—. 1939. *The Meaning of History*. New York: Scribner's.

—. 1965. *Christian Existentialism: A Berdyaev Anthology*. Ed. and trans. Donald A. Lowrie. New York: Harper and Row.

Berman, Joshua A. 2008. *Created Equal: How the Bible Broke with Ancient Political Thought*. Oxford: Oxford University Press.

Bernasconi, Robert. 2004. '"Failure of Communication" as a Surplus: Dialogue and Lack of Dialogue between Buber and Levinas'. In *Levinas and Buber: Dialogue and Difference*, pp. 65–97. Ed. Peter Atterton, Matthew Calarco and Maurice Friedman. Pittsburgh: Duquesne University Press.

Betanzos, Ramón J. 1998. *Franz von Baader's Philosophy of Love*. Vienna: Passagen Verlag.

Bettenson, Henry, ed. and trans. 1956. *The Early Christian Fathers. A Selection from the Writings of the Fathers from St. Clement of Rome to St. Athanasius*. Oxford: Oxford University Press.

Betz, John R. 2019. 'The *Analogia Entis* as a Standard of Catholic Engagement: Erich Przywara's Critique of Phenomenology and Dialectical Theology'. *Modern Theology*, 35:1, 81–102.

Bigg, Charles. 1886. *The Christian Platonists of Alexandria*. Oxford: Clarendon Press.

Bloch, Ernst. 1959. *The Principle of Hope*. 3 vols. Trans. Neville Plaice, Stephen Plaice and Paul Knight. Cambridge, MA: MIT Press, 1995.

Blumenthal, James. 2004. *The Ornament of the Middle Way. A Study of the Madhyamaka Thought of Santaraksita*. Ithaca: Snow Lion.

Boehme, Jacob. 1623. *De Electione Gratiae oder von der Gnaden-Wahl. Jacob Boehme Sämtliche Schriften, Bd. 6*. Faksimile-Neudruck der Ausgabe von 1730 in elf Bänden. Ed. Will-Erich Peuckert. Stuttgart: Frommanns, 1960. English: *De Electione Gratiae and Quaestiones Theosophicae*. By Jacob Böhme, with a biographical sktech by H.A. Fechner. Trans. John Rolleston Earle. London: Constable, 1930.

Boenke, Michaela, ed. 1995. *Schelling. Ausgewählt und vorgestellt von Michaela Boenke*. Berlin: Diederichs.

Bornkamm, Günther. 1960. *Jesus of Nazareth*. New York: Harper and Row.

Bowie, Andrew. 1993. *Schelling and Modern European Philosophy*. London: Routledge.

Bradley, F. H. 1897. *Appearance and Reality: A Metaphysical Essay*. 2nd edn. London: Allen and Unwin.

— . 1914. *Essays on Truth and Reality*. Oxford: Oxford University Press.

Bradley, James. 1979a. 'Hegel in Britain Part I'. *Heythrop Journal*, 20:1, 1–24.

— . 1979b. 'Hegel in Britain Part II'. *Heythrop Journal*, 21:2, 163–88.

— . 1999. 'God and Argument: Strong and Weak Theories of Existence'. In *God and Argument: A Collection of Essays*, pp. 17–26. Ed. William Sweet. Ottawa: University of Ottawa Press.

— . 2009. 'Beyond Hermeneutics: Peirce's Semiology as a Trinitarian Metaphysics of Communication'. *Analecta Hermeneutica*, 1. <https://journals.library.mun.ca/ojs/index.php/analecta/issue/view/1/showToc> (accessed 1 July 2020).

— . 2012. 'Philosophy and Trinity'. *Symposium*, 16:1, 155–78.

— . 2021. *Essays in Speculative Philosophy*. Ed. Sean J. McGrath. Edinburgh: Edinburgh University Press, forthcoming.

Brown, Robert. 1972. *The Later Philosophy of Schelling: The Influence of Boehme on the Works of 1809–1815*. Lewisburg, PA: Bucknell University Press.

Bruff, Kyla, trans. 2020. 'Schelling's Late Political Philosophy: Translation of Lectures 22–24 of the Presentation of the Purely Rational Philosophy'. *Kabiri*, 2: 93–135.

Buchheim, Thomas. 2017. '"Auch wir behaupten eine Prädestination, aber in ganz anderm Sinn" – Schellings Aufnahme und Umwendung von Luthers Theorem'. Unpublished conference paper, consulted with permission of the author. Conference of the Bayerischen Akad. der Wissenschaften zum Lutherjahr, 2 June 2017.

— . 2020. 'The Method and Systematic Structure of Schelling's Late Philosophy'. *Kabiri*, 2: 117–57.

Bullerwell, Peter. 2020. 'Divine Decree and Matter Indifferent: Elizabethan Polity as Neoplatonic Emanation in Richard Hooker'. Unpublished paper presented at McGill University, School of Religious Studies, 10 March 2020.

Bultmann, Rudolf. 1948. *The Theology of the New Testament*. Trans. Kendrick Grobel. Waco: Baylor University Press, 2007.

— . 1975. *Primitive Christianity in its Contemporary Setting*. Philadelphia: Fortress Press.

Burbridge, John. 1992. *Hegel on Logic and Religion: The Reasonableness of Christianity*. Albany: State University of New York Press.

Caird, G. B. 1955. *The Apostolic Age*. London: Gerald Duckworth.

Camus, Albert. 1955. *The Myth of Sisyphus and Other Essays*. Trans. Justin O'Brien. New York: Random House.

Candlish, Stewart. 2007. *The Russell/Bradley Dispute and its Significance for Twentieth-Century Philosophy*. Basingstoke: Palgrave Macmillan.

Caputo, John. 1987. *Radical Hermeneutics: Repetition, Desconstruction, and the Hermeneutic Project*. Bloomington: Indiana University Press.

Carnap, Rudolf. 1932. 'Überwindung der Metaphysik durch Logische Analyse der Sprache'. *Erkenntnis*, II, 60–81.

Chadwick, Henry. 1993. *The Early Church*. Rev. edn. New York: Penguin.

Charlesworth, M. J., ed. 1979. *St. Anselm's Proslogion: With a Reply on Behalf of the Fool by Gaunilo and the Author's Reply to Gaunilo*. South Bend: University of Notre Dame Press.

Chlup, Radek. 1997. 'Two Kinds of Necessity in Plato's Dialogues'. *Listy filologické / Folia philologica*, 120:3/4, 204–16.

Cleary, J. C. 2006. *Swampland Flowers: The Letters and Lectures of Zen Master Ta Hui*. Boulder, CO: Shambala.

Cochrane, Charles Norris. 1944. *Christianity and Classical Culture: A Study of Thought and Action from Augustus to Augustine*. Oxford: Oxford University Press.

Collingwood, R. G. 1940. *An Essay on Metaphysics.* Oxford: Clarendon Press.

Copleston, Frederick. 1965. *A History of Philosophy.* Vol. 7. *Modern Philosophy. Part I: Fichte to Hegel.* Garden City, NY: Doubleday.

Courtine, Jean-François. 1990. *Extase de la raison. Essais sur Schelling.* Paris: Éditions Galilée.

— , ed. 2010. *Schelling.* Paris: Les Éditions du Cerf.

Cowell, E. B., et al., eds. 1894. *Buddhist Mahayana Texts.* New York: Dover, 1969.

Coyle, Justin Shaun. 2020. 'Heterodox Hegels: Heresiology in de Lubac and Bulgakov'. *Scottish Journal of Theology,* 73, 31–42.

Cusanus, Nicolas. 1440. *Of Learned Ignorance.* Trans. Germain Heron. London: Routledge and Kegan Paul, 1954.

Danz, Christian. 1996. *Die philosophische Christologie F.W.J. Schellings.* Stuttgart: Frommann-Holzboog.

Das, Saitya Brata. 2016. *The Political Theology of Schelling.* Edinburgh: Edinburgh University Press.

Deleuze, Gilles, and Félix Guattari. 1983. *Anti-Oedipus: Capitalism and Schizophrenia.* Trans. Robert Hurley, Mark Seem and Helen R. Lane. Minneapolis: University of Minnesota Press.

— . 1987. *A Thousand Plateaus: Capitalism and Schizophrenia.* Trans. Brian Massumi. Minneapolis: University of Minnesota Press.

Derrida, Jacques. 1996. *The Gift of Death.* Trans. David Wills. Chicago: University of Chicago Press.

— . 1997. *Politics of Friendship.* London: Verso.

— . 2005. *Rogues: Two Essays on Reason.* Trans. Pascale-Anne Brault and Michael Naas. Stanford: Stanford University Press.

Descartes, René. 1641. *Meditations on First Philosophy.* Trans. Donald A. Cress. Indianapolis: Hackett, 1998.

Dierauer, Walter. 1986. *Hölderlin und der spekulative Pietismus Württembergs. Gemeinsame Anschauugnshorizonte im Werk Oetingers und Hölderlins.* Zurich: Juris.

Dilthey, Wilhelm. 1988. *Introduction to the Human Sciences.* Trans. Ramon J. Betanzos. Detroit: Wayne State University Press.

Drobb, Sanford. 2000. *Symbols of the Kabbalah: Philosophical and Theological Perspectives.* North Vale, NJ: Jason Aronson.

Duque, Félix. 2007. 'Nature–in God, or the Problems of a Dash: Schelling's Freiheitsschrift'. *Research in Phenomenology,* 37:1, 56–74.

Durand, Emmanuel. 2012. 'Perichoresis: A Key Concept for Balancing Trinitarian Theology'. In *Rethinking Trinitarian Theology: Disputed Questions and Contemporary Issues in Trinitarian Theology,* pp. 177–92. Ed. Robert J. Wozniak and Giulio Maspero. New York: T & T Clark.

Durner, Manfred. 1979. *Wissen und Geschichte bei Schelling. Eine Interpretation der ersten Erlangen Vorlesung.* Munich: Johannes Bergmans.

Eckhart, Meister. 1963. *Deutsche Predigten und Traktate.* Ed. Josef Quint. Munich: Carl Hanser Verlag.

—. 1986. *Meister Eckhart. Teacher and Preacher.* Ed. Bernard McGinn. Mahwah, NJ: Paulist Press.

—. 2009. *The Complete Works of Meister Eckhart.* Ed. and trans. Maurice O'C. Walsh. New York: Crossroad.

Enders, Markus. 1993. *Das mystische Wissen bei Heinrich Seuse.* Munich: Ferdinand Schöningh.

Esposito, Joseph L. 1977. *Schelling's Idealism and Philosophy of Nature*. Lewisburg, PA: Bucknell University Press.

Fackenheim, Emil. 1967. *The Religious Dimension in Hegel's Thought*. Bloomington: Indiana University Press.

— . 1996a. 'Schelling's Philosophy of Religion'. In *The God Within: Kant, Schelling, and Historicity*, pp. 92–108. Toronto: University of Toronto Press.

— . 1996b. 'Schelling's Concept of Positive Philosophy'. In *The God Within: Kant, Schelling, and Historicity*, pp. 109–21. Toronto: University of Toronto Press.

Fichte, Johann Gottlieb. 1794. *The Science of Knowledge*. Ed. and trans. Peter Heath and John Lachs. Cambridge: Cambridge University Press, 1982.

— . 1797. '[First] Introduction to the *Wissenschaftslehre*'. In *Fichte: Introduction to the Wissenschaftslehre and Other Writings*, pp. 1–118. 2nd edn. Ed. and trans. Daniel Breazeale. Indianapolis: Hackett, 1998.

Fink, Bruce. 1995. *The Lacanian Subject. Between Language and Jouissance*. Princeton: Princeton University Press.

Ford, Lewis S. 1965. 'The Controversy Between Schelling and Jacobi'. *Journal of the History of Philosophy*, 3:1, 75–89.

Frank, Manfred. 1975. *Der unendliche Mangel an Sein. Schellings Hegelkritik und die Anfänge der Marxschen Dialektik*. Frankfurt am Main: Suhrkamp.

— . 1977. Einleitung zu F. W. J. Schelling, *Philosophie der Offenbarung 1841/42 (Paulus Nachscrift)*, pp. 9–84. Ed. Manfred Frank. Frankfurt am Main: Suhrkamp.

— . 2004. 'Schelling and Sartre on Being and Nothingness'. In *The New Schelling*, pp. 151–66. Ed. Judith Norman. New York: Continuum.

Franks, Paul. 2015. 'Peirce's "Schelling-Fashioned Idealism" and "the Monstrous Mysticism of the East"'. *The British Journal of the History of Philosophy*, 23:4, 732–55.

Fuhrmans, Horst. 1940. *Schellings letzte Philosophie. Die negative und positive Philosophie im Einsatz des Spätidealismus*. Berlin: Hans Triltsch.

— . 1954. *Schellings Philosophie der Weltalter. Schellings Philosophie in den Jahren 1806–1821. Zum Problem des Schellingschen Theismus*. Düsseldorf: L. Schwann.

—. ed., 1975. *F.W.J. Schelling: Briefe und Dokumente*. 3 vols. Bonn: Bouvier.

Gabriel, Markus. 2011. *Transcendental Ontology. Essays in German Idealism*. London: Bloomsbury.

—. 2015. *Fields of Sense: A New Realist Ontology*. Edinburgh: Edinburgh University Press.

Gabriel, Markus, with Slavoj Žižek. 2009. *Mythology, Madness and Laughter: Subjectivity in German Idealism*. New York: Continuum.

Gallaher, Brandon. 2009. 'The Christological Focus of Vladimir Solov'ev's Sophiology'. *Modern Theology*, 25:4, 617–46.

Gaskin, Richard. 2008. *The Unity of the Proposition*. Oxford: Oxford University Press.

Gauchet, Marcel. 1985. *The Disenchantment of the World: A Political History of Religion*. Trans. Oscar Burge. Princeton: Princeton University Press, 1999.

Gilson, Etienne. 1936. *The Spirit of Medieval Philosophy*. Trans. A. H. C. Downes. South Bend: University of Notre Dame Press, 1991.

— . 1952. *Being and Some Philosophers*. 2nd edn. Toronto: Pontifical Institute for Medieval Studies, 2016.

— . 2002. *Thomism: The Philosophy of Thomas Aquinas*. 6th edn. Trans. Laurence K. Shook and Armand Maurer. Toronto: Pontifical Institute of Medieval Studies.

Grant, George. 1960. *Philosophy in the Mass Age*. In *The Collected Works of George Grant, Vol 2: 1952–1959*. Ed. Arthur Davis. Toronto: University of Toronto Press, 2002.

— . 1971. *Time as History*. Ed. Wilham Christian. Toronto: University of Toronto Press, 1995.

Grant, Iain Hamilton. 2006. *Philosophies of Nature after Schelling*. London: Continuum.

— . 2013a. 'The Law of Insuperable Environment: What is Exhibited in the Exhibition of the Process of Nature?' *Analecta Hermeneutica*, 5. <https://journals.library.mun.ca/ojs/index.php/analecta/issue/view/92> (accessed 1 July 2020).

— . 2013b. 'The Remains of the World: Grounds and Powers in Schelling's Later *Naturphilosophie*'. *Schelling Studien*, 1, 3–24.

Grant, Iain Hamilton, with Jeremy Dunham. 2010. *Idealism: A History*. London: Routledge.

Gratton, Peter. 2014. *Speculative Realism: Problems and Prospects*. London: Bloomsbury.

Gratton, Peter, with Paul J. Ennis, eds. 2015. *The Meillassoux Dictionary*. Edinburgh: Edinburgh University Press.

Gulyga, Arsenij. 1989. *Schelling. Leben und Werk*. Trans. Elke Kirsten. Stuttgart: Deutsche Verlags-Anstalt.

Habermas, Jürgen. 1954. *Das Absolute und die Geschichte: Von der Zwiespältigkeit in Schellings Denken*. Bonn: Dissertation.

— . 2008. 'Notes on a Post-Secular Society'. <http://www.signandsight.com/features/1714.html> (accessed 1 July 2020).

Hankey, Wayne. 1987. *God in Himself: Aquinas' Doctrine of God as Expounded in the Summa Theologiae*. Oxford: Oxford University Press.

Harris, H. S. 1989. Review of Vincent A. McCarthy, *Quest for a Philosophical Jesus: Christianity in Rousseau, Kant, Hegel, and Schelling. International Journal for Philosophy of Religion*, 26:1, 62–4.

Hart, David Bentley. 2013. *The Experience of God: Being, Consciousness, Bliss*. New Haven: Yale University Press.

— . 2019. *That All Shall Be Saved: Heaven, Hell, and Universal Salvation*. New Haven: Yale University Press.

Hart, Ray. 2016. *God Being Nothing: Toward a Theogony*. Chicago: University of Chicago Press.

Hayes, Victor C. 1995. *Schelling's Philosophy of Mythology and Revelation. Three of Seven Books Translated and Reduced with General Introduction*. Armidale, NSW: The Australian Association for the Study of Religions.

Hedley, Douglas. 2000. *Coleridge, Philosophy and Religion: Aids to Reflection and the Mirror of the Spirit*. Cambridge: Cambridge University Press.

Hege, Brent. 2017. *Myth, History, and German Protestant Theology*. Eugene, OR: Wipf and Stock.

Hegel, G. W. F. 1801. *The Difference Between Fichte and Schelling's System of Philosophy*. Trans. H. S. Harris and Walter Cerf. Albany: State University of New York Press. 1988.

— . 1802. *Faith and Knowledge*. Trans. Walter Cerf and H. S. Harris. Albany: State University of New York Press, 1977.

— . 1807. *Hegel's Phenomenology of Spirit*. Trans. A. V. Miller. Oxford: Oxford University Press, 1977.

— . 1827. *Hegel's Lectures on the Philosophy of Religion. The Lectures of 1827*. Ed. Peter C. Hodgson. Trans. R. F. Brown, P. C. Hodgson and J. M. Stewart. Berkeley: University of California Press, 1988.

— . 1830–31. *The Philosophy of History*. Trans. J. Sibree. New York: Dover, 1956.

— . 1845. *Hegel's Philosophy of Mind. Being Part Three of the Encyclopedia of the Philosophical Sciences (1830). Together with the Zusätze in Boumann's Text*. Trans. A. V. Miller. Ed. William Wallace. Oxford: Oxford University Press, 1971.

— . 1896a. *Philosophy of Right*. Trans S. W. Dyde. Kingston: Queen's University Press.

— . 1896b. *Hegel's Lectures on the History of Philosophy*. Vol. 3. Trans. E. S. Haldane and Francis H. Simson. London: Routledge and Kegan Paul.

— . 1948. *Early Theological Writings*. Trans. Richard Kroner and T. M. Knox. Chicago: University of Chicago Press.

— . 1996. *Hegel's Lectures on the History of Philosophy*. Trans. E. S. Haldane and Frances H. Simson. Abridged Student Edition. Atlantic Highlands, NJ: Humanities Press.

Heidegger, Martin. 1919. *Zur Bestimmung der Philosophie*. In Martin Heidegger, *Gesamtausgabe*, vol. 56/57. Ed. Bernd Heimbüchel. Frankfurt am Main: Klostermann, 1999.

— . 1920–21. *The Phenomenology of Religious Life*. In Martin Heidegger, *Gesamtausgabe*, vol. 60. Trans. Matthias Fritsche and Jennifer Anna Gosetti-Ferencei. Bloomington: Indiana University Press, 2004.

— . 1922. 'Phenomenological Interpretations in Connection with Aristotle: An Indication of the Hermeneutical Situation'. Trans. John van Buren. In *Martin Heidegger: Supplements. From the Earliest Essays to Being and Time and Beyond*, pp. 111–46. Ed. John van Buren. Albany: State University of New York Press, 2002.

— . 1924. 'The Problem of Sin in Luther'. Trans. John van Buren. In *Martin Heidegger: Supplements. From the Earliest Essays to Being and Time and Beyond*, pp. 105–10. Ed. John van Buren. Albany: State University of New York Press, 2002.

— . 1927a. *Being and Time*. Trans. John Macquarrie and Edward Robinson. New York: Harper and Row, 1962.

— . 1927b. 'Phenomenology and Theology'. Trans. James G. Hart and John C. Maraldo. In Martin Heidegger, *Pathmarks*, pp. 39–62. Ed. William McNeil. Cambridge: Cambridge University Press, 1998.

— . 1929. 'What is Metaphysics?' In Martin Heidegger, *Basic Writings*, pp. 89–110. Ed. David Farrell Krell. London: Harper Collins.

— . 1936. *Schelling's Treatise on the Essence of Human Freedom*. Trans. Joan Stambaugh. Athens: Ohio University Press, 1985.

— . 1966. *Discourse on Thinking*. Trans. John Anderson. New York: Harper and Row.

Heisig, James W. et al., eds. 2011. *Japanese Philosophy: A Source Book*. Honolulu: University of Hawaii Press.

Hemmerle, Klaus. 1968. *Gott und das Denken nach Schellings Spätphilosophie*. Freiburg/Vienna: Herder.

Henrich, Dieter. 1982. *Selbstverhältnisse*. Stuttgart: Reclam.

Henry, Michel. 1963. *The Essence of Manifestation*. Trans. Gerard Etzkorn. The Hague: Martinus Nijhoff, 1973.

Heraclitus. 2019. *Fragments*. Ed. Samuel Béreau. <http://philoctetes.free.fr/heraclite.pdf> (accessed 1 July 2020).

Hildebrand, Stephen M. 2011. 'The Trinity in the Ante-Nicene Fathers'. In *The Oxford Handbook of the Trinity*, pp. 95–108. Ed. Gilles Emery and Matthew Levering. Oxford: Oxford University Press.

Hogrebe, Wolfram. 1989. *Prädikation und Genesis. Metaphysik als Fundamentalheuristik im Ausgang von Schellings* Die Weltalter. Frankfurt am Main: Suhrkamp.

Horner, Robyn. 2001. *Rethinking God as Gift: Marion, Derrida, and the Limits of Phenomenology*. New York: Fordham University Press.

Husserl, Edmund. 1913. *Ideas Pertaining to a Pure Phenomenology and to a Phenomenological Philosophy*. Trans. F. Kersten. The Hague: Nijhoff, 1982.

— . 1931. *Cartesian Meditations: An Introduction to Phenomenology*. Trans. Dorion Cairns. The Hague: Nijhoff, 1999.

Hutter, Axel. 1996. *Geschichtliche Vernunft: Die Weiterführung der Kantischen Vernunftkritik in der Spätphilosophie Schellings*. Frankfurt am Main: Suhrkamp.

Jacobi, Friedrich Heinrich. 1803. 'On Faith and Knowledge in Response to Schelling and Hegel'. In *Philosophy of German Idealism*, pp. 142–57. Ed. Ernst Behler. New York: Continuum, 2002.

—. 1811. *Von den Göttlichen Dingen und ihrer Offenbarung*. Leipzig: Gerhard Fleischer.

—. 1815. *Friedrich Heinrich Jacobi's Werke*. Vol. 2. Leipzig: Gerhard Fleischer.

—. 1994. *The Main Philosophical Writings and the Novel Allwill*. Ed. and trans. George Di Giovanni. Montreal: McGill Queen's University Press.

Jacobs, Wilhelm G. 1998. 'Schelling im Deutschen Idealismus. Interaktionen und Kontroversen'. In *F.W.J. Schelling*, pp. 66–81. Ed. Hans Jörg Sandkühler. Stuttgart: J.B. Metzler, 1998.

Janicaud, Dominique. 1991. *Le Tournant théologique de la phénoménologie française*. Combas: Éditions de l'Éclat.

Jankélévich, Vladmir. 1933. *L'Odysée de la conscience dans la dernière philosophie de Schelling*. Paris: Félix Alcan.

Jaspers, Karl. 1955. *Schelling: Größe und Verhängnis*. Munich: R. Piper.

Johnston, James Scott. 2015. 'Against Strong Reductionism in Neuroscience Education: A Three Pronged Argument'. *Studia Pedogogica Ignatianum*, 18, 177–20.

Jung, C. G. 1934. 'The Development of Personality'. In *The Collected Works of C.G. Jung*, vol. 17, pp. 165–86. Princeton: Princeton University Press, 1954.

—. 1963. *Memories, Dreams, Reflections*. Ed. Aniela Jaffé. Trans. Richard and Clara Winston. New York: Vintage, 1989.

Kant, Immanuel. 1787. *The Critique of Pure Reason*. Trans. Norman Kemp Smith. New York: Palgrave Macmillan, 2003.

—. 1799. *Religion within the Limits of Reason Alone*. Trans. Theodore M. Greene and Hoyt H. Hudson. New York: Harper and Row, 1960.

Kasper, Walter. 1965. *Das Absolute in der Geschichte. Philosophie und Theologie der Geschichte in der Spätphilosophie Schellings*. Mainz: Grünwald.

Kearney, Richard. 2001. *The God Who May Be: A Hermeneutics of Religion*. Bloomington: Indiana University Press.

Kierkegaard, Soren. 1843. *Fear and Trembling / Repetition*. Ed. and trans. Howard v. Hong and Edna H. Hong. Princeton: Princeton University Press, 1983.

—. 1844. *Philosophical Fragments / Johannes Climacus*. Ed. and trans. Howard v. Hong and Edna H. Hong. Princeton: Princeton University Press, 1985.

—. 1846. *Concluding Unscientific Postscript*. Ed. and trans. Alistair Hannay. Cambridge: Cambridge University Press, 1992.

—. 1848. *The Sickness unto Death: A Christian Psychological Exposition for Upbuilding and Awakening*. Ed. and trans. Howard v. Hong and Edna H. Hong. Princeton: Princeton University Press, 1980.

—. 1849. *The Sickness Unto Death*. Trans. Walter Lowrie. Princeton: Princeton University Press, 1941.

—. 1850. *Practice in Christianity*. Ed. and trans. Howard v. Hong and Edna H. Hong. Princeton: Princeton University Press. 1991.

—. 1970. *Journals and Papers*. Vol. 2. Bloomington: Indiana University Press.

Kojève, Alexandre. 1980. *Introduction to the Reading of Hegel. Lectures on The Phenomenology of Spirit*. Assembled by Raymond Queneau. Ed. Allan Bloom. Trans. James H. Nichols, Jr. Ithaca: Cornell University Press.

Kosch, Michelle. 2006. *Freedom and Reason in Kant, Schelling, and Kierkegaard*. Oxford: Oxford University Press.

Koslowski, Peter. 2001. *Philosophien der Offenbarung. Antiker Gnostizismus, Franz von Baader, Schelling*. Munich: Ferdinand Schöningh.

Krell, David Farrell. 2005. *The Tragic Absolute*. Bloomington: Indiana University Press.

Lacan, Jacques. 1998. *The Four Fundamental Concepts of Psycho-analysis: The Seminar of Jacques Lacan, Book XI*. Trans. J. Alain-Miller. Ed. A. Sheridan. New York: W. W. Norton.

— . 2002. *Écrits. A Selection*. Trans. Bruce Fink. New York: W.W. Norton.

Laughland, John. 2007. *Schelling versus Hegel: From German Idealism to Christian Metaphysics*. Aldershot: Ashgate.

Lawrence, Joseph. 1989. *Der ewige Anfang. Zum Verhältnis von Natur und Geschichte bei Schelling*. Würzburg: Königshausen & Neumann.

— . 2019. 'Translator's Introduction'. In F. W. J. Schelling, *The Ages of the World (1811)*. Trans. Joseph P. Lawrence. Albany: State University of New York Press.

Leibniz, Gottfried. 1710. *Theodicy: Essays on the Goodness of God, the Freedom of Man and the Origin of Evil*. Trans. E. M. Hubbard. Ed. Austin M. Farrer. New York: Cosimo Classics, 2009.

Lenoir, Frederick. 2003. *Les Métamorphoses de Dieu. La nouvelle spiritualité occidentale*. Paris: Editions Plon.

Levinas, Emmanuel. 1961. *Totality and Infinity*. Trans. Alphonso Lingis. Pittsburgh: Duquesne University Press, 1969.

— . 1974. *Otherwise than Being or Beyond Essence*. Trans. Alphonso Lingis. Pittsburgh: Duquesne University Press, 2002.

— . 1998. *Of God Who Comes to Mind*. Trans. Bettina Bergo. Stanford: Stanford University Press.

Lewis, C. S. 1970. *God in the Dock: Essays on Theology and Ethics*. Grand Rapids: Eerdmans.

Livingstone, E. A., and F. L. Cross, eds. 2005. *The Oxford Dictionary of the Christian Church*. Oxford: Oxford University Press.

Loewenich, Walther von. *Luther's Theology of the Cross*. Trans. Herbert J. A. Bouman. Belfast: Christian Journals, 1976.

Løland, Ole Jacob. 2018. *The Reception of Paul the Apostle in the Works of Slavoj Žižek*. Basingstoke: Palgrave Macmillan.

Lonergan, Bernard. 1957. *Insight: A Study of Human Understanding. The Collected Works of Bernard Lonergan*, vol. 3. Toronto: University of Toronto Press, 1992.

— . 1967. *Verbum: Word and Idea in Aquinas. The Collected Works of Bernard Lonergan*, vol. 2. Toronto: University of Toronto Press, 1997.

— . 1971. *Method in Theology*. Toronto: University of Toronto Press.

— . 2000. *Grace and Freedom: Operative Grace in the Thought of St. Thomas Aquinas. The Collected Works of Bernard Lonergan*, vol. 1. University of Toronto Press.

Lossky, Vladimir. 2005. *The Mystical Theology of the Eastern Church*. Cambridge: Cambridge University Press.

Löwith, Karl. 1949. *Meaning in History*. Chicago: University of Chicago Press.

Luther, Martin. 1955–86. *Luther's Works*. Vol. 31. *Career of the Reformer*. Ed. Jaroslav Pelikan and Helmut T. Lehmann. Philadelphia: Fortress Press.

Mackintosh, H. R. 1937. *Types of Modern Theology*. London: Collins, 1964.

Magee, Glenn Alexander. *Hegel and the Hermetic Tradition*. Ithaca: Cornell University Press, 2001.

Mander, W. J. 2011. *British Idealism: A History*. Oxford: Oxford University Press.

Marion, Jean-Luc. 1992. 'Is the Ontological Argument Ontological? The Argument According to Anselm and its Metaphysical Interpretation According to Kant'. *Journal of the History of Philosophy*, 30:2: 201–18.

— . 2002. *Being-Given: Toward a Phenomenology of Givenness*. Trans. Jeffrey L. Kosky. Stanford: Stanford University Press.

Maritain, Jacques. 1945. *Scholasticism and Politics*. Trans. Mortimer Adler. London: Geoffrey Bles.

— . 1956. *Existence and the Existent: An Essay on Christian Existentialism*. Trans. Lewis Galantrie and Gerald B. Phelan. Garden City, NY: Image Books.

Marquet, Jean-François. 1973. *Liberté et existence. Étude sur la formation de la philosophie de Schelling*. Paris: Gallimard.

Marsh, Charles. 1996. *Reclaiming Dietrich Bonhoeffer: The Promise of his Theology*. Oxford: Oxford University Press.

Mason, Steve, and Tom Robinson, eds. 2004. *Early Christian Reader. Christian Texts From the First and Second Centuries in Contemporary English Translations*. Peabody, MA: Hendrickson.

Matthews, Bruce. 2007. Introduction to F. W. J. Schelling, *The Grounding of the Positive Philosophy. The Berlin Lectures*, pp. 1–87. Albany: State University of New York Press.

— . 2011. *Schelling's Organic Form of Philosophy: Life as the Schema of Freedom*. Albany: State University of New York Press.

Maurer, Armand. 1993. Introduction to Etienne Gilson, *Christian Philosophy: An Introduction*, pp. ix–xxv. Toronto: Pontifical Institute for Medieval Studies.

May, Eric. 1946. 'The Logos in the Old Testament'. *The Catholic Biblical Quarterly*, 8:4, 438–47.

Mayer, Paola. 1999. *Jena Romanticism and its Appropriation of Jakob Böhme*. Montreal: McGill-Queen's University Press.

McGinn, Bernard. 2001. *The Mystical Theology of Meister Eckhart*. Chestnut Ridge, NY: Crossroad.

McGrath, Sean J. 2002. 'The Forgetting of Haecceitas: Heidegger's 1915–16 *Habilitationsschrift*'. In *Between the Human and the Divine: Philosophical and Theological Hermeneutics*, pp. 355–77. Ed. Andrzej Wiercinski. Toronto: The Hermeneutic Press.

— . 2006a. *The Early Heidegger and Medieval Philosophy: Phenomenology for the Godforsaken*. Washington, DC: Catholic University of America Press.

— . 2006b. 'Böhme, Schelling, Hegel, and the Hermetic Theology of Evil'. *Philosophy and Theology*, 18:2, 257–85.

— . 2008. *Heidegger. A (Very) Critical Introduction*. Grand Rapids: Eerdmans.

— . 2010. 'Schelling on the Unconscious'. *Research in Phenomenology*, 40, 72–91.

— . 2012. *The Dark Ground of Spirit: Schelling and the Unconscious*. London: Routledge.

— . 2013a. 'The Logic of Indirection in Aquinas and Heidegger'. *Heythrop Journal*, 54:2, 268–80.

— . 2013b. 'The Tyranny of Consumerism and the Third Age of Revelation', *Analecta Hermeneutica*, 5. <https://journals.library.mun.ca/ojs/index.php/analecta/issue/view/92> (accessed 1 July 2020).

— . 2014a. 'The Psychology of Productive Dissociation, or What Would a Schellingian Psychotherapy Look Like?' *Comparative and Continental Philosophy*, 6:1, 35–48.

— . 2014b. 'Secularism and the Tyranny of the Homogeneous State'. *Bhartiya Manyaprad. International Journal of Indian Studies*, 2, 90–106.

— . 2014c. 'The Theology of Consumerism'. *Analecta Hermeneutica*, 6. <https://journals.library.mun.ca/ojs/index.php/analecta/issue/view/113> (accessed 1 July 2020).

— . 2014d. 'The Late Schelling and the End of Christianity'. *Schelling Studien*, 2, 63–77.

— . 2014e. 'The Question Concerning Metaphysics: A Schellingian Intervention into Analytical Psychology'. *International Journal of Jung Studies*, 6:1, 23–51.

— . 2015. 'Schelling and the History of the Dissociative Self'. *Symposium. The Journal of the Canadian Society for Continental Philosophy*, 19:1, 52–66, special section, 'Schelling After Theory', ed. Tilottama Rajan and Sean J. McGrath.

— . 2016a. 'Is the Late Schelling Still Doing Nature-Philosophy?' *Angelaki*, 21:4, 121–41, special issue, 'Nature, Speculation, and the Return to Schelling', ed. Daniel Whistler and Tyler Tritten.

— . 2016b. 'On the Difference Between Schelling and Hegel'. In *Rethinking German Idealism*, pp. 247–70. Ed. Sean J. McGrath and Joseph Carew. Basingstoke: Palgrave Macmillan.

— . 2017a. 'The Ecstatic Realism of the Late Schelling'. In *Continental Realism and its Discontents*, pp. 38–58. Ed. Marie-Eve Morin. Edinburgh: Edinburgh University Press.

— . 2017b. 'Populism, Ideology, and the Late Schelling on Revelation'. *Analecta Hermeneutica*, 9. <https://journals.library.mun.ca/ojs/index.php/analecta/issue/view/129> (accessed 1 July 2020).

— . 2018. 'Friedrich Christoph Oetinger's Speculative Pietism'. *Kabiri*, 1, 175–92.

— . 2019. *Thinking Nature: An Essay in Negative Ecology*. Edinburgh: Edinburgh University Press.

McGrath, Sean J., with Jason Wirth. 2015. 'A Report on the North American Schelling Society'. *Schelling Studien*, 3, 195–200.

Meillassoux, Quentin. 2009. *After Finitude: An Essay on the Necessity of Contingency*. Trans. Tay Brassier. New York: Continuum.

Merton, Thomas. 1999. *The Intimate Merton: His Life from his Journals*. Ed. Patrick Hart and Jonathan Montaldo. New York: Harper Collins.

— . 2007. *New Seeds of Contemplation*. New York: New Directions.

Millbank, John. 2006. *Theology and Social Theory: Beyond Secular Reason*. Chichester: Wiley-Blackwell.

Mohanty, Sachidananda, ed. 2012. *Sri Aurobindo: A Contemporary Reader*. London: Routledge.

Moltmann, Jürgen. 1967. *The Theology of Hope. On the Grounds and Implications of a Christian Eschatology*. Trans. James W. Leitch. New York: Harper and Row.

— . 1973. *The Crucified God*. London: SCM Press.

— . 1985. *God in Creation*. Trans. Margaret Kohl. Minneapolis: Fortress Press, 1993.

— . 1993. *The Trinity and the Kingdom: The Doctrine of God*. Trans. Margaret Kohl. Minneapolis: Fortress Press.

Mostert, Christiaan. 2002. *God and the Future: Wolfhart Pannenberg's Eschatological Doctrine of God*. London: T & T Clark.

Mouffe, Chantal. 1999. *The Challenge of Carl Schmitt*. London: Verso.

Nancy, Jean-Luc. 1991. *The Inoperative Community*. Ed. Peter Connor. Minneapolis: University of Minneapolis Press.

Newman, John Henry (Cardinal). 1864. *Apologia Pro Vita Sua*. London: J.M. Dent & Sons, 1912.

Nietzsche, Friedrich. 1895. *The Antichrist*. In *The Portable Nietzsche*, pp. 565–656. Trans. and ed. Walter Kaufmann. New York: Viking, 1954.

Norris Clarke, William. 2001. *The One and the Many: A Contemporary Thomist Metaphysics*. South Bend: University of Notre Dame Press.

Oetinger, Friedrich Christoph. 1776. *Biblisches und Emblematisches Wörterbuch*. Ed. Gerhard Schäfer. Section VII, vol. 3. Berlin: De Gruyter, 1999.

O'Meara, Thomas. 1982. *Romantic Idealism and Roman Catholicism: Schelling and the Theologians*. South Bend: University of Notre Dame Press.

O'Regan, Cyril. 1994. *The Heterodox Hegel*. Albany: State University of New York Press.

— . 2001. *The Gnostic Return of Modernity*. Albany: State University of New York Press.

— . 2002. *Gnostic Apocalypse: Jacob Boehme's Haunted Narrative*. Albany: State University of New York Press.

— . 2011. 'The Trinity in Kant, Hegel, and Schelling'. In *The Oxford Handbook of the Trinity*, pp. 254–66. Ed. Gilles Emery and Matthew Levering. Oxford: Oxford University Press.

Owens, Joseph. 1965. 'Quiddity and Real Distinction in Thomas Aquinas'. *Medieval Studies*, 27, 1–22.

Pannenberg, Wolfhart. 2004. *Systematic Theology*. Trans. Geoffrey W. Bromley. Grand Rapids: Eerdmans.

Pannenberg, Wolfhart, et al. 1968. *Revelation as History*. Trans. David Granskou. London: Macmillan, 1991.

Pareyson, Luigi. 1975. *Schelling*. Bologna: Marietti.

— . 2010. 'La Stupeur de la raison selon Schelling'. In *Schelling*, pp. 481–540. Ed. Jean-François Courtine. Paris: Les éditions du Cerf.

Peirce, C. S. 1901. 'Abduction and Induction'. In *Philosophical Writings of Peirce*, pp. 150–6. Ed. Justus Buchler. Mineola, NY: Dover, 1955.

— . 1903a. 'Pragmatism as the Logic of Abduction'. In *The Essential Peirce. Selected Philosophical Writings*. Vol. 2 *(1893–1913)*, pp. 226–41. Ed. the Peirce Edition Project. Bloomington: Indiana University Press, 1998.

— . 1903b. 'The Principle of Phenomenology'. In *Philosophical Writings of Peirce*, pp. 74–97. Ed. Justus Buchler. Mineola, NY: Dover, 1955.

— . 1908. 'A Neglected Argument for the Reality of God'. In *The Essential Peirce. Selected Philosophical Writings*. Vol. 2 *(1893–1913)*, pp. 434–50. Ed. the Peirce Edition Project. Bloomington: Indiana University Press, 1998.

— . 1931–35. *The Collected Papers of Charles Sanders Peirce: Vols. I–VIII*. Ed. Charles Hartshorne and Paul Weiss. Cambridge: Cambridge University Press.

Peterson, Erik. 1935. 'Monotheism as a Political Problem. A Contribution to Political Theology in the Roman Empire'. In Erik Peterson, *Theological Tractates*, pp. 68–105. Ed. and trans. Michael J. Hollerich. Stanford: Stanford University Press, 2011.

Pickstock, Catherine, with John Milbank and Graham Ward, eds. 1998. *Radical Orthodoxy: A New Theology*. London: Routledge.

Pieper, Josef. 1957. *The Silence of St. Thomas*. South Bend: St. Augustine's Press.

Popper, Karl. 1963. *Conjectures and Refutations. The Growth of Scientific Knowledge*. London: Routledge, 2002.

Proclus. 1992. *The Elements of Theology*. Ed. E. R. Dodds. Oxford: Oxford University Press.

Przywara, Erich. 1952. *Humanitas. Der Mensch gestern und morgen*. Nürnberg: Glock und Lutz.

Rahner, Karl. 1941. *Hearer of the Word*. Trans. Joseph Donceel. New York: Continuum, 1994.

— . 1978. *Foundations of Christian Faith: An Introduction to the Idea of Christianity*. Trans. William V. Dych. New York: Crossroad.

Rasmussen, Anders Moe. 2003. 'The Legacy of Jacobi in Schelling and Kierkegaard'. In *Kierkegaard und Schelling: Freiheit, Angst und Wirklichkeit*, pp. 209–22. Ed. Jochem Hennigfeld and Jon Stewart. Berlin: De Gruyter.

Ratzinger, Cardinal Joseph. 1973. 'Concerning the Notion of Person in Theology'. Trans. Michale Waldstein. *Communio*, 17 (1990), 439–54.

Reeves, Marjorie. 1999. *Joachim of Fiore and the Prophetic Future: A Medieval Study in Historical Thinking*. Stroud: Sutton.

Reinhold, Karl Leonhard. 1789. *Versuch einer neuen Theorie des menschlichen Vorstellungsvermögens*. Prague: Widtmann und Manke.

— . 1791. *Über das Fundament des philosophisches Wissen*. Prague: Widtmann und Manke.

Reno, R. R. 2017. 'The Return of the Strong Gods'. *First Things*, May 2017. <https://www.firstthings.com/article/2017/05/return-of-the-strong-gods> (accessed 1 July 2020).

Richardson, Cyril C., ed. 1953. *Early Christian Fathers*. Philadelphia: Westminster Press.

Ringgren, Helmer. 1966. *Israelite Religion*. Trans. David Green. London: SPCK.

Rockmore, Tom. 2012. 'The Pittsburgh School, the Given and Knowledge'. *Social Epistemology Review*, 2:1, 29–38.

Roseneau, Hartmut von. 2003. 'System und Christologie: Schellings und Kierkegaards Kritik des systematischen Denkens'. In *Kierkegaard und Schelling: Freiheit, Angst und Wirklichkeit*, pp. 185–208. Ed. Jochem Hennigfeld and Jon Stewart. Berlin: De Gruyter.

Rosenzweig, Franz. 1930. *The Star of Redemption*. Trans. Barbara E. Galli. Madison: University of Wisconsin Press, 2005.

Rush, Fred. 2014. 'Schelling's Critique of Hegel'. In *Interpreting Schelling: Critical Essays*, pp. 216–37. Ed. Lara Ostaric. Cambridge: Cambridge University Press.

Sallis, John. 1999. 'Secluded Nature: The Point of Schelling's Re-inscription of the *Timaeus*'. *Pli*, 8, 71–85.

Sandkühler, Hans-Jörg. 1968. *Freiheit und Wirklichkeit*: Zur Dialektik von Politik und Philosophie bei Schelling. Mynster: Suhrkamp.

Sartre, Jean-Paul. 1943. *Being and Nothingness*. Trans. Hazel E. Barnes. New York: Washington Square Press, 1993.

Schelling, F. W. J. 1794. 'Timaeus'. Trans. Adam Arola, Jena Jolissaint and Peter Warnek. *Epoché*, 12:2 (2008), 205–48.

— . 1797a. *Ideas for a Philosophy of Nature*. Trans. Errol E. Harris and Peter Heath. Cambridge: Cambridge University Press, 1988.

— . 1797b. 'Ideas on a Philosophy of Nature as an Introduction to this Science'. *Sämtliche Werke*, vol. 2, pp. 1–73. In *Philosophy of German Idealism*, pp. 167–202. Trans. Priscilla Hayden-Roy. Ed. Ernst Behler. The German Library, vol. 23. New York: Continuum, 1987.

— . 1799a. *First Outline of a System of the Philosophy of Nature*. *Sämtliche Werke*, vol. 3, pp. 1–268. Trans. Keith R. Peterson. Albany: State University of New York Press, 2004.

— . 1799b. 'Introduction to the Outline of a System of the Philosophy of Nature, or, On the Concept of Speculative Physics and the Internal Organization of a System of this Science'. *Sämtliche Werke*, vol. 3, pp. 269–326. In F. W. J. Schelling, *Outline of a System of the Philosophy of Nature*, pp. 193–232. Trans. Keith R. Peterson. Albany: State University of New York Press, 2004.

— . 1800. *System of Transcendental Idealism*. *Sämtliche Werke*, vol. 3, pp. 327–634. Trans. Peter Heath. Charlottesville: University of Virginia Press, 1978.

— . 1803. *On University Studies*. *Sämtliche Werke*, vol. 5, pp. 207–352. Trans. E. S. Morgan. Ed. Norbert Guterman. Athens: Ohio University Press, 1966.

— . 1804a. 'System of Philosophy in General and of the Philosophy of Nature in Particular'. *Sämtliche Werke*, vol. 6, pp. 131–576. In [selection] *Idealism and the Endgame of Theory. Three Essays by F.W.J. Schelling*, pp. 139–94. Ed. and trans. Thomas Pfau. Albany: State University of New York Press, 1994.

— . 1804b. *Philosophie und Religion*. *Sämtliche Werke*, vol. 6, pp. 11–70. *Philosophy and Religion*. Trans. Klaus Ottmann. Putnam, CT: Spring Publications, 2010.

— . 1806. *Aphorismen zur Einleitung in die Naturphilosophie*. *Sämtliche Werke*, vol. 7, pp. 127–288.

— . 1809. *Philosophical Inquiries into the Essence of Human Freedom*. *Sämtliche Werke*, vol. 7, pp. 331–416. Trans. Jeff Love and Johannes Schmidt. Albany: State University of New York Press, 2006.

— . 1810a. 'Stuttgart Seminars'. *Sämtliche Werke*, vol. 7, pp. 417–86. In *Idealism and the Endgame of Theory. Three Essays by F.W.J. Schelling*, pp. 195–243. Ed. and trans. Thomas Pfau. Albany: State University of New York Press, 1994.

— . 1810b. *Clara or, On Nature's Connection to the Spirit World. Sämtliche Werke*, vol. 9, pp. 1–110. Trans. Fiona Steinkamp. Albany: State University of New York Press, 2002.

— . 1811. *The Ages of the World (1811).* From *Die Weltalter. Fragmente. In den Urfassungen von 1811 und 1813.* Ed. Manfred Schröter. Munich: Biederstein, 1946. Trans. Joseph Lawrence. Albany: State University of New York Press. 2019.

— . 1812. *Denkmal der Schrift von den göttlichen Dingen, etc. des Herrn Friederich Heinrich Jacobi und der ihm in derselben gemachten Beschuldigung eines absichtlich täuschenden, Lüge redenden Atheismus. Sämtliche Werke*, vol. 8, pp. 19–138.

— . 1815a. *The Ages of the World.* 3rd draft. *Sämtliche Werke*, vol. 8, pp. 195–344. Trans. Jason M. Wirth. Albany: State University of New York Press, 2000.

— . 1815b. 'The Deities of Samothrace'. *Sämtliche Werke*, vol. 8, pp. 345–426. Trans. Robert Brown. In *Schelling's Treatise on the Deities of Samothrace*. Missoula, MT: Scholars Press for the American Academy of Religion, 1977.

— . 1821. 'Erlanger Vortäge'. *Sämtliche Werke*, vol. 9, pp. 207–52.

— . 1827. *System der Weltalter: Müncher Vorlesung 1827/8 in einer nachschrift von Ernst Lasaulx.* Ed. Siegbert Peetz. Frankfurt am Main: Klostermann, 1990

— . 1830. *Einleitung in die Philosophie.* Ed. Walter Erhardt. Stuttgart: Frommann-Holzboog, 1989.

— . 1831. *Urfassung der Philosophie der Offenbarung.* Ed. Walter E. Ehrhardt. Frankfurt am Main: Meiner, 2010.

— . 1832. *Grundlegung der positive Philosophie: Münchener Vorlesung* WS 1832/33 and SS 1833. Ed. H. Fuhrmans. Turin: Bottega D'Erasmo, 1973.

— . 1833. *On the History of Modern Philosophy. Sämtliche Werke*, vol. 10, pp. 1–200. Trans. Andrew Bowie. Cambridge: Cambridge University Press, 1994.

— . 1841. *Philosophie der Offenbarung 1841/42 (Paulus Nachschrift).* Ed. Manfred Frank. Frankfurt am Main: Suhrkamp, 1977.

— . 1842a. *Historical-Critical Introduction to the Philosophy of Mythology. Sämtliche Werke*, vol. 11, pp. 1–252. Trans. Mason Richey and Markus Zisselsberger. Albany: State University of New York Press, 2007.

— . 1842b. *Philosophie der Mythologie. Erstes Buch. Der Monotheismus. Sämtliche Werke*, vol. 12, pp. 1–132.

— . 1842c. *Philosophie der Mythologie. Zweites Buch. Die Mythologie. Sämtliche Werke*, vol. 12, pp. 133–674.

— . 1842d. *The Grounding of the Positive Philosophy. The Berlin Lectures. Sämtliche Werke*, vol. 13, pp. 1–174. Trans. Bruce Matthews. Albany: State University of New York Press, 2008.

— . 1843. 'Schelling's Introductory Lecture in Berlin'. *The Dial*, 3:3, 398–404.

— . 1850. 'On the Source of the Eternal Truths'. *Sämtliche Werke*, vol. 11, pp. 573–90. Trans. Edward A. Beach. *The Owl of Minerva*, 22:1 (1990), 55–67.

— . 1853. 'Dokumente zur Schellingforschung IV: Schellings Verfügung über seinen literarischen Nachlass'. *Kant-Studien*, 51 (1959/60), 14–26.

— . 1854a. *Einleitung in die Philosophie der Mythologie (Darstellung der reinrationalen Philosophie). Sämtliche Werke*, vol. 11, pp. 253–572.

— . 1854b. *Philosophie der Offenbarung. Erster Theil. Kurze Darstellung der Philosophie der Mythologie. Sämtliche Werke*, vol. 13, pp. 175–530.

— . 1854c. *Philosophie der Offenbarung. Zweiter Teil. Sämtliche Werke*, vol. 14, pp. 1–334.

—. 1856–61. *Sämtliche Werke*. Ed. K. F. A. Schelling. Stuttgart: J.G. Cotta.
    Vol. 1. (erste Abtheilung, erster Band, 1856), 1792–97.
    Vol. 2 (erste Abtheilung, zweiter Band, 1857), 1797–98.
    Vol. 3 (erste Abtheilung, dritter Band, 1858), 1799–1800.
    Vol. 4 (erste Abtheilung, vierter Band, 1859), 1800–2.
    Vol. 5 (erste Abtheilung, fünfter Band, 1859), 1802–3.
    Vol. 6 (erste Abtheilung, sechster Band, 1860), 1804.
    Vol. 7 (erste Abtheilung, siebenter Band, 1860), 1805–10.
    Vol. 8 (erste Abtheilung, achter Band, 1861), 1811–15.
    Vol. 9 (erste Abtheilung, neunter Band, 1861), 1816–32.
    Vol. 10 (erste Abtheilung, zehnter Band, 1861), 1833–50.
    Vol. 11 (zweite Abtheilung, erster Band, 1856), *Einleitung in die Philosophie der Mythologie*.
    Vol. 12 (zweite Abtheilung, zweiter Band, 1857), *Philosophie der Mythologie*.
    Vol. 13 (zweite Abtheilung, dritter Band, 1858), *Philosophie der Offenbarung* (1).
    Vol. 14 (zweite Abtheilung, vierter Band, 1858), *Philosophie der Offenbarung* (2).
—. 1991. *Philosophie de la Révélation*. 3 vols. Trans. Jean-François Marquet and Jean-François Courtine. Paris: Presse Universitaires de France.
—. 2020. *Philosophy of Revelation (1841–42) and Related Texts*. Trans. Klaus Ottmann. Thompson, CT: Spring Publications.
Schlegel, Friedrich von. 1828. *The Philosophy of History*. 7th edn. Trans. James Burton Robertson. London: George Bell & Sons, 1885.
Schleiermacher, Friedrich. 1799. *Speeches on Religion: To its Cultured Despisers*. Ed. and trans. Richard Crouter. Cambridge: Cambridge University Press, 1996.
—. 1830. *The Christian Faith*. Ed. H. R. Mackintosh and J. S. Stewart. New York: Harper and Row, 1963.
Schlitt, Dale M. 2016. *German Idealism's Trinitarian Legacy*. Albany: State University of New York Press.
Schmitt, Carl. 1934. *Political Theology*. 2nd edn. Trans. George Schwab. Chicago: University of Chicago Press, 2005.
—. 1970. *Politische Theologie II. Die Legende von der Erledigung jeder Politischen Theologie*. Berlin: Duncker & Humblot.
Schneider, Robert. 1938. *Schelling und Hegels schwäbischen Geistesahnen*. Würzburg: K. Triltsch.
Scholem, Gershom. 1974. *Kabbalah*. New York: Penguin, 1978.
Schulz, Michael. 1997. *Sein und Trinität: Systematische Erörterung zur Religionsphilosophie G. W. F. Hegels*. St. Ottilien: Eos Verlag.
Schulz, Walter. 1955. *Die Vollendung des deutschen Idealismus in der spätphilosophie Schellings*. Stuttgart: Kohlhammer.
—. 1977. 'Freiheit und Geschichte in Schellings Philosophie'. In *Schellings Philosophie der Freiheit. Festschrift der Stadt Leonberg zum 200. Geburtstag des Philosophen*, pp. 36–7. Stuttgart: Kohlhammer, 1977.
Schulze, Wilhelm August. 1955. 'Jacob Boehme und die Kabbala'. *Judaica. Beiträge zum Verständnis des Jüdischen Schicksals*, 11:12–29, 209–16.
—. 1957a. 'Schelling und die Kabbala'. *Judaica. Beiträge zum Verständnis des Jüdischen Schicksals*, 13:65–98, 143–70, 210–32.
—. 1957b. 'Oetinger's Beitrag zur Schellingschen Freiheitslehre'. *Zeitschrift für Theologie und Kirche*, 54, 213–25.

Schwab, Philipp. 2013. 'Nonground and the Metaphysics of Evil. From Heidegger's First Schelling Seminar to Derrida's Last Reading of Schelling (1927–2002)'. *Analecta Hermeneutica*, 5. <https://journals.library.mun.ca/ojs/index.php/analecta/issue/view/92> (accessed 1 July 2020).

Sellars, Wilfred. 1963. 'Philosophy and the Scientific Image of Man'. In *Empiricism and the Philosophy of Mind*, pp. 1–40. London: Routledge and Kegan Paul.

Sloterdijk, Peter. 1988. *Critique of Cynical Reason*. Trans. Michael Eldred. Minneapolis: University of Minnesota Press.

Snow, Dale. E. 1996. *Schelling and the End of Idealism*. Albany: State University of New York Press.

Spinoza, Benedict de. 1955. *The Chief Works of Benedict de Spinoza*. Vol. II. Trans. R. H. M. Elwes. New York: Dover Publications.

Stewart, Jon, ed. 2017. *Kierkegaard Research: Sources, Reception and Resources. Volume 18, Tome IV: Kierkegaard Secondary Literature: Finnish, French, Galician, and German*. London: Routledge.

Strawbridge, Jennifer R. 2015. *The Pauline Effect: The Use of Pauline Epistles by Early Christian Writers*. Berlin: De Gruyter.

Taubes, Jacob. 1947. *Occidental Eschatology*. Trans. David Ratmoko. Stanford: Stanford University Press, 2009.

Taylor, Bron, 2009. *Dark Green Religion: Nature Spirituality and the Planetary Future*. Berkeley: University of California Press.

Taylor, Charles. 2007. *A Secular Age*. Cambridge, MA: Harvard University Press.

Thomas, Mark J. 2014. 'The Mediation of the Copula as a Fundamental Structure in Schelling's Philosophy'. *Schelling Studien*, 2, 20–39.

Tillich, Paul. 1910. *The Construction of the History of Religion in Schelling's Positive Philosophy: Its Presuppositions and Principles*. Trans. Victor Nuovo. Lewisburg, PA: Bucknell University Press, 1974.

— . 1912. *Mysticism and Guilt-Consciousness in Schelling's Philosophical Development*. Trans. Victor Nuovo. Lewisburg, PA: Bucknell University Press, 1974.

— . 1967. *Systematic Theology*. Chicago: University of Chicago Press.

Tilliette, Xavier. 1970. *Une philosophie en devenir*. Paris: J. Vrin.

— . 1987. *L'Absolu et la philosophie: essais sur Schelling*. Paris: Presses Universitaires de France.

— . 1999. *Schelling. Biographie*. Paris: Calmann-Lévy.

Tolkien, J. R. R. 1942. *Tolkien on Fairy-Stories*. Ed. Verlyn Flieger and Douglas A. Anderson. London: Harper Collins, 2014.

Tomberg, Valentin. 1985. *Meditations on the Tarot: A Journey into Christian Hermeticism*. Trans. Robert A. Powell. New York: Penguin.

Torwesten, Hans. 1991. *Vedanta: Heart of Hinduism*. New York: Grove Press.

Tritten, Tyler. 2012a. *Beyond Presence: The Late F.W.J. Schelling's Criticism of Metaphysics*. Boston: De Gruyter.

— . 2012b. 'Schelling's Doctrine of the Potencies: The Unity of Thinking and Being'. *Philosophy and Theology*, 24:2, 217–53.

— . 2014. 'Christ as Copula: On the Incarnation and the Possibility of Religious Exclusivism'. *Analecta Hermeneutica*, 6. <https://journals.library.mun.ca/ojs/index.php/analecta/issue/view/113> (accessed 1 July 2020).

— . 2017. *The Contingency of Necessity: Reason and God as Matters of Fact*. Edinburgh: Edinburgh University Press.

— . 2018. 'On Matter: Schelling's Anti-Platonic Reading of the Timaeus'. *Kabiri*, 1, 93–114.

Vasilyev, Tikhon. 2019. 'Aspects of Schelling's Influence on Sergius Bulgakov and Other Thinkers of the Russian Religious Renaissance of the Twentieth Century'. *International Journal of Philosophy and Theology*, 80:1–2, 143–59.

Vater, Michael. 2014. 'Reconfiguring Identity in Schelling's *Würzburg System*'. *Schelling Studien*, 2, 127–44.

Vattimo, Gianni. 1992. *The End of Modernity: Nihilism and Hermeneutics in Post-modern Culture*. Chichester: John Wiley.

Von Balthasar, Hans Urs. 1995. *Presence and Thought: An Essay on the Religious Philosophy of Gregory of Nyssa*. San Francisco: Ignatius Press.

— . 2000. *Theo-Logic I: Truth of the World*. Trans. Adrian J. Walker. San Francisco: Ignatius Press.

Von Rad, Gerhard. 1962. *Old Testament Theology*. Trans. D. M. G. Stalker. Edinburgh: Oliver and Boyd.

Walsh, Maurice O'C., and Bernard McGinn, ed. and trans. 2009. *The Complete Mystical Works of Meister Eckhart*. New York: Crossroad.

Watson, John. 1882. *Schelling's Transcendental Idealism*. Chicago: S. C. Griggs.

Watt, Paul B. 2016. *De-mythologizing Pure Land Buddhism. Yasuda Rijin and the Shin Buddhist Tradition*. Honolulu: University of Hawaii Press.

Weber, Max. 2002. *The Protestant Ethic and the 'Spirit' of Capitalism*. Trans. Peter R. Baehr and Gordon C. Wells. New York: Penguin.

Weeks, Andrew. 1991. *Böhme. An Intellectual Biography of the Seventeenth-Century Philosopher and Mystic*. Albany: State University of New York Press.

Werner, Martin. 1941. *Die Entstehung des christlichen Dogmas*. Leipzig: P. Haupt.

White, Lynn, Jr. 1967. 'The Historical Roots of Our Ecological Crisis'. *Science*, 155, 1203–7.

Whitehead, Alfred North. 1929. *Process and Reality. An Essay in Cosmology*. Cambridge: Cambridge University Press.

Whiteley, Giles. 2018. *Schelling's Reception in Nineteenth Century British Literature*. Basingstoke: Palgrave Macmillan.

Whitson, Robley Edward. 1971. *The Coming Convergence of World Religions*. New York: Newman Press.

Wiercinski, Andrzej. 2010. *Hermeneutics between Philosophy and Theology: The Imperative to Think the Incommensurable*. Münster: LIT Verlag.

Williams, Rowan. 1987. *Arius: Heresy & Tradition*. Grand Rapids: Eerdmans.

— . 2018. *Christ, the Heart of Creation*. London: Bloomsbury.

Wirth, Jason. 2003. *The Conspiracy of Life: Meditations on Schelling and his Time*. Albany: State University of New York Press.

— . 2015. *Schelling's Practice of the Wild: Time, Art, Imagination*. Albany: State University of New York Press.

— . 2020. 'Schelling and the Satanic: On Naturvernichtung'. *Kabiri*, 2: 81–92.

Wishart, Ian S. 2019. *Schleiermacher's Interpretation of the Bible: The Doctrine and Use of the Scriptures in the Light of Schleiermacher's Hermeneutical Principles. Analecta Hermeneutica*, 11. <https://journals.library.mun.ca/ojs/index.php/analecta/issue/view/145/showToc> (accessed 1 July 2020).

Wittgenstein, Ludwig. 1922. *Tractatus Logico-Philosophicus*. Trans. C. K. Ogden. London: Routledge and Kegan Paul.

Wolf, A. 1966. *The Correspondence of Spinoza*. London: Allen and Unwin.

Wright, N. T. 1992. *The New Testament and the People of God: Christian Origins and the Question of God*. Minneapolis: Fortress Press.

— . 2018. *Paul: A Biography*. New York: Harper Collins.

Yu-Lan, Fung. 1947. *The Spirit of Chinese Philosophy*. Trans. E. R. Hughes. Boston: Beacon Press.

Žižek, Slavoj. 1991. *For They Know Not What They Do: Enjoyment as a Political Factor*. London: Verso.

— . 1996. *The Indivisible Remainder: On Schelling and Other Matters*. London: Verso.

— . 1997. *The Abyss of Freedom*. Ann Arbor: University of Michigan Press.

— . 2000. *The Fragile Absolute – or, Why is the Christian legacy worth fighting for?* London: Verso.

— . 2003. *The Puppet and the Dwarf: The Perverse Core of Christianity*. Cambridge, MA: MIT Press.

— . 2006. *The Parallax View*. London: Verso.

— . 2015. 'Some Thoughts on the Divine Ex-sistence'. *Crisis & Critique*, 2:1, 12–34.

Žižek, Slavoj, with John Milbank. 2009. *The Monstrosity of Christ: Paradox or Dialectic?* Ed. Creston Davis. Cambridge, MA: MIT Press.

Zizioulas, John. 1985. *Being as Communion: Studies in Personhood and the Church*. New York: St. Valdimir's Seminary Press.

Zöller, Günter. 2014. 'The Church and State: Schelling's Political Philosophy of Religion'. In *Interpreting Schelling: Critical Essays*, pp. 200–15. Ed. Lara Ostaric. Cambridge: Cambridge University Press.

Zovko, Marie-Elise. 1996. *Natur und Gott: Das wirkungsgeschichtliches Verhältnis Schellings und Baaders*. Würzburg: Königshausen & Neumann.

Zunic, Nikolaj. 2021. 'The Processes of *Universio* and *Katabolé* in the Creation of the World'. *Kabiri*, 3, forthcoming.

Index

religion
  academic study of, 135
  as key to history, 153
  free, 210
  natural, 163, 182, 183, 195, 217;
    see also mythology
  revealed, 119, 194–207
Reno, R. R., 222
resurrection, 4, 5, 128n77, 135,
    186n5, 209, 238
revelation, 140, 203
  actual, 194–207
  biblical, 3
  defined, 133
  as *explanans* of history, 159, 194,
    199
  as free act, 59, 106, 134
  passive potency for, 53, 120n6
  possible, 132–41
  and reason, 172
  as secular, 171
  theology of, 11, 121n18, 136, 140,
    192n47
  third age of, 16, 108, 174, 180
  unprethinkable, 52
revolution, 1, 16, 230, 234, 235, 240
  French, 226, 232
Rosenzweig, Franz, 41n13, 242n23,
    126n70
Russel, Bertrand, 26, 27

samsara, 233
Sandkühler, Hans-Jörg, 188n17, 239
Santaraksita, 116–17
Sartre, Jean Paul, 78
Satan, 127n72, 151
satisfaction, criterion of *see* adequacy
satori, 117
saturated phenomenon, 135–40
Schelling, I and II, 31–2, 35, 37, 38,
    49, 50, 58, 130, 171, 227–8,
    239, 247
Schelling's turn to the positive of, 49
Schlegel, Caroline, 46n52, 248
Schlegel, Friedrich, 8, 9

Schleiermacher, Friedrich, 30, 187n7,
    195
Schmitt, Carl, 124n47, 229, 232
Scholasticism, 33, 53, 67, 70, 75, 84,
    88–94, 170, 181, 250
Schulz, Walter, 32–5, 243n33
Scotus, Duns, 27, 28, 45n43, 89, 90,
    193n58, 242n20
secularism, 2, 6, 9, 196, 202, 210, 224
self-consciousness, 97, 126n67, 215,
    216
Shankara, 113, 115–16
sin, 5, 15, 108, 131, 182, 185, 205,
    227, 228, 234, 239, 242n20, 246
society, civil, 223, 234
Socrates, x, 3, 56, 113, 115, 191n34,
    212, 241n14
Soloviev, Vladimir, ix, 41n13, 122n28
Sophia, divine wisdom, 151–2,
    188n19, 188n21
Sophiology, 41n13
sovereignty, 124n47, 181, 185, 207,
    231, 232–3
speculative pietism, 72, 121n16
Spinoza, 24, 36, 63–5, 68, 71, 75, 81,
    92, 102, 112, 155, 158, 167–9,
    186n1, 191n35, 196, 197, 245,
    248
spirit, 36–7
Stalin, 100
State, the, 9, 15, 114, 217, 230–6
Stoicism, 84
subject-object distinction, 54,
    121n13, 133
subjectivity, 130, 131, 139
subordinationism, viii, 50, 96, 102,
    206, 207
Sufism, 117
sunyata, 247
system, open or living, 157

Taoism, 113, 117
teleology, 33, 50, 104, 109, 234
theology of the cross (*theologia crucis*),
    180–6